Democratic Drift

Democratic Drift

Majoritarian Modification and Democratic Anomie in the United Kingdom

Matthew Flinders

OXFORD
UNIVERSITY PRESS

OXFORD
UNIVERSITY PRESS

Great Clarendon Street, Oxford OX2 6DP

Oxford University Press is a department of the University of Oxford.
It furthers the University's objective of excellence in research, scholarship,
and education by publishing worldwide in

Oxford New York

Auckland Cape Town Dar es Salaam Hong Kong Karachi
Kuala Lumpur Madrid Melbourne Mexico City Nairobi
New Delhi Shanghai Taipei Toronto

With offices in

Argentina Austria Brazil Chile Czech Republic France Greece
Guatemala Hungary Italy Japan Poland Portugal Singapore
South Korea Switzerland Thailand Turkey Ukraine Vietnam

Oxford is a registered trade mark of Oxford University Press
in the UK and in certain other countries

Published in the United States
by Oxford University Press Inc., New York

British Library Cataloguing in Publication Data

Data available

Library of Congress Cataloging in Publication Data

Data available

Typeset by SPI Publisher Services, Pondicherry, India
Printed in Great Britain
on acid-free paper by the
MPG Books Group, Bodmin and King's Lynn

ISBN 978–0–19–927159–7

1 3 5 7 9 10 8 6 4 2

Charlie, Indigo, Agnes, and Queenie—thanks for teaching me what really matters in this world.

Contents

Contents

Part III: Bi-constitutionalism and the Governance of Britain

Acknowledgements

As with most ventures of this kind, I have called upon a great number of friends, colleagues, and scholars in the course of writing this book. In terms of thanking and recognizing some of these individuals it would be remiss of me not to begin by thanking Arend Lijphart. This debt of gratitude relates not only to his original scholarship in the sphere of democratic analysis but also to his willingness to engage and support younger scholars as they seek to develop his initial framework and cultivate new intellectual terrains. In this context I would also like to highlight the support I have received from Peter Mair. This book grew from an article I was commissioned to write for *West European Politics* in 2005 and Professor Mair has remained a constant source of stimulation and inspiration throughout the course of this project.

Many other people have provided guidance and feedback on specific parts of this book, as well as the broader arguments I seek to make. These include Andrew Gamble, Ben Seyd, Mark Evans, Richard Heffernan, Charles Pattie, Meg Russell, Andrew Taylor, Paul Chaney, Sean Carey, Alix Kelso, Stuart Weir, John Morison, Anthony Barnett, Patrick Dunleavy, Fliss Matthews, Francesca Gains, Alistair McMillan, Gerry Stoker, Adrian Vatter, Glenn Gottfried, Colin Hay, Andrew Russell, Roger Mortimer, Ben Page, Guy Lodge, Dion Curry, Peter Jones, Richard Wyn Jones, Roger Scully, David Moon, Michael Cole, Michael Gallagher, Michael Thrasher, Rick Wilford, Robin Wilson, Mark Sandford, and Robert Hazell. I also owe a debt of gratitude to the staff of the House of Commons Library, the Bank of England, and Ipsos/MORI for the provision of statistical data. The monitoring reports provided by the Constitution Unit were also an invaluable resource throughout the writing of this book.

Various elements of this book were presented as papers at departmental seminars and conferences around the world between 2006 and 2009 and I would like to thank the participants at these events for their insightful comments and suggestions for improvement. I was also involved in a

Acknowledgements

number of international research networks and colloquia that helped sharpen my arguments and theories in a number of ways. It is in this context that I would like to thank David Erdos of Oxford University's Centre for Socio-Legal Studies for coordinating a project on Charter 88 and democratic change; Steven Fielding of Nottingham University for convening a conference on the Conservative Party under David Cameron; and Iain McLean and Varun Uberoi of Nuffield College, Oxford University, for inviting me to contribute to the Future Options II project. I was also fortunate enough to be involved with the Political Studies Association's formal response to the *Governance of Britain* green paper and a series of subsequent events on the theme of constitutional reform under Gordon Brown.

During the course of this project I was also fortunate enough to hold a Leverhulme Trust Research Fellowship which afforded me a break from my teaching and administrative responsibilities at the University of Sheffield, and also access to a critical mass of documents and interviewees. The sections of this book on parliamentary scrutiny and forms of legislative oversight between 1997 and 2007 also drew upon research undertaken alongside Alex Brazier and Declan McHugh of the Hansard Society under a Nuffield Foundation funded audit of parliamentary modernization.

Finally, I would like to thank Dominic Byatt and Lizzy Suffling at Oxford University Press for their editorial advice and guidance throughout this project.

Matthew Flinders
May 2009

List of Figures

List of Figures

List of Tables

List of Tables

List of Abbreviations

AM	Assembly Member
AMS	Additional Member System
CWN	Cukierman, Webb, and Neyapti
DCA	Department for Constitutional Affairs
ECHR	European Convention on Human Rights
FOI	Freedom of Information
FPTP	First Past the Post
GLA	Greater London Assembly
GMT	Grilli–Masciandaro–Tabellini
HLAC	House of Lords Appointments Commission
IRA	Irish Republican Army
JCHR	Joint Committee on Human Rights
MMP	Mixed-Member Proportional
MPC	Monetary Policy Committee
MSP	Members of the Scottish Parliament
NAW	National Assembly for Wales
NIA	Northern Ireland Assembly
NIE	Northern Ireland Executive
PLP	Parliamentary Labour Party
PPR	Public Policy Research
RC	Regional Chambers
RDA	Regional Development Agency
SGP	Scottish Green Party
SSCUP	Scottish Senior Citizens Unity Party
SSP	Scottish Socialist Party
STUC	Scottish Trade Unions Congress

List of Abbreviations

STV	Single Transferable Vote
TUC	Trades Union Congress
UK	United Kingdom
UUP	Ulster Unionist Party
WAG	Welsh Assembly Government

Part I:

History, Theory, and Method

Chapter 1

Constitutional Anomie

The constitution of the UK lives on, changing from day to day for the constitution is no more and no less than what happens. Everything that happens is constitutional. And if nothing happened that would be constitutional also.[1]

Democracies around the world exist in a constant process of adaptation and change. Although severe crises, such as war, disease, or natural disasters may provoke 'mega-political' change in the sense of a fundamental shift in the principles and institutional structures through which a country is governed, the general pattern of democratic evolution is based upon incremental shifts in the nature of a democracy. This stability is rooted in institutional and cultural path-dependencies that tend to ensure that reforms are designed and implemented within a fairly narrow-bounded rationality. Put slightly differently, most democracies possess, either implicitly or explicitly, a form of constitutional morality which define the key principles or values underlying the distribution of powers and political relationships within that country. This constitutional morality provides a form of socio-political roots or glue that, in turn, shape and mould not only institutional arrangements, but also reform proposals.

For centuries the United Kingdom (UK) was regarded as the 'Mother of Democracy' and its institutional framework and socio-political culture were exported along colonial channels throughout the world. Its constitutional morality was clear and broadly accepted—it was a power-hoarding or majoritarian form of democracy. And yet at the beginning of the twenty-first century, the nature and future of democracy in the UK are highly contested. The election of New Labour in 1997 led to the introduction of a number of constitutional reforms that have been interpreted as deconstructing, even 'vandalising', the UK's traditional Westminster Model democracy.[2] It is this debate that forms the context for this book.

1.1 Aims and arguments

This book seeks to gauge and understand the manner in which the nature of democracy in the UK altered after the election of New Labour in 1997, and is therefore a piece of constitutional political analysis. It achieves this by drawing on the tools, language, and methods of comparative political science in order to plot the degree and direction of democratic change. More specifically, it draws upon Lijphartian political analysis in order to provide a sharper account of New Labour's statecraft in relation to constitutional reform and democratic renewal. Sharper in the sense that the contemporary nature of democracy in the UK cannot be captured in simplistic statements concerning a shift from one democratic model to another, but must instead be interpreted and understood through a lens that is sensitive to the existence of parallel and incongruent models of democracy. Indeed, it is the tension or grating between these coexisting and competing forms of democracy, intended as they are to deliver quite different governing principles, that explains many of the current challenges within domestic politics and emerging frameworks of multilevel governance.

In order to understand the manner in which New Labour approached the topic of constitutional reform and democratic renewal, and therefore how the UK came to be institutionally configured, it is necessary to appreciate both the political tradition in the UK and the historical mentality of the Labour Party. In this sense, New Labour came to power in 1997 within a context that was to some degree path-dependant. This created a critical tension for the government between their pre-election rhetoric of 'fundamental' or 'radical' constitutional change, and their post-election determination to retain the power of a strong state in order to protect their governing capacity in terms of driving-through new policies and ensuring delivery. New Labour responded to this tension in a typically British manner: by 'muddling through' in the sense of ad hoc pragmatic responses to specific challenges, but without any clear statement of overall intent or principled foundation. 'Muddling through', however, can be interpreted as an inadequate response to the challenges of modern governance at the cusp of the twenty-first century. Instead of reconnecting the governed and the governors or revitalizing politics, the available data and survey evidence suggest that trust in traditional politics, politicians, and political institutions appears to have declined during 1997–2007. It is in explaining why such a significant number of constitutional reforms should have failed to rebuild public trust in politics that this book is concerned.

The focus of the explanation offered in this book rests on the distinction (or gap) between *rhetorical principles* and *governing practice* and combines to generate a clear thesis concerning what is termed 'constitutional anomie'. Constitutional anomie in this context relates to the manner in which New Labour failed to offer an explicit account of what they were seeking to achieve in the sphere of democratic reform, or why measures were viewed as legitimate and acceptable in some areas or in relation to some issues but not others. Put simply, between 1997 and 2007 the Labour governments of Tony Blair suffered from constitutional anomie, and a series of reforms were implemented with little appreciation of: (*a*) what (in the long run) the government was seeking to achieve; (*b*) how reform in one sphere of the constitution would have obvious and far-reaching consequences for other elements of the constitutional equilibrium; or (*c*) any detailed analysis of the nature or model of democracy that existed towards the end of the twentieth century and particularly after eighteen years of Conservative government.

Prime Minister Tony Blair made no speeches on the constitution and a white paper on the constitution was never forthcoming. Blair was never a constitutional entrepreneur with a driving passion for change or a clear vision of what a reformed model of democracy in the UK would look like. The Lord Chancellor for much of this period, Lord Irvine, responded to criticisms that the reform programme was disjointed and opaque in terms of under-pinning values by stating that the government had no intention of 'returning to first principles'. 'Cobbled together on the back of an envelope' may well have been Hennessy's apt description of constitutional design and reform in the UK, but it arguably reached its zenith during 2001–5 as a lack of consultation, inadequate preparatory work, and poor media management led to the government being perceived as floundering, ill-prepared, overhasty, and, at times, simply shoddy in relation to constitutional reform.

It is this accusation of constitutional anomie that provides the context or backcloth on which this book is written. The central question this book seeks to answer—and therefore around which its theoretical and empirical arguments revolve—is how exactly did New Labour alter the nature of democracy in the UK during 1997–2007?

In this context, the publication of the *Governance of Britain* green paper in July 2007, just weeks after Tony Blair resigned and was replaced by Gordon Brown marks a significant point in the constitutional history of the UK.[3] As Chancellor of the Exchequer, Brown had always been more sensitive to the existence and implications of constitutional anomie, and during the government's second term (2001–5) he signalled his anxieties in a number of speeches and statements in which he called for a 'new constitutional settlement'.[4] *Governance of Britain* can therefore be located within a broader narrative concerning the evolution and future of democracy. In terms of style there is a distinct change of emphasis in two clear ways: first, there is an explicit engagement and willingness to promote a discussion about the primary values and principles that should underpin the UK's constitutional arrangements; and, second, there is an emphasis on broad consultation in relation to both underpinning values and elements of 'unfinished business' (electoral reform for the House of Commons, reform of the second chamber, etc.). However, the green paper also provides an intriguing glance into the executive mentality and particularly how members of the government and senior civil servants frame certain issues in terms of key questions. In this regard it is possible to suggest that the document is misdirected. The foreword by the Prime Minister, Gordon Brown, and Secretary of State for Justice and the Lord Chancellor, Jack Straw, states that the *Governance of Britain* is focused on two fundamental questions:

1. How should we hold power accountable?
2. How should we uphold and enhance the rights and responsibilities of the citizen?

However, it is possible to suggest that these two questions continue to suggest a degree of constitutional anomie because they are secondary or meso-level questions that can only be answered once broader macro-political questions regarding what sort of democracy, what specific model or form, we are seeking to evolve towards have been settled. Put slightly differently, there are many ways of holding power to account and there are many mechanisms through which rights and responsibilities can be entrenched and secured but these variations tend to flow—like branches from a tree—from the specific form of democracy (parliamentary, presidential, majoritarian, consociational) deployed within that polity. Adopting the metaphor of a journey, the government's questions are akin to discussing what form of transport we might use (train, bus, plane, tram, etc.) before we have decided where we want to go. Following this line of argument it is possible to suggest that if the government is truly committed to forging 'a new relationship between government and citizen, and beginning the journey towards a new constitutional settlement' then a more constructive approach would take a more expansive and grounded stanae by asking two quite different questions:

1. What kind of constitution and democracy do we have in the UK at the beginning of the twenty-first century?
2. What are we attempting to achieve through the reform process?

These questions are clearly interrelated as answering the second requires at least some attempt at resolving the first. Both questions also involve normative and empirical dimensions which, in turn, force us to consider the tools of political analysis, and particularly those that offer the capacity to assess the *sum impact* of a series of constitutional measures. This raises epistemological and methodological questions concerning the concepts, theories, and frameworks through which it is possible to deduce *subtle, moderate,* or *fundamental* changes in a democratic system. However, the significance of these questions of political analysis and the need for explicitly theorized systematic research on the impact/legacy of reforms during 1997–2007 is demonstrated not just by the current Labour government's position on constitutional reform, but also by the failure of the now burgeoning academic literature on this topic to come to any sort of shared conclusion about the impact of these measures.

A clear polarization of opinion can be identified within the scholarly analysis between those who have interpreted New Labour's impact on the constitution as fundamental and those more sceptical observers who view the very same reforms as involving a far less radical, even cosmetic effect on democracy in the UK. In this context Peter Mair observes, 'New Labour is currently engaged in what amounts to a full-blooded constitutional revolution, dragging the political system away from an extreme version of majoritarian democracy towards a more institutionally consensual model' while Mark Evans rejects such an interpretation and argues that 'Third Way democracy is elite democracy in disguise'.[5] This polarization of opinion is intriguing because it forces us to reflect on the methods and tools of political analysis that can be utilized in order to tease apart and disentangle a complex patchwork of reforms, and thereby reveal the underlying drivers or consequences of this process.

This vast body of work provides the backdrop against which this book stands. The central epistemological and methodological argument of this book is that a binary distinction between consensual or majoritarian models of democracy is inappropriate because it fails to reflect the true complexity that currently exists. As a result this book develops the concept of 'meta-constitutional orientations' in order to argue that the distinctive element of New Labour's approach to constitutional engineering is not that it has shifted the nature of democracy in the UK from one model to another, but that it has sought to apply different models at the periphery and core: bi-constitutionality. Revealing the existence of overlapping or intertwined models of democracy provides a sharper understanding of the realities of modern governance through which it is possible to understand the polarization of academic opinion and many of the key challenges facing democracy in the UK.

In order to provide depth (in terms of a conceptual and theoretical framework) and breadth (in terms of a structure through which it is possible to identify the interrelationship between specific reforms) this book utilizes Arend Lijphart's framework for measuring patterns of democracy.[6] This contributes a deeper understanding and more fundamental analysis to the broader debate about how the constitution and nature of democracy has altered in the UK since May 1997. It therefore provides a way of teasing apart and understanding the roots of the academic debate on the cumulative impact of New Labour's reforms and through this provide an answer to the first question mentioned earlier ('What kind of constitution and democracy do we have in the UK at the beginning of the twenty-first century?'), that will itself aid our understanding of the trajectory of UK politics and from this provide a clearer foundation and basis from which to debate the second question ('What are we attempting to achieve through the reform process?').

Briefly focusing on this latter question at this early stage is useful for a number of reasons, but not least because it encourages us to reflect on New Labour's original aims and ambitions and then consider the degree to which they have been achieved. This then sets out the broader context or background within which not only *Governance of Britain* was published by the government in July 2007, but also within which the research in this book was conducted. It is for this reason that Section 1.2 focuses on the analysis of levels of public trust in politics.

1.2 The Democratic legacy, 1997–2007

In January 2006, the Minister for Constitutional Affairs, Harriet Harman, emphasized that '[A] healthy democracy is one that has the active engagement of its citizens. Our democracy lacks legitimacy if, whatever the formal rules about universal suffrage and the right to vote, people don't make it a reality by turning out to vote'.[7] The Minister went on to lament the contemporary existence of 'democracy deserts' in the UK where high-levels of social exclusion are compounded by low-levels of democratic engagement. If we adopt the minister's emphasis on electoral turnout as a reflective indicator of a healthy democracy, then we can observe from the result of the 2005 General Election that democracy is not very healthy in the UK, and that major questions exist concerning its legitimacy. The Labour government won just 35.2 per cent of the popular vote, which was translated by the simple-plurality electoral system into 55 per cent of seats (355, a majority of 65). Not only was this the lowest share of the vote won by any governing party since 1923, but it was also the lowest share of the popular vote of any party to gain a majority in modern times.

In this context Gordon Brown's core message—'I will restore trust in politics'—during his leadership campaign in May 2007, an emphasis that was widely interpreted as an implicit criticism of Tony Blair's period in office, is significant. Rebuilding public trust and confidence in politics was a defining ambition of New Labour. In 1996 Tony Blair emphasized the need to 'construct a new and radical politics to serve the people in the new century ahead...where power is pushed down to the people instead of being hoarded centrally'.[8] This emphasis formed part of the broader 'Third Way' narrative whereby 'reform of the state and government should be a basic orientating principle—a process of the deepening and widening of democracy'[9] or what Anthony Giddens would later refer to as 'a second wave of democratization...the democratization of democracy'.[10] The Labour Party manifesto for the 1997 General Election declared, 'We shall fight the general election *inter alia* on democratic renewal as an essential element in our project: the modernization of Britain'.

If the central aim of New Labour was to rebuild public trust and confidence in politics then it is difficult to avoid the conclusion that it has been unsuccessful. In coming to this conclusion it is sufficient to draw upon three authoritative sources. First, the Electoral Commission's annual audit of political engagement provides a detailed barometer of public opinion vis-à-vis trust, confidence, and satisfaction with politics. Although the statistics are generally fairly stable between each of the four years (2003–7) the baseline is not very impressive. In the latest audit only 27 per cent of the public trusted politicians generally, and 33 per cent thought 'the present political system of governing works well'.[11] These findings complement those of the Hansard Society's audits which reveal very little public knowledge or public interest in constitutional issues. As Figure 1.1 illustrates, the Hansard Society's audits suggest that although public satisfaction with politics is higher than it was in the mid-1990s

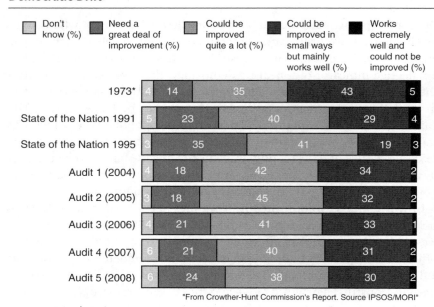

Figure 1.1 Public Attitudes on the political system in the UK, 1973–2008
Source: Hansard Society (2008) *Audit of Political Engagement* 5 London, p. 37.

before New Labour were elected, it has subsequently waned to the point at which only 32 per cent are generally satisfied with the status quo.

The British Social Attitude Survey's longitudinal research on public attitudes also provides a rich vein of data on the public's attitude to politics that chimes with the findings of other surveys. The most recent British Attitudes Survey indicates a decline in public trust in politicians and political institutions. In 2008, the proportion of the public who simply do not trust the government to put the interests of the country above those of their party increased to its highest level (33.6%) since the data set began in 1986. The ESRC's Democracy and Participation Programme provides a final source of detailed quantitative and qualitative data on public attitudes that helps us dissect and understand the issue in greater detail. This research reveals that the public are not disinterested with politics per se, but they are lacking in trust when it comes to the motivations of politicians, and are increasingly utilizing non-traditional forms of political participation and engagement. Non-traditional in the sense that instead of voting, joining a political party, or contacting their MP members of the public, especially young people are likely to engage in quite different activities, like consumer involvement in buying or boycotting products or events in order to express their opinion.[12] In short, they are likely to chose channels of influence that lie beyond the traditional representative politics and those which are more single-interest, direct, and possibly reliant on new forms of technology. In short, the evidence suggests that New Labour's constitutional reforms have failed to reconnect the governed with the governors. Levels of public distrust and disengagement remain high. This was the driving force behind the Independent Inquiry into Britain's Democracy (*The Power Report*) in 2006 and which led Colin Hay, in his influential 2007 book *Why We Hate Politics*, to state quite simply that 'Politics is a dirty word'.[13]

The data and evidence of heightened public distrust of politicians and political institutions alongside a more general sense of public apathy and disengagement, particularly among certain social groups, during 1997–2007 is fundamental in relation to this book's focus on constitutional anomie. Although the UK is by no means unique amongst advanced liberal democracies in being a 'disaffected democracy', the available data do pose distinct questions about the nature and manner in which New Labour approached the issue of constitutional reform and democratic renewal. The absence of any clear underlying logic or variables combined with evidence that the government was committed to a far-reaching shift in the nature of democracy in *principle but not in practice* alienated large sections of the public and reinforced existing beliefs about the trustworthiness of politicians. Constitutional anomie therefore eviscerated the potential rewards of reform in terms of rebuilding trust because it confused the public in terms of the driving logic or consequences of each specific measure as well as frequently cultivating an image of a government constantly devolving power with one hand, only to claw it back through the imposition of exemptions, opt-outs, or ministerial veto at the implementation stage. This last point reveals the existence of what commentators have labelled the 'Blair paradox', and it is exactly this paradox which forms an important explanatory variable behind the constitutional anomie thesis. In order to set out how this book underpins its arguments concerning constitutional anomie, bi-constitutionalism, and the changing of democracy in the UK, Section 1.3 outlines the structure of this book.

1.3 Structure

Gordon Brown's first steps as Prime Minister have been anchored to the idea of restoring trust in politics. That is, restoring public confidence in the integrity, vitality, and capacity of the agents, institutions, and processes of *conventional* representative politics.[14] This restored emphasis on trust is a direct response to the erosion of public trust and increase in disenchantment that occurred during the final years of New Labour. This book examines Brown's constitutional inheritance and provides a framework for mapping and considering future options. It is divided into three parts and sixteen chapters. The core arguments of each chapter and how they combine to offer a distinctive account of constitutional reform and democratic renewal in the UK can be summarized as follows:

(Chapter 1)—During 1997–2007, the constitution of the UK was modified, but not fundamentally reformed. New Labour suffered from constitutional anomie due predominantly to intra-executive confusion regarding what it was seeking to achieve.

↓

(Chapter 2)—The 'Blair paradox' reflects not a simple shift in orientations (i.e. from majoritarian power-hoarding *to* consensual power-sharing) but a multifaceted attempt to inject a new meta-constitutional orientation, in terms of a set of core values, principles, and assumptions about the distribution of power and the relationship between political actors, *within* the existing version (i.e. bi-constitutionalism).

↓

(Chapter 3)—The Labour Party has traditionally been aligned with a power-hoarding model of democracy, and its rhetorical commitment to constitutional reform in the mid-1990s was largely an *act-contingent* strategy to win power.

↓

(Chapter 4)—The political studies community in the UK has traditionally adopted a distinctive and insular approach, in terms of theory and methods, to constitutional research, but there is a pressing need to embrace alternative tools of political analysis. This book utilizes Lijphartian political analysis in order to inject a more theoretically driven account of change.

↓

(Chapter 5)—There is no such thing as *the* party system in the UK, but an embryonic multilevelled hierarchy of party *systems*. The existence of different party systems, founded and perpetuated by electoral systems that have been designed to inculcate a quite different value-set, raises

terms of a coherent set of principles, or an explanation of why many of the reforms appear to pull in quite different directions. More broadly, at the beginning of the twenty-first century nobody seems able to articulate as to what actually is meant by constitutional reform. In this sense, the UK is suffering from an illness known as constitutional anomie, and neither the Labour government's *Governance of Britain* initiative or the Conservative Party's plans, combined with the behaviour of politicians, appears to be able to respond to this diagnosis. Constitutional anomie is a debilitating illness. Its symptoms include the introduction of reforms in a manner bereft of any underlying logic or explicit principles, combined with the inability to adopt a strategic approach which is sensitive to the interrelated nature of any constitutional configuration. Constitutional anomie is therefore an ailment of both mental and physical health vis-à-vis the body politic. Social and political anxiety, confusion, and frustration emerge with the result that reforms that were designed to enhance levels of public trust and confidence in politics, politicians, and political institutions can actually have the opposite effect. The prognosis for constitutional anomie depends on a complex range of factors but not least on the creation of specific anomalies and inconsistencies that are likely to augment to the point at which the pressure for more fundamental measures and the articulation of a revised constitutional morality becomes inevitable.

This book is of methodological importance, not simply because it assesses the cumulative impact of recent reforms through the application of Lijphart's methodological and conceptual framework, but because it critically reflects on the utility of this tool of political analysis and from this criticizes the existing body of literature on constitutional reform in the UK since 1997. It is of conceptual importance because the results of the systematic analysis add further weight to the accusation of constitutional anomie while also allowing the development of a new conceptual tool, namely bi-constitutionality, which offers significant analytical leverage in terms of understanding longstanding debates, such as the 'Blair paradox'. This book is of normative importance because it avoids the descriptive-prescriptive approach to constitutional literature that has dominated political studies in the UK throughout the twentieth century, and it is relevant for comparative politics because it replicates and takes forward a methodology that has been applied around the world and in doing so provides a critical case of executive-politics and statecraft vis-à-vis constitutional reform.

Notes

1. Griffiths, J A G (1979) 'The Political Constitution', *Modern Law Review*, 42(1), 19.
2. 'New Labour' for the purposes of this book relates to the period in which Tony Blair was Leader of the Party (i.e. 1994–2007).
3. Cm. 7170 *Governance of Britain*. London: HMSO.
4. See *The Guardian* 27 February 2006.
5. Mair, Peter (2000) 'Partyless Democracy: Solving the Paradox of New Labour', *New Left Review*, 2 March/April, 34; Evans, M (2003) *Constitution-Making and the Labour Party*. London: Palgrave, p. 5.
6. Lijphart, A (1984) *Democracies*. London: Yale University Press; see also Lijphart, A (1999) *Patterns of Democracy*. London: Yale University Press; Lijphart, A (2008) *Thinking About Democracy*. London: Routledge.
7. Harman, Harriet (2006) *A New Deal for Democracy*. Speech to the Hansard Society, 16 January (www.dca.gov.uk/speeches/2006/sp060116.htm).
8. Blair, Anthony (1996) 'My Vision for Britain', in Giles Radice, ed, *What Needs to Change*. London: Harper Collins, p.3. See also Blair, Anthony (1996) *New Britain: My Vision of a Young Country*. London: Fourth Estate; Blair, Anthony (1998) *The Third Way*. London: Fabian Society.
9. Giddens, Anthony (2000) *The Third Way and Its Critics*. Cambridge: Polity, p. 69.
10. Giddens, *The Third Way*, p. 61.
11. See Electoral Commission (2006) *An Audit of Political Engagement 3*. London: Electoral Commission, p. 7. See also Mortimore, R, Clark, J, and Pollard, N (2008) *Blair's Britain: The Political Legacy*. London: IPSOS/MORI.
12. Whiteley, Paul and Seyd, Patrick (2002). *High Intensity Participation: The Dynamics of Party Activism in Britain*. Ann Arbor, MI: University of Michigan Press.
13. Hay, Colin (2007) *Why We Hate Politics*. Cambridge: Polity, 1.
14. See Kennedy, C (2007) 'Britain After Blair: The Issue of Trust', *British Politics*, 2, 435–40.

Chapter 2

Meta-constitutional Orientations

There has been little enthusiasm at any time since 1789 in Britain for fundamental constitutional change.[1]

This chapter argues that the correlation between specific constitutional reforms and the nature of democracy in a given country is an empirical question rather than an assumed fact. Consequently, it is possible for a government to embark upon an apparently wide-ranging programme of constitutional reform with little actual commitment to changing the nature of democracy—what I refer to below as *cosmetic reform*. It is equally possible that a government may wish to shift the balance of power within the constitutional configuration of a country to some degree while still retaining control over core components and power centres, such as the voting system and legislature—*moderate reform*. Rarely, and usually in response to a major political crisis or incident, a government may wish to embark upon a far-reaching reform process in which the infrastructure of the constitution is amended in such a way that power is either concentrated or dispersed in a manner which marks a stark departure from the previous constitutional arrangement—*fundamental reform*.

Should New Labour's reforms be assessed as constituting *fundamental* reform of the British political system, as some scholars argue, or more pessimistically should they be viewed as *moderate*, even *cosmetic* amendments or adjustments to the British constitutional order? This forms the central question of this book, but in order to provide an answer or, at the very least, understand how and why different scholars have come to such contrasting, in some cases diametrically opposed conclusions, it is necessary to understand the history and nature of the British constitution. However, it is not the intention of this chapter (indeed, nor of this book) to attempt to review and synthesize that vast body of literature which exists on the British constitution. The objective here is quite different. This chapter draws upon the concept of a 'meta-constitutional orientation' in order to tease out and expose how constitutions inculcate and reflect certain specific principles or judgements about how a polity should be governed. The first section of this chapter focuses on the meta-constitutional orientation of what we might term the UK's *traditional* constitution. Although many of the institutional characteristics of this constitutional configuration are well-known, the emphasis here is on exposing the deeper values and assumptions underlying this model of democracy. It is only through revealing the meta-constitutional orientation of the traditional constitution that we can understand the roots and drivers of the constitutional anxieties and frustrations that emerged towards the end of the twentieth century. It is these latter 'constitutional fuels' that form the focus of the second half of this chapter.

2.1 Meta-constitutional orientations

A constant process of low-level, incremental constitutional change is ongoing in virtually all democracies at the meso- or micro-levels (as outlined in Table 2.1). However, when constitutional debates move well beyond disputing the merits of specific proposals and instead address the very nature and principles of a political community, they become an aspect of what might be termed 'mega-' or 'meta-politics'—precisely because of the fundamental nature of the issues in dispute.[2] Hirschl defines 'mega-politics' as 'matters of outright and utmost political significance that often define and divide whole polities. These range from electoral outcomes and corroboration of regime change to matters of war and peace, foundational collective identity questions, and nation-building processes pertaining to the very nature and definition of the body politic'.[3] The distinction between what counts as 'mega-politics' and what counts as 'ordinary' politics is often, as Hirschl notes, 'intuitive and context-specific rather than analytical or universal' but reform of this nature is exceptionally emotional and intense due to the fact that it touches on issues of self-worth and identity amongst the public while also demarcating the prerequisites of democratic governance.[4] It is in this sense that Russell's concept of a 'mega-constitutional orientation' refers to a pact or settlement on the identity and fundamental principles of a body politic.[5]

During the 1990s a range of countries were engaged in 'meta-constitutional' upheavals—much of Eastern Europe, South Africa, Belgium, Canada,

Table 2.1 Gradations of constitutional reform

Level	Definition	Examples	Geological stratum
Meta-constitutional	Underpinning elements of the constitution which provide the foundation of the system while also and generally ascribing a pattern or model of democracy.	• Electoral system (proportional versus disproportional). • State system (unitary versus federal). • Constitution (codified versus unwritten).	Core
Meso-constitutional	Secondary elements of the constitutional order which are shaped or stem from the primary meta-constitutional dynamic.	• Incorporation of human rights legislation (while retaining a ministerial veto and maintaining the sanctity of parliamentary sovereignty). • Creating a 'Supreme Court' (but without the power to strike down legislation). • Introduction of Freedom of Information Legislation (while retaining a ministerial veto). • Facilitating sub-national regional devolution (within the bounds of a unitary state).	Mantle
Micro-constitutional	Third-order elements that amend existing arrangements, codify long-standing conventions, or represent executive-led concessions to specific constitutional actors.	• Granting more resources to legislative scrutiny committees. • The publication of internal official guidance documents that have previously been confidential. • Decisions that involve the creation, abolition, or amalgamation of public bodies.	Lithosphere (crust)

New Zealand—while the twenty-first century began with a major meta-constitutional debate concerning the utility of a written constitution for the European Union. Indeed, this last example illustrates the point that a polity's meta-constitutional orientation may be explicit in the form of a codified constitution or may exist in a more implicit and cryptic form through conventions, standard operating procedures, and historical precedent. However, whether explicit or implicit the meta-constitutional orientation of a polity is likely to be embedded within the dominant political culture of a regime which itself inculcates and prioritizes certain values and judgements. Consequently, meta-constitutional politics focuses on debates concerning the basic foundations, framework, or 'rules of the game' that, in turn, set certain parameters—a form of constitutional bounded rationality—within which meso- and micro-constitutional arguments would be based (see Table 2.1).

In this sense, the meta-constitutional orientation of a democracy is akin to what David Easton refers to as a 'legitimizing ideology'—'the ethical principles that justify the way power is organized, used, and limited and that defines the broad responsibilities expected of participants of particular relationships'.[6] The UK's meta-constitutional orientation from the seventeenth century until the final decade of the twentieth century was the Westminster Model.[7] The Westminster Model, or what King refers to as the 'traditional constitution', consists of a number of key tenets that combine both descriptive and normative elements. The model therefore seeks to outline not only how democracy in the UK operates, but also how it *should* operate.

There is a great wealth of literature on the Westminster Model and it is sufficient here to list its core characteristics: parliamentary sovereignty; two-party system; simple plurality electoral system; cabinet government; individual ministerial responsibility; a dominant executive; weak second chamber; and a unitary state. We return to many of these characteristics in the second part of this book when we examine how they have been modified by New Labour's constitutional reforms but what is really necessary at this stage, however, is to drill down beneath the visible features of the UK's traditional constitution in order to reveal the underlying values, principles, and judgements. The meta-constitutional orientation casts a heavy shadow not just over the way that the political system operates, but also (and potentially more importantly for the focus of this book) on how the executive interprets demands for constitutional reform or adjustment. Therefore in order to obtain greater analytical traction or leverage from the concept of a 'meta-constitutional orientation' it is useful to highlight five underlying and mutually self-reinforcing values or principles:

1. Belief in the value of an unwritten or 'small-c' constitution.
2. An emphasis on pragmatic adaptation and flexibility.
3. The 'Good Chaps' theory of government.
4. A Political Constitution.
5. Majoritarianism.

The first and possibly the most well-known feature of this system was that it was *unwritten*. Not unwritten in the sense that none of its components were never set down on paper in the form of statutes or Cabinet papers but unwritten in terms of there not being one definitive collective constitutional declaration that was accepted as demarcating a 'higher order' statement that could only be amended through an explicit and demanding process. It was and remains a 'small-c' constitution and not a 'capital-C' constitution as favoured by the founding fathers in the United States or several mainland European countries.[8] As Dicey famously declared, 'There is in the English constitution an absence of those declarations or definitions of rights so dear to foreign constitutionalists'.[9] This unwritten aspect of the British constitution leads into a consideration of the second broad theme—an emphasis on pragmatic adaptation and flexibility. This was linked to a Whiggish belief and commitment to self-adjustment, and therefore there was a reluctance to codify or develop a distinct strand of constitutional law in favour of a more organic approach.

> Our constitution is not based upon any fixed or immutable laws, nor do we require any special procedure to change it. This so-called flexibility is our greatest asset, it should enable the constitution to adapt itself momentarily to the desires and wishes of the people.[10]

This vaunted adaptive quality of the constitution was cherished by a host of constitutional theorists and commentators including Dicey, Low, and Jennings and was founded on a high degree of governing confidence, bordering on smugness, which allowed them to view the constitutional malleability offered by a 'small-c' constitution as a positive asset.[11] The absence of a formal codified constitution was viewed as a positive reflection of the 'self-evident superiority' and commonsense basis of politics in the UK.[12] The constitution was based upon tacit understandings and even though 'the understandings are not always understood', as Low remarked, they provided a way of maintaining the mystique of the constitution while also protecting the position of a socially exclusive political elite. Rather like the governance of the Universities of Oxford and Cambridge, the constitution remained incomprehensible to outsiders. If you needed to ask how something worked then you were probably not supposed to know.

This rather self-satisfied and commonsensical approach to politics was tightly connected to our third broad theme—the '"Good Chaps" theory of government'. This maintained that the UK did not need a 'capital-C' constitution because the political elite, of either political party, knew what was proper and right in terms of standards and behaviour and could therefore be trusted to work within a largely self-regulating political environment.[13] 'The British Constitution' Gladstone emphasized in 1879 'depends on the good sense and the good faith of those who work it'. The 'Good Chaps' theory of government provided a form of constitutional glue or social capital that reinforced the belief that a written constitution was unnecessary in the British context while also exposing the elitist nature of democracy in the UK. 'The atmosphere of British government was that of a club, whose members trusted each other to observe the spirit of the club rules; the notion that the principles underlying the rules should be clearly defined and publicly proclaimed was profoundly alien'.[14]

This 'Good Chaps' theory resonates with Jellineck's notion of 'auto-limitation' by reason not so much of constitutional law but by political morality, shaped in part by social principle and in part by that political prudence which is instinctively aware of the limits beyond which a legislature or executive cannot safely go without encountering the risk of political breakdown.[15] The Westminster Model therefore established, maintained, and protected a highly elitist, predemocratic form of club-government that was characterized by informal modes of operation, beliefs concerning personal integrity, mutual respect and dependence, high-trust relationships, the internalization of cultural norms and a distaste for legal controls or sanctions.[16] This latter point is critical. The UK's 'traditional' constitution was a political constitution (our fourth theme). This confidence and acceptance of political self-regulation explains Griffiths' famous assertion that the British constitution was 'a political constitution'.[17] Whereas supreme or constitutional courts in other polities, including Austria, France, Italy, and Germany had been established with the power to strike down primary legislation as unconstitutional, the judiciary in the UK had no such constitutional role. The executive was responsible and accountable to the legislature.

The final hallmark of the UK's meta-constitutional orientation was a normative belief in the value of centralization—both territorially and politically. The Westminster Model was therefore a 'power hoarding' or 'power concentrating' model of democracy. Territorially the constitution of the UK was (and theoretically remains) a unitary state. Although sub-national tiers of governing have existed in a variety of forms for centuries their existence is derived (and protected) not from the explicit provisions of a 'capital-C' constitution, as is the case with the German Lander or the American states, but solely through a more precarious reliance on the good-will and confidence of the national government. Politically, power is centralized through Bagehot's 'efficient secret': the lack of a clear separation of powers and the drawing of the executive from the legislature.[18]

The modern constitution of the UK was forged during the middle of the nineteenth century during a critical historical phase between the Great Reforms Acts. The Reform Act of 1832 enlarged the electorate by 50 per cent. The House of Commons was liberated from the discipline of the Crown influence and, with parties in an embryonic stage, the House entered into more than three decades of making and unmaking governments. The House of Commons was free of Crown influence and not yet constrained by strict party discipline; departments were still small enough for ministerial responsibility to be strictly applied without dispute; and MPs felt empowered to play a more active role in government due to their popular support in the country. As Maitland's *Constitutional History of England* (1908) demonstrates, Parliament displayed a determined ability to hold ministers to account and '... exercised a constant supervision of all governmental affairs'. It was expected that ministers would have to work to maintain the confidence of the House. Forced resignations were common. The MPs collaborated in shaping government measures as well as heavily amending and rejecting legislation. After the second Reform Act, the relationship between parliament and the executive shifted in the latter's favour. Within and beyond parliament, party control of its members became much tighter. Moreover, the procedural reforms within parliament in the early 1880s considerably strengthened the position of the executive and restricted the opportunities for backbenchers to table amendments. Constitutional writers at the time—Bagehot, Dicey, and Maitland—may well have overstated the success of the convention of ministerial responsibility in order to demonstrate a workable theory of accountability to accommodate a constitution in which parliament was supreme, both as a legislature and check on the executive.[19] A *political* constitution based on a parliamentary convention as a method for ensuring accountability also reassured the ruling elite that the government of the country would remain in its hands—for the essence of conventions is that they are developed and controlled by those who operate the system and are not imposed externally.

The Westminster Model was therefore constitutionally insular. The convention of parliamentary sovereignty ensured that no limits or restrictions could be imposed by external actors on the capacity of the legislature while at the same time the shift in the balance of power from the House of Commons to the executive that occurred in the second half of the nineteenth century ensured that British parliamentary government was something of a veil for executive government.[20] However, for around one hundred and fifty years from the middle of the nineteenth century to the end of the twentieth century the meta-constitutional orientation in the UK remained undisputed. The disadvantages of a power-hoarding model—limited public participation, a lack of legal protections, etc.— were viewed as being outweighed by the advantages—governing capacity, executive stability, public clarity, clear lines of accountability, etc. The main political parties broadly accepted the logic and principles of this model and consequently British constitutional history is, unlike many other countries, largely devoid of meta-constitutional politics. Incremental changes at the meso and micro levels occurred (reforms of the House of Lords in 1911, secession of Southern Ireland in 1921), but the central framework remained solid and largely uncontested. Section 2.2 focuses on why this historic satisfaction with the UK's constitutional system waned towards the end of the twentieth century.

2.2 Constitutional disquiet

The Westminster Model is a highly centralized form of democracy that is clear in terms of the clarity and logic of its underlying principles. It emphasizes governing capacity over other competing principles (such as participation or fairness) and this meta-constitutional orientation provides the backbone from which choices about specific institutional configurations (electoral systems, territorial models, etc.) can be made and legitimated. This issue of legitimation is critical because the Westminster Model acted as a frame; that is 'an interpretive schema that simplifies the world by selectively punctuating and encoding objects, situations, events, experiences and sequences of actions within one's present and past environment'.[21] For the public this frame set out a chain of delegation through which legitimate political power could be conferred and an adequate level of accountability secured. The links in this chain moved from the public to their MPs, from MPs to the executive, and from the executive to the bureaucrats that implemented policies on their behalf. Arguably, the most important link in this chain was the convention of individual ministerial responsibility which acted as Bagehot's 'buckle' between parliament and the wider bureaucracy.[22] In constitutional terms this reassured the public that for any error or omission there would be a clear and indivisible point of accountability in the form of the responsible minister. For the political elite, the Westminster Model was equally significant because, as noted before, it provided a form of bounded rationality and a frame through which current and proposed arrangements could be interpreted and assessed. More significantly, for an incumbent executive, the Westminster Model provided a powerful legitimating tool through which reform proposals that were designed to dilute the power of the executive or strengthen other actors could be rejected. It is in this vein that Judge has written of the 'negative executive mentality' and the way it has inverted the logic of ministerial responsibility and employs the convention as a tool of 'strong' government with which to eviscerate the participatory claims of reformers.[23]

Proposals to move towards a more power-sharing model of democracy are therefore dependent on the support of a dominant executive that is unlikely to support measures that will weaken its capacity to implement the policies on which it was elected, or increase the resources of the opposition. It is therefore possible to identify a historical trend throughout the twentieth century whereby incoming governments generally move rapidly away from any commitment to power-sharing reforms and embrace the benefits of the 'power-hoarding' model; while outgoing governments that had rejected decentralizing measures while in office suddenly discover a passionate zeal for power-sharing initiatives. In many ways the central ambition of this book is to discover the degree to which this 'swing thesis' remains true for New Labour and in order to achieve this we need to understand the dynamics behind its transition from being a party that was historically committed to the principles of the Westminster Model to being one that was elected on 1 May 1997 on the basis of a commitment to 'new politics'.

Returning to the role of the Westminster Model and its role as a frame or legitimating framework provides a way into understanding not only the Labour Party's attitude and approach in office to constitutional reform, but also the broader social dynamics that the party was attempting to respond to. The Westminster Model entrenched an ethos or a set of underlying assumptions and beliefs (forged in the nineteenth century in the context of a minimal state and market liberalism) that have became historically and structurally preserved through institutional relationships and patterns of behaviour. Throughout the twentieth century the Westminster Model concealed profound changes in the form and substance of the state and it also sought to veil the existence of clear anomalies through the language and notions of constitutional propriety.[24] However, the fact that the constitutional model was something of a straw man and contained many clear inconsistencies was unproblematic while it was widely viewed as delivering its core tenets in terms of governing capacity, executive stability, public clarity, clear lines of accountability, etc.—the essence of its meta-constitutional orientation. The Westminster Model in this sense provided a guiding narrative or a loose framework and its innate elitism, centralization, and opacity were simply the costs incurred for receiving those benefits. However, as Marquand's *Unprincipled Society* (1988) underlines, 'club government' is only tenable as long as customs are accepted, conventions are respected, and ambiguities remain uncontested. Once the populace start to look beneath the veil or refuse to accept that the existing constitutional configuration delivers an acceptable degree of, for example, responsiveness or accountability then arrangements based on hazy foundations are liable to collapse.

> The ambiguities inherent in them will be exposed, without being cleared up, the discrepancies will come out into the open and it will become more and more apparent that the question of principle they pose cannot be answered with precision or authority.[25]

During the final two decades of the twentieth century the British constitutional order did not collapse—the UK has not experienced a first-order constitutional crisis since 1688—but it did become the topic of sustained and widespread disquiet.[26] The roots of this disquiet were varied and a substantial literature exists which seeks to map out the variables which stimulated interest in constitutional reform. In this context, Foley's identification of ten 'constitutional fuels' provides a valuable review (Table 2.2).

Although these ten 'fuels' provide a useful overview of many of the issues which became politically salient in the 1990s and as a result created a sense of constitutional anxiety, the most striking aspect of this list of fuels—and one rarely noted in the wider literature—is that many of them are neither new nor particularly problematic in terms of the UK's traditional constitution. The disproportional translation of votes into seats by the simple-plurality electoral system, for example, was not accidental but was designed to ensure that elections resulted in a governing majority.

More broadly, the governance of the UK had always arguably been char-acterized by secrecy, centralization, and an emphasis on executive govern-ing capacity. The critical element in understanding the politics of the constitution in the 1990s lies not in the identification of specific incidents or issues—these are merely the visible symptoms of a deeper malady—but in the recognition that for the first time in 150 years the UK's meta-constitutional orientation, in terms of the core values and principles upon which institutional relationships had been constructed, was ques-tioned.

It was questioned because there was increasing evidence that it was not working. This point brings us back full circle to Marquand's arguments in the *The Unprincipled Society*. Although democracy in the UK was not *un-principled*—the Westminster Model embraces a relatively clear set of prin-ciples—Marquand was correct to highlight how democracy was essentially elitist and in many ways pre-democratic. For much of the nineteenth and twentieth centuries this did not matter. The public were willing to defer to a social elite and play a limited role in politics because they believed that the constitution was effective and provided for an acceptable balance between *representative* and *responsible* government. By the end of the twentieth century, however, there was a growing body of evidence that the traditional constitution was not working.

> The number of calls for radical change increased as a function of a growing sense that the existing constitutional order was not only insufficiently responsive to people's opinions and wishes, and was not only insufficient-ly participatory, but was, perhaps worst of all, increasingly ineffective.[27]

The roots of this sense of ineffectiveness can be traced back to the litera-ture on de-legitimation, ungovernability, and overload in the 1970s, through to the 'Britain in decline' discourse of the 1980s, and through to the body of work set out in the fourth column of Table 2.2.[28] In the late 1970s James Callaghan was already treading on thin ice when he re-sponded to constitutional criticism by retorting 'Well it works doesn't it? So I think that is the answer, even if it is on the back of an envelope'.[29] By the 1990s a significant body of opinion doubted whether the constitution still worked. The willingness of significant sections of the British public to acquiesce vis-à-vis the anomalies and opacity of the constitutional frame-work diminished as evidence of its failure to deliver stable and effective government increased. Moreover, as the internal structure of the British state became more complex, due to the centrifugal pressures of New Public Management, and increasingly enmeshed in supra-national projects, most

Table 2.2 Constitutional fuels

Fuel	Essence	Evidence	Key text
1. Electoral inequity	Criticism of the manner in which the disproportional plurality system discriminates against smaller parties. Thereby fuelling concern that significant minorities of the population were not being represented.	1983 General Election. SDP-Liberal Alliance win 25.4% of the national vote but receive just 3.5% (23) seats.	Bogdanor's *Power to the People*, 1997.
2. Government excess	Concern that the executive had transgressed the bounds of acceptable conduct in relation to the balance between governing authority and individual human rights.	Frequent use of the Official Secrets Act (e.g. 1984, 1985).	Ewing and Gearty's *Freedom Under Thatcher*, 1990.
3. Centralization	The weakening of 'intermediate' social institutions—trade unions, local government, universities, etc.—had deconstructed the intricate network of checks and balances.	Abolition of metropolitan counties and the Greater London Council in 1986.	Jenkins' *Accountable to None*, 1995.
4. Governmental misuse	Evidence that the government had repeatedly contravened its own internal rules of conduct which cast doubt on the reliability of the 'good chaps' theory of government.	Pergau Dam Affair (1988–94).	Norton-Taylor et al.'s *Knee Deep in Dishonour*, 1996.
5. Secrecy	Concern arising from a number of incidents in which ministers had deployed Public Interest Immunity Certificates for private political reasons.	Arms to Iraq Inquiry (1994–6).	Ponting's *Secrecy in Britain*, 1990.
6. Personal misconduct	A broad and diffuse sense of social morality where the personal conduct, sexual behaviour or financial affairs of politicians can give rise to broader	'Cash for Questions' Affair (1994).	Vulliamy and Leigh's *Sleaze: The Corruption of Parliament*, 1997.

	concerns about political efficacy and public trust.		
7. Systemic dysfunction	Incidents that undermine public confidence in the capacity of the political system to deliver good government.	Poll Tax 1986–92; Child Support Act 1991; Dangerous Dogs Act 1991.	Butler et al.'s *Failure in British Government*, 1994.
8. Transcendent innovation	Evidence of developments that cannot be located within the precepts of the traditional constitution.	Growth in judicial review; increased creation of quangos.	Jowell and oliver's *The Changing Constitution*, 1994.
9. External imposition	Constitutional anxiety and disruption created by the increasing influence of incompatible external forces.	Pressures emanating from UK's membership of the EU.	Holme and Elliot's, *1688– 1988, Time for a New Constitution*, 1988.
10. Traditional anomalies	The existence of historical anomalies in stark contradiction of established liberal democratic standards.	Hereditary Peers; the Monarchy.	Nairn's *The Enchanted Glass*, 1994.

Source: Derived from Foley, M. (1999). *The Politics of the British Constitution*. Manchester: Manchester University Press.

notably the European Union, the Westminster Model's constitutional elasticity appeared exhausted to many observers. Consequently the traditional constitution's capacity to provide a guiding narrative or frame through which the public could make sense of and understand political structures and relationships was weakened. This fed into a surge in public disenchantment with politicians, political institutions, and political processes more generally and manifested itself in a number of forms but most notably through declining levels of electoral turnout.

The argument and content of this chapter can be summed up in two simple statements:

1. The meta-constitutional orientation of the traditional British constitution emphasized power-hoarding and governing capacity.
2. Towards the end of the twentieth century a number of factors conspired to stimulate a period of 'meta-constitutional' politics in which the basic values, principles, and assumptions of the British constitution were contested.

Neither of these comments is particularly original nor uncontestable. However, before we proceed to examine the position of the Labour Party vis-à-vis the UK's traditional constitution and how the Labour governments between 1997 and 2007 reformed the constitution, it is necessary to emphasize one key point in relation to British constitutional history in the twentieth century: there was no constitutional crisis. This is a significant point. As we shall see in Chapter 3, mega-politics, defined as core political controversies that define the boundaries of the collective and therefore the very definition of a polity, is generally driven by a definitive event or incident—civil war, natural disaster, invasion, etc.—which leads to a seismic shift in governing and public attitudes. The notion of a governing crisis is therefore tied into analyses of regime change and meta-constitutional politics, but in the UK there was no crisis. As Table 2.2 indicates, a variety of issues and incidents certainly raised questions about the efficacy of the UK's constitutional framework and the values that it inculcated but there was no specific event which made change of some sort inevitable. It might therefore be suggested that the most important constitutional fuel was missing—any sense of crisis.

Constitutional reform was never an issue of great *public* debate. Constitutional policy has never been a core issue, like health, race relations and immigration, education, crime, taxation, and unemployment, when it comes to public interest and voting intentions. The UK's relationship with Europe has consistently been the most salient constitutional issue, but this is generally regarded as a quite separate issue to domestic aspects of the reform programme (which have consistently been rated as less important than 'animal welfare'). Drilling down still further survey-evidence suggests that beneath the issue of Europe only those of Scottish and Welsh devolution, and local government and tax are consistently identified by the public as 'important issues' facing the UK today. And yet the proportion of adults raising these issues remained well below 5 per cent throughout the period 1997–2007.[30] It is therefore relatively uncontroversial to suggest that arguments pertaining to the need for constitutional reform during the 1990s were largely the preserve of the political elite. Indeed, with the exception of the work of the Scottish Constitutional Convention there was rarely any attempt to engage with the public about the values on which a twenty-first century constitution might be based. Neil Kinnock alluded to this fact as Leader of the Labour Party in 1988 when he allegedly described the founders of Charter 88 as 'wankers, winers and whingers'.[31] Public pressure is a core variable in relation to reform trajectories. Put simply, a new government that does not face strong public pressure for change enjoys greater choice in relation to the manner and extent of constitutional adjustment. Conversely, for proponents of constitutional reform, strong public support can be deployed as a resource or tool through which pressure for remodelling or modernization can be deployed. New Labour did not attain office in a period of constitutional crisis. New Labour did not attain office as whole-hearted advocates of far-reaching reform.

2.3 Constitution morality

This chapter has examined the meta-constitutional orientation of the UK's traditional constitution and how it came to be questioned towards the end of the twentieth century. Questioned, but not rejected. The essence of the UK's meta-constitutional orientation in terms of the set of values and attitudes that prevailed for a significant period of time can be captured in the notion of the constitutional morality. In simple terms, the constitutional morality of the UK was relatively clear and internally coherent. It was based upon the utility of centralized and powerful governance structures, high-levels of social deference towards the political elite, and limited notions of public participation. It was this constitutional morality which provided the authority and framework within which second- and third-order decisions were taken. Indeed the importance of the constitutional morality stems from its role in demarcating an implicit code of conduct consisting of certain rules, ethics, beliefs, and expectations—a theme eloquently captured in Pollard's (1920) statement that how the constitution operates is not so much conditioned by its form 'but upon the spirit which informs it'.[32]

To introduce the notion of constitutional morality as in some way capturing the spirit of culture of the constitution in the UK is therefore not without precedent. For Dicey to define an act or proposal as 'unconstitutional' was to suggest, 'that the act in question is, in the opinion of the speaker, opposed to the spirit of the British constitution'; moreover 'the constitutional morality of the day' was maintained and upheld through the interpretation and observance of conventions. This theme and language of constitutional morality was further developed by later scholars including Maitland, Dunham, and Marshall.[33] Although the notion of constitutional morality is dissected and further explored in Chapter 16, it is useful at this stage to emphasize the manner in which it forms a counterpoint or antithesis to this book's argument concerning New Labour and constitutional anomie. New Labour has rejected elements of the UK's longstanding meta-constitutional orientation (i.e. the Westminster Model) but has failed to replace it with any other coherent set of values, principles, or institutional architecture. More significantly, the institutional and cultural dynamics frequently flow in divergent directions and the UK remains, as Bogdanor notes, 'constitutionally speaking, in a half-way house'[34] or as King more starkly concludes 'a mess'.[35] This book's argument regarding constitutional anomie is therefore seeking to build upon and develop elements of the wider literature. In order to understand the trajectory of democracy in the UK it is necessary to understand the relationship between the Westminster Model and the Labour Party; particularly the tensions and anomalies that have always been embedded within this relationship. This forms the topic of Chapter 3.

Notes

1. Harrison, B (1995) *The Transformation of British Politics, 1860–1995*. Oxford: Oxford University Press.
2. Russell, P (1993) 'The End of Mega-Constitutional Politics in Canada?', *PS: Political Science and Politics*, 26, 33–7.
3. Hirschl, R (2008) 'The Judicialization of Mega-Politics and the Rise of Political Courts', *Annual Review of Political Science*, 11, 94.
4. Ibid., p. 108
5. See Russell, P (1992) *Constitutional Odyssey* Toronto: University of Toronto Press.
6. Easton, D (1965) *A Systems Analysis of Political Life*. New York: Wiley, p. 292.
7. On this see: Greenleaf, W (1983–7) *The British Political Tradition, Parts 1, 2 & 3* London: Methuen; Jennings, I. (1966) *The British Constitution*. Cambridge: Cambridge University Press; Mackintosh, J (1977) *The Politics and Government of Britain*. London: Hutchinson; Gamble, A (1990) 'Theories of British Politics' *Political Studies*, 38, pp. 404–20; Judge, D (1993) *The Parliamentary State*. London: Sage.
8. See King, A (2001) *Does the United Kingdom have a Constitution?* London: Sweet and Maxwell.
9. Dicey, A (1915) *Introduction to the Study of the Law and the Constitution* 8th edn. London, p. 144
10. Cole, G D H (1932) *A Plan for Britain*. London: Clarion Press, p. 39.

11. See Wolf-Philips, L (1984) 'A Long Look at the British Constitution', *Parliamentary Affairs*, 37(1), 385–402.

12. Shell, D (1993) 'The British Constitution 1991–1992' *Parliamentary Affairs*, 46(1), 1–16.

13. See Hennessy, P (1994) 'Harvesting the Cupboards', *Transactions of the Royal Historical Society*, 4, 203–19; See Hennessy, P (1995) *The Hidden Wiring*. London: Gollancz.

14. Marquand, D (1988) *The Unprincipled Society*. London: Jonathan Cape, p. 178.

15. See Catlin, G (1955) 'Considerations on the British Constitution', *Political Science Quarterly*, 70(4), 481–97.

16. On 'club government', see Moran, M (2003) *The British Regulatory State*. Oxford: Oxford University Press.

17. Griffiths, J A G (1979) 'The Political Constitution' *Modern Law Review*, 42(1), 1–21.

18. Bagehot, A (1867) *The English Constitution*.

19. Schaffer, B (1957) 'The Idea of the Ministerial Department: Bentham. Mill and Bagehot', *The Australian Journal of Politics and History*, 3(1), 60–78.

20. Flinders, M (2002) 'Shifting the Balance? Parliament, the Executive and the British Constitution', *Political Studies*, 50(2), 23–42.

21. Snow, D and Benford, R (1998) 'Master Frames and Cycles of Protest' in Morris, A and McClurg, C, eds., *Frontiers in Social Movement Theory*. London: Yale University Press, p. 127.

22. Flinders, M (2000) 'The Enduring Centrality of Individual Ministerial Responsibility Within the British Constitution', *Journal of Legislative Studies*, 6(3), 73–91.

23. Judge *op. cit.* (1993); see also Beattie, A (1998) 'Why is the Case for Parliamentary Reform in Britain so Weak', *Legislative Studies*, 4(2), 1–16; Tant, A (1990) 'The Campaign for Freedom of Information', *Public Administration*, 68, 477–91.

24. Flinders, M (2008) *Delegated Governance and the British State*. Oxford: Oxford University Press.

25. Marquand *op. cit.* (1998), p. 198.

26. Harden, I (1991) 'The Constitution and Its Discontents', *British Journal of Political Science*, 21, 489–510.

27. King, A (2007) *The British Constitution*. Oxford: Oxford University Press, p. 68.

28. See King, A (1975) 'Overload: Problems of Governing in the 1970s', *Political Studies*, 23(2), 284–96; Gamble, A (1981) *Britain in Decline*. London: Macmillan.

29. Quoted in Hennessy, P and Coates, S (1991) 'The Back of an Envelope', Strathclyde Analysis Paper, No. 5, 18.

30. See Ipsos/MORI Political Monitor, May 1997 – May 2007.

31. See Giddy, P (2000) 'We Need a Brand New Constitution', *New Statesman*, 26 June.

32. Pollard, A (1926) *The Evolution of Parliament*. London, p. 378.

33. Dicey *op. cit.* (1915) 516; Dunham, W (1971) 'The Spirit of the British Constitution', *University of Toronto Law Journal*, 21(1), 44–66; Marshall, G (1984) *Constitutional Conventions*. Oxford: Clarendon.

34. Bogdanor, V (2003) 'Conclusion', in V. Bogdanor, ed., *The British Constitution in the Twentieth Century*. London: British Academy, p. 719.

35. King *op. cit.* (2007) p. 345.

Chapter 3

Old Labour, New Labour, 'Blair Paradox'

It is very British, this revolution. It is a revolution without a theory. It is the messy, muddled work of practical men and women, un-intellectual when not positively anti-intellectual, apparently oblivious of the long tradition of political and constitutional reflection of which they are heirs, responding piecemeal and ad hoc to conflicting pressures—a revolution of sleepwalkers who don't quite know where they are going or why.[1]

Constitutions are made up of a number of layers and as such can be understood and studied with reference to the geological construction of the Earth. This is indicated in the fourth column of Table 2.1 in which each of the constitutional levels is assigned a geological stratum. In geological terms micro-constitutional elements of the constitution resemble the Earth's lithosphere because not only are these the most visible elements of the configuration, but they are also the ones most amenable to change. Minor reforms are relatively common, can be conceded by a dominant executive without creating any deeper threat to the democratic order, and are frequently used by governments as a form of constitutional pressure-valve. Beneath this layer of operational or day-to-day constitutional practices, procedures, or relationships exist a layer of more significant secondary elements which in geological terms represents the Earth's second (much thicker) layer—the mantle. Although this is made of solid rock, a process known as plasticity ensures that over geological time this layer actually behaves like a sticky liquid, and is therefore dynamic and fluid. As we shall see in later chapters, the relative rigidity of secondary elements of a constitution and the need for significant pressures to exist to provoke reform make meso-level components similar to the Earth's mantle. Finally, underpinning elements of the constitution which provide the foundation of the system while also and generally ascribing a pattern or model of democracy—meta-constitutional elements—are comparable to the Earth's solid inner core.

There are clearly limits to the value of such cursory geological metaphors but at the same time the analogy of the Earth's layers does provide an accessible framework, and particularly a language and discourse, from which it is possible to read across into the sphere of constitutional politics. Change takes place at a number of levels, some more visible than others. Change is dynamic: although modern constitutional history in the UK is well known for stability, and the absence of meta-constitutional debate there has always been an ongoing process of low-level reform and amendment combined with more infrequent examples of second-order change. This relates to the fact that meta-constitutional demands and reforms (i.e. mega-politics) require the existence of *extreme* societal pressures, just as earthquakes, volcanic eruptions, and tsunamis emanate from extreme geological events, which cannot be vented through meso- or micro-constitutional responses. This brings us back to our focus on the decade 1997–2007, and whether the reforms enacted during this period were *fundamental* (i.e. did they reach down and reform the very core of the constitution in terms of altering those components that reflect the meta-constitutional orientation and ascribe a pattern or model of democracy?) Or were the reforms actually less far-reaching (although *significant*) because the Labour government retained an attachment to the Westminster Model as the dominant meta-constitutional orientation which, in turn, restricted the reach and ambition of its reform programme?

We have already concluded at the end of Chapter 2 that although a number issues and incidents had put the issue of constitutional reform on the political agenda in the mid-1990s, this situation should not be confused with one of extreme social pressure for change. Constitutional reform was not a public debate, but an elite debate.

This is a critical point. Meta-constitutional reforms that affect and modify the core values of the constitution (Table 2.1) tend to be driven by some degree of popular unrest. The Great Reform Act 1832, for example, was passed as a result of popular agitation. The Parliament Act 1911 was the topic of intense political and public debate which dominated the run-up to two general elections (January and December 1910).[2] As such, it is possible to suggest that the absence of a constitutional crisis (real or perceived) provided New Labour with a degree of choice in 1997 in relation to democratic renewal. A radical approach might seize the opportunity to reform core elements of the constitution in order to create a quite different (i.e. power-sharing) model of democracy which inculcated an alternative meta-constitutional orientation than the traditional constitution. A less radical approach might attempt to deliver a form of modified majoritarianism which devolved some powers and created new checks and balances, but within a framework which retained executive dominance. The former strategy would undoubtedly represent a seismic shift or 'big bang'—a constitutional revolution—whereby the reform programme permeated the very core of the constitution. The latter strategy would be less momentous.

Within this debate this chapter seeks to substantiate three core arguments:

1. The Labour Party has historically been wedded to the Westminster Model and New Labour, in general, and Tony Blair, in particular, was always ambivalent about the merits of constitutional reform.
2. In office New Labour maintained rather than rejected the Labour Party's historical attachment to the Westminster Model.
3. The existence of constitutional anomie, and particularly the discrepancy between the *principles* and *practice* of New Labour in relation to constitutional reform, have become crystallized in the notion of a 'Blair paradox'.

Section 3.1 examines the history of the Labour Party and emphasizes how constitutional reform became enmeshed within a broader modernization process that occurred in the 1990s. Having outlined Tony Blair's misgivings vis-à-vis constitutional reform the second section proceeds to outline the behaviour of New Labour in office. The aim of this section is not to *describe* each reform in detail but to drawout and reveal the underlying approach to statecraft adopted by New Labour, and assess what this tells us about the executive mentality and whether an alternative meta-constitutional orientation was ever delineated or implemented. As the quote from David Marquand at the head of this chapter suggests, New Labour approached the constitution in a typically British manner—ad hoc, unprincipled, and apparently content to 'muddle through'. However, academic opinion on the sum impact of New Labour's reforms is deeply polarized between those who view 1997–2007 as a critical juncture in which the constitution of the UK was fundamentally reformed, and those more sceptical observers who highlight continuity rather than change. Reviewing this broader body of literature on democratic renewal under New Labour in the final section allows the chapter to reiterate and develop the central argument of this book. That is, the distinctive element of 'New' Labour's approach to constitutional engineering is not that it has shifted the nature of British democracy from one model to another, but that it has instead sought to apply different models at the periphery and core: bi-constitutionality.

3.1 Old Labour

The Labour Party had enjoyed a 'history of satisfaction' with the constitutional configuration and, in particular, the influential Fabian tradition within the party advocated the Westminster Model as providing a strong foundation through which socialist reforms could be delivered.[3] It is exactly this strand of thought which is prominent in the later work of Harold Laski and, as such, *A Grammar of Politics* (1925), *Democracy in Crisis* (1933), *Parliamentary Government in England* (1939), and most notably, *Reflections on the Constitution* (1951) each in their own way promote the benefits and sanctity of executive government.[4] The party's first experience of majority government (1945–51) was widely viewed as confirming the capacity of the existing constitutional system to deliver socialist goals (a view linked with the influential 1954 work of Herbert Morrison *Government and Parliament*). Meta-constitutional reforms were rejected on the basis that they would dilute the capacity of a future Labour government to drive through its socialist measures. That is not to say that proponents of radical constitutional reform were not to be found within the party. The proposals of Fred Jowett (1906), G D H Cole (1917) and notably, Sidney and Beatrice Webb in their (1920) *A Constitution for the Socialist Commonwealth of Great Britain*, for example, all rejected the Westminster Model and proposed meta-constitutional reforms.[5] But despite the influence of this current of opinion Evans notes,

> Traditionally the Labour leadership has supported functional elite democracy: state collectivism forwarded through an electoral majority; a constitution which legitimizes executive dominance; and constitutional arrangements which are amenable to manipulation by the executive.[6]

In the 1980s and early 1990s, the Labour Party's attitude to constitutional reform was strongly influenced by the views of its Deputy Leader, Roy Hattersley, who was a staunch opponent of any measures that would shift the balance of power away from the executive. For Hattersley a written constitution was 'a badly thought-out counsel of despair—a desperate attempt to stop the excesses of Thatcherism infecting this country forever'.[7] During the late 1980s, however, a process of constitutional revisionism occurred in which the notion of renewed democracy, delivered through a process of constitutional reform, became a central component of the party's then embryonic modernization strategy. This internal revisionist strategy complemented the changing political context as, for the first time, the UK's relative economic decline, territorial tensions, and a broader sense that the Conservative governments of Mrs Thatcher had exposed the dangers of unrestricted state power had led to a debate concerning the utility of the Westminster Model.[8] However, it is critical to understand that the Labour Party's engagement with constitutional reflection was always bounded by a commitment to executive government. It is in this vein that Wright states that the party's policy review of 1987–9 may have produced a 'shopping list' of constitutional reforms but it did not suggest that a need existed for any 'fundamental alterations'.[9] This is reflected in the fact that the review rejected the need for a Bill of Rights, and the topic of electoral reform was ruled out even for discussion by the review process.

By the mid-1990s, a combination of further electoral defeat (in 1992), and the campaigning of the Institute for Public Policy Research and Charter 88 convinced many within the senior echelons of the party, and particularly the new leader, John Smith, of the merits of constitutional reform. In 1993 Smith told a Charter 88 conference 'I want to see a fundamental shift in the balance of power between citizens and the state—a shift away from an overpowering state to a citizens' democracy where people have rights and powers and where they are served by accountable and responsive government'.[10] Eight months later, the Labour Party published *A New Agenda for Democracy: Labour's Programme for Constitutional Reform* which committed the party to a range of measures including a Bill of Rights, freedom of information legislation, and parliamentary reform.

Under Tony Blair (from 1994 onwards) the political philosophy of the Labour Party became intertwined with the notion of a 'third way'—an attempt to transcend both old style social democracy and neo-liberalism—of which democratic renewal was a core element.[11] Although Faux describes the third way as 'an intellectually amorphous substance' it is possible to glean the core components of a distinct third-way meta-constitutional orientation from the literature and speeches of influential social theorists, commentators and politicians during the mid-1990s.[12] A fairly predictable starting point for such a process would begin with the work of Anthony Giddens, who suggested that the UK's problems stemmed not from a crisis of democracy, but from not being democratic enough. The 'third way' for Giddens was built upon the introduction of 'new politics', indeed 'reform of the state and government should be a basic orientating principle of third-way politics—a process of the deepening and widening of democracy'[13] or what he would later refer to as 'a second wave of democratization . . . the democratization of democracy'.[14] The core tenets of this approach were participation, openness, transparency, devolution, explicit constitutional rules, diluted executive power, a more balanced relationship between the executive and legislature, and forms of democracy 'other than the orthodox voting process'.[15] These core themes provided the central DNA of the great majority of third-way prescriptions published at the time, and also permeated a broader body of work on the nature of British democracy and the need for constitutional change.[16] They also underpinned the writings and speeches of New Labour politicians. For example, Mandelson and Liddle's *The Blair Revolution* (1996)[17] repeated the 'new politics' narrative and set out the need not just for the formal sharing of power, but also for the development of a more consensual and less adversarial political system, while Tony Blair wrote of the need to 'construct a new and radical politics to serve the people in the new century ahead . . . where power is pushed down to the people instead of being hoarded centrally'.[18] The meta-constitutional orientation of the third way was therefore intended to be quite distinct from the existing Westminister Model. Where the latter was elitist and centralist, the third-way vision of a new democracy was participatory and pluralist.[19]

In moving towards this revisionist strategy, the Labour Party was clearly evolving towards a position on the constitution that had traditionally been held by the Liberal Democrats. Consequently, the two parties agreed a pact (the Cook–Maclennan Pact) on the constitution in the run up to the 1997 general election, whereby the Labour Party agreed to implement devolution, introduce proportional representation for European Parliament elections, pass a Human Rights Act and a Freedom of Information Act, as well as make less-clear commitments in relation to electoral reform for Westminster and reform of the House of Lords.[20] The pact played a role in encouraging Labour Party members to vote for the Liberal Democrats in seats where they had very little support (and often did not campaign), and vice versa. The Labour Party manifesto for the 1997 General Election declared, 'We shall fight the general election *inter alia* on democratic renewal as an essential element in our project: the modernization of Britain' and went on to commit the party to a broad programme of constitutional reform.[21]

However, it is important to treat these political statements and commitments with a measure of political realism. Although the Labour Party shifted during the 1990s towards a reconsideration of the UK's meta-constitutional orientation a rational-actor model would predict that a strong executive who had gained power through the extant configuration would resist measures that may weaken their position. Indeed, the broader comparative literature on models of democracy and reform demonstrates that constitutions, and particularly meta-political aspects, tend to be notoriously resistant to change. As Lijphart notes, 'fundamental constitutional changes are difficult to effect and therefore rare'.[22] The core issue for this book rests on the degree to which the Labour Party was actually committed to replacing the traditional Westminster Model of the constitution with a more consensual, pluralist, and participatory form or whether it was only *rhetorically* committed to reforms while still harbouring its traditional commitment to majoritarian politics at a less visible level. Put slightly differently, was there a significant distinction between the Labour Party's commitment in *principle* and in *practice*?

In order to develop this point in more detail it is useful to draw upon a distinction developed in the field of comparative electoral studies. Specifically, the distinction between *outcome-contingent* and *act-contingent* factors in relation to electoral reform processes as this provides a useful heuristic tool for understanding and explaining executive actions and non-actions in relation to meta-constitutional politics.[23] *Outcome-contingent* factors encourage incumbent executives to pursue a programme of strategic reform because they prefer the anticipated outcome of the modified system to the status quo. Examples include the introduction of electoral reform in France in 1981 and 1986, and in Italy in 2006. *Act-contingent* factors, by contrast, emphasize style over substance, and the potential benefits of being *seen* as pro-reform by the public in order to benefit from perceived electoral support irrespective of whether or not any deeper attachment exists.

Reviewing the actual performance and governing mentality of New Labour in office will aid our understanding in relation to whether the party was pursuing an outcome-contingent strategy, or had simply attached themselves to the cause of constitutional reform and democratic renewal as an act-contingent electoral strategy. However, it is important at this stage to (re)emphasize three elements of this debate: (*a*) the Labour Party's historical support for the Westminster Model; (*b*) the fact that the shadow cabinet contained many individuals who were notably less enthusiastic about the merits of reform; and (*c*) Tony Blair was amongst these individuals. After Blair became Leader of the Labour Party, several senior voices advised him to drop the constitutional reform agenda because they saw it as a distraction from New Labour's prime focus on the economy and public services. These members of the shadow Cabinet argued that constitutional reform was not an important issue for the electorate, and that valuable parliamentary time should not be sacrificed in their first two legislative sessions.[24] As Riddell notes,

> [T]he Labour Party, and in particular Tony Blair himself, have never fully embraced constitutional reform and a pluralist view of politics. At times, it has seemed that constitutional reform has been additional to, and separate from, the main New Labour programme.[25]

This last point is particularly significant. With the exception of Northern Ireland, Blair was disinterested in constitutional reform. According to one senior official whenever the issue of constitutional reform was raised in a meeting, Blair's eyes 'just glazed over' and as Prime Minister he adopted an instrumental tick-box mentality towards democratic renewal that failed to articulate a clear vision of the form of constitution he was attempting to construct.[26] With the benefit of hindsight the antecedents of this governing mentality are identifiable during Blair's period as Leader of the Opposition prior to becoming Prime Minister (1994–7). Jack Straw, one of the less passionate members of the shadow cabinet regarding constitutional reform was appointed Shadow Home Secretary, and the strongly pro-reform party spokesman for constitutional affairs Graham Allen was replaced by the markedly less enthusiastic Kim Howells. Allen was well aware of the implication of these internal strategic manoeuvrings and expressed his concern in January 1995 by writing, 'without the personal impetus supplied by John Smith, both the witting and unthinking centralists will halt the process of policy development on democracy'.[27] Section 3.2 considers the actions, attitude, and approach of the Labour Party in government from 1 May 1997 onwards.

3.2 New Labour

The concept of a 'meta-constitutional orientation' helps us dig beneath the visible exterior of a constitutional framework and identify the underlying assumptions, values, and principles on which a polity is based. Meta-constitutional debates (or what Hirschl calls 'mega-politics') focus on the utility of underpinning elements of the constitution which provide the foundation of the system while also and generally ascribing a pattern or model of democracy. Identifying the existence of secondary or competing meta-constitutional orientations creates questions concerning their genesis. Indeed, understanding the logic behind the design, advocacy, and influence of alternative meta-constitutional orientations is likely to explain the manner in which they are subsequently accepted or rejected—or certain elements are cherry-picked—by the political elite.

As historical institutionalism seeks to emphasize, over time power tends to become embedded in institutional configurations which has a constraining effect on future action. Past decisions establish a framework, funnel, or channel that is likely to augment the recurrence of a specific pattern in the future. This constraining or shaping effect—'path dependency'—leads to a degree of continuity, shared norms, bounded rationality, or what March and Olsen describe as a 'logic of appropriateness'.[28] The structural characteristics of institutions are therefore arguably characterized by inbuilt biases against change, a position which would resonate with the emphasis on the Westminster Model's enduring qualities, as mentioned in Chapter 2.[29] However, significant change did occur during the decade after 1997. And yet the existence of change is of little value without a consideration of the process, pace, and extent of change and in order to tease apart these dimensions it is useful to break the decade 1997–2007 into three distinct periods (Table 3.1).

Table 3.1 New Labour and the constitution: three phases

Phase	Dates	Characterization	Core content
1.	May 1997 to June 2001 (1st full term).	Upheaval followed by Anomie.	The introduction of a large number of reforms in the early sessions followed by growing concern regarding a lack of clarity regarding underpinning principles or what the government was seeking to achieve.
2.	June 2001 to September 2005 (2nd full term).	Failure and anomie.	Attempts to complete 'unfinished business' were unsuccessful, major reform announcements were made without adequate detailed planning or consultation, growing disquiet about the government's apparently shoddy and half-hearted approach to constitutional reform.
3.	September 2005 to June 2007 (3rd term up to the resignation of Blair).	Marginalization and anomie.	Constitutional reform becomes a key issue between Blair and Brown.

What each of the following three sub-sections (one on each of the phases) seeks to demonstrate is the existence of constitutional anomie as a continuing theme of governance under Labour.

3.2.1 *Phase 1: constitutional upheaval, 1997–2001*

Having swept into power on 1 May 1997 with a working majority of 178, New Labour unleashed an almost frantic programme of constitutional reform. No less than twenty bills relating to constitutional reform were steered through parliament during the first three parliamentary sessions facilitating devolution to Scotland and Wales, incorporation of the European Convention on Human Rights in a Human Rights Act, freedom of information legislation, reform of the House of Lords, operational independence to the Bank of England, and a range of other measures (see Table 3.2).

This degree of constitutional (hyper)activity was driven by two factors: first, implementing a number of these reforms, notably devolution, was irresistible due to a combination of popular pressures and long-standing pre-election commitments; and, (second) the government's commitment to stay within the previous Conservative administration's spending limits restricted major social and economic policy initiatives, thereby allowing the parliamentary timetable to accommodate a large amount of constitutional legislation without intense pressure from other members of the Cabinet for legislative space. However, the government was unwilling, even unable, to draw together the distinct elements of the reform process within one coherent package or narrative.[30] The government did not publish a white paper on constitutional reform in order to set out what is was trying to achieve.

Towards the end of the 1997 Parliament, however, a degree of constitutional fatigue set in. A number of senior ministers felt that constitutional issues had taken up too much time, were of little interest to the general public, and may have created a range of constitutional hurdles that may later thwart the government in pushing forward with major social, economic, and public sector reforms. It is also important to understand that Tony Blair had never been a fully fledged supporter of constitutional reforms. Many of the policies implemented during the first time were the legacy of John Smith's period as Leader of the Labour Party to which Blair felt he had a moral and political duty to see through, albeit in a more limited manner than John Smith may have envisaged. As a result 'the calm after the storm' might usefully sum up the general feeling in relation to

Table 3.2 New Labour's constitutional reforms 1997–2007

Legislation	Reform
Referendums (Scotland and Wales) Act 1997	Facilitated public referendums on devolution to Scotland and Wales.
Scotland Act 1998	Established a Scottish Parliament.
Government of Wales Act 1998	Established a Welsh Assembly.
Bank of England Act 1998	Increased the independence of the Bank of England and reduced the role of ministers.
Human Rights Act 1998	Incorporated the European Convention on Human Rights into British law.
Northern Ireland (Elections) Act 1998	Established an Assembly in Northern Ireland.
Regional Development Agencies Act 1998	Established a network of non-elected semi-autonomous bodies to promote regional development.
Greater London Authority Act 1998	Established an elected regional assembly for London.
Registration of Political Parties Act 1998	Created an independent Electoral Commission and regulatory framework for political parties.
European Parliament Elections Act 1999	Changed the electoral system for electing MEPs.
House of Lords Act 1999	Removed the majority of hereditary peers from the House of Lords.
Representation of the People Act 2000	Allowed voters to request postal votes and enabled local authorities to pilot schemes for electoral arrangements.
Freedom of Information Act 2000	Established a statutory freedom of information regime.
Local Government Act 2000	Require local authorities to adopt a executive model system and also introduced a new ethical framework and independent regulator.
Political Parties, Elections and Referendums Act 2000	Created an independent Electoral Commission to keep electoral law and practice under review.

the constitution at the end of New Labour's first term in office. A great number of potentially far-reaching reforms had been enacted but there was a sense that the time had come to allow these changes to 'bed in'. It is, however, possible to identify two critical issues in relation to New Labour's statecraft during its first term. The first of these relates directly to the issue of constitutional anomie: a broad sense of concern and anxiety that the constitutional project lacked clarity with regard to both principles and outcomes. The basis upon which reform decisions had been taken were far from clear, particularly because 'in its genesis and implementation the government's enterprise of constitutional reform deliberately eschewed any engagement with first principles, with grand plans and templates, or with the creation of new constitutional machinery to underpin the arrangements it was busily putting in place'.[31] Although Seldon suggests that it was Lord Irvine, rather than Blair, who was 'committed to filling [John] Smith's legacy' as Lord Chancellor from 1997–2003, Lord Irvine was never willing to engage in the articulation of core values,

> The strands do not spring from a single master plan, however much that concept might appeal to purists. We prefer the empirical genius of our nation: to go, pragmatically, step by step, for change through continuing consent. Principled steps, not absolutist master plans, are the winning route to constitutional renewal in unity and in peace.[32]

In December 2002, Lord Irvine used a speech in the House of Lords to set out the government's approach to constitutional reform which can be summarized as follows:

1. The United Kingdom should remain a parliamentary democracy with the Westminster Parliament supreme and within that the Commons the dominant chamber.
2. To encourage greater public participation by 'developing a maturer democracy with different centres of power, where individuals enjoy greater rights and where government is carried out closer to the people'.
3. To devise a solution to each problem on its own terms.[33]

For Lord Norton this announcement signalled that 'the principled approach was, at once, to retain power at the centre, not to retain power at the centre, and to decide as one goes along' but the critical element of this statement relates to the manner in which it reflects a second critical theme of New Labour's statecraft: a commitment to work within the parameters of the Westminster Model. This is an issue which permeates the second part of this book, and it is sufficient here to note the manner in which New Labour sought to implement its reforms while at the same time seeking to maintain core elements of the UK's traditional constitution, notably the notion of parliamentary sovereignty and the convention of ministerial responsibility. These tenets of the Westminster Model were deployed in order to legitimate the need for ministers or the House of Commons to have the final decision on all matters and as a result the constitutional legislation set out in Table 3.2 is replete with exemptions, opt-outs, or potential ministerial vetos. The disparity between the government's pre-election rhetoric and the manner in which specific elements of the reform agenda were designed and implemented stimulated concern that New Labour had in fact been act-contingent and possessed little enthusiasm to move towards a power-sharing model of democracy based upon a quite different meta-constitutional orientation. It was in this vein that Weir and his colleagues noted,

> The government's reluctance to accept the need to redress the balance of power between executive and parliament matches its attitude towards devolution, elections to Westminster, the Human Rights Act, and freedom of information. The Prime Minister and his ministers and 'No.10 Downing Street' are united in their determination to maintain the power of the central state and political executive.[34]

How these issues and themes played out during New Labour's second term is the topic of the next sub-section.

3.2.2 Phase 2: constitutional failure, 2001–5

In June 2001 New Labour was re-elected with a Commons majority of 166. However, it was clear that the party's priorities had changed and also that the wider political context had altered. Domestically, the government's commitment to public services and specifically its emphasis on delivery prioritized results over processes and rested on a belief that the public are less interested in participation and scrutiny but do want high-quality public services delivered at the lowest possible cost.[35] Indeed, the pressure on the government to deliver on health, education, etc., created an environment that favoured strong government. The international context had also altered. The September 2001 suicide attacks in London altered the political climate and promoted the strengthening of centralized executive power over its dispersal. The emphasis on public service delivery within a broader context that was painfully aware of heightened security risks combined to re-focus attention on the benefits of strong government arguably above more liberal values.

The first two sessions of Labour's second term included a limited package of parliamentary modernization, further government papers, and statements on the future of the Lords, and the publication of a white paper on devolution to English regions. Constitutional matters were not, therefore, a priority for the government. Paradoxically, the importance of this period lies not in any reforms but in the sustained criticism and pressure on the government. Attention focused on areas where the government was seen as failing to implement meaningful reform (e.g. reform of the House of Commons), or was constantly avoiding making decisions or firm announcements (e.g. introducing a Civil Service Act or considering reform of the electoral system for Westminster). The Labour government's attempts via the whips to manipulate the composition of the Commons select committees in July 2001, combined with the subsequent tensions between Parliament and the executive over the deployment of troops to Iraq created considerable anxiety, and constitutional observers began to detect a clear shift in the governing mentality of New Labour that could arguably be interpreted as a swing from an executive mentality with at least some degree of sympathy for a power-sharing model of democracy to one that was more firmly focused on the governing merits of a power-hoarding model.

In response to these concerns and more established criticisms relating to the core principles underlying the process the government attempted to seize the initiative in June 2003. The catalyst came in the form of a government re-shuffle that included the removal of Lord Irvine and the announcement that the post of Lord Chancellor was to be abolished and most of the responsibilities of the Lord Chancellor's Department transferred to a new Department for Constitutional Affairs (DCA) headed by Lord Falconer. However, far from reassuring the public that the government was in control of the agenda, the reforms further reinforced the view that the government was confused and divided over the aims and future of the reform process. The public statement by the Prime Minister took many members of the Cabinet by surprise and once again it was clear that detailed consultations and preparatory planning had not preceded the announcement.[36] For example, it was initially announced that the Scottish Office and the Welsh Office would be subsumed within the DCA but hours later the government reversed this decision and announced that the territorial departments and their Secretaries of State would continue to exist.

In the Queen's next speech at the opening of the 2003–4 parliamentary session, the DCA received the major share of the legislative timetable. Moreover, the government's future legislative programme included two major constitutional bills—the House of Lords Bill and the Constitutional Reform Bill. Not only did these reforms attempt to tidy up Whitehall in the aftermath of devolution, but they also represented an attempt, in the form of Lord Falconer, to situate the reform programme on the shoulders of an individual who would be willing to engage in debates concerning the values and principles behind the constitutional changes. A distinct feature of Lord Falconer's tenure as Lord Chancellor and Secretary of State for Constitutional Affairs (2003–7) was his willingness, in direct opposition to his predecessor, to engage in retrospective reasoning in order to try and reassure the public and commentators that the constitutional reform programme did indeed have a coherent and clear principled foundation and rationale.

> [T]the constitutional issue at stake is one of the most important in a liberal democracy—the relationship between citizens and the state ... Since 1997 this Government has been involved in a sustained attempt to revive and redefine that relationship for the twenty-first century. Three progressive values have underpinned our approach: the first has been to enhance the credibility and effectiveness of our public institutions; the second has been to strengthen our democracy and public engagement with decision-making; and the third has been to increase trust and accountability in public bodies.[37]

Not only did these 'progressive values' represent a marked dilution of the 'revolutionary' rhetoric and discourse on which New Labour had been elected in 1997, but it was also difficult to reconcile them with manner in which the government had managed the reform process. Public trust and the credibility of the government's reform initiatives were damaged by the government's failure to undertake detailed preparatory work or consult the public ahead of major announcements. These weaknesses, combined with poor media management, led to the government to be perceived as floundering, ill-prepared, over-hasty (even desperate), and, at times, simply shoddy. This fuelled further criticism that the government lacked any coherent vision of the reformed constitution as a whole or appreciation of the possibly negative consequences of reforms in one area for other aspects of the constitutional configuration. Norton interprets 2003–5 as the period in which Tony Blair attempted to take personal control of the constitutional reform agenda and that the lack of consultation or detailed planning in advance of announcement was symptomatic of a broader style of governing, and to some extent 'Too much vigour, not enough rigour' is a suitable epithet for New Labour's approach to the constitution during its second term.[38] This might explain why a striking feature of this period was the government's failure to complete most of the 'unfinished business' carried over from Phase 1. If anything, the overall situation was more confused, bordering on the chaotic, at the end of the second term: the future of the House of Lords remained unclear; the Constitutional Reform Act 2005 had been passed, but only in an eviscerated manner; plans for elected regional government in England were in disarray (particularly after the resounding no vote in the North East regional referendum in November 2004); and the issue of electoral reform for Westminster remained firmly marginalized. Added to this was evidence that public trust in politics, politicians, and political institutions had declined to pre-1997 levels. The degree to which New Labour's third term addressed these issues is the topic of the next sub-section.

3.2.3 *Phase 3: constitutional spillover, 2005–7*

This third phase focuses on the period from when New Labour was elected to a third term in office (with a much-reduced majority of 66) in September 2005 to the resignation of Tony Blair on 27 June 2007 and can be interpreted as a period in which the existence of constitutional anomie became most clear. The dynamics, anomalies, and inconsistencies created by New Labour's first-wave of reforms (1997–2001) began to spill over and spill back, and as a consequence demanded some sort of coherent response from the government as to how each element of the reform programme was intended to hang together or, at the very least, why one model or form of democracy was viewed as appropriate for certain levels of governance but not others. Not only did the government appear unable to provide a response to these questions, but it was also unable (or unwilling) to proceed with those elements of 'unfinished business' that had now been on the agenda for nearly a decade. Rather than setting the agenda and demonstrating any strategic capacity the government appeared to be fire-fighting in response to external events.

The Richard Commission on the powers of the Welsh Assembly and evidence of electoral malpractice in relation to postal voting in the 2005 General Election, for example, led the government to introduce the Government of Wales Act 2006 and the Electoral Administration Act 2006 respectively, while the 'no' votes in the Dutch and French referendums on the European Constitution led the government to cancel its plans for a referendum in the UK. The 'Cash for Peerages' affair in 2006 was hugely damaging for a government that had been elected into office to restore public trust and refocused attention on the issue of Lords reform. However, progress on this issue had been blocked by the failure of the government to be able to convene a committee of both houses to examine the issue. Pressure for change was also growing within the Palace of Westminster. In November 2005 the Prime Minister had been introduced to the challenges of governing with a small majority by the government's first defeat on a whipped vote (on the Terrorism Bill) since New Labour had come to power in May 2007. A number of private members bills in the Commons and Lords, like David Chaytor's *Electoral Choice Bill* and Lord

Lester's *Constitutional Reform (Prerogative Powers and the Civil Service) Bill*, had also signalled parliamentary disquiet with the executive's failure to move forward in certain areas. The pressure on the government vis-à-vis prerogative powers increased in July 2006 with the Lords' Committee on the Constitution's report *Waging War: Parliament's role and responsibility*.[39] In February 2007, the long-awaited white paper on Lords reform was published and recommended an equal but mixed composition of elected and appointed members.[40] But during the subsequent vote on 7 March the 50:50 proposal was rejected by 418 votes to 155, while the vote for a fully elected chamber received the most support. Not only was a fully elected chamber, however, the least palatable option for the Prime Minister, but it also raised broader questions about the legitimacy and role of each house, and the relationship between the two. As a result, the government announced that further work on Lords reform would not proceed until after the next General Election in 2009 or 2010.

Beyond the Palace of Westminster the court decision to overrule the proposed deportation of nine Afghan hijackers prompted the Prime Minister to order an official review into whether primary legislation was needed to address the issue of court rulings which overrule the government in a way that was inconsistent with other EU countrifes' interpretation of the European Convention on Human Rights. If the Human Rights Act had shifted the balance of powers in ways that New Labour had not originally anticipated, then the May 2007 elections to the Scottish Parliament provided an equally testing case of constitutional dynamics with the election of a Scottish National Party government under the leadership of Alex Salmond. The potential consequences of this development were underlined in August 2007 when the First Minister announced the publication of *Scotland's Future—A National Conversation* which proposed a single referendum on Scottish independence. However, for the purposes of this section and this book, the election of a minority SNP government in Edinburgh marks the final constitutional event of Tony Blair's tenure as the figurehead of New Labour. The Unionist parties' response, establishing a Scottish Constitutional Commission to examine the present constitutional arrangements, was the first cross-border initiative involving Gordon Brown and David Cameron.

More importantly, this cross-border and cross-party collaboration on the management of constitutional dynamism and reform reflected a change in Prime Ministerial style and thinking in relation to constitution issues, the roots of which might be dated back to Gordon Brown's involvement with Charter 88 in the mid-1990s but which had resurfaced from the beginning of New Labour's third term. Indeed, Tony Blair's final years as Prime Minister were arguably ones in which the existence of constitutional anomie were most obvious and a tipping-point arguably occurred around Easter 2006 when the existence of intra-executive tensions and frustrations became public, and the issue of constitutional reform became a central element of the long-standing friction between Tony Blair and Gordon Brown over the succession process. This surfaced for the first time in a newspaper article by Brown in which he signalled that a priority for the government was 'to work out the detail of the next steps for both local democracy and long-term constitutional reform' and move towards 'a new constitutional settlement...a radical shift of power from the centre...[and] a renewed debate on issues including the role of parties and electoral reform', which was widely interpreted as a veiled attack on Blair's disinterest in constitutional issues.[41] At the same time similar issues were raised by the Leader of the Opposition, David Cameron, who declared 'the time is right for a serious thoughtful programme of institutional and constitutional reform...not knee-jerk and reactionary' and launched a 'Democracy Taskforce' chaired by Kenneth Clarke.[42]

These party political statements overlapped with the work of the Independent Inquiry into Britain's Democracy—the Power Report. Published in March 2006, the report concluded that power had become more centralized under New Labour and therefore called for a number of power-sharing measures and more public participation. The report was, however, devoid of specific recommendations and perpetuated a number of highly contested myths about governance in the UK.[43] What was particularly significant in light of the approach of this book was the manner in which the approach and language of the inquiry was shaped and bounded by the very precepts of the Westminster Model it was implicitly attempting to deconstruct. In this regard the report exhibited little awareness and sensitivity to the inbuilt impediments to achieving significant reform. In this regard the Power Report exhibited many of the weakness of a pseudo-journalistic descriptive–prescriptive approach that has dominated the study of the constitution within British political studies for much of the twentieth century (a theme developed in Chapter 4).

This section has examined the behaviour of New Labour in office vis-à-vis constitutional reform. The analysis of each of the three phases discussed earlier suggests that although New Labour were committed to implementing reforms of some kind, they were never clear about what exactly they were attempting to achieve. Rhetorically the party was clearly associated with a commitment to create a more consensual and participatory model of democracy, but support for this vision had always been half-hearted. Tony Blair was not a constitutional entrepreneur and as the challenges of governing in the twenty-first century, in both domestic and international terms, became more apparent, support for reforms that would dilute the executive's governing capacity waned. In this sense although constitutional anomie had always existed within the political psychology of New Labour, it became increasingly obvious over time as the government appeared unable or unwilling to articulate a vision of what exactly it was seeking to achieve. And it is in this context that Hazell has called for a 'new narrative' that would offer a better justification than the 'bland word of modernisation' and thereby weave the various threads of the constitutional reform programme together.[44]

It would be an error, however, to label New Labour's approach as un-principled and more accurate to argue that the central dilemma for the government was the inconsistency between the meta-constitutional orientation it rhetorically attached itself to in opposition, and the one it sought to maintain and protect in office. The central anomaly or incon-sistency of New Labour was rooted in its attempt to forge a more consen-sual and participatory form of power-sharing constitution *within* the parameters of an essentially elitist and centralized power-hoarding consti-tution. This is a critical point. The central contribution of this book rests in the fact that it departs from the wider literature by rejecting the utility of a binary-axis between power-hoarding and power-sharing democracies and instead argues that the situation is far more complex. New Labour did not attempt to shift the constitution of the UK from one dominant model of democracy to another, but instead adopted a strategy of bi-constitutionalism involving an attempt to apply different meta-constitu-tional orientations at different levels of governance. The great value of this argument regarding the notion of bi-constitutionality is that it provides a way of explaining and understanding what has been termed the 'Blair paradox' and the analytical polarization that has occurred in relation to the significance of New Labour's constitutional reforms.

3.3 The Blair paradox

Identifying meta-constitutional orientations and being aware of their potential incompatibility provides a useful tool for exploring what has been described as the 'Blair paradox'. How can a government, which has set in train a great number of major constitutional reforms that involve the devolution or transference of some degree of political power be seen, at the same time, as having a strong centralizing and controlling approach to governing which conflicts with the centrifugal thrust of many of the constitutional reforms? It is this vein that Marquand has noted the 'mixture of boldness and timidity' and 'the contradictions of modernisation' which have characterized New Labour's approach to the constitution.[45] King states that 'For people so often accused of being power hungry they have been behaving, to say the least, oddly' while Norris goes further and states,

> For all the commissions and committees, the reviews and the reports, employing the great and the good, there is no over-arching master plan but rather a perfect exemplification of British muddling through. This remains a work in progress, although the Blair government's defining achievement during their first term in office, characterised schizophrenically by courage and timidity, radicalism and conservatism, devolution and centralization, often with two steps unexpectedly forwards and one back.[46]

As Section 3.2 demonstrated, there is no doubt that during 1997–2007, New Labour was exceedingly active in relation to constitutional reform. And yet an intense debate exists concerning the *degree* to which the nature of democracy in the UK has changed, and whether political power has actually become more dispersed. It is beyond the bounds of this section to review the existing literature in great depth and it is sufficient to highlight the fact that two largely coherent groups of scholars can be identified. The first group—the Revolutionary Theorists—argue that fundamental reforms have been implemented; while the second group—the Sceptical Theorists—emphasize the continuing role and influence of the Westminster Model, and therefore assess the impact of New Labour's reforms as markedly less significant than the first group.

The Revolutionary Theorists consists of a body of scholars who are broadly of the opinion that during 1997–2007 New Labour implemented *fundamental* reforms (see Table 2.1) that remodelled the UK's traditional constitution along more pluralist lines. It is in this vein that Peter Mair wrote, 'New Labour is currently engaged in what amounts to a full-blooded constitutional revolution, dragging the political system away from an extreme version of majoritarian democracy towards a more institutionally consensual model'.[47] From a similar perspective Maer and her colleagues suggest that 'constitutional law is growing into a more distinct body of fundamental law. Although technically these constitutional laws have no higher status, politically they are entrenched in a way that ordinary statute law is not'.[48] McDonald opens his *Reinventing Britain* (2007) by stating 'The proposition behind this book is a simple one. Since the election of the New Labour government in 1997, the British state has undergone radical change'; while Bogdanor similarly states that 'the Labour government, elected in 1997, implemented the most radical programme of constitutional reform that Britain had seen since the Great Reform Act'.[49]

In direct opposition to this view is King's analysis of 'Britain's New Constitution' which he concludes 'remains essentially a power-hoarding or power concentrating constitution'.[50] Peter Riddell, Chief Political Editor of *The Times*, similarly suggests 'At root, Blair has shown himself as much a majoritarian in his instincts as Thatcher'.[51] This point chimes with the view of Theakston that 'Blair's 'modernization' rhetoric cannot disguise a strong personal attachment to the fundamentals of an executive-dominated parliamentary regime'.[52] Johnson takes on the Fundamental Theorists directly by stating that 'Despite the best efforts of the protagonists to present the changes as the fulfilment of a radical reform programme there are few grounds for accepting such a view of the matter. The constitution has not been reshaped, or cast in a new form.'[53] Lord Norton's view that 'The Westminster model has been modified, perhaps vandalised but it has not been destroyed' corresponds with Nairn's conclusion that 'the mainframe has remained sacrosanct' and Morison's opinion that 'the government may style itself New Labour but it is very old constitutionalism that informs its reform programme'.[54] Taylor similarly states that, 'The Westminster Model, despite criticism and (apparent) reform, remains the authoritative description of how politics should operate and what the distribution of power should be' while Judge concludes that 'the majoritarianism of the parliamentary system was not seen as a problem by New Labour Governments'.[55] Evans argues that 'Third Way democracy is elite democracy in disguise'.[56] Byrne and Weir conclude their democratic audit by stating that 'The Labour government's reform programme since 1997 has retained central powers on which 'elective dictatorship' or Jack Straw's 'executive democracy' depends', while Morrison similarly notes '... despite all the reforms to the periphery, the core of the British political system of elective dictatorship has remained intact'.[57]

Although seeking to specify two dominant views on the nature and extent of New Labour's constitutional reforms' risks exaggerating the degree of coherency that actually exists, it is possible to argue that a constellation of values and assumptions can be identified in each case. Furthermore, what is significant about these analyses is the degree to which a distinct polarization is relatively clear. Even those scholars who adopt a more nuanced and less extreme position can generally be located on the margins of one pole or another. Gamble's analysis, for example, concludes that 'the UK today is less centralist and less unitary than it was, but it is still a long way from a political system that is truly federal and decentralized, and many doubt it will ever arrive' would fall, albeit softly, within the sceptical camp.[58] In contrast, the work of Dunleavy on electoral behaviour and reform in which he suggests that Britain is experiencing a transition towards full multi-party politics would fit within the Revolutionary Theorists' camp.[59]

Both camps agree that New Labour's reforms have been far-reaching and have altered to some degree the nature of British democracy. No one is arguing that the reforms are cosmetic: the debate relates to the issue of degree. And yet so far the Fundamentalists and Sceptical camps have largely talked past each other and there has been little attempt to connect, understand, or weave together their respective positions as part of a broader coherent analysis of the constitution as it exists today.

However, a major ontological and epistemological problem with this debate is that it has become polarized around a binary distinction *between* consensual or majoritarian meta-constitutional orientations, when in fact the contemporary reality is far more complex. The 'Blair paradox' actually reflects not a simple shift in orientations, but a multifaceted attempt to overlay a new meta-constitutional orientation on top of the existing version. This is the creation of a multi-level polity based upon a more consensual model of democracy *within* what is, admittedly, an increasingly frail conception of the Westminster model. And it is this constitutional engineering, or more precisely the attempt to blend arguably incompatible meta-constitutional orientations that explains not only the manner in which certain reforms have been implemented, but also why the government has sought to block or marginalize certain issues. This line of argument forces us to reflect back on the tools of political analysis that have been deployed to date in order to understand how New Labour has altered democracy in the UK, and it is exactly this issue that forms the focus of Chapter 4.

Notes

1. Marquand, David (1999). 'Populism or Pluralism? New Labour and the Constitution', Mishcon Lecture, UCL.

2. See Bogdanor, V (2004) 'Our New Constitution', *Law Quarterly Review*, 120, 242–62.

3. See Taylor, M (2000) 'Labour and the Constitution' in Tanner, D Thane, P and Tiratsoo eds. *Labour's First Century* Cambridge: Cambridge University Press; Wright, A (1990) 'British Socialists and the British Constitution'; *Parliamentary Affairs*, 43, 322–40; Dorey, P. (2008) *The Labour Party and Constitutional Reform*. London: Palgrave.

4. Kavanagh, D (2009) 'Antecedents' in Flinders, M Gamble, A Kenny, M and Hay, C eds. *The Oxford Handbook of British Politics* Oxford: Oxford University Press.

5. See Wright, A (1990) 'British Socialists and the British Constitution', *Parliamentary Affairs*, 43, 322–40.

6. Evans, M (2003) *Constitution-Making and the Labour Party*, Basingstoke: Palgrave, 20.

7. *The Guardian* 12 December 1989; see also *The Guardian* 19 December 1989.

8. See, for example, Marquand, D (1988) *The Unprincipled Society*. London: Fontana.

9. Wright, A (1990) 'British Socialists and the British Constitution', 322.

10. Smith, J (1993) *A Citizens' Democracy* London; Charter 88.

11. Giddens, A (1998) *The Third Way*, Cambridge: Polity, 26.

12. Faux, J (1999) 'Lost on the Third Way', *Dissent*, 46, 75.

13. Giddens, *The Third Way*, 69.

14. Giddens, A (2000) *The Third Way and Its Critics*, Cambridge: Polity, 61.

15. Giddens, *The Third Way*, 73–4.

16. See, for example, Hargreaves, I and Christie, I (1998) *Tomorrow's Politics: The Third Way and Beyond*. London: Demos; Halpern, D and Mikosz, D (1998) *The Third Way*, London: Nexus; Leadbetter, C (1999) *Living on Thin Air*, London: Viking. For a discussion see, Finlayson, A (1999) 'Third Way Theory', *Political Quarterly*, 70, 271–9; Barnett, A (1997) *This Time*, London: Vintage; Mulgan, G (1997) *Life After Politics*, London: Demos; Hutton, W (1995) *The State We're In*, London: Jonathan Cape.

17. Mandelson, P and Liddle, R (1996) *The Blair Revolution*, London: Faber & Faber.

18. Blair, T (1996) 'My Vision for Britain', in Giles Radice, ed., *What Needs to Change?*, London: Harper Collins, 3. See also Blair, T (1996) *New Britain*, London: Fourth Estate; Blair, T (1998) *The Third Way*, London: Fabian Society.

19. See Giddens, A (2002) *Where Now for New Labour?* Cambridge: Polity, 80.

20. Cook, R and Maclennan, R (2005) Looking Back, Looking Forward: The Cook-Maclennan Agreement Eight Years On. London: New Politics Network.

21. Labour Party (1997) *New Labour: Because Britain Deserves Better*, London: Labour Party.

22. Lijphart, A (2008) *Thinking About Democracy*. London: Routledge, 178.

23. See Shugart, M and Wattenberg, M eds. (2001) *Mixed-Member Electoral Systems*, Oxford: Oxford University Press.

24. See Seldon, A (2004) *Blair*. London: Free Press, 205.

25. Riddell, P (2007) 'Labour's Conversion to Constitutional Reform', in McDonald, A ed. *Reinventing Britain,* London: Politicos, 31.

26. Quoted in Norton, P (2007) 'Tony Blair and the Constitution', *British Politics*, 2, 269. Interestingly Harden also states that 'Mrs Thatcher's eyes were reported to glaze over at the mention of Constitutional reform'. See Harden, I (1991) 'The Constitution and its Discontents', 510.

27. Allen, G (1995) Reinventing Democracy: Labour's Mission for a New Century.

28. March, J and Olsen, J (1989) *Rediscovering Institutions,* New York: Free Press.

29. Dunleavy, P (2006) 'The Westminster Model and the Distinctiveness of British Politics', in Dunleavy, P Heffernan, R Cowley, P and Hay, C eds, *Developments in British Politics 8,* London: Macmillan, 315–41.

30. See McDonald, A and Hazell, A 'What Happened Next' in McDonald, A ed. *Reinventing Britain,* London: Politicos.

31. Gamble, A and Wright, T (2000) 'Modernising Government?', *Political Quarterly*, 71(3), 265.

32. Irvine, Lord. (1998) Lecture to the Constitution Unit, 8 December 1998. See Seldon, A (2004) *Blair* London: Free Press, 205.

33. HL Hansard 18 December 2002, col.692.

34. Beetham, D Ngan, P and Weir, S (2001) 'Democratic Audit: Labour's Record So Far' *Parliamentary Affairs*, 54 (2), 389.

35. See Shaw, E (2004) 'What matters is what works' in Hale, S Leggett, W and Martell, L (eds.) *The Third Way and Beyond*, Manchester: Manchester University Press.

36. Seldon *op cit.* (2004), 562–3.

37. Falconer, Lord. 'Constitutional Reform Speech', University College London, 8 December 2003; Falconer, Lord. 'Human Rights and Constitutional Reform', Law Society and Human Rights Lawyers' Association, London, 17 February 2004; Falconer, Lord. 'Constitutional Reform: Strengthening Democracy and Rights', Inaugural Leslie Falconer WS Memorial Lecture, Signet Library, Edinburgh, 20 February 2004.

38. See Norton *op cit.* (2007).

39. HL 236 Waging War: Parliament's role and responsibility.

40. CM 7072 (2007) *The House of Lords: Reform* London: HMSO.

41. *The Guardian* 27 February 2006.

42. Cameron, D 'A Programme for Conservative constitutional reform', speech delivered at the Carlton Club, London, 26 July 2005.

43. See Riddell, P 'Toothless Parliament is fighting fit', *The Times* 28 February 2006.

44. Hazell, R (2007) 'The Continuing Dynamism of Constitutional Reform', *Parliamentary Affairs*, 60(1), 3–25.

45. Marquand, D (2000) 'Democracy in Britain', *Political Quarterly*, 268–76. See also Marquand, D (1998) 'The Blair Paradox', *Prospect*, 30; Marquand, D (2000) 'Revisiting the Blair Paradox', *New Left Review*, 3, 73–9.

46. King, A (2007) *The British Constitution*. Oxford: Oxford University Press, 355. Norris, P (2001) 'The Twilight of Westminster?', *Political Studies*, 49, 879.

47. Mair, P (2000) 'Partyless Democracy: Solving the Paradox of New Labour', *New Left Review*, 2 (March–April), 34.

48. Maer, L et al. (2004), 'The Constitution', *Parliamentary Affairs*, 57(2), 254.

49. McDonald *op cit.* (2007), vii; Bogdanor, *op cit.* (2003), 690. See also Bogdanor, V. (2004) 'Our New Constitution', *Law Quarterly Review*, 120, 242–62.

50. King *op cit.* (2007), 352.

51. Riddell, P (2007) 'Labour's conversion to constitutional reform' in McDonald *op cit.* (2007) 53.

52. Theakston, K (2005) 'Prime Ministers and the Constitution', *Parliamentary Affairs*, 58(1), 38.

53. Johnson, N (2004) *Reshaping the British Constitution,* London: Palgrave Macmillan, 308.

54. Quoted in Morrison, J (2001) *Reforming Britain,* London: Pearson Education, 509–10; Morison, J (1998) 'The Case Against Constitutional Reform?' *Journal of Law and Society*, 4, 525.

55. Taylor, A (2006) 'The Strategic Impact of the Electoral System and the Definition of 'Good' Governance', *British Politics,* 1, 25–43; Judge, D (2006) 'This is What Democracy Looks Like' *British Politics*, 1, 370. See also Judge, D (2004) 'What ever happened to parliamentary democracy in the United Kingdom?', *Parliamentary Affairs*, 57(3), 682–701.

56. Mair *op cit.* (2000), 34; Evans, M (2003) *Constitution-Making and the Labour Party* London: Palgrave, 5.

57. Byrne, I and Weir, S (2004) 'Democratic Audit', *Parliamentary Affairs*, 57 (2), 453–68; Morrison *op cit.* (2001), 501.

58. Gamble, A (2006) 'The Constitutional Revolution in the United Kingdom' *Publius,* 36(1), 33.

59. Dunleavy, P (2005) 'Facing Up to Multi-Party Politics' *Parliamentary Affairs*, 5(3), 503–32; See also Dunleavy, P and Margetts, H (2001) 'From Majoritarian to Pluralist Democracy', *Journal of Theoretical Politics*, 3, 295–319.

Chapter 4

Democratic Analysis

We do not know anything about constitutions here, at least not in the sense that they are known about elsewhere. We are not even familiar with the basic language of constitutional debate. The British enjoy a marvellous constitutional illiteracy. They think pluralism is a lung disease.[1]

In 1998, the Leader of the Conservative Party, William Hague, commented that 'Labour has embarked on a journey of constitutional upheaval without a route map'.[2] This was not simply a partisan point. It tapped into a much broader concern that New Labour was reforming the polity of the UK in a manner that was not only devoid of underlying principles, but was also opaque in terms of the aims or ambitions of this process. This approach was reflected in the government's tendency to reform aspects of the constitution in isolation without any apparent awareness of the inter-related nature of the constitution and in its failure to complete elements of 'unfinished business' during its second term. Equally if not more significant, was the government's apparent commitment to implementing its reforms *within* the parameters of the traditional Westminster Model. It is exactly this attempt to institute elements of a quite different model or form of democracy—one which emphasizes legally protected rights, public participation, new checks and balances, etc.—within a traditional democratic framework that inculcates a quite different meta-constitutional orientation which forms the basis of the 'Blair paradox' and the polarization of opinion that was set out in Chapter 3.

This chapter focuses on the tools of political analysis that have been used, and could be used in order to deepen our understanding of these issues. More specifically, it attempts to set out a methodology with the capacity to not only assess and gauge the nature of reform as it relates to specific elements of the constitution, but also to assess the cumulative impact of a number of specific reforms on the overall model or form of democracy. It achieves this by reviewing what might be termed the dominant tradition of studying the constitution within UK political studies in the first section. This identifies a common pattern by which scholars of UK politics have almost without exception adopted a normative descriptive–prescriptive institutionally focused approach. While this provides us with a certain form of knowledge, it arguably fails to provide a rigorous and coherent methodological framework with the capacity to map or trace the impact of constitutional reforms on a democratic system over time. Moreover, this traditional approach also tends to work, either implicitly or explicitly, within the conceptual bounds (and certainly within the discourse) of the Westminster Model. It therefore provides a form of disciplinary straightjacket which may well be inappropriate to furnish a broader or more rounded understanding of the new constitutionalism and it is in this context that Section 4.2 reviews Lijphart's framework for assessing and mapping patterns of democracy. This methodology, it is argued, aids understanding in relation to the 'Blair paradox', provides a more subtle and fine-grained account of change, and through this allows us to assess the degree to which New Labour's reforms should be conceived as *significant* or *fundamental* alterations to the polity of the UK. It also allows scholars to locate developments in the UK within a broader comparative context. Adopting Lijphart's methodology is no panacea to the challenges of political analysis but in the context of *The Governance of Britain* green paper and the two basic questions this book set out in Chapter 1—What kind of constitution and democracy do we have in the UK at the beginning of the twenty-first century? What are we attempting to achieve through the reform process?—this methodology for conceptual and empirical mapping provides a powerful and as yet unrivalled tool.

4.1 Approaches

Although Evan's may have been overstating the case in 2001 when he suggested that 'talking about constitutional politics has become "sexy"' in the UK it is certainly true that New Labour's constitutional reforms have been the focus of a large amount of literature and elements of this body of work, with its severe analytical polarization, which were briefly reviewed in Section 3.3. The existence of such a stark divergence of opinion raises questions about the theories, methods, and approaches that were deployed in order to reach these conclusions. The significance of these traditions in the context of this chapter stems from the fact that dominant approaches inculcate certain values, not just regarding the nature of knowledge in the social sciences, but specific ideas and beliefs regarding the object of analysis and how it should be studied. They also utilize quite different frames of reference, discourses, and methods in order to validate their theory of knowledge epistemologically. But in order to understand the power and role of certain approaches or traditions in the study of the constitution in the UK it is necessary to reflect on the heritage of political studies in this field. It is for this reason that the following three sub-sections review the dominant tradition in the study of the UK's constitution in three distinct phases of the disciplines history. The aim of these sub-sections is not to provide an authoritative account of every piece of writing published in each phase, but simply to tease out the main theories, methods and approaches through which knowledge on the UK's constitution was obtained and framed.

4.1.1 *Phase 1, 1850–1950*

Since the middle of the nineteenth century, writing about the constitution has been primarily concerned with describing political and governmental institutions and how they work.[3] The aim of these studies was to shed light on the inner workings of the state and the principles on which certain relationships and procedures were founded. Paradigms of this genre include Bagehot's *The English Constitution* (1867), Hearn's *Government of England* (1867), Todd's *Parliamentary Government in England* (two volumes: 1867 and 1869), and Freeman's *The Growth of the English Constitution* (1872) which each in their own way were written in a form of Whig historiography which entrenched what would come to be accepted as the Westminster Model.[4] A closely related sub-strand of legal scholarship focused on those norms and rules which might loosely be collected under the umbrella of 'constitutional law'—Dicey's *Introduction to the Study of the Law of the Constitution* (1885) and Anson's *The Law and Custom of the Constitution* (1886) providing classic and early examples—but this was far removed from the body of technical constitutional and public law which was developing in continental Europe. In fact, there was very little within this body of work which is not essentially focused on mapping and understanding *political* relationships, albeit possibly supported by a closer relationship with judicial decisions and case law, and the dominance of political and institutional approaches clearly reflected the character of the constitution in the UK itself (i.e. it was a *political* constitution).

The work of eminent constitutional theorists such as Dicey and Bagehot was significant because it set in train a form of disciplinary path-dependency, and as a result the first half of the twentieth century witnessed the publication of a number of texts that continued this historical-descriptive approach. This included: Jennings' *The Law and the Constitution* (1933) and *The British Constitution* (1941); Greaves' *The British Constitution* (1938); Amery's *Thoughts on the Constitution* (1947), Harrison's *The Government of Britain* (1948); Laski's *Reflections on the Constitution* (1951); and Morrison's *Government and Parliament* (1954), to name just a few exemplar texts. Until the 1960s, the mainstream approach to constitutional studies in the UK was therefore what Johnson labels 'institutional realism', the characteristics of which include:

1. Institutional description (i.e. 'rich' description).
2. Historical evidence and/or case studies.
3. A focus on the day-to-day workings of the constitution.
4. The lack of a distinctive methodology.
5. An (implicit or explicit) normative bias in favour of the existing constitution.

During the first half of the twentieth century, the majority of those writing on the constitution were disinclined to debate the fundamental principles on which the UK was governed, and were instead content to provide an objective account of particular aspects of the constitution rather than petition for any specific changes. This is reflected in Bogdanor and Skidelsky's statement in *The Age of Affluence* (1970) that 'one of the most striking characteristics of the 1950s was the absence of any major intellectual challenges to the dominant political assumptions'.[5]

However, the second half of the twentieth century witnessed both *continuity* and *change* in relation to the study of the constitution of the UK.

4.1.2 Phase 2, 1950–97

Continuity was exhibited in relation to the tools of political analysis (theories, approaches, and methods) that were deployed by commentators to understand and write about the constitution. Descriptive institutional studies that drew upon historical and precedent-based evidence and tended to focus on individual actions or specific decisions dominated the field. As such, semi-structured elite interviews, biographical analysis, and case studies were conventional research methods. To some extent the methods and approaches related to the nature of the constitution did little to lend themselves to quantitative methods or to the formal deductive modelling techniques that were promoted by public choice theorists. However, although explicit theoretical modelling, hypotheses testing, and deductive social-scientific techniques were not part of the UK's political tradition in constitutional analysis, it would be mistaken to label this approach as atheoretical. Studies of the constitution in the UK were implicitly set against, and within the theory of the Westminster Model.[6]

Emphasizing the role of the Westminster Model, not just in terms of its role of ascribing certain 'real world' relationships, but also in terms of its role and influence in shaping the way scholars approached the study of the constitution feeds into the first element of *change* that can be identified during the second half of the twentieth century. Change in this case relating to the normative foundation of analyses, particularly in relation to the efficacy of the Westminster Model as a workable and acceptable meta-constitutional orientation for the UK. Marshall and Moodie's *Some Problems of the Constitution* (1959), Chapman's *British Government Observed* (1963), and Crick's *The Reform of Parliament* (1964) signalled anxiety and frustration with the current situation and the start of the descriptive—prescriptive approach that would dominate the study of the constitution in the second half of the twentieth century. This approach can be traced from Crick through to Norton's *The Constitution in Flux* (1982) and Marshall's *Constitutional Conventions* (1984), and right through to the body of descriptive–prescriptive literature that was published in the 1990s and is set out in the final column of Table 2.2.

The literature identified in this table feeds into the second element of change that can be identified within literature on the constitution in the second half of the twentieth century—the development of a much broader constituency of writers on the constitution. Although there is little to be gained from attempting to delineate this body of work in anything apart from fairly broad categories, it is worth highlighting a number of specific sub-fields and their contribution to debates. One of the most significant developments in the 1980s was the increasing role of legal scholars within constitutional debates in the UK—Graham and Prosser's *Waiving the Rules* (1988), Lewis' *Hapy and Glorious: The Constitution in Transition* (1990), McAuslan and McEldowney *Law, Legitimacy and the Constitution* (1985), Brazier's *Constitutional Reform* (1991), and Oliver's *Government in the United Kingdom* (1991)—many of which advocated a normative preference for an increased role for the judiciary as a response to the perceived failure of the 'political constitution'. In this regard, much of the legal scholarship of the 1990s was overtly prescriptive and normative political scholarship.

The second key sub-strand of writing emanated from a number of non-academic authors on the constitution. This would include influential works by journalists—Mount's *The British Constitution Now* (1992), Hutton's *The State We're In* (1995), and Riddell's *Parliament Under Pressure* (1997). It is also possible to locate the work of individuals who have made the transition from journalism into academia within this grouping—Marquand's *The Unprincipled Society* (1988) and Hennessy's *The Hidden Wiring* (1995)—because they share a certain verve and accessibility which took their arguments to a much broader audience. This notion of reaching a wider audience and connecting with the public in terms of moulding or steering anxieties about the workings of the constitution leads us to consider the origins of a third sub-strand of writing which emerged during the 1980s—pro-reform advocacy groups and think-tanks. This body of work ranged from single-issue groups like the Campaign for Freedom of Information and Liberty, to organizations that were committed to achieving a broad programme of constitutional reforms. Central actors within this latter group included Charter 88, the Constitution Unit, DEMOS, Democratic Audit, and the Institute for Public Policy Research (IPPR).[7] In terms of promoting constitutional reforms, one of the roles and achievements of organizations like Charter 88 and the IPPR was their capacity to bring together representatives of many of these different advocacy networks (academics from a range of disciplines, journalists, former politicians, etc.) within specific campaigns that would, in turn, be discussed in the broadsheet media.[8]

Although the actual influence and role of these campaign groups on the Labour Party is a matter of debate, it is undoubtedly true that they played a role, amongst other factors, in stimulating debate about the need for change. As the debate intensified during the 1990s, support for constitutional change of some form emerged in the most unexpected quarters. For example, Vibert's *Britain's Constitutional Future* (1991), Hurd's *Conservatism in the 1990s* (1991), and Patten's *Rolling Constitutional Change* (1993) represented a strand of reformist Conservative thinking on the constitution which, although modest in terms of its ambitions and prescriptions for change, were notable for their existence and contribution to a broader campaign.

However, what is of critical importance for this book is the fact that although the normative foundation of much of the literature on the constitution in the second half of the twentieth century may have shifted from a position of implicitly supporting to explicitly critiquing the Westminster Model, the core tradition in terms of scholarship remained remarkably stable and apparently resilient to the influence of new theories, approaches, and methods that were evolving elsewhere in the world. The theoretical framework remained the Westminster Model, the dominant approach was institutional descriptive–prescriptive, and the main research methods involved historical analysis, case studies, and semi-structured elite interviews. Whether this changed in relation to the analysis of New Labour's decade in office is the topic of the next sub-section.

4.1.3 *Phase 3, 1997–2007*

The previous sub-sections have described a body of analysis and writing which has been strongly shaped by its focus of analysis. During the first half of the twentieth century, the existence of consensus regarding the 'rules of the game' amongst the two main parties 'depoliticized' the topic to some extent, and certainly created little stimulus and few incentives for academics to engage in radical thinking about the shape and form of democracy in the UK (let alone the way it is studied).[9] This changed in the second half of the century as exogenous and endogenous factors conspired to stimulate interest in constitutional reform. However, as Sub-section 4.1.2 emphasized, this wave of literature remained locked-in to the traditional narrative of constitutionalism and consequently largely failed to scratch beneath the surface of debates in order to expose and question the dominant meta-constitutional orientation. With only one or two exceptions, this body of work remained resolutely insular. As such, it failed not only to look abroad for comparative evidence or research that could inform debates in the UK but also to draw upon theories, approaches, and methods that had evolved in the sphere of constitutional theory and practise elsewhere, and could, with some adaptation, have delivered new insights and perspectives within the context of the UK. The challenge for the UK's political studies community at the end of the twentieth century was, as Dearlove stressed, to 'bring the constitution back in' as a field of political studies 'in ways that avoid the limitations of the constitutional approach and narrow legalism' through the creation of 'a new, or at least greatly refurbished language of constitutionalism'.[10]

Even the most cursory analysis of the vast body of work on the constitution since the election of New Labour in 1997 suggests that this has not occurred: Nash, in this vein observes 'a lamentable lack of theoretical and conceptual grounding'.[11] Although questions about the *method* to be used in studying the constitution were fundamental to writers like Dicey and Jennings, more recent scholars, with a small number of exceptions, have neglected any detailed reflection on their tools of political analysis.[12] The dominant approach remains one of 'institutional realism' in which the vast majority of texts are past-descriptive, present-descriptive, or future-prescriptive and provide little by way of explicit theoretical modelling or reflection on the tools of political analysis, and exhibit great consistency in terms of theories and methods.[13] Table 4.1 provides an overview of the key strands (and representative texts) which make up this body of work. The aim here is not to discuss them in any detail but simply to provide a gist of each strand and locate them within the broader argument that writing on the UK's constitution during 1997–2007 failed to look up and beyond its traditional approach.

The *past-descriptive* texts—such as Catterall, Kaiser, and Walton-Jordan's *Reforming the Constitution* (2000)—generally seek to provide an evolutionary account of the UK's constitution within a lose commentary on unifying themes and issues. The most significant contributions within this genre include: Bogdnaor's *The British Constitution in the Twentieth Century* (2003) with its interdisciplinary and historical attempt to evaluate New Labour's reforms; Evan's *Constitution-Making and the Labour Party* (2003) which provides an authoritative account of internal party dynamics and revisionism; and McLean and McMillan's *State of the Union* (2005), which provides a meticulous study of unionism since 1707 up to the dawn of the twenty-first century.

The *present-descriptive* category of third-wave literature on the constitution represents the largest body of work, and as such it comes in a variety of forms which all share the central goal of casting light on the workings of the constitution as it has been reformed under New Labour. Carving up the vast body of literature into component parts is clearly difficult and open to challenge, but a first starting point is those texts that are essentially public/practitioner-orientated policy-relevant studies or reviews. The numerous publications emanating from the Constitution Unit, for example, have provided an authoritative and detailed account, almost survey-like, of how the reform process has unfolded.[14] Forman's *Constitutional Change in the UK* (2002) provides a survey of change, while Bogdanor's *Power to the People* (1997) and Barnett's *Britain Unwrapped* (2002) seek to provide a layman's guide or user handbook on the constitution.

The second form of *present-descriptive* work on New Labour's reforms adopts an empiricist Whig narrative which is often both highly personalized and normative. Leading examples of this genre include Johnson's *Reshaping the British Constitution* (2004) and King's *The British Constitution* (2007) which, each in their own way demonstrates the capacity of this

Table 4.1 Strands of third-wave literature on the UK's constitution

Strand	Present-descriptive					Future-prescriptive
	Past-descriptive	Public policy	Political	Legal	Journalistic/practitioner	
Key texts	Catterall, Kaiser and Walton-Jordan's *Reforming the Constitution* (2000) Bogdnaor's *The British Constitution in the Twentieth Century* (2003) Evan's *Constitution-Making and the Labour Party* (2003) McLean and McMillan's *State of the Union* (2005)	Hazell's *State of the Nations* (2001) Forman's *Constitutional Change in the UK* (2002)Barnett's *Britain Unwrapped* (2002)Hazell's *State of the Nations* (2003)	Weir and Beetham's *Democratic Audit* (1998 & 2002) Johnson's *Reshaping the British Constitution* (2004) Ward's *The English Constitution* (2004) King's *The British Constitution* (2007)	Leyland's *Public Law in a Multi-Layered Constitution* (2003) Hazell and Rawling's *Devolution, Law Making and the Constitution* (2005) Oliver's *Constitutional Reform in the UK* (2003)Tomkins' *Our Republican Constitution* (2005)	Redwood's *The Death of Britain* (1999)Hitchens' *The Abolition of Britain* (1999)Heffer's *Nor Shall My Sword* (1999)Sutherland's *The Rape of the Constitution* (2000) McDonald's *Reinventing Britain* (2007)	Freedland's *Bringing Home the Revolution* (1999)Hazell's *Constitutional Futures* (1999) Foley's *The Politics of the British Constitution* (1999) Nairn's *After Britain* (2000)
Dominant approach	Institutionally focused Qualitative Research Methodology					

approach to provide insights into the discrepancies between constitutional theory and constitutional practice, as well as the role of interpersonal
relationships. The classic example of this genre is Bagehot's *The English
Constitution*, and although King and Johnson exhibit a subtle and nuanced
understanding of the subject of analysis, the danger of a less astute author
adopting this approach is that it risks becoming little more than a quasi-
journalistic narrative, like Ward's *The English Constitution* (2004), which
does not provide any analytical space, obscures as much as it elucidates,
and perpetuates well-known (but frequently false) idioms and maxims.

Interest in constitutional theory and practice within UK law schools was
undoubtedly stimulated by the increasing influence of European constitutionalism and jurisprudence during the 1980s and 1990s. As an increasing
number of judicial decisions and speeches included reference to specific
rights and duties and notably 'higher order laws', it became clear that
the traditional boundary between politicians and the judiciary was growing more opaque. Incorporation of the European Convention of
Human Rights in 1998, as we shall see in Chapter 13, altered the nature
of the constitution and it is unsurprising that the third strand of *present-
descriptive* literature emphasizes elements of legal constitutionalism and is
generally written by scholars of public and constitutional law. This involves studies that focus on legal aspects of devolution and mechanisms of
conflict resolution—Leyland's *Public Law in a Multi-Layered Constitution*
(2003); Hazell and Rawling's *Devolution, Law Making and the Constitution*
(2005)—to broader introductory texts which set out recent reforms from a
more legalistic standpoint—Brazier's *Constitutional Practice* (1999); Black-
burn and Plant's *Constitutional Reform* (1999); and Oliver's *Constitutional
Reform in the UK* (2003)—to more esoteric texts which seek to promote
legal constitutionalism—Allan's *Constitutional Justice* (2001). It is, however, possible to identify a generation of younger legal scholars who are not
only willing to challenge the assumptions and arguments of those who
seek to promote legal constitutionalism—as reflected in Tomkins' *Our
Republican Constitution* (2005)—but are also willing to draw upon theories
and approaches that were originally devised abroad—like Erdos' work on
'aversive constitutionalism'.[15]

The final strand of *present-descriptive* writing contains an eclectic range
of books in which a range of observers including former or serving politicians, journalists, judges, and senior civil servants discuss various elements or themes relating to New Labour's reforms. From Redwood's *The
Death of Britain* (1999), Hitchen's *The Abolition of Britain* (1999), Heffer's
Nor Shall My Sword (1999), Sutherland's *The Rape of the Constitution* (2000)

through to McDonald's *Reinventing Britain* (2007), the value of this genre of writing is highly variable. Although considered reflective and provocative, contributions by those who have previously worked within Whitehall and Westminster can provide unparalleled insights, notably into the role of political cultures on the process of reform, many contributions fail to achieve this standard and instead become highly personal polemical arguments with little analytical depth or practical utility.

The *future-prescriptive* mode of writing draws upon a rich heritage to combine detailed (but largely descriptive) institutional accounts with normative arguments about how the process of reform should, or might unfold in the future. Freedland's *Bringing Home the Revolution* (1999), for example, represents an argument in favour of moving towards a more republican constitutional framework that embraces an active citizenship and a clearer separation of powers; while Nairn's *After Britain* (2000) focuses on the long-term consequences of devolution. If Freedland and Nairn's books are leading examples of a journalistic element of this genre, then Hazell's *Constitutional Futures* (1999) provides arguably the strongest academic reference point. However, they also display the analytical challenges of seeking to derive the existence of social pressures or drivers, gauge the cumulative impact of reforms, or the direction of travel in terms of the trajectory of a reform process. In this context, Hazell's *Constitutional Futures Revisited* (2008) provides a critical and distinctive reference point due to the manner in which it departs from the conventional approach, and instead seeks to adopt a more systematic and theoretically driven methodology. However, the insights offered by Hazell are circumscribed by a failure to locate the analysis within a frame that can be located within both longitudinal and comparative perspectives. What this section has attempted to demonstrate is that scholars of the UK's constitution, both historically and more recently, have operated largely within the contours of a very narrow analytical frame that remains attached to institutionally focused descriptive approaches. This leads to a certain sameness or prosaic quality about much of the literature. Moreover, this lack of a body of literature that offers conceptual or ideological depth is particularly curious, in light of the fact that a key criticism levelled at New Labour by scholars and other commentators is that their constitutional reform measures have been devoid of any clear statement of principles or underlying rationale. It is at this point that a conjunction occurs between the concept of the 'Blair paradox' and the dominant tradition (in terms of methods, theories, and approaches) within political studies in the UK that is trying to explain and deconstruct this issue into its component parts.

The dominant tradition appears ill-equipped to undertake this task. This is reflected in the fact that a great number of books and articles on New Labour's constitutional reforms (many of which have been mentioned earlier) highlight the existence of a certain strain of incoherence within the government's approach, but appear unable to drill down and expose this anomaly in any detail.

Moreover, most analyses have tended to focus on the nature of New Labour's reform agenda rather than what has *not* happened. Put slightly differently, a more rounded and subtle account of change might seek to explore aspects of non-decision making alongside decision making. This point concerning agenda-setting and non-decision making is particularly pertinent in light of New Labour's marginalization of certain issues. This raises distinct questions regarding executive veto capacity and strategic manoeuvring that may be of relevance far beyond the UK. Therefore, it is in explaining and understanding both action and non-action in relation to constitutional reform in the UK that a conceptually informed and theoretically robust analysis may be particularly beneficial.

This argument resonates with the work of scholars such as Evans and Dearlove who have argued for some time that what is required is a new type of thinking on the UK's constitution. This approach would avoid *past-*, *present-*, and *future-descriptive* accounts and would instead seek to provide a broader canvas on which to make sense of the new constitutionalism. This would, in turn, facilitate understanding of the manner in which alterations to specific elements may spill over and affect other parts of the constitution configuration, as well as affect the overall model of democracy itself. It may also offer a way of explaining and understanding the polarization of opinion surrounding the impact of New Labour's reforms. The ambition being not to decide which of these opposing camps is 'correct', but instead to offer a more sophisticated account that goes beyond binary yes/no, right/wrong conclusions and instead explains the counter-intuitive suggestion that both camps are in fact correct—a conclusion which leads into a discussion of bi-constitutionalism and raises a host of issues concerning dynamic variables (the focus of Chapters 15 and 16).

Emphasizing the need to reflect on the tools of political analysis and suggesting that the dominant approach within political studies in the UK has clear limitations is not in any way to decry the existing body of knowledge, or to suggest that any 'superior' methodological framework exists. It is simply to state that different methods and different approaches to political analysis will yield different forms of knowledge—none of which are necessarily any 'better' or 'worse' than others—which will, in turn, allow us to understand the manner in which different approaches:

1. Inculcate certain epistemological assumptions about the collection and validation of knowledge vis-à-vis constitutional change.
2. Offer both strengths and weaknesses in terms of measuring specific variables (notably in relation to locating specific constitutional reforms within a broader methodological framework thereby exposing secondary impacts on other elements of the constitution as well as on the form of democracy more broadly).
3. And therefore contribute a layered quality in terms of building up a body of knowledge.

In many ways this is a Darwinian argument about disciplinary evolution: as the UK's constitution evolves, so must the tools of political analysis through which we seek to understand it. This need not involve a shift towards rational-choice-inspired deductive and predominantly quantitative techniques; nor must it involve a return to the 'po-faced' style which King ascribes much of the legalistic literature on this topic.[16] But there is no way of avoiding the argument that students of the constitution of the UK need to recognize the limitations of the dominant tradition in order to create 'a new, or at least greatly refurbished language of constitutionalism'.[17] As such, the aim of this section has not been to provide an exhaustive account, but simply to steer a course through the existing literature in order to expose the existence and parameters of this dominant tradition. A student of constitutional theory schooled in mainland Europe or North America would quite probably bring with them a quite different set of methods, theories, and approaches—a different tradition—if they were to seek to understand the impact of New Labour upon democracy during 1997–2007. Their initial literature review would undoubtedly be surprised to find that so much literature had been published with so little explicit discussion of: how the constitution should be defined; the tools of political analysis and their respective strengths and weaknesses; issues of ontology or epistemology in the context of constitutional theory and analysis; or any detailed discussion of the meaning and measurement of power. It is in this vein that Johnson emphasized that there had been little *serious* effort in post-1997 analyses to elaborate and justify the principles on which past, current, and prospective constitutional practises are based.

> Yet so far, there has been little sign of an effort to provide a coherent statement of whatever may be the unifying principles underpinning the

new settlement, to justify them as a foundation of what might become a new body of constitutional law, and to set out the normative presuppositions of such guiding principles along with a philosophical grounding for them. No doubt this would be a daunting task, but one to which a political theorist or philosophically minded jurist might feel called.[18]

The twentieth century does, however, provide us with one incisive text that seeks to look beneath the visible surface of the constitution and expose not only the role and power of dominant ideas and political cultures, but also the manner in which the UK's constitution was founded upon not one but two sets of core values. Although Birch's *Representative and Responsible Government* (1964) was written clearly within the dominant tradition of political studies it made a significant contribution to our broader understanding of the constitution by highlighting the manner in which it has historically been fused around two competing and diametrically opposed sets of values which he termed the 'liberal' and 'Whitehall' views. Put simply, the 'liberal' view incorporated power-sharing related values such as openness, participation, accountability, and inclusion whereas the 'Whitehall' view promoted a set of values—strong government, insulation, control, stability—that were facets of a more power-hoarding orientated model of democracy.[19]

This simple framework is significant in the context of this book because it forces us to reflect on the basic spirit or morality of the constitution in terms of what exactly it is intended to deliver—*representative* or *responsible* government. The insight provided by Birch's historical analysis is rooted in the fact that the constitutional architects of the mid-nineteenth century were able to argue, and to some degree demonstrate, that a constitution founded upon political conventions could deliver a workable balance between the two views outlined in Table 4.2. However, as the authoritative texts of Muir (1930), Jennings (1934), Fell (1935), Ross (1943), Hollis (1949), Benemy (1965), Wiseman (1966), Crick (1968), and Butt (1969), to name but a few, emphasized the gradual shifting of power from the legislature to the executive that occurred from the mid-nineteenth century onwards resulted in an increased emphasis on the Whitehall view. However, the reforms advocated within these works and those outlined in the final column of Table 2.2 are addressed almost solely to the problems and values of the 'Liberal' view of the constitution. Thus, much of the reform literature contained a naiveté which ignored the normative claims and practical influence of the 'Whitehall' view. The attraction to successive governments is that the current constitutional structure

Table 4.2 Birch's liberal and Whitehall views

Liberal	Whitehall
Parliamentary government	Strong government
Representative	Responsible
Inclusion	Exclusion
Responsiveness	Distance
Participation	Stability
Accountability	Realism
Direction	Control
Exposure of ministers	Insulation of ministers
Dualistic	Monistic
Power-sharing	**Power-hoarding**
consensus	**majoritarian**

provides both flexibility and a strong platform from which to implement their policies. Reforms designed to move towards a more power-sharing model of democracy are dependent upon the support of an executive that has few incentives to dilute its own governing capacity.[20]

Table 4.2 provides us with the embryonic parameters of a lens or organizing perspective (to be developed later) through which we can start to locate certain positions or trace patterns. John Smith's views on the constitution and therefore his plans for constitutional reform resonate to some extent with the Liberal view of the constitution.[21] And yet as we have seen in Chapter 3, during 1997–2007 New Labour did implement a number of constitutional reforms which devolved power, created new checks and balances, and which sought to strengthen the position of parliament and the public vis-à-vis the executive. The Blair paradox, however, makes us aware that at the same time New Labour was unwilling or unable to press ahead with reform in several other areas. Moreover, the shadow of the Westminster Model affected the implementation of the government's reform programme by protecting and insulating the continuing role of ministers, thereby diluting the radical potential of many of the measures. The question is, how can we understand the statecraft of New Labour in relation to the constitution? What methods, discourse, or approaches might complement the body of research that currently exists? How can we assess the cumulative significance of New Labour's reforms? Section 4.2 argues that Lijphart's analytical framework for mapping and tracing models of democracy provides a valuable and timely answer to these questions.

4.2 Patterns of democracy

Arend Lijphart's career has been dedicated to the study and understanding of democratic regimes and constitutional change. *Democracies* (1984) provided his first major analysis of patterns of majoritarian and consensus governments and was subsequently revised and updated in *Patterns of Democracy* (1999). Lijphart's central thesis is that democratic systems can be placed on an axis, which has majoritarianism at one extreme and consensualism at the other.[22] Most democratic systems, Lijphart suggests, can be located on a continuum between these poles. The majoritarian-consensus contrast therefore forms the foundation of Lijphart's framework (thereby forming a direct link with the debate outlined in Section 4.1). These two poles can be understood as meta-constitutional orientations as they prescribe or inculcate a set of core beliefs, values, and assumptions—the core of any constitutional configuration.

In the majoritarian model or Westminster Model—Lijphart uses the terms interchangeably—political power is concentrated. It is a power-hoarding model. Dominant institutional characteristics therefore include: concentration of power in one-party executives, executive dominance, a two-party system, disproportional electoral systems, a winner-takes-all executive mentality, an adversarial political culture, centralized government, constitutional flexibility, and stability between elections. This form of democracy is, at its foundation, therefore highly elitist, based to some extent on mass-exclusion, and has little emphasis on public participation. The consensus model of democracy, by contrast, is based upon a rather different value-slope that emphasizes inclusion, participation, multi-party systems, proportional electoral systems, decentralized government, power sharing in coalition cabinets, and a broadly balanced relationship between the executive and legislature. It is a power-sharing model of democracy.

As mentioned in the earlier chapters, the meta-constitutional orientation of a polity shapes and conditions secondary elements of the constitutional infrastructure and, as such, the majoritarian and consensus models are, as Lijphart demonstrated, both rational and logically coherent. The institutional characteristics of the Westminster Model derive logically from the basic meta-constitutional orientation of power-hoarding. Conversely, all the features of the consensual system flow, like branches from a tree trunk, logically follow from the basic core political value that power should be dispersed and shared in a number of ways.[23] The two rational models do not always coincide with the logical extremes on each specific dimension due to the existence of cultural, historical, or contextual limits within each specific polity but a high degree of internal validity is generally observable. Both models are also prescriptive in terms of the fact that they involve a set of basic core choices that have to be made about the central values which a constitution will seek to promote above any number of secondary variables. The potential tensions arising from the existence of deep and far-reaching ethnic, religious, or linguistic cleavages within a society—like Northern Ireland, Iraq, Canada, Belgium, etc.—might therefore lead constitutional engineers to favour a consensual model of democracy with the capacity to promote inclusion and collaboration, rather than a winner-takes-all majoritarian approach that would further entrench societal polarization by creating a set of 'winners' and 'losers'.[24] The majoritarian and consensual models, as we shall see here, therefore offer a blueprint in the form of an explicit set of core values out of which a series of logical choices, or at the least a bounded range of options, arise.

Having argued that the two models are both *rational* and *prescriptive*, it is also possible to follow Lijphart's lead and suggest that they are also *empirical* models. Empirical in the sense that as the meso-constitutional elements flow from an internally coherent meta-constitutional orientation, it is reasonable to predict a pattern across the specific institutional features or variables (see later) in the sense that they are interconnected, 'we may expect them to occur *together* in the real world' (emphasis added).[25] This prediction of clustering proved correct in relation to Lijphart's 1984 analysis of nine variables in twenty-two countries, and was later substantiated using a slightly modified framework in his 36-country analysis in 1999. However, before examining the ten variables (across two dimensions) employed in that study, and which will therefore be replicated in this study, it is worth noting a final feature of the majoritarian and consensual models of democracy that Lijphart arguably underemphasizes—the *normative* dimension. In this sense both models go much further than inculcating certain values, thereby initiating a form of constitutional path-dependency, because they are also deployed by various epistemic communities in the form of normative arguments about how democracies *should* be governed. This dimension has already been alluded to earlier, in relation to the view propounded by many politicians and scholars during the nineteenth century that the Westminster Model was a superior form of democracy deserving of admiration and replication around the world.[26] Lijphart's own research and writing has similarly gone beyond simple description and analysis and into the value-laden terrain of promoting consensual forms of democracy as the most effective way to ensure both *responsible* and *representative* government (to take us back to the work of Birch discussed in Section 4.1.3). Indeed, the link between Birch and Lijphart, although not intuitively obvious, becomes apparent if we return to the Liberal and Whitehall views of the constitution set out in Table 4.2. Birch's Liberal Model resonates directly with Lijphart's notion of a consensual democracy; while the Whitehall model is synonymous with a power-hoarding majoritarian democracy.

In terms of setting out the parameters of Lijphart's analytical frame it is important to recognize that the variables have been modified from the original eight variables employed in *Democracies* (1984) to the ten variables used in *Patterns of Democracy* (1999). This latter list of variables (the ones examined in this book) is set out in Table 4.3. Each variable is studied in close detail and then operationalized into a quantitative indicator. The aim being to capture the 'reality' of the political phenomenon as closely as possible (we will return to this methodological challenge later). The characteristics for each variable on each of the two dimensions are then averaged to form two summary characteristics. These can then be used to place a country on the two-dimensional map of democracy (Figure 4.1).

Table 4.3 Two dimensions and ten characteristics

Executive–parties dimension

1. Concentration of executive power in single-party majority cabinets versus executive power-sharing in broad multiparty coalitions.
2. Executive legislative relationships in which the executive is dominant versus executive-legislative balance of power.
3. Two-party versus multiparty systems.
4. Majoritarian and disproportional electoral systems versus proportional representation.
5. Pluralist interest group systems with free-for-all competition among groups versus coordinated and 'corporatist' interest group systems aimed at compromise and concertation.

Federal–unitary dimension

6. Unitary and centralized government versus federal and decentralized government.
7. Concentration of legislative power in a unicameral legislature versus division of legislative power between two equally strong but differently constituted houses.
8. Flexible constitutions that can be amended by simple majorities versus rigid constitutions that can be changed only by extraordinary majorities.
9. Systems in which legislatures have the final word on the constitutionality of their own legislation versus systems in which laws are subject to a judicial review of their constitutionality by supreme or constitutional courts.
10. Central banks that are dependent on the executive versus independent central banks.

Source: Lijphart (1999), **Patterns of Democracy**, pp. 3–4.

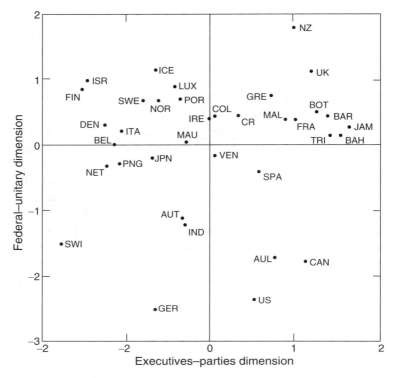

Figure 4.1 Two-dimensional map of democracy
Source: From Lijphart (1999), *Patterns of Democracy.*

The horizontal axis represents the executives–parties dimension and the vertical axis the federal–unity dimension. Each unit on these axis represents one standard deviation; high values indicate majoritarianism, and low values consensus. Most of the prototypical cases of majoritarianism or consensus democracy are in the expected positions (respectively top/right bottom/left) on the conceptual map. It is not necessary at this stage to review the detailed findings and explanations offered by Lijphart for the position of specific countries or groups of countries (although we return to these in Chapter 15 when we come to analyse the updated position of the UK from a comparative perspective) on the conceptual map. Figure 4.1 illustrates that prior to the election of New Labour, the UK was a highly majoritarian polity, and this book is essentially attempting to gauge the manner in which the UK has moved (if at all) across the conceptual map of democracy during 1997–2007. This will then provide an authoritative response in the context of the polarized debate between what were referred to (above) as the Revolutionary Group and the Sceptical Camp. The former arguing that the UK has been repositioned from an extreme form of majoritarianism to a consensual model of democracy (i.e. a diagonal shift on Figure 4.1 from the top/right corner to a position in the bottom/left quadrant); while the more sceptical observers suggest a less significant repositioning, possibly towards the central axis, but still squarely within the top/right quadrant (i.e. modified majoritarianism).

This notion of democratic drift or evolution over time encourages us to reflect on Lijphart's key findings. First, despite the ideational dominance of majoritarianism or 'majority rule' forms of democracy, there are actually very few ideal-type examples of this model of democracy. Secondly, Lijphart's detailed analysis suggested that, contrary to popular belief, consensual systems do not commonly suffer from pluralistic stagnation in which the decision-making processes become overly complex leading to economic inefficiency.[27] At the same time (third) consensus systems delivered significantly higher scores in terms of the quality of democracy, in terms of public trust and engagement, etc.[28] Lijphart's overall conclusion, as stated in the conclusion to his *Thinking About Democracy* (2008), is worth restating in full,

> On the basis of theoretical arguments in the political science literature as well as some preliminary empirical tests, my thinking was that consensus democracy.... would have a substantial advantage over majoritarian democracy with regard to democratic quality, and that it would be roughly equal in terms of effective government, although I anticipated that majoritarian democracy might have a slight edge. In both respects, the evidence turned out to be much more favourable to consensus democracy. It is consensus rather than majoritarian democracy that has the slight edge with regard to effective policy making, and the performance of consensus democracy with regard to the indicators of democratic quality is not just superior, but vastly superior—confirmed by clear results of statistical tests.[29]

This conclusion presents an intriguing puzzle vis-à-vis the evolution of democracy in the UK during 1997–2007, because if New Labour have in fact been committed to a more consensual model of democracy in theory but not in practice, then this may help us understand the decline in public trust and faith in politics, politicians, and political institutions (as

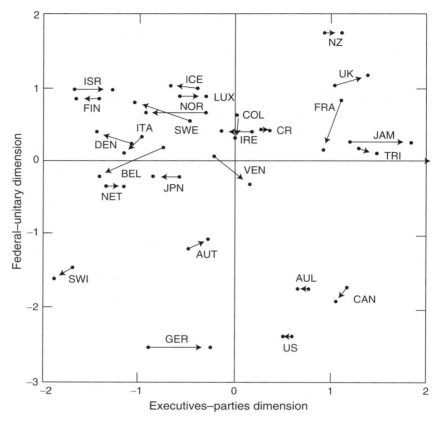

Figure 4.2 Shifts on the two-dimensional map from the period before 1971 to the period 1971–96

Source: From Lijphart (1999), *Patterns of Democracy*.

discussed in Chapter 1). Keeping the focus on Lijphart's research as it applies to the UK is also useful in terms of this line of argument because the results of his first and second studies allowed the changing nature of different country's democratic regimes to be traced over time (see Figure 4.2). A significant feature of Figure 4.2 is that it suggests that the UK actually evolved towards a more extreme power-hoarding version of majoritarian democracy under the Conservative governments during the 1980s and 1990s. This analysis would correspond with the concerns of constitutional commentators and reformers (discussed in Chapter 2) regarding the manner in which political power had become increasingly centralized towards the end of the twentieth century.

The aim of Part II of this book is therefore to reassess each of the ten variables set out in Table 4.3 in order to determine the position of the UK in Figure 4.2 in 2007. Chapter 16 will also assess how this situation has altered as a result of the *Governance of Britain* reform agenda initiated by Gordon Brown towards the end of 2007.

By now it should be reasonably clear why and how Lijphart's framework and methodology provides not only a new language and discourse through which to discuss and understand the new constitutionalism, but it also provides a broad framework with the capacity to assess the cumulative impact of a series of reforms, despite the fact that they may have been designed and implemented in an ad hoc and piecemeal manner. A project of this nature is also timely for three other reasons: (*a*) Lijphart's last analysis of developments in the UK focused on the period between 1971 and 1996 and therefore needs updating; (*b*) although Norris adopts the language of Lijphart to frame her thoughts about democratic change in the UK under New Labour, she does not apply or replicate his study in detail and so this book will test her thesis concerning a shift on the federal–unitary dimension but not on the executive–parties dimension; (*c*) the *Governance of Britain* green paper and the white paper on constitutional renewal (in July 2007 and April 2008, respectively) represents a period of constitutional reflection and consolidation in which theoretically informed policy-relevant research can play a valuable role in understanding the impact of previous reforms and informing future policy decisions.[30]

A Lijphartian approach to understanding New Labour's impact on the UK's constitution is not necessarily 'better' or 'worse' than more traditional forms of analyses, but it will offer a new perspective and a rounded view with the capacity for future replication and refinement. The approach of this book therefore concurs with Aldo Leopold's much cited advice that 'The first rule of intelligent tinkering is to keep all the parts' (1945). Continuing with this pluralistic approach to political analysis—and in the context of the earlier statement about Lijpart's framework not being a panacea—alerts us to the fact that possibly the most critical element of any methodological design is the honesty with which its progenitors acknowledge the existence of certain potential weaknesses or issues around which a degree of epistemological and methodological debate are inevitable. In this regard, Lijphart's approach has been constructively critiqued and developed in two main areas—variables and measurement.

In terms of the ten variables included in Table 4.3, it is quite apparent that any number of additional variables could have been added. The existence of freedom of information legislation, local government, or the role of the monarchy, for example, could have been included. The use of referendums was included in Lijphart's original 1984 analysis but dropped in favour of two new variables—interest groups and central banks—in his second expanded 1999 analysis. The simple fact about the selection and number of variables rests with the need to acknowledge the need for some limits on the realistic number of variables that can be analysed, and that widespread agreement on which variables deserve examination will always be disputed. In this context, the ten variables selected by Lijphart offers breadth and depth and arguably captures many of the most critical dimensions.[31] The work of Vatter has, however, attempted to build upon Lijphart's methods by integrating direct democracy as an additional dimension.[32]

The issue of quantitative scoring is more problematic. Table 4.4 sets out the specific data-score for each of the ten dimensions across the two time periods studied by Lijphart.

The aim of Part II is therefore to arrive at updated variable scores for the final column of Table 4.4. However, there are no neutral observable facts. Even with dimensions that appear straightforward and readily quantifiable, such as the number of actors in the party system (V1) or the proportion of cabinets involving power sharing (V2), debate can be found at the margins. The level of debate becomes greater as analysts seek to ascribe scores in relation to those variables that involve a normative judgement. The issue of the balance of power between the legislature and the executive (V3) or the role of the judiciary (V9), for example, cannot be determined in any indisputable manner. The issue of assigning quantitative scores to specific variables is particularly problematic in relation to New Labour's period in office due to the fact that ministers used the conventions of parliamentary sovereignty and ministerial responsibility to parliament to ensure that the vast majority of measures enacted in legislation included specific ministerial opt-outs, exemptions, vetoes, or final decision-making capacities.

However, this methodological challenge can be overstated. Hazell suggests that 'it is a weakness of Lijphart's classification that it focuses narrowly on the formal powers granted to institutions, and can miss the significance of culture and behaviour'.[33] This is incorrect. As Part II of this book will demonstrate, it is quite possible for data scores to take into account changes in relation to both formal powers and actual behaviour. Indeed, in an attempt to achieve a higher degree of validity and reliability for each variable score some scholars, including De Winter (2005), Lorenz

Table 4.4 Lijphart's analysis of democracy in the UK, 1945–96

Variable	Majoritarian	Consensus	1945–96	1971–96	1997–2007
V1. Party system	Two party system.	Multiparty system.	2.11	2.20	
V2. Cabinets	Single party majority cabinets.	Power-sharing multiparty coalitions.	96.7	93.3	
V3. Executive–legislative relationship	Dominant executive.	Executive–legislature balance of power.	5.52	5.52	
V4. Electoral system	Disproportional first-past-the post system.	Proportional representation.	10.33	14.66	
V5. Interest groups	Informal pluralist interest group interaction.	Coordinated and 'corporatist' interest group interaction.	3.38	3.50	
V6. Federal–unitary dimension	Unitary and centralized government.	Federal and decentralized government.	1.0	1.0	
V7. Unicameralism–bicameralism dimension	Concentration of power in a unicameral legislature.	Division of power between two equally strong but differently constituted houses.	2.5	2.5	
V8. Constitutional amendment	Flexible constitution that can be amended by simple majorities.	Rigid constitutions that can be changed only by extraordinary majorities.	1.0	1.0	
V9. Legislative supremacy	Legislature has the final word on the constitutionality of legislation.	Legislation subject to a judicial review of their constitutionality by a supreme or constitutional court.	1.0	1.0	
V10. Central bank	Dependent on the executive.	Independent central bank.	0.31	0.28	
D1. Executive–Parties			1.21	1.39	
D.1 Federal–Unitary			1.12	1.19	

(2005) and Vatter (2009) have modified the technique for scoring some of the variables. In order to protect the longitudinal integrity of this study, each of the chapters in Part II replicates Lijphart's methods for variable scoring.[34] This approach is, however, supplemented by two secondary forms of triangulation: (a) where other methods have been developed with the aim of securing a more accurate and credible score for a specific variable, the result derived from these alternative formulae will be calculated and compared with that given by Lijphart's original method. Where significant differences occur, these will be subject to further analysis and discussion; (b) all variable scores were subjected to a peer-review process whereby each chapter in Part II was assessed by two subject specialists. Each reviewer was asked to comment on:

1. The factual accuracy of each chapter.
2. The degree to which the chapter captured the key debates and arguments within the specific field.
3. If they felt that the suggested variable score for 1997–2007 was fair and accurate.

Where factual inaccuracies were identified, they were corrected. If critical debates and arguments had been overlooked, the relevant chapter was revised to include them. Where a reviewer was of the opinion that the variable score was inaccurate, an attempt was made within the text to either explain the contentious nature of ascribing a score in relation to the variable, and therefore the basis on which the reviewer challenged the initial score, or if a general consensus emerged from all the reviews that significant issues had been underemphasized which would affect the variable's score, then this would be incorporated within the text and the score altered accordingly.

Lijphart's framework allows us to unpack and therefore understand a number of issues that have been noted by observers, but not really understood with any precision. Two issues demonstrate this point: (a) as mentioned earlier, Lijphart's previous research demonstrates a clear clustering of variables along two dimensions. If this clustering no longer exists in relation to democracy in the UK, this may help us understand the roots of the 'Blair paradox'; (b) Lijphart's research makes very strong claims about citizen satisfaction and specific models of democracy, 'citizens in consensus democracies are significantly more satisfied with democratic performance in their countries than citizens in majoritarian democracies; the difference is approximately 17 percentage points'.[35] This finding, which is supported by other studies, may provide important clues in relation to explaining the apparent decline in public trust in conventional political institutions, processes, and politicians that was highlighted in Chapter 1. In essence, if New Labour increased public expectations regarding moving towards a more power-sharing consensus based model but then failed to deliver on these commitments, or the public *perceives* they have failed to deliver, this might explain the low contemporary levels of public trust.

This section has argued that political studies in the UK has adopted a distinctive approach to the analysis of the constitution that has involved little explicit systematic analysis, and therefore struggles to provide any structured interpretation of the cumulative impact of distinct measures on the overall model of democracy. It is for this reason that Lijphart's framework offers a rich and valuable epistemological and methodological tool for the analysis of developments during 1997–2007. The framework is particularly appropriate in relation to the UK because: (*a*) it has always been presented as an exemplar of the majoritarian model; (*b*) the election of New Labour on 1 May 1997 is often portrayed as a critical juncture that challenges Lijphart's characterization of the UK as a majoritarian democracy; and (*c*) Lijphart's scholarship provides a conceptual framework through which the reform of institutions, structures, and to some extent cultures can be mapped in order to understand the trajectory of democratic change.

4.3 Constitutional cartography

This chapter has examined the issue of political analysis in the sphere of constitutional reform. The first section demonstrated the existence of a very clear tradition within British political studies in relation to how constitutional change and reform is studied. This is reflected in the existence of a proliferation of overly descriptive, frequently normative, and generally empiricist studies that neglect explicit theoretical perspectives or methodological considerations. This is not an original argument. Indeed, to adopt this line of reasoning is to work within the contours of a much broader debate concerning the distinction between British political *studies* and the ontological, epistemological, and methodological positions of those scholars who prefer the label political *science*.[36] The specific point, however, made within this chapter relates to the manner in which the traditional Whig narrative and Westminster-Model-framed approach combined with a certain an 'anti-intellectual aversion to theoretically informed debate' has limited and restricted our understanding of how democracy has been reshaped in the UK since 1997.[37]

In order to contribute a broader theoretically informed methodology with the capacity to measure and gauge the impact of specific reforms on the overall model of democracy this book adopts a Lijphartian approach. As such, although this book rejects the idea of a pure science of politics, it does at least seek to employ the techniques of classification, typologies and models, and use the language of variables and relationships to make generalizations and statements about complex political phenomena. It seeks to interpret a body of factual knowledge within a broader theoretical framework in order to identify trends or patterns, and as a result deepen our knowledge. This point takes us back to the concept of constitutional anomie. We have seen in earlier chapters that New Labour approached the constitution in an instrumental and disparate manner, allowing the constitution to drift in the currents produced by a number of reforms, but without any clear objective or destination in terms of the model of democracy it was attempting to create. At the same time, this chapter has suggested that scholars operating in the field of constitutional studies and reform have failed to look beyond the limitations of a narrow dominant tradition and forge the tools of political analysis that offer the capacity to map and understand both the new constitutionalism and the continuing influence of the traditional constitution. There is a need to think critically and holistically about the way we understand the constitution if we are to answer the two central questions set out in Chapter 1 in the context of the *Governance of Britain* green paper. Specifically,

1. What kind of constitution and democracy do we have in the UK at the beginning of the twenty-first century?
2. What are we attempting to achieve through the reform process?

If Tony Blair has reformed the constitution without a map, then we need to engage in an exercise of cartography in order to understand exactly where we are in order to consider whether to stay there or embark on further reforms. It is to this mapping exercise that we now turn by analysing the nature of reform in relation to each of Lijphart's ten variables. The aim of each of the proceeding variable-focused chapters is not, however, to provide a detailed account of reform in each area—there are already many authoritative reviews of change—but to assess the cumulative impact and direction of change. For this reason the chapters that make up Part II have been deliberately written as concise narratives of change with the sole aim of updating Lijphart's methodology and data-set. It is for this reason that we now turn to the issue of the party system (V1).

Notes

1. Wright, T (2003) *British Politics*. Oxford: Oxford University Press, p. 17.
2. Hague, W (1988) 'Change and Tradition: Thinking Creatively about the Constitution'. Speech to the Centre for Policy Studies, 24 February.
3. See Johnson, N (2000) 'Then and Now: the British Constitution', *Political Studies*, 48, 118.
4. See Bevir, M (2008) 'The Westminster Model, Governance and Judicial Reform', *Parliamentary Affairs*, 61(4), 559–77.
5. Bogdanor, V and Skidelski, R (1970) *The Age of Affluence 1951–1964*. London: Macmillan, p. 11.
6. See Ridley, F (1990) 'There is no British Constitution', *Parliamentary Affairs*, 41, 340–61.
7. See *Parliamentary Affairs*. Special Issue.
8. As occurred, for example, in relation to Barnett, A, Elliss, C, and Hirst, P (1993) *Debating the Constitution*. Oxford: Polity.
9. Bogdanor *op. cit.* (2003) notes 'It was not until the party system came gradually to unfreeze, in the years following 1974, that the constitution once again entered the political agenda, and reformers rediscovered the liberal critique of the constitution, whose challenge had been evaded rather than resolved by the settlement of the years 1911–22' (p. 693).
10. Dearlove, J (1989) 'Bringing the Constitution Back In', *Political Studies*, 37, 521–39.
11. Nash, F (2002) 'Devolution Dominoes', *The Times Higher*, 1 February, 30.
12. See Harden *op cit.* (1991).
13. This distinction comes from Mount, F (1992) *The British Constitution Now*. London: Mandarin.
14. See Hazell, R (2000) ed. *The State of the Nations*. Exeter: Imprint; Trench, A (2001) ed. *The State of the Nations 2001*. Exeter: Imprint; Hazell, R (2003) ed. *The State of the Nations 2003*. Exeter: Imprint; Trench, A (2004) ed. *Has Devolution Made a Difference?* Exeter: Imprint.
15. Erdos, D (2007) 'Aversive Constitutionalism in the Westminster World', *International Journal of Constitutional Law*, 5(2), 343–69.
16. King *op. cit.* (2007), p. vii.
17. Dearlove *op. cit.* (1989).
18. Johnson *op. cit.* (2000), p. 127.
19. Birch, A (1964) *Representative and Responsible Government*. London: Unwin, pp. 65–81.
20. See Judge, D (1993) *The Parliamentary State*. London: Sage.
21. See Stuart, M (2005) *John Smith: A Life*. London: Politicos, p. 295.

22. Lijphart, A (1984) *Democracies*. London: Yale University Press; Lijphart, A (1999) *Patterns of Democracy*. London: Yale University Press.

23. See Lijphart *op. cit.* (1984), pp. 207–22.

24. Lijphart's arguments concerning the benefits of consociational arrangements in divided societies has, however, been challenged. See Roader, P and Rothchild, D (2005) eds. *Sustainable Peace: Power and Democracy after Civil Wars*. Ithaca, NY: Cornell University Press.

25. *Op. cit.*, p. 211.

26. See Rose, R (1974) 'A Model of Democracy, in R, Rode (ed.), *Lessons from America*. New York: Wiley; Kavanagh, D (1974) 'An American Science of British Politics', *Political Studies*, 22(3), 251–70.

27. On the relationship between majoritarian and consensual regimes and economic policy see, Persson, T and Tabellini, G (2005) *The Economic Effects of Constitutions*. Cambridge, MA: MITI Press.

28. On Lijphart's views about 'gentler and kinder' forms of democracy see: Armingeon, K (2002) 'The Effects of Negotiation Democracy', *European Journal of Political Research*, 41(1), 81–105; Andeweg, R (2001) 'Lijphart versus Lijphart', *Acta Politica*, 36(2), 117–28.

29. Lijphart *op. cit.* (2008), p. 270.

30. Norris, P (2001) 'The Twilight of Westminster?', *Political Studies*, 49, 877–900.

31. On this topic see the following scholarly exchange: Taagepera, R (2003) 'Arend Lijphart's Dimensions of Democracy', *Political Studies*, 51(1), 1–19; Lijphart, A (2003) 'Measurement Validity and Institutional Engineering', *Political Studies*, 51(1), 20–5.

32. Vatter, A (2009) 'Lijphart Expanded', *European Political Science Review,* 1(1), 125–54.

33. Hazell, R (2008) *Constitutional Futures Revisted*. Houndmills: Palgrave, 299.

34. See Vatter *op. cit.* (2009); Lorenz, A (2005) 'How to Measure Constitutional Rigidity?', *Journal of Theoretical Politics*, 17(3), 339–61; De Winter, L (2005) 'Theoretical, Conceptual and Methodological Problems in Applying Lijphart's Patterns of Democracy to Autonomous Regions in Europe'. Paper presented to the ECPR Joint Sessions, Granada, 14–15 April.

35. Lijphart *op. cit.* (2008), p. 95.

36. See Hayward, J, Barry, B, and Brown, A (1999) eds. *The British Study of Politics in the Twentieth Century*. Oxford: Oxford University Press.

37. Kerr, P and Kettell, S (2006) 'In Defence of British Politics', *British Politics*, 1(1), 6.

Part II:

Patterns of Democracy

Chapter 5

V1. Party System

I can conceive of nothing more corrupting or worse for a set of ignorant people than that two combinations of well-taught and rich men should constantly offer to defer to their decision, and should compete for office of executing it.[1]

The first four chapters of this book have been concerned with setting out the conceptual, historical, and methodological foundations of this study. The aim of the next ten chapters (Part II) is to generate the data through which Lijphart's analysis of democracy in the UK can be updated. The first of the ten variables is the difference between two-party and multiparty systems. The party system epitomizes the nature of power within any democracy and is a key variable for the executive-parties dimension. It is therefore intertwined with other variables assessed in later chapters—notably single-party cabinets versus multiparty coalition cabinets (V2), executive–legislative relationships (V3), and majoritarian versus proportional electoral systems (V4)—and through this forms a central aspect of the internal coherence that specific models or forms of democracy are expected to display under Lijphart's framework. As Chapter 4 indicated, stable two-party systems are a central aspect of the majoritarian model of democracy and it was in this vein that Lijphart quotes Lowell's 'axiom of politics' that legislatures should contain 'two parties, and two parties only . . . in order that the parliamentary form of government should permanently produce good results'.[2] The question that this chapter seeks to answer is whether Lijphart's 1996 conclusion that the UK was essentially a two-party state remains true after a decade of New Labour.

The challenge in answering this question lies in the deliberate mistake included in the final sentence of Chapter 4—there is no such thing as *the* party system in the UK but an embryonic multilevelled hierarchy of party *systems*. Not only does this present new challenges for politicians and political parties, but it also undermines, or at least complicates, traditional conceptual lenses through which party politics in the UK has traditionally been studied. It also presents the first potential weakness in terms of the utility of Lijphart's framework vis-à-vis the shifting nature of democracy in the UK. A focus on the party system at the national level risks overlooking the existence of significant developments or new cleavages at the sub-national or supra-national level, and the potential spillovers or pressures that such a development may create.

And yet an awareness of this issue alongside an attempt to build a multilayered account within the analysis actually reveals one of the key benefits of Lijphart's framework in terms of its sensitivity to the impact of reform in one area on other aspects of the constitutional configuration. In this case the relationship between electoral systems and electoral reform, asymmetrical devolution, and the evolution of party systems. The central conclusion of this chapter is that the UK remains a two-party system, or more precisely a 'two-party-plus' system, at the national level.

How this situation remains the case despite the creation of multiparty systems above and below the national level provides insights into executive politics, strategic majoritarian modification, and the politics of constitutional reform. In order to deepen our understanding of elements of both continuity and change in relation to the party system(s) this chapter is divided into three sections. The party system at the national level forms the focus of the first section and reveals that a 'two-party-plus system' remains an apt characterization of the UK after a decade of New Labour. However, a broader analytical lens reveals the existence of significant change above and below the nation state through the creation of complex and dynamic multiparty systems and this forms the focus of the second section. The final section locates the findings of this chapter back within Lijphart's framework, while also reflecting on the possible spillover and spillback effects that multiparty systems above and below the national level may produce.

5.1 From two-party to two-party plus

The concept of a party system seeks to define a 'particular pattern of competitive and cooperative interactions displayed by a given set of political parties'.[3] A party system is therefore the product of a rich mixture of institutional, electoral, ideational, and socio-economic factors. Unsurprisingly at the national level in the UK political parties and the party system reflects the values and assumptions of the dominant meta-constitutional orientation—the Westminster Model. As Shaw and Laffin have emphasized, although Scottish and Welsh devolution has served to 'semi-federalize' the intra-party organizational arrangements of the national parties the main political parties still project a majoritarian impulse not to separate power.[4] However, as the work of a number of leading scholars like Kirchheimer (1966), Sartori (1976), and Mair (1983) has demonstrated, in terms of the factors that shape party systems the institutional and constitutional environment, specifically the electoral system(s), are crucial.[5] Not only does the electoral system establish and maintain the political opportunity structure within which inter-party competition will be controlled and mediated, but it also governs the transition between votes cast and legislative seats awarded. As Chapter 8 will discuss in more detail, First Past the Post (FPTP) simple-plurality elections encourage voters to concentrate their votes and tends to penalize third and fourth choice parties, a characteristic enshrined in Duverger's Law. The FPTP is designed and intended to be a disproportional electoral system that creates an artificial majority for the party usually receiving the largest minority of votes (i.e. plurality rule).

With only a few exceptions the dominant pattern of government during the first half of the twentieth century was coalition or minority government.[6] The party system in the period 1945–70, however, epitomized Sartori's two-party system with the Labour Party and Conservative Party attracting over 91 per cent of the vote in the eight general elections during this period and nearly 98 per cent of legislative seats. Between 1950 and 1970 minor parties and independents won a combined total of just ten seats. After 1970 a combination of factors—partisan and class de-alignment, the growth of issue-voting, the development of a credible third party (the Liberal Democrats and before them the Liberals and Social Democratic Party), and the emergence of nationalist parties—affected the purity of this model by diluting the position of the two main parties. The outcome of these factors was a transition from a two-party system to one that became characterized as a 'two-party-plus' system. However, despite the emergence of these alternative parties and evidence of greater electoral volatility on behalf of the electorate, the UK remained a two-party system at the national level (albeit now of the 'plus' variety to indicate a degree of change). The *degree* of change is not to be understated (an issue to be examined below) but at the same time it should not be overstated. As Heffernan emphasizes,

In Westminster elections, as opposed to European, Scottish and Welsh second order elections, the old two-party system no longer exists...but the two-party 'plus others' system presently persists. It persists, thanks to SMPS [single-member plurality system], in terms of Commons seat share and by making it almost certain that—short of a hung parliament—only Labour or the Conservatives can secure the necessary sufficient support to form a single-party government.

The manner in which an electoral system facilitates and perpetuates a certain party system (while also shaping the electorate's views in relation to whether and how to vote) is reflected in electoral data for the general elections in 1997, 2001, and 2005 (Table 5.1).

The data in Table 5.1 allow us to recalculate the UK's score for V1. Lijphart employed the Laakso and Taagepera Index in order to gauge both the number of parties within a system and their relative strength.[7] In a two-party system with two equally strong parties, the effective number of parties is exactly 2.0; whereas in a system where one party is stronger than another, with respective seat shares of 60 and 40 per cent, the index score would be 1.6. This would support an intuitive belief that the system was closer to a one-party system than one in which the two dominant parties were equally balanced. Using this index, Lijphart calculated that for the period 1945–96 (14 general elections) the House of Commons scored 2.11 (2.20 for 1971–96) therefore indicating that the UK was essentially a two-party system. Replicating Lijphart's work using the data in Table 5.1 produces a mean score of 2.28 for the results of the 1997, 2001, and 2005 general elections which would support the conclusion that the UK remains a 'two-party-plus' system at the national level (a view supported by the historical analysis provided in Figure 5.1).

As Table 5.2 shows, the mean index score of effective political parties from 1974–2005 is 2.23. A score of 2.28 can therefore be entered into the final column of Table 4.4 for V1, and could be taken at face value to suggest that little change has occurred. However, as noted earlier, the UK no longer has *a* party system but a number of party systems, the existence of which raises questions about the value of a methodological framework that is focused solely at the national level. The existence of multiparty systems above and beyond the nation state forces us to acknowledge the existence of certain dynamics or pressures which may in time build up to the point at which a future executive is forced to concede change at the national level. It is in this vein that Dunleavy draws upon comparative research in order to suggest that the UK is experiencing a form of 'Colomer transition towards full multiparty politics, with the advent of either full PR elections for

Table 5.1 British general election statistics, results May 1997, June 2001, and May 2005

	1997 General election			2001 General election			2005 General election		
Turnout	71.3% (31.3 m/43.9 m)			59.4% (26.4 m/44.4 m)			61.3% (27.0 m/44.2 m)		
Total No. of parties standing	**38**			**78**			**118**		
% of votes received by three main parties	**90.7%**			**90.7%**			**89.6%**		
	Votes (million)	Vote share (%)	Seats won/ prop. seats won	Votes (million)	Vote share (%)	Seats won/ prop. seats won	Votes (million)	Vote share (%)	Seats won/prop. seats won
Con.	9.6	30.7	165/25%	8.36	31.7	166/ 25.2%	8.7	32.4	198/30.7%
Lab.	13.52	43.2	418/ 63.4%	10.72	40.7	412/ 62.5%	9.55	35.2	355/55.0%
Lib. Dem	5.24	16.8	46/6.9%	4.81	18.3	52/7.9%	5.99	22.0	62/9.6%
PC/SNP	0.78	2.5	10/1.5%	0.66	2.5	9/1.3%	0.59	2.2	9/1.4%
Other	2.14	6.8	19/3%	1.81	6.9	20/3%	2.24	8.2	22/3.4%
Total	*31.29*	*100*	*659/100%*	*26.37*	*100*	*659/100%*	*27.15*	*100*	*646/100%*
Working majority (seats)	**178**			**166**			**71**		
Winning Party's share of registered electors	**30.81%**			**24.2%**			**21.6%**		

Note: 'Other' includes Ulster Unionist Party, Ulster Democratic Unionist Party, Social and Democratic Labour Party, Sinn Fein, UK Unionist Party, and two MPs elected as independents.

Sources: (1) House of Commons Library *UK Election Statistics 1945–2007*, Research Paper 08/12, Feb. 2008. (2) www.psr.keele.ac.uk. (3) Electoral Commission (2005) *Election 2005: Turnout.*

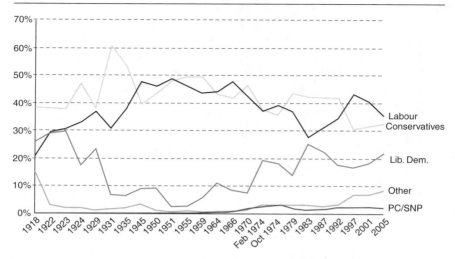

Figure 5.1 Share of the vote: UK general elections, 1918–2005
Source: House of Commons Library (2008) *Election Statistics*: UK 1918–2007.

Westminster or some other fundamental rebalancing of the national constitution'.[8] In order to explore this issue in more detail, Section 5.2 examines party systems above and below the nation state.

5.2 From a party *system* to party *systems*

The introduction of devolution since 1997 based on a variety of proportional electoral systems (discussed in Chapter 8) has created a multilevelled hierarchy of party-systems, each of which not only display a range
of parties but also different relationships (formal and informal) between
those parties. It is for this reason that Dunleavy criticizes much of the
wider literature on party systems in the UK because 'exponents of the
orthodoxy believe that the UK is still somehow a "two party system",
where only bipolar conflict of the two largest contenders at general elections "really" matters'.[9] However, the debate that Dunleavy seeks to construct is arguably artificial. A close reading of the work of those scholars
who Dunleavy accuses of promoting a dated 'orthodox view' generally
reveals a more nuanced position in which they confirm that a variant of
the two-party system remains at the national level (as we have seen earlier)
while also acknowledging the emergence of more fluid multiparty systems
at the sub-national level. It is in this context that Heffernan states,

Table 5.2 Effective number of parties at UK general elections, 1974–2005

Year	Con. vote %	Con. seats	Lab. vote %	Lab. seats	Lib. vote %	Lib. seats	Others votes %	Others seats	ENEP	ENPP
1974 (Feb)	37.9	297	37.2	301	19.3	14	5.6	23	3.13	2.25
1974 (Oct)	35.8	277	39.2	319	18.3	13	6.7	26	3.17	2.26
1979	43.9	339	36.9	269	13.8	11	5.4	16	2.87	2.15
1983	42.4	397	27.6	209	25.4	23	4.6	21	3.12	2.09
1987	42.3	376	30.8	229	22.5	22	4.4	23	3.08	2.18
1992	41.8	336	34.2	271	17.9	20	6.1	24	3.09	2.27
1997	30.7	165	43.4	419	16.8	46	9.3	29	3.21	2.15
2001	31.7	166	40.7	413	18.3	52	9.3	28	3.33	2.19
2005	32.2	197	35.2	355	22.0	62	10.5	32	3.61	2.51
Mean 1974–2005	**37.6**	**283**	**36.1**	**309**	**19.4**	**29**	**6.9**	**25**	**3.18**	**2.23**

Notes: (1) ENEP = effective number of electoral parties; (2) ENPP = effective number of parliamentary parties; (3) Liberal includes SDP/Liberal Alliance (1983–7) and Liberal Democrat (1992–2005). Northern Ireland MPs are included as 'Others'.

Source: Lynch, P (2008) 'Party System Change in Britain', *British Politics*, 2(3), 326.

> The British party system has changed, but in many ways remains the same... The established party system has changed, but is has been fragmented, not overturned... That is why, at the same time as it can no longer be described as a classical two-party system, Britain cannot be described as a genuine multi-party system... Britain may be described as a 'two-party plus' system, particularly as multi-party systems can be discerned as coming into being in the devolved assemblies in Scotland and Wales.[10]

The party system has changed. But it has changed, or more precisely it has been strategically manipulated by a dominant executive, in a way that has sought to block or prevent change at the national level—thereby retaining a two-party system—while actively promoting the creation of multiparty systems at the sub-national regional level. Dunleavy's argument is actually more influential for the manner in which it emphasizes how the tradition of studying party systems in the UK still tends to focus on national elections while paying very little attention to intervening elections at the local or sub-national levels. This intellectual heritage is reflected by the manner in which Scottish, Welsh, and local elections are commonly referred to as 'secondary elections'—a feature of Heffernan's work—and labelling the Liberal Democrats as a minor party despite their significant and consistent share of the vote (Table 5.1).[11]

The polarization between the scholars Dunleavy accuses of perpetuating an outdated 'orthodox view'—Richard Heffernan, Philip Lynch, and Robert Garner, Paul Webb, etc.—and his own argument that the UK has become a genuine multiparty system is therefore false and arguably unhelpful because the contemporary reality is more complex.[12] Put slightly differently, the semantic construction of polarized debates, exactly like that which has emerged between the 'Revolutionary Theorists' and the 'Sceptical Theorists' that was outlined in Chapter 3, is that it masks a situation that is actually displaying elements of both *continuity* and *change*. The discussion earlier about the *continuing* existence of a 'two-party plus' system reveals a degree of continuity; but in terms of *change* it is reasonably clear that a combination of partisan and class dealignment fused with the creation of a new democratic arenas built upon proportional electoral systems has fostered multiparty politics at the supra- and sub-national level with the number of effective parties in competition averaging between 5.5 and 6.0.[13] In elections to the European Parliament, for example, the change in electoral system from FPTP to a regional list system in England, Scotland, and Wales from the 1999 elections onwards significantly altered the party balance of MEPs representing the UK (see Table 5.3).[14] As a result the index score for effective political parties for the 2004 elections to the European Parliament was 4.4.

In Wales, elections to the National Assembly for Wales (NAW) are decided using an Additional Member System (AMS). Voters have two ballots. The first is used to elect forty constituency Assembly Members (AMs) under a traditional FPTP system and the second is used to elect four AMs from five electoral regions, thereby allowing split-ticket voting.[15] These additional AMs are elected so that the total representation from each geographical area, including those members elected under FPTP, corresponds more closely to the share of the votes cast for each political party in the region. Table 5.4 provides a summary of the results of elections to the NAW in 1999, 2003, and 2007.

The Labour Party still dominates in terms of constituency contests but the smaller parties, in this case the Conservatives, Plaid Cymru, and the Liberal Democrats, achieved most of their seats on the regional lists. Research suggests that the electorate utilize the proportional electoral system in order to express distinctive voting preferences and this is reflected in the fact that the Labour and Conservative Party attract less support in elections to the NAW than for comparable General Elections (the same is true for elections to the Scottish Parliament).[16] Consequently, analysing the statistics for Wales through the Laakso and Taagepera index results in scores of 3.03, 3.08, and 3.33 for the assembly elections in 1999, 2003, and 2007, respectively, leading to a mean score of 3.15.

Table 5.3 UK MEPs by party, 1979–2004

	1979	1984	1989	1994	1999	2004
Labour	17	32	45	62	29	19
Conservative	60	45	32	18	36	27
Lib. Dem.	—	—	0	2	10	12
SNP	1	1	1	2	2	2
Plaid Cymru	—	—	0	0	2	1
Green	—	—	—	0	2	2
UKIP	—	—	—	—	3	12
Dem. Union.	1	1	1	1	1	1
Sinn Fein	—	—	—	—	—	1
SDLP	1	1	1	1	1	0
Ulster Unionist	1	1	1	1	1	1
Total	**81**	**81**	**81**	**85**	**87**	**78**

Not surprisingly a similar pattern can be identified in Scotland where seventy-three constituency Members of the Scottish Parliament (MSP) and fifty-six list-elected MSPs (seven from each of the eight electoral regions) are delivered using AMS. Although voting statistics confirm that the electorate generally vote for one of the main four parties in Scotland they are far more likely to give their second regional list vote to a smaller party. This was a particularly distinctive feature of the second round of elections to the Scottish Parliament in 2003 when the Scottish Green Party (SGP), Scottish Socialist Party (SSP), and Scottish Senior Citizens Unity Party (SSCUP) had candidates elected (seven, six, and one, respectively) in addition to the election of three independent MSPs.[17] As Table 5.5 shows, during the 2007 elections the smaller parties and independent candidates faired less well with the SGP losing five seats and the SSP and the SSCUP failing to return any of their candidates, and just one independent candidate was elected.

Analysing the statistics for Scotland through the Laakso and Taagepera index results in the following party system scores for 1999, 2003, and 2007, respectively—3.23, 4.23, and 3.41 (a mean score of 3.62).

The party system in Northern Ireland is the most distinctive in the UK due to the major cleavage between the nationalist and unionist parties. The 1998 Good Friday Agreement focused on this cleavage and sought to promote co-operation between these two groups through a range of measures. The Single Transferable Vote (STV), the division of executive posts to reflect party strength in the assembly, and requirements for parallel consent are designed to foster consociational rather than majoritarian politics.[18] The Northern Ireland Assembly (NIA) was first elected in July 2008, but devolution was suspended on 14 October 2002 under the terms of the *Northern Ireland Act 2000*. Assembly elections next took place on 26 November 2003. The Assembly elected in 2003 finally convened in May 2006 solely for the purpose of choosing Northern Ireland ministers, but without any legislative powers. The Assembly was dissolved on 30 January 2007 and the subsequent elections took place on the 7 March 2007. The results of these elections are set out in Table 5.6.

The index results for Northern Ireland are therefore 5.41, 4.54, and 4.30 for the 1998, 2003, and 2007 elections, respectively, producing a mean score of 4.75—the highest number of effective political parties in the UK. However, this score veils the fact that electors remain firmly attached to the traditional representatives of their communities. The STV may have increased the choices available to voters in Northern Ireland, but the electorate still prefers to utilize that choice within their respective

Table 5.4 Elections to the National Assembly for Wales (constituency and regional lists combined): 1999, 2003, and 2007

	Number of votes			Per cent share of votes				Seats won			
	1999 (000s)	2003 (000s)	2007 (000s)	1999 (%)	2003 (%)	2007 (%)	Change (%)	1999	2003	2007	Change
Labour	746	651	604	36.5	38.3	30.9	−7.4	28	30	26	−4
Plaid Cymru	603	348	424	29.5	20.5	21.7	+1.2	17	12	15	+3
Con.	330	332	428	16.2	19.5	21.9	+2.4	9	11	12	+1
Lib. Dem.	266	228	259	13.0	13.4	13.3	−0.2	6	6	6	0
Other	100	141	238	4.9	8.3	12.2	+3.9		1	1	0
Total	2,045	1,700	1,953	100	100	100	—	60	60	60	

Table 5.5 Elections to the Scottish Parliament (constituency and regional lists combined): 1999, 2003, and 2007

| | Number of votes | | | Per cent share of votes | | | | Seats won | | | |
	1999 (000s)	2003 (000s)	2007 (000s)	1999 (%)	2003 (%)	2007 (%)	Change	1999	2003	2007	Change
Labour	1,695	1,225	1,244	36.2	32.0	30.6	−1.4	56	50	46	−4
SNP	1,311	855	1,298	28.0	22.3	32.0	+9.6	35	27	47	+20
Con.	724	615	619	15.5	16.1	15.2	−0.8	18	18	17	−1
Lib. Dem.	624	520	557	13.3	13.6	13.7	+0.1	17	17	16	−1
Others	327	614	342	7	16.0	8.4	−7.6	3	17	3	−14
Total	4,681	3,830	4,059	100	100	100	—	129	129	129	—

Table 5.6 Results of elections to the Northern Ireland Assembly: 1999, 2003, and 2007

	First preference votes (000S)			Votes (%)				Seats			
	1998	2003	2007	1999	2003	2007	Change	1999	2003	2007	Change
SDLP	178	118	105	22.0	17.0	15.2	−1.8	24	18	16	−2
Ulster Unionists	172	157	103	21.3	22.7	14.9	−7.7	28	27	18	−9
Dem. Unionists	147	178	208	18.1	25.7	30.1	+4.4	20	30	36	+6
Sinn Fein	143	163	181	17.6	23.5	26.2	+2.6	18	24	28	+4
Alliance	53	25	36	6.5	3.7	5.2	+1.6	6	6	7	+1
UK Unionists	37	6	10	4.5	0.8	1.5	+0.7	5	1	0	−1
Prog. Unionist Party	21	8	4	2.5	1.2	0.6	−0.6	2	1	1	0
Others	60	38	43	7.5	5.5	6.3	+0.8	5	1	2	+1
Total	**810**	**692**	**690**	**100**	**100**	**100**	—	**108**	**108**	**108**	—

Table 5.7 Results of elections to the London Assembly (seats)

	2000	2004	2008
Conservative Party	9	9	11
Labour Party	9	7	8
Liberal Democrats	4	5	3
Green Party	3	2	2
UK Independence Party	0	2	0
British National Party	0	0	1
Total	**25**	**25**	**25**

sectarian bloc of political parties, be they nationalist or unionist.[19] Non-sectarian minor parties, like the Alliance Party and the Women's Coalition, have made little progress.

In England the creation of the Greater London Assembly using an alternative vote electoral system has produced and similarly increased the range of effective political parties. The London Assembly has twenty-five members. There are fourteen constituency members topped-up by eleven London-wide members. Voters have two votes (one for a constituency candidate and one for a party or independent candidate). The results of the 2000, 2004, and 2008 elections are set out in Table 5.7 and produce an Index score of 3.4, 3.8, and 3.2, respectively.

The aim of this section has not been to provide a detailed account of party politics and political change in the constituent countries of the UK but simply to demonstrate that although a 'two-party-plus' system continues to exist at the national level it is possible to identify the existence of multiparty systems above and below the nation state. Whether a relationship exists between these party systems that may in time reveal elements of spillover and spillback forms the focus of Section 5.3.

5.3 Party system change

The UK did not become a genuine multiparty system during 1997–2007. The variable score for the national level was 2.28, a result which differs little from Lijphart's 1996 score of 2.11 (2.20 for 1971–96). We have yet to see the final demise of the two-party system, although Dunleavy's thesis does highlight the existence of anomalies and dynamics that may in time lead to a multiparty system at the national level. As Table 5.1 shows, the number of parties and organizations fielding candidates at recent general elections has increased significantly, at the same time the combined vote share of the two main parties has fallen to around 75 per cent (reaching a low of 67% in 2005), and the statistics suggest that minor parties are attracting more votes. In short, there are developments that suggest that a more competitive and open electoral arena is emerging. And yet Lynch is correct to emphasize the simple fact that,

> There remain flickers of life in the two-party system, largely because the simple plurality electoral system acts as an artificial life support machine providing Labour and to a lesser extent the Conservatives with some protection from the advance of multi-party politics.[20]

Indeed, the effect of electoral systems on either facilitating or preventing the development of multiparty politics is underlined by the data set out in Figure 5.2. This reflects the fact that the devolved party systems are closer to Sartori's model of 'moderate pluralism' because many parties compete for votes and the number of effective parliamentary parties is significantly higher than Westminster.[21]

Returning directly to Lijphart's methodology it is possible to state that the 1997–2007 score for V1 is 2.28, but if we take the mean of the scores for the same variable at the sub-national regional level (i.e. Scotland, Wales, and N.I.) then we arrive at a score of 3.84. Clearly the existence of multi-party systems alongside a 'two-party-plus' system at the national level not

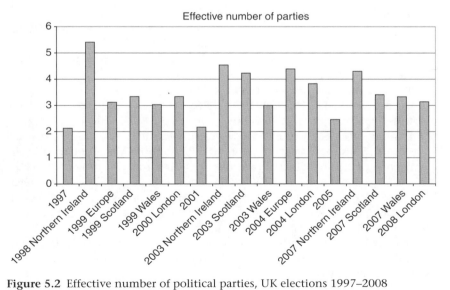

Figure 5.2 Effective number of political parties, UK elections 1997–2008

only feeds into a broader thesis concerning the bi-constitutionality of New Labour's statecraft, but it also provokes a series of questions concerning the long-term dynamics and stability of parallel party systems that reflect and are constructed upon quite different meta-constitutional orientations. Party systems do not exist in isolation and as Dunleavy states, 'The coexistence of plurality rule and PR elections is progressively accentuating and accelerating the transformation of both voters' alignments and parties strategies'.[22] Although we will return to these issues of statecraft and dynamics in Part III of this book it is now necessary to turn to Lijphart's second variable and one that is directly related to the nature of the party system—cabinets (V2).

V1 Effective number of parliamentary parties conclusion

Lijphart's UK score 1945–96	2.11
Lijphart's UK score 1971–96	2.20
Updated UK score 1997–2007	2.28
Devolved tier score 1998–2007	3.84

Notes

1. Bagehot *op. cit.* (1867).
2. See Lijphart *op. cit.* (1999), p. 64.
3. Webb, P (2000) *The Modern British Party System*. London: Sage, p. 1.
4. Laffin, M and Shaw, E (2007) 'British Devolution and the Labour Party', *British Journal of Politics and International Relations*, 9(1), 55–72.
5. Sartori, G (1976) *Parties and Party Systems*. Cambridge: Cambridge University Press.
6. The exceptions being 1906–10, 1922–3, 1924–9, and 1935–40.
7. Laakso, M and Taagepera, P (1979) 'Effective Number of Parties: A Measure with Application to Western Europe', *Comparative Political Studies*, 12, 3–27.
8. Dunleavy, P (2005) 'Facing Up to Multi-party Politics', *Parliamentary Affairs*, 5 (3), 530. See also Dunleavy, P (2006) 'The Westminster Model and the Distinctiveness of British Politics', in P Dunleavy, R Heffernan, P Cowley, and C Hay, eds., *Developments in British Politics 8*. London: Palgrave, pp. 315–41. The reference to Colomer is in relation to (2005) 'It's Parties that Chose Electoral Systems (or Duverger's Law Upside Down)', *Political Studies*, 53(1), 1–21.
9. Dunleavy *op. cit.* (2005).
10. Heffernan, R (2003) 'Political Parties and the Party System', in P Dunleavy, A Gamble, R Heffernan, and G Peele, eds., *Developments in British Politics 7*. London: Palgrave, p. 97.

11. Heffernan, R (2009) 'The Party System' in M Flinders, C Hay, A Gamble, and M Kenny, eds., *Oxford Handbook of British Politics*. Oxford: Oxford University Press.

12. Lynch, R and Garner, R (2005) 'The Changing Party System', *Parliamentary Affairs*, 58(3), 533–54; Webb, P (2002) 'Parties and Party Systems: More Continuity than Change?', *Parliamentary Affairs*, 55(2), 363–76; Webb, P (2003) 'Parties and Party Systems', *Parliamentary Affairs*, 56(2), 283–96.

13. Dunleavy *op. cit.* (2005), pp. 503–32; see also Denver, D (2003) *Elections and Voting in Britain*. London: Palgrave.

14. Northern Ireland elections to the European Parliament are held under a regional list system.

15. See Johnston, R and Pattie, C (2002) 'Campaigning and Split-Ticket Voting in New Electoral Systems', *Electoral Studies*, 21(4), 583–600; Rallings, C and Thrasher, M (2003) 'Explaining Split Ticket Voting at the 1979 and 1997 General and Local Elections in England', *Political Studies*, 51(3), 558–72.

16. See Wyn Jones, R and Scully, R (2006) 'Devolution and Electoral Politics in Scotland and Wales', *Publius*, 36(1), 115–34.

17. Dennis Canavan (Falkirk West), Jean Turner (Strathkelvin and Bearsden), and Margo MacDonald (Lothians region).

18. Mitchell, P (2001) 'Transcending an Ethnic Party System?' in R Wilford, ed., *Aspects of the Belfast Agreement*. Oxford: Oxford University Press, pp. 28–48.

19. Electoral Reform Society (2007) *STV in Practice: A Briefing on the Northern Ireland Assembly Election*. Edinburgh: Electoral Reform Society.

20. Lynch, P (2008) 'Party System Change in Britain: Multi-Party Politics in a Multi-level Polity', *British Politics*, 2(3), 323.

21. See Bennie, L and Clarke, A (2003) 'Towards Moderate Pluralism' in C Rallings, P Webb, R Scully, and J Tonge, eds., *British Elections and Parties Review*. London: Frank Cass.

22. Dunleavy *op. cit.* (2005), p. 505.

Chapter 6

V2. Cabinets

England does not love Coalitions.[1]

Chapter 5 focused on the spread of political parties operating within a given polity. V2 develops this theme by analysing the breadth of party-representation within the executive branch of government. The difference between one-party majority governments and broad multiparty coalitions encapsulates to a large extent the contrast between the majoritarian principle of concentrating power and the consensus principle of power-sharing. Coalition theory offers three broad classifications that are pertinent to this discussion: (*a*) *minimal winning cabinets*, 'winning' in the sense that the party or parties in the cabinet controls a majority of parliamentary seats in the lower house but 'minimal' to reflect the fact that no other parties contribute to the executive; (*b*) *oversized cabinets*, which do contain more parties than are actually necessary for majority support in the legislature; and (*c*) *minority cabinets*, which do not enjoy the support of a parliamentary majority.[2] The most majoritarian form of cabinet is single-party and minimal winning (i.e. a one-party majority cabinet). A multiparty and oversized cabinet is, by contrast, the most consensual form.

The simple finding of this chapter is that the cabinet system in the UK remained a minimal winning cabinet throughout the period under observation (i.e. 1997–2007). This finding, however, needs to be set against the fact that, as with V1, the introduction of devolution based upon proportional electoral systems has led to minority or 'under-sized' cabinets at the sub-national level. In order to explore this argument and its implications in more detail this chapter is divided into three sections. The first section focuses on developments and cabinet-dynamics at the national level in order to update Lijphart's data for this variable. The existence and potential repercussions of alternative cabinet systems at the sub-national level forms the focus of the second section. The final section locates the specific findings of this chapter back within the broader contours of both Lijphart's framework and the central thesis of this book.

6.1 The British cabinet 1997–2007

The notion of parliamentary systems of government is founded on the idea that it will be possible to draw from the legislature a cabinet or executive that will enjoy both the confidence and support of a parliamentary majority. In most cases where a political party enjoys a majority of seats in the legislature they will form a one-party cabinet, but there are examples of majority parties forming coalitions with one or more parties (i.e. an oversized cabinet).[3] Lijphart's analysis of political history in the UK between 1945 and 1996 established that the executive had been a minimal winning cabinet for 93.3 per cent of this period and a one-party cabinet for all (100%) of this period resulting in a mean of 96.7 per cent. For the period 1997–2007 New Labour enjoyed a minimal winning cabinet with parliamentary majorities of 178, 166, and 71 after the 1997, 2001, and 2005 general elections, respectively (see Table 5.1).

As Chapter 3 noted, during the mid-1990s New Labour entered into negotiations with the Liberal Democrats regarding the creation of a minority and oversized cabinet should the forthcoming general election produce no clear legislative majority.[4] The result of the 1997 election, combined with the adversarial, almost tribal, political culture created few incentives for New Labour to form an oversized cabinet that included representatives from another party. Consequently one-party cabinet bolstered by a large parliamentary majority has been the dominant (100%) form of government during 1997–2007. The figure of 100 per cent for V2 suggests that on this variable the UK has become more majoritarian since 1997 rather than less. Indeed, increasing the period of analysis from 1945 to 2007 increases the mean figure from Lijphart's 96.7 per cent, to around 98 per cent. Paradoxically then V2 suggests a move not away but towards greater majoritarianism during New Labour's decade in power. A deeper analysis of developments beneath the national level, however, allows us to detect the existence of significant trends and dynamics in relation to V2. This is particularly true where recent developments have created complex party-bargaining relationships and have led to the formation of coalition cabinets.

6.2 Cabinet systems

Just as we have already seen that there is no such thing as *the* party system in the UK it is also possible to suggest that any discussion of *the* cabinet system risks underemphasizing the creation, dynamics, and potential consequences of multiparty coalition governments in Scotland, Wales, and Northern Ireland. The first part of this section reviews the main theories of coalition formation in order to allow us to tease apart and identify the distinctive qualities of coalition politics in each nation.[5] The latter half of this section reviews the development and nature of coalition formation in Scotland, Wales, and Northern Ireland. It is at this point that the broader theoretical literature on the formation and durability of government coalitions becomes relevant and in this regard Lijphart synthesizes the vast literature to isolate six kinds of coalition (Table 6.1).

As Chapter 5 illustrated, the use of a proportional AMS electoral system in Scotland has led to a multiparty system. In the 1999 election, the seats were distributed to the four largest parties, as well as one each for the Greens, Socialists, and an independent candidate. The 2003 elections saw a move towards a 'rainbow parliament' in a shift towards smaller parties

Table 6.1 Forms of coalition government

Coalition type	Central criterion	Key reference
Minimal winning coalitions	Only those numbers of parties that are necessary to construct a bare statistical majority of legislative seats will be invited to join the coalition.	Riker, *The Theory of Coalitions*, 1962.
Minimum size coalitions	Parties will prefer the mixture of coalition partners that maximizes its proportional share of power.	Deemen, 'Dominant Players and Minimum Size Coalitions' 2006.
Smallest number of parties	Because coalitions demand bargaining and negotiating there is a rational incentive to involve the smallest number of parties.	Groennings and Leiserson *The Study of Coalition Behaviour*, 1970.
Minimal range coalitions	It is easier to bargain, negotiate, and trust coalition partners with similar policy preferences.	de Swaan, *Coalition Theories and Cabinet Formations*, 1970.
Minimal connected winning coalitions	Coalitions will form with parties that are both ideologically 'connected' but only until a majority coalition is formed.	Axelrod, *Conflict of Interest*, 1970.
Policy-viable coalitions	A policy-viable coalition is one that cannot be defeated by any other coalition representing a policy position preferred by a legislative majority.	Strom, *Minority Government and Majority Rule*, 1990.

and independents and away from Labour and the SNP, but the final result was a continuation of the Labour-Party–Liberal-Democrat minimal-winning coalitions which had since 1999 provided a relatively smooth transition into the potential incompatibilities afforded by an embryonic system of multilevel government. Inter-party collaboration had been facilitated by the pre-devolution Labour-Party–Liberal-Democrat co-operation in the Scottish Constitutional Convention. In this context the governing coalition executive in Scotland has largely functioned within the framework of the broad contours of the national Labour government's programme, albeit with some specific departures.[6]

After the 1999 election the Liberal Democrats gained two ministerial portfolios in the eleven-strong Scottish executive (with the Leader of the Scottish Liberal Democrats, Jim Wallace, appointed Deputy First Minister), and two out of eight deputy ministers. However the Labour Party's decision at the national level to remain within the spending restrictions of the previous Conservative government for its first two years meant that 'the 1999–2000 Scottish budget contained little slack'.[7] In retrospect the Liberal Democrat negotiators may well have felt they had achieved little in 1999, but after the 2003 election the balance of power shifted slightly in their favour due to the fact that their share of seats in the legislature remained stable at 17, while the Labour Party's fell from 56 to 50. As a result the Liberal Democrats were able to claim a third seat in the Scottish executive (and a third junior ministerial post).

Overall, however, the coalition executive that governed in Scotland during 1999–2007 provided a high degree of stability which surprised many observers. The underlying reason for this stability, however, lay not solely within Scotland but was due in many parts to the favourable public spending settlements provided to Scotland, courtesy of the Barnett Formula, following the Westminster Labour government's significant public sector spending increases from 2000 onwards.[8] The increased fiscal resources facilitated the high-cost demands of the Liberal Demo-crats—free prescriptions, no student fees, free personal care for the elder-ly—without creating the political frictions that would have occurred in a more restrained financial environment. It was also true that the Liberal Democrats were conscious of the meagre rewards they enjoyed from keeping Labour in power nationally in the Lib–Lab pact of 1977–8 and therefore bargained very hard as the junior coalition partner. They insisted upon using explicit public partnership agreements that set out a policy programme and some specific demands at the beginning of each coalition government in order to 'stem the tide of policy erosion by executive decision in cabinet'.[9]

The real challenges of multiparty coalition politics in Scotland were therefore widely expected to occur once the Labour Party were excluded from office. In this context the resignation of Jim Wallace and subsequent appointment of Nicol Stephen as Leader of the Scottish Liberal Democrats in June 2005 proved critical. Buoyed by the unexpected victory of the party in the Dunfermline Westminster by-election (overturning an 11,000 Labour majority on a 15% swing) Stephen announced a strategic shift in the governing strategy of the party in which the historic strategy of equidistance was reinstated after the previous tactic of adjacency to the Labour Party that had been followed by Paddy Ashdown at Westminster and Jim Wallace in Edinburgh.[10] As such a new phase of 'new politics plus' was signalled in the run up to the 2007 Scottish elections when the Liberal Democrats indicated that they would not in future form a coalition with either the Labour Party or the SNP. As Table 6.2 shows, the results of the 2007 election were critical because the trend towards small parties was reversed, and the SNP won the largest plurality of seats with 47 out of 129. In this situation the comparatively relaxed rules governing coalition formation in the Scottish Parliament proved significant (particularly when compared with the complex and entrenched rules in Northern Ireland). There is no need for the affirmation of a coalition but there is a need to decide who should be the First Minister within twenty-eight days of the election. Standing Orders also require that the first vote on a First Minister should be within fourteen days and this may depend on the prior election of a Presiding Officer at its first meeting.

With two dominant parties and two smaller parties (both of which had announced their intention not to join a future coalition) the explanatory value of much coalition theory (Table 6.1) earlier was not tested. Although the two major parties could theoretically have formed a coalition this was effectively ruled-out because it is doubtful that they could have been described as a 'connected winning coalition' due to their differences on key policies, particularly Scottish independence. Moreover, the logic of minimal winning coalitions makes such an agreement extremely inefficient for both parties as only sixty-five seats are necessary for a majority but their combined number of seats would be ninety-three (72% of the legislature) thereby significantly reducing the relative performance-reward ratio for each coalition partner. The Liberal Democrats could have offered to join a coalition with one of the large parties but a significant number of its MSPs believed that the party could make significant policy gains through ad hoc deals with a minority government.

Table 6.2 Scottish Assembly, party strengths: 1999, 2003, and 2007

	1999	2003	2007
Labour	56	50	46
SNP	35	27	47
Con.	18	18	17
Lib. Dem.	17	17	16
Green Party	1	7	2
Socialist Party	1	6	0
Independent MPs	1[28]	3[29]	1[30]
Scottish Senior Citizens Unity Party	0	1	0
Total legislative seats	129	129	129
Subsequent executive formation	Minimal-winning (Lab.9/LD2)	Minimal-winning (Lab.8/LD3)	Single-Minority SNP
Total executive seats	11	11	11

Consequently the SNP formed a single-minority administration. The outcome of the 2007 Scottish elections was therefore a relatively weak executive bereft of the legislative majority commonly associated with majoritarian politics that could not expect to achieve all or even most of its manifesto pledges. Control of just 36 per cent of legislative seats also placed the executive under constant threat of a vote of no confidence which would, in turn, make governing in Scotland the focus of ongoing and complex negotiations on every issue. As such the role of the legislature would be enhanced vis-à-vis the executive (V3—the focus of Chapter 7) but at a cost of what might be termed 'strong', 'effective', or 'stable' government. Devolution to Scotland has therefore been significant in terms of the functioning of cabinet government. One-party majority rule has not existed post-1998. Two terms of minimal-winning coalition government were followed by a period of single-party minority rule.

In Wales the first elections to the NAW resulted in no party gaining an overall majority of assembly seats in 1999 (Table 6.3).[11] With twenty-eight seats the Labour Party were three seats short of a majority but appeared reluctant to form a coalition because as Deacon suggests 'the concept of a coalition government was quite alien to its [the Labour Party in Wales] nature'.[12] Research suggests, however, that Labour, or more precisely its

Table 6.3 National Assembly for Wales, party strengths: 1999, 2003, and 2007

	1999	2003	2007
Labour	28	30	26
PC	17	12	15
Con.	9	11	12
Lib Dem.	6	6	6
Other	—	1	1
Total legislative seats	60	60	60
Subsequent executive formation	1999–2000 minority Labour executive 2000–3 Lab./LD coalition (Labour 7/LD 2).	2003–5 Labour executive 2005–7 Labour minority executive	2007– Lab./PC coalition (Lab. 6/PC 3).
Total executive seats	9	9	9

Leader in the NAW, were not opposed to forming a coalition in principle but were simply of the opinion that the demands of the Liberal Democrats to enter a coalition—two executive seats out of nine for the support of their six AMs—were too high.[13] Alun Michael therefore formed a minority-executive that was heavily reliant on the informal support of Plaid Cymru. This administration proved short-lived. Specific concerns regarding Treasury match funding for EU support for the West Wales and Valleys Region acted as a lightning rod for broader concerns with Michael's style of leadership and a perception that he was insufficiently robust in his dealings with the government in Westminster. This led Plaid Cymru to withdraw their support and table a no confidence motion at the end of the NAW's budget debate in February 2000. This was passed by thirty-one votes to twenty-seven (with one Labour abstention).[14]

In October 2000 the Labour Party, under the leadership of Rhodri Morgan, formed a majority coalition government with the Liberal Democrats under the auspices of the 'Putting Wales First' partnership agreement; a document modelled closely on the Scottish Parliament's partnership between the Labour Party and the Liberal Democrats. However, despite private negotiations between the parties dating back to August 2000 coalition politics came as something of a culture shock to many members of the Labour Party in Wales and many AMs were made aware of the agreement just one day before it was formally announced. For many Labour politicians and activists bringing the Liberal Democrats into the executive, and especially conceding to so many of their policy demands, were flawed by the First Minister. The cost for the Labour Party of negotiating from a position of weakness was that they were forced to concede to almost every Liberal Democrat policy's demand to secure their commitment to a coalition.

Despite public unpopularity regarding the Iraq War, the Labour Party (+2 seats) was clearly the winner of the Welsh Assembly elections in 2003 and Plaid Cymru (−5 seats) was the loser (see Table 6.3). When the positions of the Presiding Officer and Deputy Presiding Officer are removed from the equation it is possible to argue that thirty seats is a working, if not clear cut, majority in the NAW and therefore the Labour Party decided to form a single-minority government.[15] However, the subsequent resignation of Peter Law from the Labour Party in May 2005, and his subsequent siding with the opposition, meant that the combined opposition now had thirty-one seats and Labour were effectively a minority party. After this point the Welsh assembly government could effectively be defeated whenever the opposition could unite on a common topic, as they did when they rejected the 2005 draft budget and when the assembly voted 30/29 in favour of a Conservative motion not to introduce top-up fees in Wales.

However, as coalition theory makes clear, minor parties who hold the balance of power due to the larger party's need to acquire their support in order to form a government can exert a weight in excess of their statistical representation. In that case the price paid by the Labour Party for securing the informal support of the Liberal Democrats over many issues during 2006 was a firm commitment and formal pathway for an enhanced degree of autonomy for Wales. This was delivered in the form of the *Government of Wales Act 2006* that provided for a further referendum on greater legislative powers once certain criteria had been achieved (discussed in Chapter 10).

In the run up to the 2007 elections the Labour Party's election strategy offered the electorate a straight choice between themselves and the Conservatives (despite the fact that surveys suggested Plaid Cymru was their main challenger). Plaid Cymru sought to exploit the incumbency fatigue associated with the Labour Party and encouraged voters to 'kick them into touch'; while at the same time ruling out any possible coalition with a Conservative-led administration. The Welsh Conservatives hoped to gain votes not only from their support for greater powers for the Welsh Assembly, but also due to the broader surge in interest in the party since David Cameron had been appointed leader. The Liberal Democrats campaigned in the hope that they might gain a small number of seats and through this become a critical actor in a future coalition government.

As Table 5.4 shows, although the Labour Party's share of the vote declined in 2007 it benefited from the fact that its opposition is divided between Plaid Cymru and the Conservatives, and because the electoral system gives more weight to constituency contests where the Labour Party still dominates. Although initially some senior members of the Labour Party in Wales believed that a minority administration could be sustained, this position quickly gave way to the inevitability of some form of coalition government. The critical question was who the Labour Party should seek to work with and in this respect two possible partners were obvious—the Liberal Democrats or Plaid Cymru.

By mid-May with negotiations between Labour and these two partners apparently faltering, the prospect of a 'rainbow' coalition led by Plaid Cymru with the Conservatives and Liberal Democrats emerged. An 'All-Wales Accord' document was produced by the three parties in which the main aims and policy commitments of the potential coalition were set out, but at that stage internal tensions within the Liberal Democrats led them to withdraw from the proposal and as a result a minority-Labour administration was installed on the 25 May 2007. However, the relatively weak position of the minority administration encouraged the Labour Party to reopen negotiations with Plaid Cymru over a possible coalition government and, after much internal debate and discussion within both parties, a new Cabinet containing ministers from both parties was appointed on 19 July 2007 under the 'One Wales' agreement.[16] The coalition government enjoys a majority of eleven with Plaid Cymru taking three seats in the Welsh Assembly Government (plus one deputy minister) against Labour's six.

The significance of the 2007 assembly elections in Wales lay not just in the statistical results but also because of the complexity and length of the post-election coalition-formation strategies that followed. At various points the negotiations involved each of the four main parties and led to an unexpected coalition alliance between Labour and Plaid Cymru. Moreover, as McAllister and Cole emphasize, 'The negotiations showed more parallels with those in European states than they did anything based on traditional British politics'.[17] The notion of 'traditional British politics' in this context being a clear reference to strong, clear single-party majority governments underpinned by majoritarian logic. But before examining the contemporary relevance and ubiquity of this logic it is necessary to shift the focus of our empirical analysis to a polity that has in recent years been modelled on consociational logic—Northern Ireland.

Since the introduction of direct rule in 1972 (and arguably well before this date) the politics of Northern Ireland has always formed a spectacularly distinct element of the UK's politics, and the election of New Labour on 1 May 1997 did little to dampen this distinctiveness. The deep sectarian cleavages that shaped and defined the governance of the province stood apart from any tensions that could be found on the mainland, and Northern Ireland represented the only sphere of constitutional politics in which Tony Blair took a leading and very personal role. Of particular significance, given the methodological frame of this book, the constitutional settlement that had been planned in negotiations dating back to 1996 was explicitly based upon consociational thinking, and particularly Lijphart's work on divided societies.[18]

> The Belfast Agreement has, in its 'internal' and 'strand one' dimension, a 'consociationalist' character embodying the conventional Lijphartian wisdom of grand-coalition government, mutual-veto arrangements, 'segmented autonomy', and proportionality in public employment.[19]

The structure of the consociational agreement in Northern Ireland was based upon four key characteristics: cross community power-sharing; the proportionality rule; segmental autonomy; and, the mutual veto. Each of these characteristics was designed to enable and deliver effective governance within a divided society where majority rule had proved highly problematic.

In relation to cabinet government and party representation within the executive, the principles of power sharing and proportionality were delivered through the Belfast Agreement's stipulation that the composition of the executive would reflect that of the Northern Ireland Assembly (NIA). Translating the theory of consociational constitutional design into practice, however, proved difficult as the first attempt to form a coalition executive in July 1998 was abandoned due to the Ulster Unionist Party's (UUP) refusal to work with Sinn Fein. The deadlock was eventually broken in November of that year when the leader of the UUP, David Trimble, won support from his party's Ruling Council to join the executive on the basis that he would resign if Irish Republican Army (IRA) decommissioning did not occur early in the New Year. The outcome was a new coalition government, formally known as the Executive Committee, consisting of six unionist/loyalist ministers and six nationalist/republican ministers (detailed in Table 6.4).

Despite the beginning of a new phase of devolved government in Northern Ireland the long-standing sectarian tensions continued to cast

Table 6.4 Northern Ireland Assembly, party strengths: 1999, 2003, and 2007

	Legislative seats		
	1999	2003	2007
Social and Democratic Labour Party (SDLP)	24	18	16
Ulster Unionists Party (UUP)	28	27	18
Democratic Unionists Party (DUP)	20	30	36
Sinn Fein (SF)	18	24	28
Alliance	6	6	7
UK Unionists (UKU)	5	1	0
Progressive Unionists Party (PUP)	2	1	1
Others	5	1	2
Total legislative seats	108	108	108
Subsequent executive structure	UU 3 SDLP 3 DUP 2 SF 2	None (Direct Rule)	DUP 4 SF 3 UU 2 SDLP 1
Total executive seats	10		10

a long shadow over the practical day-to-day operations of the first coalition executive. The two DUP members refused to meet or negotiate directly with the two SF members of the executive, and throughout the first half of 2000 the leader of the UUP fought hard to persuade his party to remain in the executive despite the perceived failure of SF/IRA to decommission their weapons. During the same period the position of the DUP became more strident as it declared that not only would it boycott the executive, but it would also rotate its ministers.

The first NIA coalition government was therefore extremely fragile with proxy-sovereignty issues (policing, flags, decommissioning, resource targeting, etc.) not only hampering the executive but also fuelling popular cynicism and bolstering support for those parties adopting a more strident sectarian position.[20] This became clear as early as September 2000 when the UUP lost its second safest Westminster seat to the DUP in a by-election, and was further underlined in the June 2001 local and general elections when the DUP and SF made significant gains at a cost to the more moderate sectarian parties (the UUP and SDLP). The summer of 2001 saw the peace process falter as the First Minister, David Trimble, resigned over the lack of progress on decommissioning and the Secretary of State for Northern Ireland, John Reid, was forced to suspend devolution for a short time in order to re-engage the various parties to the peace process. The most surprising element of the first term of the devolved government in NI was not the regular occurrence of extreme and often surreal crises and several temporary suspensions of devolution, but the fact that when looked at in broad terms some semblance of a governing, if fragile, regime continued. The paradox was that coalition government within Stormont appeared to be inflaming rather than dampening sectarian tensions outside it.

The NIA was again suspended on 14 October 2002 after the DUP resigned from the executive after evidence of an IRA spying ring operating within Stormont was discovered. Direct rule was reinstated by the Secretary of State, by this time Paul Murphy, under the terms of the Northern Ireland Act 2000. The NIA elections of November 2003 underlined the extent of sectarian polarization in the province and as a result the Secretary of State did not convene the assembly. In fact fifty-five months passed before devolution was restored to Northern Ireland. However the coalition partners that emerged in the new Executive Committee—the DUP and SF—would have been unthinkable at the end of the twentieth century.

The 2007 assembly elections underlined the popular shift towards the DUP and Sinn Fein and this resulted in, following the St Andrews Agreement of October 2006, a new super-coalition majority involving the DUP, SF, UUP, and SDLP forming a ruling executive committee (with 4, 3, 2, and 1 seats, respectively) with Ian Paisley (DUP) as First Minister and Martin McGuiness (SF) as Deputy First Minister. As such Northern Ireland entered into its first phase of relative stability since the introduction of devolution in 1998. This is not to say that there have not been tensions and bitter struggles within the coalition since the re-establishment of devolution in May 2007 but the critical element for this chapter lies in the manner in which a new political arena has been forged around consociationalism and the perceived benefits of coalition governments. Indeed this stark departure from the majoritarian culture of one-party minimal-winning cabinets in Westminster encourages us to return to our reworking of Lijphart's analytical framework and reflect on some of the broader implications of the research presented in this chapter.

6.3 Coalition dynamics and linkages

The concentration versus sharing of executive power has formed the focus of this chapter. As Lijphart's work emphasized, this issue is critical because it can be regarded as the most typical variable in the

majoritarian-consensus contrast: the difference between one-party majority governments and broad multiparty coalitions epitomizes the contrast
between the majoritarian principle of concentrating power in the hands of
the majority and the consensus principle of broad power sharing. This
chapter has, like Chapter 5 which focused on the party system (V1),
provided a picture of both continuity and change. Continuity in relation
to single-party majority government at the national level; but change in
relation to the establishment of coalition or single-party *minority* government in the devolved nations. As Table 6.5 illustrates, this finding can be
located within the Lijphartian methodology in a manner that underlines
the existence of patterns of democracy.

The strap-line conclusion is that although single-party majority government remains the dominant mode of governance at the national level,
coalition government has become the norm (rather then the exception) at
the sub-national level. The reasons for this situation include: the use of a
proportional electoral system that makes winning an absolute majority in
the legislature much more difficult; and the existence of strict rules within
NI on the composition of coalitions. Returning to the various forms and
theories of coalition cabinets and theories as set out in Table 6.1 provides a
way of deepening this analysis and explaining specific scores. And yet it is
possible to suggest that the theories outlined earlier and analysed by Lijphart
underplay the fiscal environment in which coalition negotiations take
place. Put slightly differently, the coalition theories tend to focus on agency
to the detriment of structural and contextual factors. This line of reasoning is
substantiated by the developments in Scotland Wales discussed earlier. The
critical factor in the formation of coalitions, and in the identification of
viable coalition partners, after the 1999 elections was the substantial real
terms spending increases that New Labour had just announced at the

Table 6.5 V2. Cabinets: multilevel analysis

Country	Minimal winning cabinets (%)	One-party cabinets (%)	Mean (%)
UK 1945–96	93.3	100.0	96.7
UK 1997–2007	100.0	100.0	100.0
Constituent nations post-devolution			
Scotland 1999–2007	80.0	20.0	50.0
Wales 1999–2007	50.0	50.0	50.0
Northern Ireland 1999–2007	0.0	0.0	0.0

national level in its effort to improve public services. This allowed the Labour Party groupings in Scotland and Wales to absorb the additional public spending implications of Liberal Democrat coalition demands. As Laffin notes, 'If the spending constraints had been tighter, coalition-formation and maintenance would have been considerably more difficult'.[21]

Coalition government in Scotland and Wales has clearly been based around the construction of minimal winning coalitions with the emphasis generally being placed on the Labour Party reaching an agreement with a smaller party. Coalition bargaining, however, demands new skills and competencies in relation to informal intra- and inter-party negotiations that political parties in the UK are only just beginning to develop. This is because coalition bargaining opens us a new political space; a space that parties need to attempt to proactively shape while at the same time having the capacity to act decisively within intense and convoluted rounds of bargaining. In Wales, for example, the failure of the Liberal Democrats to present a committed and credible position on their favoured coalition partners in the wake of the 2007 election not only left them out of power but also left the party and its leader damaged in terms of their public image.

The impact and demands of coalition government, however, reverberate beyond personal skill-sets or intra-party internal governance structures. The contestation and dynamics of coalition bargaining also effect socio-political relationships in terms of party-political identities and nationalist affiliations. Framed in this manner, devolution has created a new cleavage (or possibly made more explicit and salient a cleavage that has existed for centuries) in the form of a union versus nation state fault line or fracture that is increasingly affecting intra-party dynamics and party political strategies. Parties have to cultivate a nation-focused image and this is easier for some than others because their choices of strategies and tactics are heavily dependent on their ideological and historical heritage within specific constituent nations. This is clearly more problematic for the traditionally unionist parties than for the nationalist parties.

Although Hopkin (2003) has argued that national parties will adapt to the electoral threat of regional parties by 'denationalizing' their electoral strategies. Forging a distinct 'Welsh' or 'Scottish' identity, however, is easier for those parties with a federal structure, like the Liberal Democrats who are federalized with three 'state' parties (Scotland, England and Wales), than for those with a single national structure.[22] Downs was therefore correct when he stressed that sub-national party elites have to balance 'a logic of electoral competition' with a 'logic of [national] party organization'.[23] In this context the Labour Party in Wales has sought to distinguish itself from the party at Westminster by emphasizing the existence of 'clear red water' (a euphemism for policy differences between them).[24] In Scotland analysts of the 2007 elections have suggested that the Leader of the Labour Party in Scotland failed to distance the party sufficiently from the mid-term fall in popularity of the Labour government in Westminster and that this contributed heavily to the party's poor performance.[25]

The unionist–nationalist cleavage obviously runs far deeper in Northern Ireland than in the rest of the UK and it is exactly for this reason that post-devolution politics in the province provides an example not of a *minimal-winning coalition* but of a constitutionally engineered and demanded *over-sized coalition*. After the 2007 elections, for example, the four parties forming a power-sharing government enjoyed 98 out of the 108 seats in the assembly (91% of seats). After 2007 without the requirements of the Good Friday Agreement a minimal winning coalition could have after been forged by the Ulster Unionists and the Democratic Unionists, who together had fifty-four seats (one short of a majority), plus one minor party but instead the d'Hondt proportionality rule ensured that four mistrustful parties were thrust together in a consociational-style 'grand coalition'.[26]

It is also clear from the research presented in this chapter that the coalitions formed in Scotland and Wales were based upon electoral compatibilities in the vein of *minimal range coalitions* and *minimal connected winning coalitions* (Table 6.1). The stability of the Lib–Lab coalitions was sustained by leaders' perception of the parties as electorally compatible rather than simply competitive. Despite the existence of some clear tensions, the ideological proximity of both parties allowed policy bargaining to occur within a fairly fixed and harmonious framework. Although coalitions negotiations can sometimes appear incomprehensible and protracted to students and scholars schooled in the history and culture of majoritarian politics, from a more pluralist perspective these negotiations are a positive element of a consensual mode of governing and certainly reflects a pattern that is common in states where coalition government is the norm. And yet what is distinctive about contemporary UK politics is the attempt to run parallel polities that are based on quite different meta-constitutional orientations; a point which reintroduces the theme of bi-constitutionality and the central argument of this book regarding the existence and consequences of constitutional anomie. Although these broader themes will be examined in detail in later chapters, raising them at this stage reminds us that a clustering or relationship between specific

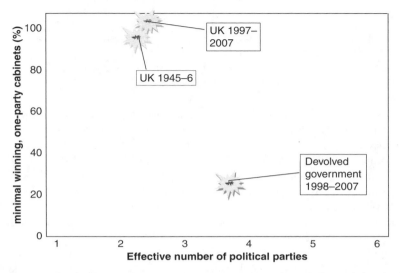

Figure 6.1 Relationship between V1 (party systems) and V2 (cabinets) for the UK and Scotland, Wales and Northern Ireland, 1997–2007

variables is often identifiable because they stem from the same governing logic. Figure 6.1 illustrates the relationship between V1 (party systems) and V2 (cabinets) for the UK and the constituent nations of Scotland, Wales, and Northern Ireland.

Although Figure 6.1 provides the first empirical glimpse or indication of the nature of bi-constitutionality in the UK it is necessary to continue with Lijphart's framework of variables in order to examine the existence of further relationships (or indeed abnormalities) in the reform agenda. It is for this reason that Chapter 7 focuses on V3, executive–legislative relationships.

V2 Minimal winning one-party cabinets (%) conclusion

Lijphart's UK score 1945–96	96.7
Lijphart's UK score 1971–96	93.3
Updated UK score 1997–2007	100.0
Devolved tier score 1998–2007	25.0

123

Notes

1. Disraeli, Benjamin (1852) Hansard, House of Commons, 16 December.
2. Lijphart *op. cit.* (1999), pp. 90–1.
3. For example, Churchill's war cabinet during the second world war (1939–45).
4. See Ashdown, P (2001) *The Ashdown Diaries 1988–1997 (Volume 1)*. London: Penguin.
5. Laver, M and Shepsle, K (1996) *Making and Breaking Governments*. Cambridge: Cambridge University Press; Laver, M and Schofield, N (1990) *Multi-Party Government*. Oxford: Oxford University Press.
6. Bonney, N (2007) 'The Settled Will of the Scottish People', *Parliamentary Affairs*, 78(2), 301–9.
7. Laffin, M (2007) 'Coalition-formation and Centre–Periphery Relations in a National Political Party', *Party Politics*, 13(6), 656.
8. McLean, I and McMillan, A (2003) 'The Distribution of Public Expenditure across the UK regions', *Fiscal Studies*, 24(1), 45–71.
9. Mitchell, P (1999) 'Coalition Discipline, Enforcement Mechanisms, and Intra-party Politics' in S Bowler, D Farrell, and R Katz, eds., *Party Discipline and Parliamentary Government*. Columbus, O: Ohio State University Press, p. 273. For a wider discussion on the use of explicit partnership agreements see Muller, W and Strom, K (2000) eds. *Coalition Governments in Western Europe*. Oxford: Oxford University Press.
10. See Joyce, P (1999) *Realignment of the Left?* Basingstoke: Macmillan.
11. For a review of this election see, McAllister, L (2000) 'Changing the Landscape', *Political Quarterly*, 71(2), 211–22.
12. Deacon, R (2007) 'The Welsh Liberal Democrats', *Political Quarterly*, 78(1), 159.
13. See Laffin *op. cit.* (2007), 651–68.
14. See Thomas, A and Laffin, M (2001) 'The First Welsh Constitutional Crisis', *Public Policy and Administration*, 16, 18–31.
15. McAllister, L (2004) 'Steady State or Second Order?' *Political Quarterly*, 75(1), 73–82.
16. Labour Party Wales / Plaid Cymru (2007) *One Wales—A Progressive Agenda for the Government of Wales*. Cardiff: Labour Party Wales / Plaid Cymru.
17. McAllister, L and Cole, M (2007) 'Pioneering New Politics or Rearranging the Deckchairs?' *Political Quarterly*, 78(4), 545.
18. Lijphart, A (1977) *Democracy in Plural Societies*. Yale: Yale University Press; Lijphart, A (1985) *Power-Sharing in South Africa*. Berkeley: University of California Press.
19. Wilford, R and Wilson, R (2005) 'Northern Ireland', in A Trench, ed., *The Dynamics of Devolution*. Exeter: Imprint Academic, p. 69.
20. On this period see Wilford, R and Wilson, R (2000) 'A Bare Knuckle Ride', in R. Hazell, ed., *The State and the Nations*. Exeter: Academic Imprint.
21. Laffin *op. cit.* (2007), 664.

22. Hopkin, J (2003) 'Political Decentralization, Electoral Change and Party Organizational Adaptation', *European Urban and Regional Studies*, 10, 227–37. On the structure and flexibility of the Liberal Democrats see, Deacon, R (1998) 'The Hidden Federal Party', *Regional Studies*, 32(5), 475–9.

23. Downs, A (1998) *Coalition Politics, Subnational Style*. Columbus, OH: Ohio State University Press, p. 47.

24. Morgan, R (2002) 'Speech by the First Minister of Wales', National Centre for Public Policy, University of Swansea, 11 December. See McAllister *op. cit.* (2003).

25. See Laffin, M and Shaw, E (2007) 'British Devolution and the Labour Party', *British Journal of Politics and International Relations*, 9, 36–54; Laffin, M, Shaw, E, and Taylor, G (2007) 'The New Sub-national Politics of the Labour Party', *Party Politics,* 13(1), 88–108.

26. See Wilford, R and Wilson, R (2003) 'Northern Ireland: Valedictory?' in R. Hazell, ed., *The State of the Nations 2003*. Exeter: Imprint Academic, pp. 79–118.

Chapter 7

V3. Executive–Legislative Relationships

*Things are not going to change under Labour. You can change the machine
but you cannot change the culture of parliament, the ambience of the House
and the ambitions of its members.*[1]

The third variable in Lijphart's schema focuses on executive–legislative
relations. The majoritarian model is one of executive dominance,
while the consensus model is generally reflected in a more balanced
relationship between the executive and the legislature. Lijphart's conclusion for the period 1945–96 was definitive for this, 'There is no good
reason to judge any cabinets to be more dominant than the British cabinet, which is the exemplar of cabinet dominance in the Westminster
Model'.[2] The central question this chapter seeks to answer is to what
extent New Labour altered the balance of power between the executive
to the legislature during 1997–2007? However, measuring the relative
power of the executive vis-à-vis a legislature is difficult due to the manner
in which the relationship is parasitical and frequently based upon informal rules, procedures, and negotiations. The quantitative analysis of formal mechanisms of legislative dissent or compliance (votes, early day
motions, etc.), therefore risks overlooking the 'internalization of dissent'
whereby ministers or party managers broker agreements on an unofficial
basis.[3] The outward appearance of a strong and stable executive, governing through a pliant and docile legislature, may therefore on occasion veil
the existence of deep parliamentary divisions that are played out largely
beyond the public eye, and are not recorded in the official legislative
record.

The measurement of constitutional relationships and the tools of political analysis at our disposal to undertake such tasks were highlighted as a
critical issue in Part I of this book, and Lijphart himself has been charac-
teristically honest and open about the challenges of gauging this variable,

'The variable that gave me the most trouble was . . . executive dominance'.[4] Lijphart adopted *cabinet durability* as the core indicator for V3; this calculated on the basis of: changes in party composition, prime ministerialship, coalition status, and new elections. This produced an 'index of executive dominance' on which the UK scored 5.52 for 1945–96, the highest score of all the countries analysed, where the mean value score was 3.32.[5] The conclusion of this chapter is that during 1997–2007, the UK remained a polity exhibiting 'executive dominance'.

In order to explain and substantiate this conclusion, the chapter is divided into four sections. The main differences between presidential and parliamentary systems as they apply to the executive–legislative relationship are examined in the first section, which flows into a detailed analysis of developments in the UK in the second section. Earlier chapters have sought to promote a thesis regarding bi-constitutionality and in order to develop this argument further, the third section analyses the nature of those executive–legislature relationships that have been created at the devolved level. The final section examines the implications and significance of this chapter and highlights how V3 logically flows into an analysis of V4, electoral systems. As the House of Commons is the dominant chamber in the UK's legislature, it forms the main arena of analysis vis-à-vis the executive in this chapter. Relations between the executive and the Upper House, the House of Lords, is the focus of Chapter 11.

7.1 Forms of government

In parliamentary systems like the UK the Prime Minister (PM) and their cabinet are responsible to and reliant on the support of the legislature in the sense that they are dependent on the legislature's confidence. The relationship is therefore much tighter and more direct than is generally found in presidential regimes where the president is not dependent on maintaining the support of a parliamentary majority. The dynamics of V3 are therefore different. This difference is also derived from the manner in which the PM is not popularly elected in parliamentary systems, but is chosen by the legislative majority. In presidential regimes, by contrast, presidents are popularly elected and may stand on platforms that are quite distinct from those of legislative colleagues, despite the fact that they wear the same party label.

A third difference between parliamentary and presidential systems is that in the former, members of the executive are generally drawn from the legislature, whereas in the latter this is not the case. The starker separation of powers in presidential regimes is generally taken to mean not only the mutual independence of the executive and legislative branches, but also the rule that an individual cannot serve in both branches concurrently. The binding between the legislature and executive is therefore that much tighter in parliamentary regimes where the separation of powers has not been fully instituted, and this has implications for both the resources and restraints that are placed on the PM. Resources in terms of a rich source of patronage, but restraints in terms of breadth of candidates.

The appointment of members of the executive from the legislature also affects the internal management and governance of executive politics because in parliamentary systems ministers will generally have legislative-based constituency duties in addition to their executive responsibilities. Moreover, within the executive, members are expected to uphold the convention of collective ministerial responsibility and the PM is, theoretically at least, first among equals. In presidential regimes, the decision-making process and the capacity of the president is far more intense and concentrated. Although members of the cabinet will advice the president they are not viewed or expected to form a collective and broadly equal political team. This distinction resonates with a debate that has arisen concerning what has been termed the 'presidentialization' of politics in the UK since 1997.[6] This argues that the PM has moved within the constitutional infrastructure from being *primus inter pares* (the position in strict constitutional theory) to Sartori's (1994) *primus solus*. Section 7.2 seeks to contribute to this debate by assessing how the distribution of powers and resources between the legislature and executive altered during 1997–2007.

7.2 New Labour, new parliament

Chapter 4 reviewed the comparative research of Lijphart as well as the historical writing of Birch on the UK in order to draw attention to a pattern of elite politics in majoritarian regimes, whereby opposition parties attached themselves to a consensual or power-sharing agenda, but once elected appear reluctant to dilute the governing capacity afforded them by a power-hoarding model of democracy. A number of questions flow out of this historical, but it is sufficient here to note the existence of the 'swing thesis' and to use it to orientate this sections' analysis of V3 during 1997–2007. New Labour were elected on a platform to 're-establish the proper balance between parliament and the executive' and within a legislative context that was supportive of parliamentary reform and yet after a decade in power, the analysis of V3 reveals a situation of continuing executive dominance.[7] However, the examination of this variable also illustrates the manner in which executive-blocking and marginalization does incur certain costs, and these can accumulate to the point at which continuing to resist change becomes self-defeating and the executive is forced to consider how best they can vent certain pressures and frustrations. This, in turn, poses new questions for the parliamentary decline thesis, and provides insights into elite politics and the resource-dependencies that surround strategic manoeuvring or eviscerate reforms.

During 1997–2001, progress in terms of shifting the balance of power between the executive and legislature was minimal. A new select committee, the Modernisation Committee, was established to '... look at the means by which the House holds ministers to account', but its inquiries focused on the legislative process and the management of the House of Commons rather than how the scrutiny capacity or resources of the legislature might be increased. Establishing the Modernisation Committee had been an element of New Labour's 1997 General Election manifesto, and the executive was therefore to some extent obliged to facilitate its creation. And yet, the capacity of the Modernisation Committee to act as a vehicle for change was reduced, and the executive's capacity to control the committee was increased through the executive's decision that it should be chaired by the Leader of the House of Commons, a member of the Cabinet. By 2001, Gregory's conclusion that 'parliamentary reform started with a bang but has ended with a whimper... with no support from Downing Street, the initial momentum quickly dissipated' was supported by a wide range of scholars, MPs, and former ministers.[8] A broad consensus existed that the balance of power had shifted since 1997, but it was in the direction of the executive not legislature.[9]

During the summer of 2001, a number of factors conspired to place great pressure on the government to institute a more balanced executive–legislative relationship. A general election had recently been held, the reports of a number of legislative committees and external commissions had provided a relatively coherent reform agenda, an all-party pressure group of MPs, Parliament First, had been established and was undertaking a high-profile campaign for change, and political leadership on the issue had been achieved by the appointment of Robin Cook as Leader of the House of Commons.[10] As Table 7.1 illustrates, such variables were present in previous reforming parliaments (defined as those in which significant reforms were introduced in an explicit *attempt* to alter the existing balance

Table 7.1 Windows of opportunities and reforming parliaments

Parliament	General election	Reform agenda	Political leadership
1966–70	31 March 1966	Emanating from members of the Study of Parliament Group (formed 1964) including works such as Crick's *The Reform of Parliament* (1964) and Wiseman's *Parliament and the Executive* (1966).	Richard Crossman (1966–8)
1979–83	3 May 1979	Procedure Committee Report HC 588 1977–8.	Norman St John Stevas (1979–81)
2001–5	7 June 2001	Norton Commission, Newton Commission, Liaison Committee Reports.	Robin Cook (2001–3)

of power), and an argument can be offered that the early sessions of the 2001–5 Parliament represented a similar occasion.

During these sessions, a number of reforms were implemented due to the guile and enthusiasm of Cook, and also due to the executive's acceptance that reform of some kind had become unavoidable. For Cook, 'good scrutiny makes for good government' and as a result the powers of select committees now formed the central focus of the Modernisation Committee's work. In February 2002, the committee published a report that explicitly attempted to re-address the balance of power between executive and legislature.[11] At the core of the recommendations lay the issue of executive control (via party managers) of appointments to legislative scrutiny committees. The controversy surrounding the government's attempts to remove two critical select committee chairs in July 2001 had augmented the feeling that reform was necessary and cemented cross-party support: 'the Executive, via the whips, ought not to select those members of the select committees who will be examining the Executive, that is crucial'.[12]

The Modernisation Committee recommended a new system for making appointments to select committees in which members would be selected by a committee consisting of existing committee chairmen.[13] The capacity of the executive to determine the composition of committees would therefore be significantly reduced. Other recommendations included the creation of a new Scrutiny Unit to support select committees, the introduction of a set of core tasks to make the work of committees more systematic, and that committee chairmen receive an additional salary in order to reflect the additional workload involved, and create an alternative career system to ministerial office.[14] These measures were clearly intended to shift the balance of power back towards the legislature. However, although the government was willing to concede *a degree of* change in the executive–legislature relationship, elements of this agenda offended the executive mentality. What is interesting about the subsequent process of intra-party and intra-legislative bargaining and negotiation that occurred is that it sheds light on a range of executive veto-tactics, while also illuminating the shared loyalties of MPs.

In May 2002, the House of Commons rejected the recommendation to sever more clearly the link between the government and select committee appointments. Hennessy captured the surprise and sentiment of many observers when he noted, '...this was a case of kissing-the-chains-that-bind which quite took one's breath away—quite the lowest moment for select committees on the road from 1979. May 2002 really was the poverty of aspirations at its malign worst'.[15] At the same time, the proposal for additional salaries for committee chairs was passed.[16] The paradox was that introducing additional payments without reducing the power of the executive via the whips, risked actually increasing the executive's influence within the House by creating an additional tier of attractive patronage appointments.[17] Other reform measures were approved: the establishment of a set of common objectives and agreement for a new staffing unit to offer select committees more resources in financial scrutiny (bolstered by secondments from the National Audit Office). A new term limit for chairs was introduced, of two parliaments or eight years, whichever is greater. Committees were also given the power to exchange papers with the Scottish Parliament and Welsh Assembly, thereby enhancing the potential for joint working.

Although 2001–5 will undoubtedly be remembered as a 'reforming parliament', what is critical about the period is the manner in which New Labour adopted two strategies: (*a*) an intra-party strategy; and (*b*) an implementation strategy—through which it could vent the legislative frustration and pressure it faced, while at the same time reducing the degree to which reforms would actually affect the executive–legislature relationship. This point takes the discussion back to a theme first raised in Chapter 1 regarding the suggestion that it is possible for an executive to support an apparently wide-ranging programme of reform with little actual commitment to changing the nature of established relationships (i.e. cosmetic reform). During 1997–2001, New Labour was able to utilize the Modernisation Committee, through the Chairman, as an executive veto-point or control mechanism through which the executive could shape, suppress, and control the agenda. This strategy had become exhausted by 2002, and new strategies were needed to control the agenda—strategies that involved a new framework of incentives and sanctions.

The failure of the vote on the floor of the House to approve the motion for a new Committee of Nomination—the example of 'kissing-the-chains-that-bind'—provides an example of the 'intra-party strategy'. As mentioned earlier, the executive–legislative relationship is for the most part played out and managed 'off stage'. No executive can afford to take its parliamentary majority for granted, and therefore any government must be sensitive to signs of intra-party dissent like those that occurred in 2002. The executive therefore adopted an intra-party strategy to give vent to this pressure by agreeing a new procedure with the Parliamentary Labour Party (PLP) by which the role of the government's whips would be significantly reduced in relation to Labour appointments to committees.[18] The executive conceded a degree of control (by giving the PLP a veto over the executive's selections), but had done this through internal party channels thereby venting the pressure and making it easier for Labour MPs not to support the proposal on the floor.

This 'internalization of dissent' underlines the argument that it is 'highly misleading to speak of "executive–legislative relations" *tout court*' (i.e. without qualification or additional information), and that scholars interested in understanding executive power need to 'think behind' this general heading in order to separate out a number of quite distinct political relationships.[19] The internalization of dissent is also critical in terms of V3 because, as this example shows, reform along one dimension (in this case *intra-party*) can undermine or at least weaken the case for reform at another (*intra-parliamentary*). The balance of power did shift between the executive and its parliamentary party but the quid pro quo for this deal was that Labour MPs would not support wider reforms that would have strengthened the legislature as a whole.

The second 'implementation strategy' involved the government seeking to ensure that the measures that had been approved but not sufficiently resourced, affect the existing balance of power. The additional salary for select committee chairs, for example, that was intended to establish an alterative career to ministerial office was introduced at just £12,500 a year despite the recommendation by the Modernisation Committee, and a range of authoritative non-parliamentary reports, that it should be established at between £40,000 and £75,000 (the salary levels of a Minister of State and Secretary of State, respectively).[20] A strategy of conceding reform, but then not supporting those measures with the necessary resources was also clear in relation to the Strategy Unit which was established, but with a staff of just eighteen people who were expected to support twenty-two select committees. The Scrutiny Unit was simply 'spread too thin' to make any significant difference, as one select committee chairman noted and is therefore a very poor relation to the National Accountability Office in the United States.[21] This strategy of under-resourcing at the implementation stage also affects the capacity of other reforms. As the Power Inquiry emphasized in 2006, 'proper resourcing' not just more reforms were necessary to shift the balance of power.[22] New Labour's implementation strategy therefore provided a mechanism through which the executive could block or dilute reforms that may have negatively affected its governing capacity.

The simple conclusion of this chapter is that during 1997–2007, the relationship between the executive and the legislature in the UK did not alter dramatically. This is not to be overly simplistic or to make any normative argument regarding the parliamentary decline thesis. Cowley and Stuart are broadly correct to state that 'much of the evidence suggests that things are getting better, not worse ... The Blair government—particularly from 2001–2005—resulted in a partial rebirth of Parliament'.[23] The key word here being 'partial': very partial. The summer of 2001 may well be remembered as a 'window of opportunity' for legislative scholars in the UK but it was hardly a critical juncture in terms of a radical departure from the pre-existing relationship.

The introduction to this chapter suggested that the parliamentary decline thesis had been overstated, and sought in its place to cultivate a more sophisticated understanding of the relationship between the executive and legislature that was sensitive to the existence of both informal and formal connections. These connections form the network through which a complex system of resource-dependencies are brokered and distributed. This dialectical relationship has been demonstrated in this section through the analysis of how legislative frustrations grew throughout New Labour's first term, and then erupted into quite a public constitutional clash during the first session of the 2001–5 Parliament. Parliament clearly matters: The executive's tight control of the legislature is a sign of the continuing centrality of Parliament, rather than its insignificance. The House of Commons still wields great *potential* power as no government can afford to take its parliamentary majority for granted, but the House uses this power sparingly and generally only in relation to issues of major public concern. In broad terms, however, the reality of parliamentary politics is that the culture, procedures, and rules of Westminster remain weighed heavily in favour of the executive, and during 1997–2007 New Labour did very little to change this basic fact. As mentioned earlier, scoring V3 is difficult due to the informal and off-stage nature of many elements of the relationship. However, repeating Lijphart's original 'cabinet-life' focused method, on the basis that the period under analysis consisted of three periods—May 1997 – June 2001 (49 months), June 2001 – May 2005 (47 months), and May 2005 – June 2007 (25 months)—during which Tony Blair was PM and two General Elections were held, generating a V3 score of 6.78.

Table 7.2 illustrates that Lijphart measures V3 using the average cabinet duration based upon the belief that a more durable executive tends to reflect the probability of a more dominant government (and vice versa). This inference is problematic, however, because it assumes that a short-lived government reflects the existence of a strong legislature when this may not in fact be the case. A number of extra-parliamentary factors may have undermined the position of the executive. Lijphart had conceded that 'I am not sure that the operational indicator I develop in *Patterns of Democracy* is satisfactory'.[24] Vatter therefore combines Siaroff's 'executive dominance' index with Schnapp and Harfst's work on effective parliamentary control capacities to produce a more sophisticated score for this variable.[25] This method also generates a scoring that is indicative of extreme executive dominance and as such, Lijphart's conclusion of 'executive dominance' and a score for V3 of 6.78—using Lijphart's method, but indicating the increased dominance suggested by Vatter's methodology—can be added to the final column of Table 4.4 and accepted as our updated score. And yet, as earlier chapters have emphasized, although Lijphart's framework provides a powerful tool for assessing specific and cumulative alterations to the nature of democracy at the national level, it is critical that any analysis is sensitive to changes at other governing levels. It is already clear from the analysis of V1 and V2 that a pattern may be emerging in which any variable score for the national level needs to be carefully set against reforms or changes that have occurred at the sub-national level. It is the discrepancy between the scores for the national and sub-national levels that underpins not only the thesis regarding bi-constitutionality, but also the accusation of constitutional anomie. It is for exactly these reasons that the next sub-section examines V3 at the sub-national level.

Table 7.2 Average cabinet duration according to two criteria (in years), the mean of these two measures, and the Index of Executive Dominance in the UK, 1945–96, 1997–2007

	Average cabinet life I	Average cabinet life II	Mean of measures I & II	Index of executive dominance
UK 1945–96	8.49	2.55	5.52	5.52
UK 1997–2007	10.16	3.4	6.78	6.78

7.3 Sub-national executive–legislative relationships

Section 7.2 concluded that in basic terms, the executive–legislative relationship at Westminster remains one of executive dominance. This section seeks to answer two questions regarding executive–legislative relationships that have been created in Scotland, Northern Ireland, and Wales:

(1) Are they less dominant and more consensual?
(2) If so, why?

These questions are particularly important because devolution was intended to deliver a 'new politics' that would be different from the 'old' (i.e. majoritarian) political culture and institutional framework of Westminster. One of the defining features of this 'new politics' was the intention that a more balanced executive–legislative relationship would be achieved. The section concludes that although strong party allegiances remain within the devolved arenas, the executive–legislative relationships are somewhat more balanced and consensual when compared to Westminster. This is due to a range of factors (the electoral system, cultural issues, scale-related dimensions, etc.). In order to explain this conclusion, it is necessary to briefly outline the roots of the 'new politics' agenda before examining the executive–legislative relationship in each of the devolved legislatures.

'New politics' is synonymous with power-sharing and a more pluralistic consensual form of politics. It therefore stands in stark contrast to the power-hoarding, adversarial majoritarianism that characterized 'old politics'. Phrased in this way, the 'New'/'Old' distinction can be overlaid with Lijphart's Consensual/Majoritarian models of democracy, respectively. The aim of devolution therefore went beyond simply attempting to secure the introduction of new institutions and procedures, and was tied to a desire for cultural change of a systemic type. As the Scottish Constitutional

Convention emphasized in 1995, '... the coming of a Scottish Parliament will usher in a way of politics that is radically different from the rituals of Westminster: more participative, more creative, less needlessly confrontational'.[26]

In Scotland, the rules, procedures, and Standing Orders of the new Parliament were based upon four principles—power sharing, accountability, equal opportunities, and openness and participation—in order to try and realize this vision of a 'new politics',[27] and in this sense Mitchell suggests that the House of Commons provided a form of 'negative template'.[28] Institutionally, a number of measures were designed to achieve a more balanced executive–legislative relationship. This included an electoral system with a proportional component that would make it more difficult for any party to secure a (dominant) majority; and a system of legislative committees with the capacity to not only scrutinize and amend the Scottish Executive's proposals, but also initiate legislation. Other notable innovations included a Public Petitions Office that fed directly to the Petitions Committee of the Parliament, and a Parliamentary Commissioner for Public Appointments with significantly stronger powers that those of the UK-wide Commissioner for Public Appointments.[29]

The outcome of these measures has been significant, but not fundamental. There is no simple causal relationship between the creation of a new parliament elected on a more proportional system and consensual politics. Historical variables, not least the fact that many of the politicians in the Scottish Parliament honed their political skills as MPs, advisers, or party operatives in the crucible of Westminster politics and the existence of enmity between the Labour Party and SNP, have cast a long shadow. And yet, at the same time it would be wrong to overlook the simple fact that the relationship between the executive and legislature in Edinburgh is qualitatively different to that at Westminster.

Different because the electoral system makes it significantly more difficult for the Scottish Executive to dominate the legislature and in practice forces it to undertake a large amount of formal and informal inter-party negotiation. And different because the legislative committee system has more powers than its Westminster counterparts. In the legislative process, for example, it is the relevant scrutiny committee, rather than the executive, that oversees the pre-legislative consultation process, considers the principles of the bill before it is presented to the House, and takes evidence on the nature and effects of the bill before considering amendments. The committees can also initiate their own legislation where the view exists that the executive is ignoring a crucial issue. In terms of scrutiny, the committees also enjoy more resources than their Westminster counter-parts. This extends beyond the provision of staff and research capacity and into the existence of agreed procedures that restrain the capacity of the executive in relation to the Scottish state. For example, members of the Scottish Executive are obliged to inform the relevant committee of the Scottish Parliament of their intention to create, amalgamate, or abol-ish Scottish public bodies and must account for their decision against a set of agreed principles.[30] No equivalent procedures, rules, or set of explicit principles exist at Westminster. Cairney therefore suggests that the Scot-tish legislative committees enjoy 'an unusual range of powers compared to Westminster and the legislatures of most West European countries', and this view is supported when the powers of the committees are weighed against Mattson and Strom's criteria for assessing legislative committee strength.[31]

The capacity of the committees to use their powers is limited by a range of factors (lack of time, membership turnover, the executive majority on each committee, party discipline), and this reflects the fact that the Scot-tish Parliament has not escaped from the majoritarian political heritage completely: but it was never supposed to. This is a critical point. The Consultative Steering Group always envisaged a situation in which the Scottish Executive would have the capacity to govern and in this sense the intention was never to completely shift the balance of power *from* the executive to the legislature, but only to create a more balanced relation-ship.[32] When compared with the situation at Westminster the executive–legislative relationship in Scotland is more balanced, and this is largely a result of the electoral system rather than institutional or cultural changes. It is in this context that Shephard and Cairney, 'found evidence of power-sharing . . . that could be used to support the arguments of the 'new poli-tics' camp'.[33] The extent of this rebalancing is likely to become more evident in 'Session 3' (i.e. after the May 2007 election) as the SNP attempts to govern through a minority administration, and is therefore forced to engage in a more consensual relationship. To paraphrase the ambitions of the Scottish Constitutional Convention, the coming of a Scottish Parlia-ment may not have ushered in a way of politics that is *radically* different from the rituals of Westminster, but has led to a more balanced executive–legislative relationship.

A similar conclusion can be drawn from the experience of governing in Northern Ireland and Wales, post-devolution. Increasing accountability was the key theme of the architects of Welsh devolution and therefore formed a central element of the 1997 A *Voice for Wales* white paper.

Ron Davies, Secretary of State for Wales at the time, told the Richard Commission,

> The construction we had ... wasn't an attempt to replicate Parliament ... it was about inclusivity, it was about power-sharing. It was based on a degree of proportionality so that the elected representatives from all the parties in Wales could be included.[34]

Like the Scottish Parliament, the NAW was intended to depart from the adversarial and majoritarian mode of governing at Westminster to some extent. This was primarily reflected in: the preference for an alternative vote electoral system, and the initial decision to establish the NAW as a single corporate body.[35] This latter decision to have a committee-based system was intended to ensure the diffusion of power across the NAW, and prevent the concentration of power in a dominant executive group. Once the NAW was operational, however, it became clear that Assembly Members (AM) wanted a clearer distinction between the Welsh Assembly Government (WAG) and the assembly. Following a cross-party review of procedures in 2001–2 the NAW voted unanimously to create a de facto separation of powers and to take this distinction as far as possible within the constraints of the *Government of Wales Act 1998*. This separation was formally recognized under the terms of the *Government of Wales Act 2006* and as a result members of the executive no longer sit as on assembly scrutiny committees.

Paradoxically, the NAW provides a critical case study of institutional evolution away from its initial highly consensual committee-based model towards a more parliamentary structure. And yet, some of the institutional features of Welsh governance continue to militate against executive dominance. These include an electoral system which promotes a significant degree of consensus-building, participation, and compromise by making it much harder when compared to the simple-plurality system for any party to gain a large majority. The issue of scale is also critical in relation to executive–legislative relations in Wales because with just sixty AMs the executive cannot be remote from its legislative arm. This is reflected in the way in which AMs and members of the WAG refer to each other on first-name terms in the NAW. The NAW's scrutiny committees are also widely viewed as being more effective than select committees at Westminster, which is a product not just of the executive having a smaller majority, but also reflects both the existence of a more consensual culture and the provision of greater resources, via the Presiding Office, to AMs and the subject committees.

As with governance in Scotland, it is important not to over-state the capacity of the NAW vis-à-vis the WAG. There have been concerns, especially in the first and second assembly terms (1999–2003, 2003–7) that the presence of the relevant member of the WAG on the scrutiny committees encouraged a preference for policy-development analysis at the expense of rigorous or challenging scrutiny. It is also true that party discipline remains high, and that the procedures of the NAW are designed to confer a certain level of governing-capacity on the WAG. Nevertheless, when viewed against the benchmark of the executive–legislative relationship at Westminster that which exists at the sub-national level in Wales does appear to be considerably more balanced.

The politics of Northern Ireland has engendered a longstanding debate concerning the most appropriate form or model of democracy for a divided society, and the Belfast Agreement of 1998 had at its core a consociationalist character.[36] Majoritarianism that might facilitate the oppression of large sections of society by the largest minority was therefore eschewed in favour of a power-sharing model of democracy involving a grand-coalition, mutual veto-points, and proportionality. The executive–legislative relationship in Northern Ireland is therefore distinct due to the manner in which posts on the Northern Ireland Executive (NIE) are distributed according to representation in the Northern Ireland Assembly (NIA). Major parties cannot, therefore, be excluded from participation in government, and power-sharing is enforced by the system. Indeed, the NIE cannot function if either of the two largest parties refuses to take part (as happened when the Ulster Unionist Party refused to work with Sinn Fein between October 2002 and May 2007). The governance of Northern Ireland has therefore since 1998 been based upon the principle of power-sharing *within* the executive (i.e. in terms of intra-executive dynamics), and also *between* the executive and assembly. This latter aspect is secured through the use of a proportional electoral system (STV) which, like Scotland and Wales, reduced the likelihood of any party securing a large majority in the assembly.

7.4 Parliamentary pressures

This chapter has examined the changing nature of executive–legislative relationships in the UK. It has concluded that whereas New Labour did not significantly alter the balance of power away from the pre-existing situation of 'executive dominance' previously identified by Lijphart, it was at the same time actively engaged in designing, building, and promoting more balanced executive–legislative relationships at the sub-national level. This analysis of V3 fits within a wider pattern that is by now beginning to emerge. This is a pattern involving a reluctance to cede power or move towards a more pluralistic and consensual model of democracy at the national level, while actively building and promoting power-sharing structures in Scotland, Wales, and Northern Ireland.

On the 'index of executive dominance' the UK scores 6.78 which chimes with the Independent Inquiry into British Democracy held during 2005–6, which concluded 'the executive has become more powerful at the expense of the House of Commons'. The index score for V3 for the Scottish Parliament, NAW, and NIA would, however, be somewhere around 3.5. Pushing this analysis still further, it is possible to detect the emergence of a certain internal coherence between V1, V2, and V3 which further supports this book's argument regarding bi-constitutionality. The three variables examined so far are interrelated, and it is therefore possible to observe a positive relationship between the number of effective political parties (V1), minimal winning one-party cabinets (V2), and executive dominance (V3). Conversely, there is a clear correlation between multiparty cabinets, coalition governments, and a more balanced relationship between the executive and legislature. This is due to the fact that these variables belong to the same cluster of features that form the executive-parties dimension on the majoritarian-consensus contrast (as discussed in Chapter 4). The relationship between V1, V2, and V3 is also intuitively direct because any party with a large legislative majority can be expected to dominate, or at least tightly manage the legislature while minority cabinets are clearly in a weaker position. In Westminster, the executive still generally governs with a solid legislative majority; whereas in Scotland and Wales, the electoral system makes achieving a legislative majority much harder; and in Northern Ireland the rules of the Good Friday Agreement formally diffuse power within the executive in addition to utilizing a proportional electoral system for the legislature.

Figure 7.1 shows the relationship between V2 and V3 as it relates to the UK. The pattern is relatively clear. Polities with more formal winning single-party cabinets also tend to be those with greater executive dominance. The paradox in the case of the UK during 1997–2007 is that divergent processes are observable. National politics has become slightly more majoritarian, whereas devolved government has been created on the basis of a quite different meta-constitutional orientation. Before pursuing this observable pattern of analysis it is useful to reflect on the relationship between this finding in relation to V3 at the national level and the debate about the presidentialization of politics in the UK as noted earlier. This thesis argues that power has shifted, not just from Parliament to the executive, but now from the executive to the PM too, and they wield a level of influence generally observed in presidential regimes. Foley's *The British Presidency* (2000) is possibly the apogee of this position, and yet as Heffernan accurately responds,

> While Prime Ministers clearly matter more than most ministers, the no-tion of presidentialism ultimately misleads. It makes little of the power-dependencies found within any system…He or she is only one actor alongside others, working within structured networks and having to share power. The presidentialism thesis particularly fails to acknowledge that institutional factors make it impossible for a Prime Minister to be-come a President'.[37]

The UK's PM may be 'first *among* equals' or 'first *above* equals', to use Sartori's terminology, but they are never 'primus solus' as is the case with the American President.[38] As the research presented in this chapter has illustrated, there is no such thing as a 'government majority' within the House of Commons as the government is a maximum of 95 MPs out of a total of 646. Therefore, although an executive can generally rely on the

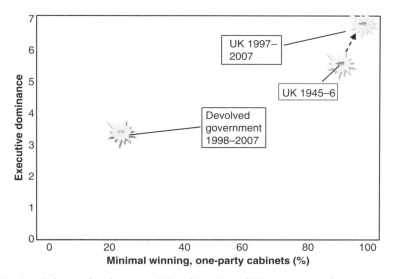

Figure 7.1 Relationship between V2 (cabinets) and V3 (executive–legislative rela-tions) for the UK and devolved government

support of their majority they cannot take it for granted and the political space in which informal intra- and inter-party bargaining and negotiation occurs, is generally more volatile than simple external observations might suggest. The presidentialization thesis therefore risks overlooking the latent power of the legislature in the UK and the existence of complex resource-dependencies. And yet, observing a correlation between low numbers of effective political parties (V1), simple-majority cabinets (V2), and a dominant executive (V3) demands an explanation in terms of what underpins and establishes these factors and their inter-relationship. It is for this reason that Chapter 8 examines possibly the most critical underlying and therefore potentially transformative element of any constitutional configuration—V4, electoral systems.

V3 Index of executive dominance conclusion

Lijphart's UK score 1945–96	5.52
Lijphart's UK score 1971–96	5.52
Updated UK score 1997–2007	6.78
Devolved tier score 1998–2007	3.5

Notes

1. Senior Labour MP (1998) Interview with the author, April.
2. Lijphart *op cit.* (1999), p. 134.
3. Cowley, P (2002) *Revolts and Rebellions: Parliamentary Voting Under Blair.* London: Politicos.
4. Lijphart, A (2003) 'Measurement Validity and Institutional Engineering', *Political Studies*, 51(1), 20.
5. Taagepera, R (2003) 'Arend Lijphart's Dimensions of Democracy', *Political Studies*, 51(1), 1–19; Tsebelis, G (2002) *Veto Players*. Princeton: Princeton University Press.
6. Foley, M (2000). *The British Presidency.* Manchester: Manchester University Press; Heffernan, R (2003) 'Prime Ministerial Predominance?' *British Journal of Politics and International Relations*, 5(3), 347–72.
7. Taylor, A (1996) 'New Politics, New Parliament'. Speech to the Charter 88 seminar on the reform of Parliament, 14 May; Weir, S and Wright, A (1996) *Power to the Back Benches?* London: Scarman Trust / Democratic Audit.
8. Gregory, D (1999) 'Style Over Substance? Labour and the Reform of Parliament', *Renewal*, 7(3), 47.
9. For a broad review of this literature, see Flinders, M (2002) 'Shifting the Balance? Parliament, the Executive and the British Constitution', *Political Studies*, 50 (2), 23–42.

10. Flinders, M (2007) 'Analysing Reform: The House of Commons 2001–2005' *Political Studies*, 55(1), 174–200.

11. HC 224 (2001–2) *Select Committees*. First Report from the Modernisation Committee, Session 2001–2.

12. Ibid.

13. Ibid., paras. 7–23.

14. See Flinders *op. cit.* (2007).

15. Hennessy, P (2004) 'An End to the Poverty of Aspirations? Parliament since 1979'. First History of Parliament Lecture, Portcullis House, London, 25 November.

16. Kelso, A (2003) 'Where Were the Masses Ranks of Parliamentary Reformers?' *Legislative Studies*, 9(1), 57–76.

17. HC 224 *op. cit.* (2001–2) para. 26.

18. See Cook, R (2003) *The Point of Departure*. London: Simon & Schuster, 28.

19. King, A *op. cit.* (1976) 'Modes of Executive-Legislative Relations', *Legislative Studies Quarterly*, 1(1), 11–36.

20. See Flinders, M, Brazier, A, and McHugh, D (2005) *New Politics, New Parliament? Parliamentary Modernisation under Labour*. London: Hansard Society.

21. Interview, September 2004.

22. Power Inquiry (2006) *Power Inquiry*. London: Joseph Rowntree Charitable Trust/Joseph Rowntree Reform Trust Ltd, p. 139.

23. Cowley, P and Stuart, M (2005) 'Parliament', in A Seldon, and A Kavanagh, (eds.), *The Blair Effect II*. Cambridge: Cambridge University Press, p. 16.

24. Lijphart, A (2002) 'Negotiation Democracy Versus Consensus Democracy', *European Journal of Political Research*, 41(1), 110.

25. Vatter *op. cit.* (2009).

26. Scottish Constitutional Convention (1995) *Scotland's Parliament, Scotland's Right*. Edinburgh: Scottish Constitutional Convention.

27. Consultative Steering Group on the Scottish Parliament (1998) *Shaping Scotland's Parliament*. Edinburgh: Consultative Steering Group on the Scottish Parliament, p. 3.

28. See Mitchell, J (2000) 'New Parliament, New Politics in Scotland', *Parliamentary Affairs*, 53, 605.

29. Flinders, M and Denton, M (2006) 'Democracy, Devolution and Delegated Governance in Scotland', *Regional and Federal Studies*, 16(1), 63–82.

30. See Flinders, M (2008) *Delegated Governance and the British State*. Oxford: Oxford University Press.

31. Cairney (2008) 'The Scottish Parliament—Actor, Arena and Agenda-Setter?', in P. McGarvey and P. Cairney, eds., *Scottish Politics*. London: Palgrave, p. 12; Mattson and Strom. *op.cit.* (2004).

32. Mitchell *op. cit.* (2000).

33. Shephard, M and Cairney, P (2004) 'Consensual or Dominant Relationships with Parliament?' *Public Administration*, 82(4), 831–55.

34. Richard Commission (2004) *Commission on the Powers and Electoral Arrangements of the National Assembly for Wales*, p. 48.

35. Laffin, M and Thomas, A (2000) 'Designing the National Assembly for Wales', *Parliamentary Affairs*, 53, 557–76; Marinetto, M (2001) 'The Settlement and Process of Devolution', *Political Studies*, 49, 306–22.

36. See Horowitz, D (2002) 'Explaining the Northern Ireland Agreement', *British Journal of Political Science*, 32, 193–220; Wilford, P (2000) 'Designing the Northern Ireland Assembly', *Parliamentary Affairs*, 53, 577–90; Lijphart, A (2004) 'Constitutional Design for Divided Societies', *Journal of Democracy*, 15(2), 96–109.

37. Heffernan, R (2005) 'Why the Prime Minister Cannot be a President', *Parliamentary Affairs*, 58(1), 53–4.

38. Sartori, G (1994) 'Neither Presidentialism or Parliamentarism', in J. Linz and A. Valenzuela, eds., *The Failure of Presidential Democracy*. Baltimore: John Hopkins University Press, pp. 106–18.

Chapter 8

V4. Electoral System

The electoral system was once seen as the 'key to the lock' of the British constitution. In this view the Conservatives and Labour kept their duopoly of power by locking the constitutional door to outsiders.[1]

The constitutional configuration of a polity conditions and shapes the nature and location of political power within that system. Institutional reform, as Tsebelis has argued is likely therefore to be 'redistributive' in that some changes 'may alter who wins and loses' and this is particularly valid in relation to electoral systems—Lijphart's fourth variable.[2] In line with the work of a number of scholars—including, for example, Nohlen, Powell, and Shugart—electoral reform is defined as the introduction of a legislative electoral system that operates towards an opposite principle from the pre-existing system (and simple-plurality and proportional systems are seen to be based on opposing principles of representation).[3] As such, the characteristics that are associated with majoritarianism—low numbers of effective political parties, single-party governments, government control of the legislature—generally form the outputs of single-member simple-plurality electoral systems, commonly known as 'first past the post' (FPTP) systems. These are winner-takes-all systems in which the candidate securing the largest number of votes wins the seat, even if they have not secured a majority of all the votes cast. The disproportionality of FPTP is not accidental, but is based on a normative desire to deliver an executive with a majority of legislative seats. Democratic criteria—such as proportionality or fairness—are therefore traded down in favour of 'governability' criteria—stability, clear majorities, and dominance in a direct reflection of majoritarian philosophy.[4] The normative values of consensualism—participation, inclusion, equity, etc.—are, by contrast, delivered by more proportional electoral systems that seek to achieve a more direct relationship between votes cast and the allocation of seats.[5] The distinction between simple-plurality and proportional electoral systems therefore underpins, and in very many ways creates and sustains the contrast between power-hoarding and power-sharing models of democracy.[6] It is in this context that Lijphart found that during 1945–96, the UK had an average electoral disproportionality score of 10.33 per cent.

Although Lijphart observed that very few democracies change from proportional to simple-plurality systems (or vice versa), in recent decades the rationale or 'mega-constitutional orientation' on which majoritarianism is based—'strong' government, clear lines of accountability and simplicity in relation to public understanding—has been the topic of sustained challenge in many countries. Concerns regarding a lack of proportionality, the dominance of the executive, the unaccountability of single-party government, an increase in third and minor parties, and evidence of growing public disillusionment with politics have encouraged some majoritarian countries to institute or at least consider electoral reform.[7] New Zealand's constitution was, for example, before the mid-1990s characterized as an 'executive paradise' but the introduction of a mixed-member proportional electoral system in 1993 has reduced the dominance of the executive and enhanced the role of the legislature.[8] Developments in New Zealand demonstrate that electoral systems effectively govern the distribution of power within a democracy: 'Changing from FPTP to PR is thus a reform that is profound, perhaps more so than any other that can be realistically imagined within an already established universal-suffrage democracy'.[9] This stimulates a consideration of when and why reforms away from majoritarianism are considered and in the UK this discussion takes a particular twist due to the manner in which the Labour governments have since 1997 imposed proportional electoral systems on Scotland, Wales, and Northern Ireland through devolution, while retaining FPTP for elections at the national level (see Table 8.1).

Table 8.1 Electoral systems in the United Kingdom, 2008

Jurisdiction	Electoral system
National (Westminster)	Single member plurality system
Scottish Parliament	Additional member system
Scottish Local Government	Single transferable vote
National Assembly for Wales	Additional member system
Northern Ireland Assembly	Single transferable vote
Greater London Assembly	Additional member system
London Mayoral Elections	Supplementary vote
European Elections	Regional list system (STV in Northern Ireland)

In order to unravel New Labour's approach to electoral reform and consider how it relates to this book's broader arguments concerning bi-constitutionalism and constitutional anomie, this chapter is divided into three sections. The first section reviews developments at the national level and particularly how the government has imposed a number of executive veto-points and marginalization tactics in order to avoid their pre-1997 commitment to hold a referendum on the electoral system for Westminster. Rational choice theoretic accounts of change would not be surprised by the behaviour of any government that reneged on a pre-election commitment to begin a process that may lead to electoral reform because few governments seek to diffuse their power-base.[10] And yet, New Labour has added a very distinct, and potentially disruptive ingredient to the constitutional mix by introducing proportional electoral systems at the sub-national level—the focus of the second section. The dynamics and relationships between electoral systems forms the focus of the final concluding section, and allows us to deepen and refine the analytical leverage of the bi-constitutionality thesis.

8.1 Westminster elections

The electoral method within a polity forms both the keystone of the system and generally ascribes a pattern or model of democracy and, as noted earlier, majoritarian systems generally employ single-member district plurality systems, while consensus systems typically operate through a proportional system. In the UK the dominance of the executive in relation to parliament (V3) has always been based on a disproportional electoral system that generally provides the party winning the largest minority of votes with a large majority of seats in the House of Commons.[11] As Figure 8.1 illustrates, during the second half of the twentieth century the disproportionality of FPTP delivered a relatively stable two-party system (evolving towards a 'two and a half' party system towards the end of the century).

As a result, electoral reform, as a way or reducing the power of the executive over the legislature, was a perennial issue in UK politics for much of the twentieth century.[12] However, for most of this period an implied deal existed between the two main parties to preserve the plurality-rule system.[13] Eighteen years of Conservative government (1979–97)—combined with evidence of partisan de-alignment and the 1983 general election result—led to a reappraisal of the Labour Party's position. From the late 1980s internal debate on the topic of electoral reform increased,

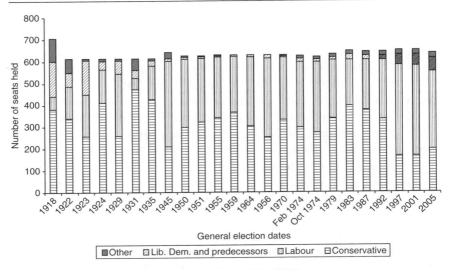

Figure 8.1 Seats won, UK general elections, 1918–2005

Source: House of Commons Library (2008) *Election Statistics*: United Kingdom 1918–2007.

particularly under the leadership of Neil Kinnock (notably in his final year), and then John Smith. At the same time, Labour-Party-affiliated trade unions also began to move away from their traditional opposition to electoral reform, thereby at least opening up political space for a policy debate.[14] In September 1990, a vote at the Labour Party annual conference carried a motion against the platform, calling for an inquiry into the electoral system which led to the establishment of a working group under the chairmanship of the eminent political scientist Professor Raymond (now Lord) Plant.[15] The Plant Report recommended a Mixed-Member Proportional System for a Scottish Parliament and Welsh Assembly, a Regional List system for European elections, and a Supplementary Vote System for elections to the House of Commons.[16] The Labour Party (now under the Leadership of John Smith) accepted the first two proposals and pledged to hold a referendum on the voting system for Westminster if it won the next election; a commitment that Tony Blair inherited when he became party leader in July 1994. The policy momentum behind electoral reform was given further emphasis during the run up to the 1997 General Election when the Joint-Consultative Committee on Constitutional Reform between the Labour Party and Liberal Democrats recommended that 'a referendum on the system for elections to the House of Commons should be held within the first term of a new Parliament'.[17] The subsequent

1997 Labour Party General Election manifesto included a commitment to 'hold a referendum on the voting system for the House of Commons', but did not include any specific time frame.[18]

On 1 May 1997, the Labour Party won 43.2 per cent of the votes cast and as a result were awarded 63.6 per cent of seats in the House of Commons (418 seats, a majority of 178), and in December established an independent commission to explore the options for electoral reform in relation to the House of Commons. The Jenkins Commission, as it became known, reported in October 1998 and recommended a hybrid combining single-member constituencies, using the Alternative Vote, with a limited top-up of 15–20 per cent of MPs.[19] However, internal conflict over the issue within the Cabinet and the wider party, stimulated to some extent by the failure of the Labour Party to win overall majority in the first round of elections in Scotland or Wales, meant that the issue was marginalized and the report's recommendations were not taken forward. The Labour government's marginalization of the issue of electoral reform for Westminster continued for the remainder of the 1997–2001 term and the Labour Party's manifesto for the 2001 general election included a weak promise to review the UK's experience with new PR systems in Scotland and Wales before proposing any changes to the electoral system for Westminster.

Pressure on the government to proceed with any discussion of electoral reform for Westminster was reduced due to the fact that the Labour Party won the 2001 General Election with 40.7 per cent of the vote, which saw them rewarded with 62.5 per cent of seats in the lower chamber (412 seats, a majority of 166). As a result, the issue of electoral reform was marginalized for the whole of the 2001–5 Parliament, despite the fact that the expected time for the promised review was after the second round of elections in Scotland and Wales in 2003. Such was the frustration created by the government's constant marginalization of the topic that the Nuffield Foundation and Joseph Rowntree Charitable Trust funded an independent and authoritative review of the experience of PR in Scotland and Wales, but the Government remained uninterested.[20] The Labour Party's manifesto for the 2005 general election simply repeated the pledge to undertake a review of the existing PR systems alongside an open statement that a referendum 'remains the right way to agree any change for Westminster'.[21] The Labour Party won the May 2005 general election with a majority of 64 seats over all the other parties combined (355 of 646 seats). However, this result was based on the Labour Party polling 9.6 million votes (35.2% of the total), the smallest share of the votes received by the winning party at a general election since 1832, and 5.5 per cent lower than in 2001. It was the equivalent of just 21.6 per cent of the total electorate, again a record low.[22] Three issues particularly concerned commentators: (a) the Labour government had experienced a substantial decrease in its share of the votes between the 2001 and 2005 elections, and yet had still won a large legislative majority; (b) in England the Conservative Party actually received more votes than the Labour Party (35.7% and 35.5%, respectively), and yet the Labour Party obtained 286 seats to the Conservatives' 194 out of a total 529 English constituencies; and finally (c) the vote–seat ratio for the third party was highly disproportional—the Liberal Democrats received 22.7 per cent of the votes but only 9.9 per cent of the seats.

The Labour Party's approach to electoral reform for Westminster during 1997 to 2005 was characterized by circumvention, delay, avoidance, and developments during 2005–7 did little to counter this argument. In the Spring of 2006, the government initiated a review of the electoral systems in Scotland and Wales but only as a desk-based internal exercise, and without the release of any supporting documentation or statement on how the results of the review would be used. A further development occurred in November 2006 when the Labour MP David Chaytor (backed by Charter 88 and the Electoral Reform Society) used the ten-minute rule to propose an Electoral Choice Bill, but this did not receive government support.[23] Towards the end of New Labour's decade in office, Kavanagh and his colleagues concluded,

> PR is effectively off the agenda and there is little prospect of a referendum in the near future. [Many New Labour ministers] still calculate that the established electoral arrangements, a key part of the traditional Westminster system and its underpinning elitism, still operates in their interests.[24]

The Labour Government's attitude has, at the very least, been consistent. As early as 1998, the Deputy Prime Minister, John Prescott, suggested that plans for voting reform should be sent out to sea 'on a viking-style funeral barge', and yet in May 2005, Mr Prescott was made responsible for the Cabinet Committee on Electoral Reform.[25] The Leader of the Liberal Democrats at the time, Charles Kennedy, responded by announcing that 'Putting John Prescott in charge of a committee looking at electoral reform is like putting Herod in charge of a maternity ward'.[26] As a result, elections to the House of Commons have continued to display a significant degree of disproportionality. This is clear from data set out in Figure 8.2 for the 2005 general election.

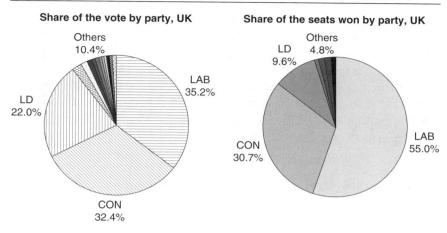

Figure 8.2 Votes cast and seats won by party, general election 2005
Source: House of Commons Library (2005) *General Election 2005*. Paper 05/33, 8.

The vote–seat ratio reflected by Figure 8.2 reflects both disproportionality and bias. This notion of bias relates to the fact that if the vote share of both the Conservative Party and the Labour Party had been reversed, their share of the seats would not have been reversed. Phrased slightly differently, if the Conservatives had received 36.2 per cent of the vote (i.e. Labour's share as opposed to the 33.2% they actually received) at the 2005 general election, they would not have been rewarded with the 56.6 per cent of the seats that the Labour Party secured. As Johnston, Rossiter, and Pattie demonstrate there have been major changes in the size and direction of bias in general election results since 1950, but in the 2001 and 2005 elections the bias favoured the Labour Party by around 141 and 111 seats, respectively.[27] This bias is produced by a mixture of demographic, social, and geographical variables amongst which constituency size and efficiency in the distribution of the Labour Party's support are critical. This 'creeping pro-Labour bias' that has been identified is critical due to the fact that it makes the costs involved in replacing the extant system with a proportional system far greater for a Labour government as they would be moving to a method where the odds were not automatically weighed in their favour in the way they currently are with FPTP.

Returning to Lijphart's schema and Table 4.4, the degree of electoral disproportionality since 1997 (Lijphart's index measure for this variable) has actually increased rather than diminished. The mean index score, using the Gallagher index, for the UK (1945–96) was 10.33. This figure increased to 14.66 during the second half of this period (1971–96). For the period 1997–2007, the index scores were 16.51, 17.77, and 16.73 for the general elections in 1997, 2001, and 2005, respectively, thereby producing an average score of 17.1. And yet, this increase in disproportionality at the national level and the marginalization of the topic in policy-terms, stood in stark contrast to developments at the sub-national level where a rich tapestry of proportional electoral systems were being established as part of New Labour's wider programme of constitutional reform.

8.2 Electoral systems at the sub-national level

As earlier chapters have discussed, the decision to base all the post-1997 political institutions on proportional electoral systems was based on an explicit desire by the Labour government to create new democratic arenas that enjoyed a more open and consensual political culture in contrast to the highly partisan and adversarial *modus operandi* of Westminster. To some extent, these ambitions have been achieved: although it is possible for one party to achieve a legislative majority, this is less likely and sub-national governance is increasingly characterized by an increased number of effective political parties (V1), multiparty coalition politics (V2), and a less dominant executive vis- à-vis the legislative assembly (V3). What this section illustrates is that the index score for disproportionality is significantly lower at the sub-national regional level than for UK-wide elections to Westminster (as shown in Figure 8.3).

The NAW has sixty members elected using the semi-proportional Additional Member System (AMS). Fixed-term (four yearly) elections clarify the timetable for campaigning and elections, and each voter has two votes. The first is used to select a constituency representative (the AM). There are forty constituencies based on the Westminster electoral boundaries, where each return one AM using the simple-plurality FPTP method. The second vote is used to elect twenty additional AMs on a regional basis (five regions, each returning four AMs). This part of the election is designed to ensure that, as far as possible, the total number of seats gained by each party reflects their share of the overall vote. The d'Hondt formula is used to calculate the allocation of regional list seats. The index scores for disproportionality for NAW elections were therefore 8.61, 10.39, and 11.36 in 1999, 2003, and 2007, respectively, producing a mean score of 10.12 (i.e. significantly more proportional than the index score of 17.1 for UK elections.

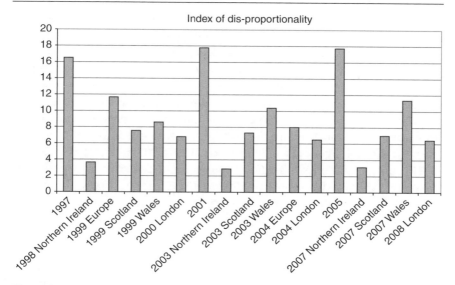

Figure 8.3 Dis-proportionality scores, UK elections 1997–2008

Elections to the Scottish Parliament are also conducted using an AMS system. Seventy-three members of the parliament are selected on the constituency-focused first votes, and a further fifty-six MSPs are elected on the second party-list based vote (seven MSPs from eight electoral regions). The larger number of seats provides the d'Hondt formula with a greater capacity to rebalance the votes/seats equilibrium, and this is reflected in lower index scores for disproportionality than were found in relation to the NAW. Specifically the disproportionality scores for elections to the Scottish Parliament for 1999, 2003, and 2007 respectively were 7.55, 7.31, and 6.99 (a mean of 7.28). The NIA is made up of 108 members and elections take place every four years. The voting system used is the single transferable vote system (STV) and six MLAs are elected in each of the eighteen UK parliamentary constituencies in Northern Ireland. The STV is a more proportional system than the AMS system used for elections to the NAW or Scottish Parliament, and this is reflected in lower levels of disproportionality with index scores of 3.66, 2.88, and 3.12 for the 1998, 2003, and 2007 elections, respectively (a mean of 3.22).

The simple finding of this section is that devolution has delivered a significantly lower index score for disproportionality, averaging out at 6.87 for Scotland, Northern Ireland, and Wales compared to 17.0

for UK elections. This result is also true in relation to the only English region with its own directly elected assembly—London. The Greater London Assembly (GLA) is elected using AMS mixed-member proportional system with fourteen of its twenty-five members representing constituencies, and the remaining eleven members being selected from party lists. As Figure 8.2 illustrates, the 2000, 2004, and 2008 elections to the GLA were far less disproportional (with respective disproportionality scores of 6.81, 6.49, and 6.44, respectively) than the general elections in 1997, 2001, or 2005 (16.51, 17.77, and 17.73, respectively). Having identified this incongruence between levels of disproportionality at the national and sub-national regional levels, Section 8.3 examines the possible consequences and implications.

8.3 Electoral dynamics

In relation to V4, the UK provides a curious mixture of majoritarian modification (at the sub-national level) alongside majoritarian stability (at the national level). Furthermore, as emphasized earlier, because electoral systems govern the transfer and distribution of power within political systems and as such can be interpreted as aspects of 'meta-constitutional' politics (i.e. they identity and reflect the fundamental principles of the body politic), it is possible to use the findings of this chapter to add weight to this book's thesis regarding New Labour's bi-constitutionalism. In this sense the bi-constitutionality of New Labour is demonstrated in the fact that it has sought to foster, develop, and apply a more pluralist meta-constitutional orientation at the sub-national level through the use of semi-proportional or highly proportional electoral systems, while seeking to retain a markedly different model of governance at the national level, a model founded on a disproportional electoral system.

In his memoirs, the former Foreign Secretary (1997–2001) and Leader of the House of Commons (2001–3), Robin Cook wrote, '...the acid test of any commitment to pluralism is whether we are prepared to allow Britain a proportional electoral system that returns a pluralist Parliament'.[28] The central finding of this chapter is that although the government passed this acid test in relation to sub-national governance, it failed to cultivate a debate about electoral reform for Westminster. In this sense, electoral system reform during 1997–2007 provides a perfect example of the 'Blair paradox' (see Chapter 3) in terms of a willingness to devolve power and orchestrate the development of 'new politics' at the periphery, while retaining a tight grip on the foundation of executive dominance (i.e. the FPTP electoral system) at the national level. The broader comparative literature on models of democracy and reform demonstrates that constitutions and electoral systems tend to be notoriously resistant to change.[29] Beneficiaries of the existing situation tend to be those whose support is also needed to deliver change. For this reason, comparative constitutional history is littered with examples of new governments that renege on pre-election promise to institute reforms that would reduce their capacity to govern. And yet, New Labour's approach is distinct exactly because it has attempted to deploy a statecraft strategy based upon constitutional coexistence and the parallel operation of markedly different models of democracy within one *unitary* polity. Before moving on to examine the last variable of the Executive–Parties dimension (V5, Interest Group Pluralism), it is therefore necessary (*a*) to reflect back on the internal coherence of the scores we have so far updated and also (*b*) to put down a thematic marker in terms of an emphasis on instability and dynamics.

In terms of internal coherence along the executive–parties dimension, a relatively clear pattern is so far observable along two dimensions (the national and devolved sub-national). At the devolved sub-national level, the internal coherence is strong with the more consensual polities in Northern Ireland, Wales, and Scotland displaying low levels of disproportionality (V4), higher numbers of effective political parties (V1), few examples of single-party majority government (V2), and finally, a more balanced executive–legislative relationship (V3). In this sense, the pattern of variable scores is in alignment because it reflects the key characteristics of a power-sharing consensual democracy. Internal coherence is also found at the national level. The main difference is that the coherence supports an opposing meta-constitutional orientation or democratic value-set (i.e. that emanating from majoritarian theory). This is reflected in our findings—high levels of disproportionality leading to manufactured majorities, low numbers of effective political parties, executive dominance of the legislature, and single-party majority cabinets for the national level during 1997–2007. The correlations between V1, V2, V3, and V4 are therefore strong (see Figure 8.4). Whether this internal coherence runs throughout all ten variables, and the implications of any outliers, will form a key strand of later chapters.

The theme of instability and dynamics (the second issue noted earlier), however, forces us to reflect on the relationship between the different patterns of democracy which are beginning to emerge in this analysis. Pushing

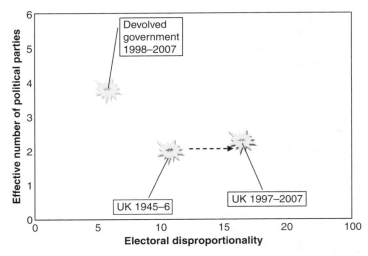

Figure 8.4 Relationship between V1 (political parties) and V4 (electoral systems) for the UK and devolved government

this line of inquiry still further, it is possible to argue that the parallel deployment of opposing electoral systems within what is formally a unitary state is unsustainable in the long-term. Put differently, at some point in the future a national government will no longer be able to (or may not want to) marginalize the issue of electoral reform for Westminster, and will either have to concede the need for change, or provide an explicit justification for why proportional systems have been deemed appropriate for Scotland, Wales, and Northern Ireland, but remain inappropriate for Westminster. Bi-constitutionalism, if accepted as a valid interpretation of recent events, therefore creates clear tensions and anomalies that are likely to fester and augment to the point at which a more systematic review or discussion about the constitutional configuration is likely to take place.

It is in this vein that Dunleavy argues that the coexistence of plurality rule and PR elections is progressively accentuating and accelerating the transformation of both voters' alignments and parties' strategies.[30] More-over, the transition to using PR systems at the sub-national level makes 'some form of transition of representation at Westminster inevitable as existing multi-party politics develops further'.[31] In offering this argument, Dunleavy draws on the comparative research of Colomer which suggests that the effective number of political parties tends to increase *before* rather than *after* the transition from plurality to proportional electoral systems.

This in itself suggests that governing elites generally only concede change when they are forced to by the electorate.[32] In this sense, the transition to a proportional system frequently has a limited effect on the party system (because the new party system was the driving force behind, rather than a result of, the reform). Placing this thesis in the UK context raises questions about the existence of multiparty politics and the longevity of executive coping-strategies, veto-points, and marginalization tactics.

A broader argument that also focuses on the dynamics that have been unleashed at the sub-national level and their possible spillover effects at the national level could draw upon Duverger's thesis regarding the social–psychological effects of electoral systems on the public.[33] If plurality systems have a mechanical effect of producing two-party systems then, Duverger suggests, they also have a related and reinforcing effect on the psychology of the electorate because voters in plurality system will be unwilling to waste their vote on small parties that have little chance of winning a seat. To ensure their vote is not wasted, voters will vote for a larger party, even if it may not be there first choice. Therefore, the number of political parties is not only reduced by the mechanics of the electoral system, but also by dominant societal assumptions about the nature of that system and corresponding strategic calculations on the part of the voter.[34] Conversely, wasted votes are less likely under proportional systems, the electorate is willing to vote for a broader range of (often small) parties, and multiparty systems are more common (as we found in relation to V1). This notion of the social–psychological impact of electoral systems complements Dunleavy's thesis, while also providing a link with Judge's suggestion that over time 'normative subsystems' and 'deviant cultures' will emerge within these devolved political arenas that will increasingly challenge, or at least stand in stark contrast to the established mega-constitutional orientation at Westminster.[35] As the earlier chapters have shown, the implementation of proportional systems has led to an increase in the number of effective political parties (V1) at the devolved level (Figure 5.2). Because the seat share more closely corresponds with the vote share, the party systems are more balanced, government formation (V2) is more complex and the executive–legislative relationship (V3) are more equal. Scotland, Northern Ireland, and Wales are diverging from the United Kingdom's power-hoarding model. And yet, although Bohrer and Krutz highlight the 'sharp differences between the British system and the Devolved settings' and Dunleavy is correct to emphasize the dynamic impulses that have been set in train via devolution, it is important not to underestimate, as Blau has emphasized, the executive's capacity for instituting veto-points, coping-strategies, and self-preservation in general, especially where the existing system sustains a favourable bias.[36]

We return to these issues in later chapters and their role at this stage has simply been to underline the point that there is no such thing as a constitutional settlement. The constitutional reforms implemented during 1997–2007 under the guise of 'modernization' and 'democratic renewal' are inconsistent for the reason that they impose power-sharing values and institutions within a power-hoarding model of democracy. Whether this proves problematic depends on how future governments seek to resolve or remedy the anomalies that have now been set in train. The themes of instability and the dynamics of change, in terms of spill-over and spill-back, therefore form a central element of Part III of this book. Chapter 9 focuses on the final fifth variable of the executive–parties dimension—interest group pluralism (V5).

V4 Index of disproportionality conclusion

Lijphart's UK score 1945–96	10.33
Lijphart's UK score 1971–96	14.66
Updated UK score 1997–2007	17.00
Devolved tier score 1998–2007	6.87

Notes

1. Blau, A (2008) 'Majoritarianism Under Pressure', in R. Hazell, ed., *Constitutional Futures Revisited*. Houndmills: Palgrave, pp. 233–48.
2. Tsebelis, G (1990) *Nested Games*. Berkeley, CA: University of California Press, p. 104.
3. Nohlen, D (1984) 'Two Incompatible Principles of Democracy', in A Lijphart and B Grofman, eds., *Choosing an Electoral System*. New York, NY: Praeger; Powell, G (2000). *Elections as Instruments of Democracy*. New Haven, CT: Yale University Press; Shugart, M (2006) 'Inherent and Contingent Factors in Reform Initiation in Plurality Systems'. Paper presented at the Plurality and Multiround Elections Conference, Montreal, 17 June.
4. Dunleavy, P and Margetts, H (1995) 'Understanding the Dynamics of Electoral Reform', *International Political Science Review*, 16(1): 9–29; See also Norris, P (1995) 'The Politics of Electoral Reform in United Kingdom', *International Political Science Review*, 16(1): 45–75.
5. Blau, A (2004) 'Fairness and Electoral Reform', *British Journal of Politics and International Relations*, 6(2), 165–81.

6. Gallagher, M and Mitchell, P (2008) *The Politics of Electoral Systems*. Oxford: Oxford University Press.

7. See Blais, A (2008) ed. *To Keep or Change First Past the Post?* Oxford: Oxford University Press.

8. The phrase 'executive paradise' is taken from Zines, L (1991) *Constitutional Change in the Commonwealth*. Cambridge: Cambridge University Press.

9. Shugart, M (2006) 'Inherent and Contingent Factors in Reform Initiation in Plurality Systems'. Paper presented at the Plurality and Multiround Elections Conference, Montreal, 17 June.

10. For a discussion see Grofmann, B and Lijphart, A (1986) eds. *Electoral Laws and Their Political Consequences*. New York: Agathon.

11. Mair, P (1992) 'The Question of Electoral Reform', *New Left Review*, I(194), 75–97.

12. See, for example, Muir, R (1930). *How the United Kingdom is Governed*. London: Constable; Finer, S (1975) *Adversary Politics and Electoral Reform*. London: Anthony Wigram; Bogdanor, V (1981) *The People and the Party System*. Cambridge: Cambridge University Press; Walkland, S (1983) 'Parliamentary Reform, Party Realignment and Electoral Reform', in D Judge, ed., *The Politics of Parliamentary Reform*. London: Heinemann; Norris, P (1997) 'Choosing Electoral Systems', *International Political Science Review*, 18(3): 297–312.

13. See Evans, M (2003) *Constitution-Making and the Labour Party*. Basingstoke: Palgrave.

14. Linton, M and Georghiou, M (1993) *Labour's Road to Electoral Reform*. London: Labour Campaign for Electoral Reform.

15. Labour Party (1993) *Representation and Elections: Report of the Working Party on Elections* [The Plant Report]. London: Labour Party.

16. Beetham, D (1992) 'The Plant Report and the Theory of Political Representation', *Political Quarterly*, 63(4), 460–7. Dummett, M (1992) 'Towards a More Representative Voting System: The Plant Report', *New Left Review*, I(194): 98–113.

17. Labour Party (1997a) *Joint Consultative Committee on Constitutional Reform—Final Report*. London: Labour Party, para. 56.

18. Labour Party (1997b) *New Labour: Because United Kingdom Deserves Better*. London: Labour Party.

19. Cm. 4090 (1998) *The Report of the Independent Commission on the Voting System*. London: HMSO. For a review, see Dunleavy, P and Margetts, H (1999) 'Mixed Electoral Systems in United Kingdom and the Jenkins Commission', *British Journal of Politics and International Relations*, 1(1), 12–38.

20. Independent Commission to Review Britain's Experience with PR Voting Systems (2003) *Changed Voting, Changed Politics: Lessons of Britain's Experience with PR Since 1997*. London: Constitution Unit.

21. Labour Party (2005) *United Kingdom: Forward Not Back, Labour's Manifesto 2005*. London: Labour Party, p. 110.

22. House of Commons Library (2005) *General Election 2005*. Research Paper 05/33.

23. The Bill would have enabled a petition of 5 per cent of the electorate to initiate either a nationwide referendum on the Westminster electoral system or a local referendum on the system to elect local councillors.

24. Kavanagh, D, Richards, D, Smith, M, and Geddes, A (2006) *British Politics*. Oxford: Oxford University Press, pp. 399–400.

25. Flinders, M (2002) 'Shifting the Balance? Parliament, the Executive and the British Constitution', *Political Studies*, 50(1), 23–42.

26. BBC News (2005) 'Kennedy attacks "Herod" Prescott', 25 May (http://news.bbc.co.uk/1/hi/uk_politics/4578159.stm).

27. Johnston, R, Rossiter, D, and Pattie, C (2006) 'The Results of the 2005 General Election in Great Britain', *Journal of Elections, Public Opinion and Parties*, 16(1), 37–54.

28. Cook, R (2003) *The Point of Departure*. London: Simon & Schuster.

29. See Lijphart, A (1994) *Electoral Systems and Party Systems*. Oxford: Oxford University Press.

30. Dunleavy, P (2005) 'Facing Up to Multi-party Politics', *Parliamentary Affairs*, 58 (3), 503–32.

31. Ibid., p. 505.

32. Colomer, J (2005) 'It's Parties that Choose Electoral Systems (or Duverger's Laws Upside Down)' *Political Studies*, 53(1), 1–21.

33. Duverger, M (1954) *Political Parties*. New York: Wiley.

34. Lijphart *op. cit.* (1994).

35. Judge *op. cit.* (2006), p. 391.

36. Bohrer, R and Krutz, G (2004) 'Duverger and Devolution', *Electoral Studies*, 23, 326; see Blau *op. cit.* (2008), p. 233.

Chapter 9

V5. Interest Groups

New Labour's political strategy has been predicated on establishing distance from the trade unions.[1]

This chapter focuses on the last of the five variables that together constitute the *executive–parties* dimension on Lijphart's methodology—interest groups. Will this exhibit significant change for the decade 1997–2007 when compared with Lijphart's original analysis up to 1996? Or will it complement the emerging pattern, whereby the analysis of interest-group pluralism at the national level reveals little change? But sub-national politics suggests that a more consensual model of politics is emerging, even in the most embryonic form. The simple conclusion of this chapter is that during 1997–2007, the Labour governments *did not* significantly (or even moderately) alter the socio-political mechanics on which this variable is based. And yet, devolution to Northern Ireland, Wales, and Scotland and tentative developments at the regional level in England does seem to have created new democratic arenas in which a more consensual and cooperative set of relationships have evolved.

In order to explain and justify these conclusions, this chapter is divided into three sections. The trade union movement formed the Labour Party in the UK and a logical hypothesis might expect that the interest-group pluralism score for the decade 1997–2007 may indicate a higher degree of corporatist-style interaction. The first section focuses on what has actually occurred during this period and reflects on why New Labour were unprepared to adopt more corporatist working-relationships. The second section moves beyond the national level and briefly examines the nature of interest-group pluralism in the post-devolution period, in order to assess whether a markedly different style of politics has emerged, or shows signs of emerging. In the final section, the topic of causal connections between the five variables on the executive–parties dimension is explored. This allows us to reflect on emergent patterns, and assess their implications in terms of those five variables to be examined under the federal–unitary dimension in the remaining chapters of Part II. Before examining the nature of interest-group pluralism in the UK during 1997–2007, it is necessary to briefly consider why Lijphart selected this variable, and also how it fits within the broader distinction between majoritarian and consensual models of democracy.

The role and capacity of interest groups to play a representational role within a polity reflects not only the institutional features of a polity, but also the governing principles on which that democracy is founded. Interest groups, as Sartori emphasized, are therefore 'channels for articulating, communicating and implementing the demands of the governed'.[2] The emblematic interest-group system of majoritarian democracy is competitive, pluralist, and uncoordinated. In contrast, the consensus model is likely to display an interest-group system that is coordinated and compromise-orientated. This latter model is commonly known as corporatism, which generally means that interest groups are relatively large in size and small in number, and tend to be coordinated into national peak or umbrella organizations. These peak organizations will enjoy privileged access to the executive, often a formalized role within the policy-making process, and agreements are considered to be binding on all parties. Corporatism is viewed as a core element of consensual types of democracy.[3] Critically corporatism has a normative socio-political basis; there is a broad ideology of social partnership and an emphasis on participation, consultation, and compromise.[4] This normative social platform clearly stands in contrast to the central tenets of the power-hoarding or the majoritarian model.

In assessing the corporatist (consensual) or pluralist (majoritarian) nature of democratic systems, Lijphart drew upon and developed the research of Siaroff which took eight basic aspects of the pluralism–corporatism contrast and rated each of twenty-four democracies using a five-point scale.[5] Siaroff then averaged these ratings to arrive at a comprehensive score for each country. Moreover, Siaroff did this for the periods 1963–70 and 1983–90 (adding Spain, Portugal, and Greece to his original twenty-one countries for the second period) in order to deduce the existence of historical shifts for this variable. Although these two periods do not match Lijphart's periods of analysis perfectly (i.e. 1945–96, 1971–96), they may be considered as representative for the long time span from the late 1940s to the mid-1990s, especially when set against complementary studies.[6]

Siaroff's five-point scale (theoretical maximum of four and minimum of zero) therefore provides an operational measure of interest-group pluralism. Using this scale, the UK was given an index score of 3.38 for 1945–96 and 3.5 for 1971–96. To put this score in a comparative context, Norway, Sweden, and Austria received the most corporatist index scores (with 0.44, 0.50, and 0.62, respectively) and Canada, Greece, and the UK the most pluralist (3.56, 3.50, and 3.38). The mean score for the 36 countries in Lijphart's study was 2.24, with the UK placed very near the pluralist end of the spectrum, a result in line with the broader acceptance of the UK as an archetypal majoritarian country. Section 9.1 assesses whether this variable score has altered since the election of New Labour in May 1997.

9.1 New Labour and interest-group pluralism

The Labour Party was created in 1903 by a collection of socialist societies and trade unions to challenge global capitalism and forge a socialist commonwealth based upon the principles of solidarity and equality, and common ownership of the means of production, distribution and exchange. For this reason, subsequent Labour governments attempted to develop a corporatist or quasi-corporatist form of political economy in which the government, the unions, and business organizations (represented by the Trades Unions Conference and the Confederation of British Industry, respectively) attempted to manage the vagaries of global economic shifts. The popular perception of these experiences, notably in 1964–70 and 1974–9, was that they had 'failed visibly and miserably'[7] and that they had been characterized by the 'union-dominance model', where unions were able to control a deferential and referential Labour government.[8] The reality, as is so often the case, was far more complex. As Minkin's *The Contentious Alliance* (1991) demonstrated, the relationship was actually based on a dense web of resource dependencies in which the unions were not as dominant as the media, the Conservative Party, and later many Labour Party modernizers liked to suggest. For these reasons, Ludlam and Tayor argue that the 'union–party bonding model' through which unions were integrated with the party, had guaranteed positions but did not dominate policy making provides a more subtle and accurate representation of interest-group dynamics.

This was not, however, an approach to managing the economy and industrial relations that New Labour were willing to adopt.[9] In terms of public perception and practical economic management, New Labour was intent on distancing themselves from the trade union movement.[10]

163

'Between 1997–2007 New Labour embraced the neo-liberal capitalist order, not in a defensively apologetically way but with a real sense of pride and swagger'.[11] Critically, price stability in the economy was not to be achieved through social contracts or an incomes policy, but through a combination of transferring responsibility over monetary policy to the Bank of England while also maintaining a deregulated labour market where wage levels would be determined mainly by market forces. The influence and political leverage of the trade unions was therefore drastically reduced because their cooperation was not needed to implement this strategy.

In April 1997, New Labour published a special manifesto for the business community in which it set out how it intended to work closely with capital and the business community in government. It was clear from this document that the Labour Party had no intention of returning to the economic statecraft of the 1970s. Tony Blair, John Smith, and other senior Labour politicians were adamant that the election of 'New' Labour would not involve the establishment of close working relationships with the TUC. The role of a Labour government would be to facilitate a dynamic and competitive business environment in which the role of the state was to support individual rights and responsibilities, while also delivering a portfolio of skills and training packages to the workforce. The trade unions would be treated with respect and would be welcome to respond to various policy statements and papers, but they would enjoy no privileged access and would certainly have no formal role in the management of the economy. The Labour Party's 1997 General Election manifesto underlined this approach by stating, 'the key elements of the trade union legislation of the 1980s will stay—on ballots, picketing and industrial action'.

In a deliberate move to emphasize his government's distance from the unions the incoming Prime Minister refused to see the TUC during his first six months in Downing Street.[12] There were, however, several longstanding Labour Party commitments that could not be easily jettisoned, and to which Tony Blair felt a personal obligation to deliver in some form. These included the promise to introduce a statutory national minimum wage, and to end the UK's opt-out from the Social Chapter of the EU's Maastricht Treaty. Although these measures were delivered, their specific method of implementation was designed to ensure that they would not disrupt or harm business activities. More broadly, New Labour was keen to avoid any activity that might be seen as 'corporatist' in nature and as a result, trade unions were significantly under-represented in the raft of policy reviews and 'task forces' established by the government during the beginning of its first term.[13] The fact that the Monetary Policy Committee of the Bank of England (see Chapter 13) was established in 1997 without a member drawn from the trade union movement was also symptomatic of a government that was committed to maintaining an arm's-length relationship with organized Labour. Tripartite bodies, like the Advisory, Conciliation and Arbitration Service, Health and Safety Commission, and the Equal Opportunities Commission remained, but faced reductions in both their budgets and functions.[14] Where the government was willing to establish new tripartite organizations, such as with the creation of the Low Pay Commission in 1998, they were formed as advisory rather than executive bodies, and during 1997–2007 the UK remained the only country in the EU that deliberately rejected the use of institutional partnerships or social dialogues between the state, capital, and labour at any level.

Employment relations and labour market strategy were always central elements of the Labour Party's process of modernization during the 1990s.[15] At the root of this policy platform, however, was a commitment to individual rights and choice within the workplace environment, rather than union rights or rights just for union members.[16] New Labour notions of 'partnership' or 'stakeholding' proved far removed from restoration of traditional union powers or ollective institutions.[17] And yet, New Labour's approach was not simply a direct continuation of Thatcherism: 'New Labour represents a continuation of neo-liberalism . . . but one required to make more concessions than its predecessor with the trade unions and social democratic policy preferences'.[18] Industrial relations therefore formed a key part of New Labour's 'third way' as it sought to find a role for the unions and retain cooperative relationships, while at the same time reassuring the public and the markets that the government was not going to empower the unions or move towards corporatist economic management.[19]

This 'third way' strategy explains the specific manner in which a number of measures and reforms were implemented during 1997–2007.[20] The Employment Relations Act 1999 formed the centrepiece of the government's industrial relations policy during its first term. This delivered a statutory right to union recognition, a reduction in the qualifying period before benefitting from claims for unfair dismissal, extended maternity leave, enhanced parental leave, etc. However, the impact of these measures was diluted through: (*a*) the government's narrow definition of 'employees' which excluded around five million temporary agency staff and those nominally self-employed; and (*b*) the imposition of a high threshold (40 per cent) for union recognition. The UK's statutory framework for regulating industrial action remained the most restrictive in the EU.

This evisceration of the potential significance of legislation through its specific implementation is a theme that has arisen in earlier chapters. For example, the Gangmasters Licensing Act 2004 introduced a regulatory system for those companies and individuals supplying workers (often foreign) to sectors of the UK's economy. And yet, in order to limit the impact of this legislation on the business community while also maintaining the UK's reputation for offering a flexible labour market, the legislation deliberately excluded those areas of the economy where gangmasters were particularly active (including caring, cleaning, catering, and hospitality). Similarly, the impact of the EU's Working-Time Regulations (stipulating that workers must not normally be required to work over 48 hours per week) was reduced through the government's decision to let workers 'waive' their rights, and through the exclusion of several occupational categories.[21] Once again the government's justification rested on a normative emphasis on individual rights and 'choice', combined with a commitment to maximize the UK's competitive advantage through the provision of a flexible labour market.

During 2001, the relationship between New Labour and the unions soured as tensions that had simmered throughout the government's first term came to the fore.[22] For New Labour the electoral success of June 2001 reflected the public's confidence in the ability of the government to manage the economy and as a result, senior labour ministers reacted strongly against those public sector unions—including the Fire Brigades Union, Communications Workers Union, Public and Commercial Services Union—who voted to take industrial action in 2002 and 2003. Strike action fuelled New Labour's suspicions about trade unions and led to their further distancing from the party.[23] As a result, anti-Labour Party feeling within the union movement increased and a new generation of younger and more explicitly militant union leaders were elected, who demanded the fundamental labour rights for workers.[24]

The Employment Act of 2002 formed the government's main second-term policy platform on industrial relations.[25] At the core of the legislation was an attempt to reform the employment tribunals system, with the aim of reducing the number of cases handled in order to reduce the compliance costs on business and employers. The Employment Act encapsulated the 'partnership' approach of New Labour, but it cannot be seen as a decisive shift in the nature of interest-group government relations in the UK, especially when weighed against New Labour's retention of much of the previous Conservative government's anti-union legislation and their rejection of the European Union's proposed national level works councils. The Warwick Accords of 2004 were negotiated between the Labour Party and the trade unions, but even these modest proposals had little impact on a government that was committed to forcing through public-sector reforms that were rooted in managerialism and a commitment to harness the perceived benefits of the market in the delivery of public services.[26] This determination became more explicit from 2004 onwards as ministers drew upon the notion of 'contestability' to emphasize that those elements of the public sector that were consistently assessed as under-performing would be transferred to alternative service providers drawn from the 'third' or private sectors.[27]

Any account of interest-group pluralism and industrial relations, especially when changes have occurred, must account for the interplay between context, agency, and structure. Although Tony Blair was undoubtedly suspicious of the trade union movement, the capacity of his governments to alter the socio-political configuration of economic management were to a large extent facilitated by institutional and contextual factors that conspired to open a 'window of opportunity'. In institutional terms the Labour government inherited a strong economy and a robust labour market in 1997. MacDonald, Attlee, and Wilson had inherited far less propitious economic circumstances; every Labour Prime Minister before Blair had been forced to bargain with the unions in order to try and manage economic pressures. Contextually, this period of economic stability coincided with a decline in trade-union strength in terms of membership (and therefore finances), as union membership as a proportion of the total workforce declined from 53 per cent in 1979 to 27 per cent in 2000. Non-unionism was now the norm rather than the exception across large sections of the workforce (particularly amongst the young, women, and part-time workers). In this context, the government felt little obligation to empower the unions with special rights and privileges.

As a result, the role of the trade unions within the political-economy of the UK altered. The issues of workplace learning, 'up-skilling', and the provision of personal services, for example, are topics where the trade unions have played a key role in delivering the government's emphasis on vocational training and 'human capital'. Although the unions have sought to portray this role as an example of close social partnership with the potential to revitalize trade-union membership and activity, less sanguine observers suggest that they have been marginalized, becoming almost agents of the state, through a focus on government-endorsed 'public administration' functions or, as Taylor suggests, 'a small and rather marginal role, mainly as voluntary learning organisations designed to help improve corporate performance'.[28]

Put simply, New Labour rejected collective economic management and corporatist structures, and sought to cultivate an individualized rights-based working environment. The 'third way' project was, however, not simply a continuation of Thatcherism. The Employment Relations Act 1999, Employment Act 2002, the incorporation of EU directives, and especially the National Minimum Wage Act 1999 were measures that were designed to respond to union demands. And yet, these concessions were only acceded to with 'generous derogations and exceptions', and the macro-political emphasis was on distancing rather than embracing the unions.[29] Indeed, New Labour sought to build a new framework of incentives and sanctions in relation to industrial relations and employment rights that did not impose labour-market rigidities or place disproportionate costs on employers which, in turn, altered both the role and position of the trade unions within the political economy of the UK.

In *Losing Labour's Soul?* Shaw argues that 'a major modification has occurred in the role Labour performs in the political system and thereby in the pattern of interest representation'.[30] This 'major modification' is not related to any attempt to reinstitute formalized patterns of union engagement within a tripartite quasi-corporatist framework. In the context of the 'union-dominance' and 'union-party bonding' models discussed earlier, it is possible to argue that 1997–2007 witnessed the emergence of a 'union-distance model'.

How then can this analysis be located within Lijphart's schema in terms of updating our score for V5? The overall situation is relatively clear: New Labour did not shift the nature of interest-group pluralism towards a more formalized, cooperative, or conciliatory position. In fact, using Lijphart's initial methodology to generate a revised variable score produces a result of 3.5 for 1997–2007, compared to 3.38 in Lijphart's analysis of 1945–96. This result is broadly in line with Vatter's attempt to design a more accurate and credible scoring for this variable.[31] However, the introduction to this chapter suggested that our analysis of the first four variables had begun to reveal a pattern in which no (or very little) change at the national level veiled the existence of more significant developments in relation to each variable at the sub-national level. It is for this reason that Section 9.2 explores the nature of interest-group pluralism at the sub-national level.

9.2 Devolution and interest-group pluralism

Devolution and regionalization offers both opportunities and threats to interest groups. Put simply, the creation of new political spaces and democratic arenas has increased the number of linkages in the democratic chain, thereby creating new conduits through which groups may seek to play a role in the policy-making process. As the General Secretary of the TUC has noted,

> Westminster no longer monopolises the political universe. Slowly but surely a new political culture is emerging within the UK, offering new opportunities for the TUC and unions to get the voice of working people heard. The new political culture looks and feels very different ... It provides a different quality of representation, often more open and accessible ... able to reach parts of the people that 'London' has failed to reach.[32]

The evolution and pattern of engagement has evolved differently in each region, but the existence of official and prescribed provisions does at least suggest that interest-group pluralism was ascribed a higher level of significance at the sub-national level than at the national level. Devolution was accompanied, for example, by explicit and formal mechanisms for interest-group pluralism—three Partnership Councils in Wales, and Civic Forums in Northern Ireland and Scotland. This in itself raises interesting questions about emergent patterns of democracy in the UK, the evolution and implications of multi-level governance, and how interest groups that may have been excluded or marginalized at the national level have attempted to take advantage of new opportunities for formalized engagement at the sub-national level. The analysis of V5 also includes a distinct English regional dimension due to the existence of areas of the country that are culturally attuned to the principles of corporatism. The northern and midlands regions, in particular, share post-industrial features in relation to social, economic, and political legacies that involve a close affinity with 'Old' Labourism and tripartite corporatist institutional frameworks.[33] As a result, trade unions retained a significant role within these regions during the 1980s and 1990s, despite the fact that industrial decline had significantly undermined their role in regional policy making.

In Scotland, a combination of administrative autonomy, legal separation, and a distinct civil society have for some time fostered a culture of 'meso-corporatism', in which government and interest groups produced a 'negotiated order'.[34] Devolution may then have allowed this longstanding heritage to flourish to some degree through both formal and informal means. Formally, the Scottish Trade Unions Congress (STUC) and the Scottish Executive have agreed and signed a 'Memorandum of Understanding' in which both parties have explicitly agreed to adopt a joint working relationship (six-monthly unions-executive meetings, annual reviews of performance, formalized consultation procedures, consultation in relation to senior quango appointments). Jeffrey notes a 'tendency under Labour [in Scotland] to nurture corporatist relationships with public sector interests ... itself projecting forward pre-devolution patterns' while[35] Keating reviews the post-devolution structures and processes of governance in Scotland more broadly and concludes,

> It would be an exaggeration to say that Scotland has developed its own version of corporatism, binding government, business and the unions... Yet in a weaker sense, there is developing a form of social concertation and a shared agenda on certain issues ... there has certainly been a change.[36]

A change has also been detected in Wales. The Government of Wales Act 1998 included a statutory duty on the WAG to consult with economic and social partners as part of its broader commitment to the European social-partnership model. The Business Partnership Council, for example, is chaired by the First Minister and includes representatives from the Welsh TUC, Business Wales, and a range of voluntary bodies to discuss strategic issues and responses to consultation. Interest groups also engage with NAW Scrutiny Committees and Regional Committees, while also working closely with members of the WAG and their officials.[37] Finally, interest groups are not only invited to respond to formal consultation processes, but many groups have also received support from the WAG-funded Social Partner Unit (itself a collaboration between business representative organizations and the WTUC). Possibly, the most politically and symbolically important development has been the signing of what has been considered a 'corporatist concordat' in the form of a Memorandum of Understanding between the WTUC and the WAG to govern not only their day-to-day working relationships, but also to identify key priority policy areas.[38] This mirrors the concordat between the Scottish TUC and the Scottish Executive, but there is no equivalent in England.

In Northern Ireland, a desire to ensure an open and formalized dialogue between a wide range of interest groups also formed a central component of the devolution legislation. The Good Friday Agreement provided for the creation of a Civic Forum that had to be established within six months of the inauguration of the NIE. Although the Forum was an advisory consultative body, the First Minister and Deputy First Minister were obliged to obtain the views of the forum on 'social, economic, and cultural matters' under Section 56 of the *Northern Ireland Act 1998*. However, despite Lord Smith's statement that Northern Ireland is 'more collectivist than Stalinist Russia, more corporatist than Mussolini's Italy and more quangosized than the Britain of two Harolds' the prescribed membership of the Forum arguably reflected a commitment to societal pluralism, echoing longstanding tensions within the province, and the requisite need to ensure cross-community engagement and participation, rather than neo-corporatist governing arrangements.[39] As such, the traditional corporatist social partners, notably trade unions and business groups comprised less than one-quarter of the total membership of sixty representatives. The remaining places were allocated to voluntary, religious, sporting, community, post-conflict resolution, and educational groups.[40]

From its establishment in October 2000, the Forum met regularly as a plenary body, and also established a range of subject-specific standing committees and working groups, but the suspension of the devolved institutions in October 2002 brought an end to the work of the Forum. During the period of suspension, the Transitional Assembly's Preparation for Government Committee came to the conclusion that the Forum may not be the most appropriate mechanism for obtaining the views of civic society in the province. Following restoration of devolution to Northern Ireland on 8 May 2007, the First Minister and Deputy First Minister decided to commission a comprehensive review of the structure, membership, and role of the Forum.

And yet, as noted earlier, an impulse towards greater partnership, inclusion, participation, and civic engagement has been a distinctive feature of emergent English regional governance regions. For the Regional Chambers (RC), sometimes called 'Regional Assemblies', consultation with a range of interest groups has not only become a key functions, but has also emerged as a tool through which it can increase its own legitimacy. RCs are voluntary, membership bodies which are generally established under the Regional Development Agencies Act 1998. All eight English regions outside London (which has a directly elected Mayor and assembly) have an RC whose primarily role is to oversee and scrutinize the work of the main executive bodies in the regions, the Regional Development Agencies (RDAs).[41] The critical features of RCs in relation to interest-group pluralism is that they were explicitly designed in order to provide trade unions, business associations, and other 'social and economic partners' with a formalized and statutory role within the policy-making process. That is systematic engagement with interest groups (employers, unions, and the 'third sector') on a structural basis during the policy formulation stage of the policy process. This is statutorily enshrined in legislation which stipulates that at least 30 per cent of RC members must be drawn from 'social and economic partners'.[42]

Although it may be possible to identify an element of quasi-corporatist constitutional engineering, it is important to acknowledge that RCs have few formal powers. Their main functions revolve around scrutiny and planning, and these are subject to RDA-veto powers (in relation to scrutiny) and government veto-powers (in relation to planning). Their role in the policy is therefore primarily advisory. It is, however, possible to suggest that two critical resources that have been carefully cultivated to increase the leverage and influence of RCs within the dense institutional architecture of English regional governance. First, the capacity of RCs to bring together a broad range of interest groups, while also promoting their active involvement through the provision of support staff, has significant symbolic value in terms of allowing the chambers to claim a certain legitimacy and representative value as the 'voice of the region'. Secondly, RCs have the potential to form powerful epistemic communities due to their capacity to obtain specialist information and data from a range of regional interests about the likely 'real-world' impact of proposals. These resources—regional representativeness, legitimacy, specialist knowledge, etc.—combine to ensure that (even in the absence of wide executive powers and a direct electoral mandate) RCs are involved in influencing and shaping regional economic and social governance.[43] This role and influence has possibly grown as central government has delegated more tasks to RCs. In 2003, for example, RCs assumed responsibility for the preparation of Regional Spatial Strategies, and Regional Emphasis Documents.[44]

This incremental development of the role and responsibilities of RCs led Sandford to consider whether post-1997 English regional governance represented a form of (neo-)corporatism.[45] There are many similarities between the role and composition of RCs and the Regional Economic Planning Boards and Councils established under Wilson's Labour government in the 1960s. These bodies were designed to promote central government policies, but in a manner that was sympathetic to regional issues and concerns. There are also affinities between corporatist sentiments and the Regional Spatial Strategies and the Regional Economic Strategies because they are both based on the explicit assertion that business and organized Labour representatives should have a leading voice in economic affairs (while broader civil society groups should also play a role, but not a systematically organized one, in wider social policy). Taking these two forms of interest-group involvement leads Sandford to draw upon the notion of 'corporate pluralism'.[46] This suggests a degree of formalized influence over the policy-making process that is frequently associated with corporatism, but within an environment in which these benefits are extended to a much wider range of groups.

English regional governance therefore exhibits a typically curious paradox in relation to interest-group pluralism. RCs have arguably been established on neo-corporatist principles and have been able to develop specific resources (legitimacy, specialist knowledge, nodality, etc.). And yet, RCs have few formal powers and they exist within a highly centralized institutional architecture in which RDAs remain the dominant regional actor. It is this theme of devolution within centralization, or what could be termed reluctant pluralism, that leads us back to a broader discussion concerning the findings of this chapter and the emergence of a bi-constitutional polity.

9.3 Causal connections and emergent patterns

The election of New Labour in 1997 did not result in a significant shift in the relationship between interest groups and the government at the national level.[47] Instead, the government developed an approach to statecraft based upon embedding a broadly neo-liberal strategy within a subtle discourse which emphasized the notions of 'partnership' and individualized rights. In democratic and constitutional terms, however, there has been no social reordering. As Smith and Morton conclude, 'Powerful trades unions have no place in New Labour's vision of the labour market, the employment relationship, or society'.[48] New Labour did not adopt a neo-corporatist model of social or economic management during 1997–2007, and for this reason the UK remains firmly located towards the higher end of the Siaroff index of interest-group pluralism with a score of 3.5.

And yet, the second part of this chapter examined the structures and processes of governance at the sub-national level and through this identified quite a different pattern of interest-group pluralism. The albeit limited research available on developments in Cardiff, Edinburgh, Belfast, and within the English regions does suggest a more cooperative and very often formalized set of working relationships between big business, the trade unions, and political decision makers. Equally important from the perspective of seeking to understand the statecraft of New Labour in relation to democratic renewal was the manner in which elements of neo-corporatist logic infused the devolution settlements. The devolution legislation created a statutory framework in which the devolved institutions were obliged to engage with certain 'economic and social partners' in a way that the government would not endorse at the national level. These interest groups (business, labour, and voluntary) are currently adapting their structures and strategies to take advantage of the more complex 'corporate pluralism' based model of multi-levelled and 'partnership-based' governance that are emerging post-devolution. These decentralized, participatory, and partnership-based forms of governance clearly 'fit' within the 'new politics' narrative that devolution was intended to deliver. And yet, they also pose distinct questions regarding why one model or approach to interest-group engagement is viewed as suitable at the sub-national level but not the national.

Stepping back, however, to locate this specific topic within the broader context of constitutional reform post-1997 suggests that we should not over-state the degree of change. It is marginal rather than significant. The UK remains a parliamentary state and the notion of 'executive devolution' captures the reserve powers and potentialities for interference that remain at the centre. It is also significant that despite the role and influence of the RCs, the government's approach to English regional government has been heavily focused on the RDAs and Government Offices in the regions. This chapter is therefore trying to make a quite subtle argument about the *extent* of change in relation to this variable. There is a significant difference between multi-level *governance* and multi-level *participation*; the former suggesting an increased role and capacity for non-state actors, while the latter suggests an increased opportunity to express certain section views, but not necessarily any actual impact on the determination of policy. In the UK the political opportunity structure for interest groups has clearly changed since 1997, but that should not automatically be conflated with a dispersal of power—especially given the nature of the majoritarian polity within which these reforms have occurred. Devolution and regionalization has for these reasons led to marginal rather than significant change and this, when measured through the lens of Siaroff's and Lijphart's methodology, would deliver a score for sub-national governance of around 2.60 ('around' reflecting the asymmetrical nature of the devolution measures). When located against the conclusions of the preceding four chapters, this conclusion appears to maintain an element of connectivity or internal coherence between the variables. Put slightly differently, the scores are clustered depending upon whether the meta-constitutional orientation is majoritarian or consensual. This clustering and coherence is illustrated by Figures 9.1 and 9.2.

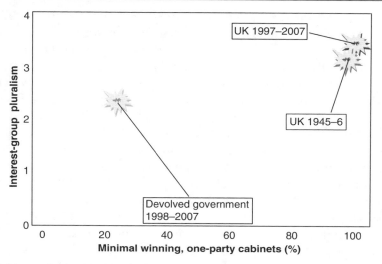

Figure 9.1 Relationship between V2 (cabinets) and V5 (interest-group pluralism) for the UK and devolved government

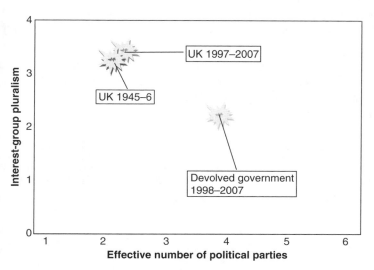

Figure 9.2 Relationship between V1 (political parties) and V5 (interest-group pluralism) for the UK and devolved government

Having assessed the nature of V5 in the UK during 1997–2007, we have completed the analysis of the first five variables which together form the executive–parties dimension. This is a suitable point to take stock and reflect on the nature of reform so far identified. In this context it is clear that Lijphart's observation that the five variables on the executive–legislature dimension tend to be inter-related to some degree appears to be upheld. More specifically, they display casual links. Electoral systems shape party systems, which in turn have a direct affect on both the nature of executive–legislative relationships, and also on the formation of cabinets. Legislative-seat distribution and the type of cabinet are also causally related to cabinet duration. Interest-group pluralism ties into this interwoven set of causal connections and Lijphart's research illustrates a close relationship between, for example, low levels of pluralism and (a) minimal winning one-party cabinets as well as (b) low levels of effective political parties. The type of interest-group system is also correlated with the electoral system and, though less strongly, with executive dominance. Having completed the analysis of variables 1–5 not only allows us to observe certain inter-relationships, but it also allows us to proceed to the second stage of Lijphart's framework by deriving the UK's position on the executive–parties dimension for the period 1997–2007 (Table 9.1).

Table 9.1 provides the first indication of how a Lijphartian analysis interprets New Labour's reforms on the conceptual map of democracy (Figure 4.1). Two basic conclusions are clear:

Table 9.1 Executive–parties dimension: 1945–96, 1971–96, and 1997–2007

Variable	Lijphart 1945–96	Lijphart 1971–96	National 1997–2007	Sub-national 1997–2007
V1 Effective no. of Parl. parties	2.11	2.20	2.28	3.84
V2 Minimal winning one-party cabinets (%)	96.7	93.3	100.0	25.0
V3 Index of executive dominance	5.52	5.52	6.78	3.5
V4 Index of disprop.	10.33	14.66	17.00	6.87
V5 Index of interest-group pluralism	3.38	3.5	3.5	2.6
Executive–parties dimension score	−1.21	−1.39	−1.62	−0.28

1. At the national level the UK actually became slightly more majoritarian along the Executive-Parties Dimension, a result that favours the Sceptical Theorists interpretation of 1997–2007.
2. Devolution has formed new democratic arenas within the UK that are based on a quite different, more consensual, meta-constitutional orientation.

This result is epistemologically bolstered due to the fact that three of the five variables behind this score (i.e. the effective number of political parties, the proportion of minimal winning one-party cabinets, and the index of disproportionality) are based upon fairly straightforward statistical analyses that are difficult to refute. In addition, the broader research-based literature on the other two variables (i.e. index of executive dominance and the index of interest-group pluralism) is fairly one-sided in that although debate exists around the margins, the overall picture is one of an executive that remains dominant over the House of Commons, and of a government that remains completely unwilling to return to any form of neo-corporatist statecraft that would involve a formalized and increased role for the trade unions.

In terms of responding to critics of Lijphart's techniques for scoring specific variables it is reassuring to note that the data contained in Table 9.1 is consistent with studies that have adopted slightly different methods for generating some variable scores. Vatter's research, for example, delivered an updated executive–parties score of −2.04 (thereby also indicating an increase in majoritarianism).[49] Taking this analysis further, what is particularly noteworthy, especially in the context of the 'Blair paradox', is that Table 9.1 suggests that the model of democracy delivered by devolution and to a lesser degree English regionalism would be located much further towards the consociational end of the executive–parties dimension (−0.28 compared to −1.62 at the national level). The 'new politics' narrative was always intended to deliver a more consensual and less adversarial model of democracy, but the extent and implications of this strategy are hard to decipher without completing the analysis of the federal–unitary dimension. It is to this endeavour that we now turn.

Notes

1. Charlwood, A (2004) 'The New Generation of Trade Union Leaders and Prospects for Union Revitalization', *British Journal of Industrial Relations*, 42(2), 391.
2. Sartori, G (1976) *Parties and Party Systems*. Cambridge: Cambridge University Press, p. 27.

3. Crepaz, M and Lijphart, A (1991) 'Corporatism and Consensus Democracy in Eighteen Countries', *British Journal of Political Science*, 21(2), 235–46. This correlation has been challenged—Keman, H and Pennings, P (1995) 'Managing Political and Societal Conflict in Democracies: Do Consensus and Corporatism Matter?' *British Journal of Political Science*, 25(2), 271–81; Crepaz, M and Lijphart, A (1995) 'Linking and Integrating Corporatism and Consensus Democracy', *British Journal of Political Science*, 25(2), 281–8.

4. See Katzenstein, P (1985) *Small States in World Markets*. Ithaca: Cornell University Press.

5. Siaroff, A (1998) 'Corporatism in Twenty-four Industrial Democracies'. Unpublished manuscript.

6. See Lijphart *op cit.* (1999), p. 171–85.

7. Cronin, J (2006) 'New Labour's Escape from Class Politics', *The Journal of the Historical Society*, 6(1), 54.

8. Ludlam, S and Taylor, A (2003) 'The Political Representation of the Labour Interest in Britain', *British Journal of Industrial Relations*, 41, 4.

9. Smith, P and Morton, G (2002) 'New Labour "Reform of Britain" Employment Law', *British Journal of International Relations*, 39(1), 119–38.

10. See Howell, C (2001) 'The End of the Relationship Between Social Democratic Parties and Trade Unions?' *Studies in Political Economy*, 65, 7–37.

11. Taylor, R (2007) 'New Labour, New Capitalism', in A. Seldon, ed., *Blair's Britain 1997–2007*. Cambridge: Cambridge University Press, p. 216.

12. Ibid., p. 227.

13. Platt, S (1998). *Government by Task Force*. London: Catalyst.

14. Taylor, R (2005) 'Third Ways: Old and New', *Political Quarterly*, 75(4), 429–48.

15. See McIlroy, J (2002) 'The Enduring Alliance: Trade Unions and the Making of New Labour, 1994–1997', *British Journal of Industrial Reelations*, 36(4), 537–64.

16. Smith and Morton *op. cit.* (2002).

17. Ackers, P and Payne, J (1998) 'British Trade Unions and Social Partnership: Rhetoric, Reality and Strategy', *International Journal of Human Resource Management*, 9(3), 529–50; Terry, M (2003) 'Can 'Partnership' Reverse the Decline in British Trade Unions?' *Employment and Society*, 17, 459–72.

18. Crouch, C (2001) 'A Third Way in Industrial Relations?' in S. White, ed., *New Labour: The Progressive Future?* Cambridge: Polity Press, p. 104.

19. Ibid., pp. 93–109.

20. Howell, C (2004) 'Is There a Third Way for Industrial Relations?' *British Journal of Industrial Relations*, 42(1), 1–22.

21. See Smith and Morton *op. cit.* (2001).

22. Undy, R (1999) 'New Labour's 'Industrial Relations Settlement', *British Journal of Industrial Relations*, 37(2), 315–36.

23. Waddington, J (2003) 'Heightening Tension in Relations between Trade Unions and the Labour Government in 2002', *British Journal of Industrial Relations*, 41(2), 335–58; Ludlam, S and Taylor, A (2003) 'The Political Representation of

the Labour Interest in Britain', *British Journal of Industrial Relations*, 41(4), 727–49.

24. Charlwood *op. cit.* (2004), pp. 379–97.
25. Hepple, R and Morris, S (2002) 'The Employment Act 2002 and the Crisis of Individual Employment Rights', *Industrial Law Journal*, 31, 245–69.
26. See Bach, S (2002) 'Public Sector Employment Relations Reform under Labour', *British Journal of Industrial Relations*, 40(2), 319–39.
27. See Flinders, M (forthcoming 2009) 'The Future of the State', *Political Quarterly*.
28. Taylor *op. cit.* (2005), p. 190; For an extensive review of this debate see McIlroy, J (2008) 'Ten Years of New Labour', *British Journal of Industrial Relations*, 46(2), 283–13.
29. Undy *op. cit.* (1999), p. 331.
30. Shaw, E. (2007) *Losing Labour's Soul*. London: Routledge, p. 141.
31. Vatter *op. cit.* (2009).
32. Brendan Barber, General Secretary, TUC (2003) Vice Chancellor's Lecture, City University, 10 June.
33. Morgan, K and Mungham, G (2000) *Redesigning Democracy*. Bridgend: Seren; Elcock, H (2001) 'A Surfeit of Strategies?' *Public Policy and Administration*, 16(1), 59–74; Robinson, F (2002) 'The North East', *City*, 6(3), 317–34.
34. Moore, C and Booth, S (1989) *Managing Competition*: Oxford: Clarendon.
35. Jeffrey, C (2009) 'Devolution', in Flinders et al., eds., *Oxford Handbook of British Politics*.
36. Keating, M (2005) *The Government of Scotland*. Edinburgh: Edinburgh University Press, p. 85.
37. Greer, S (2005) 'The Territorial Bases of Health Policymaking in the UK after Devolution', *Regional and Federal Studies*, 15(4), 501–18.
38. Pike, A, O'Brien, P, and Tomaney, J (2006) 'Devolution and the Trades Union Congress in North East England and Wales', *Regional and Federal Studies*, 16(2), 157–78.
39. Quoted in Knox, C and Carmichael, P (2005) 'Improving Public Services', *Journal of Social Policy*, 35(1), 102. See also Williamson, A, Scott, D and Halfpenny, P (2000) 'Rebuilding Civil Society in Northern Ireland', *Policy & Politics*, 28 (1), 49–66.
40. Singstad, L (2005) 'The Northern Ireland Civic Forum and a Politics of Recognition', *Irish Political Studies*, 20(2), 147–69.
41. The statutory establishment of RDAs as the lead economic development organizations also included provisions for trade unions and business representatives to have board-level representation.
42. Sandford, M (2006) 'Civic Engagement in the English Regions: Neo-corporatism, Networks, New Forms of Governance', *Regional and Federal Studies*, 16(2), 221–38.
43. Heselden, L (2001) 'Coming in from the Cold', *Antipode*, 33(5), 753–62.

44. Benneworth, P, Conroy, L, and Roberts, P (2002) 'Strategic Connectivity, Sustainable Development and the New English Regional Governance', *Journal of Environmental Planning and Management*, 45(2), 199–217.

45. Sandford *op. cit.* (2006).

46. Ibid., p. 235.

47. See Fishman, N (1997) 'Reinventing Corporatism', *Political Quarterly*, 68(1), 31–41.

48. Smith, P and Morton, G (2006) 'Nine Years of New Labour', *British Journal of Industrial Relations*, 44(3), 401–20.

49. Vatter *op. cit.* (2009).

Chapter 10

V6. Federal–Unitary Dimension

...their [New Labour] most significant achievement...the carapace of Britain's ancient regime has been broken.[1]

Chapter 9 concluded by identifying an intricate picture of majoritarian modification in which the UK's position along the executive-party dimension had actually become slightly more extreme. In 2001, Norris speculated that if Lijphart's research was replicated to analyse how New Labour was changing democracy in the UK it would likely reveal that 'the federal–unitary dimension has been transformed far more than the executive-party dimension'.[2] The aim of this chapter is to begin the process through which we can assess the nature of change along the federal–unitary dimension, and thereby judge Norris' hypothesis. Lijphart's analysis for 1945–96 was clear in relation to this variable—the UK was a unitary and centralized polity. The central conclusion of this chapter is that there has been a significant change. During 1997–2007, the UK shifted to a polity that would now be characterized as lying somewhere between a 'semi-federal' or a 'unitary and decentralized' classification. It is, however, important not to overstate the extent of change. The logic and principles of federalism have been rejected and the shadow of majoritarianism hangs over the devolved state.

10.1 The division of power

The basic feature of a majoritarian democracy is that power is concentrated, whereas in consensual polities power tends to be dispersed or non-centralized. Majoritarian democracies are therefore associated with unitary and centralized structures, while consensual democracies tend to exhibit federal or decentralized governance structures. As with so many of the variables examined in this book, the distinctions are rarely absolute and the real world is frequently messier than these distinctions suggest. And yet, at the same time these distinctions provide useful markers or reference points within which the complexities of modern governance can generally be located, understood, and compared. 'In all democracies, power is necessarily divided to some extent between central and non-central governments, but it is highly one-sided in a majoritarian democracy'.[3]

The critical element of a democratic structure is not so much *whether* some powers have been decentralized—because to a great extent the size and responsibilities of modern state systems make delegation (either functional or territorial) necessary—but *how* they have been decentralized. And it is in understanding the nature of dividing and decentralizing powers where the concept of federalism becomes salient. At the core of this concept is the notion that certain powers and responsibilities should not only be located beyond the national government, but also that the dispersal of such powers is constitutionally guaranteed. This notion of embedded rights to facilitate specified state responsibilities is vital because it brings with it a conception of governance whereby the national and regional governments are viewed as co-equals and partners in the administration of a polity. This stands in contrast to the highly centralized unitary model in which although regional and local governments may exist, they have no constitutional right to exist, their functions may be withdrawn and reallocated by the national level at any time, and the notion of embedded or guaranteed sub-national governance is alien to the principles of the constitution. It is in this vein that Elazar defines federalism as, 'the fundamental distribution of power among multiple centers...not the devolution of power from a single center or down a pyramid'.[4]

If the notion of a guaranteed and constitutionally embedded role for sub-national governments is the primary feature of federal systems, then a number of secondary features frequently accompany this aspect of constitutional design: (*a*) federal systems often involve bicameral legislatures in which a role of the second chamber is to represent constituent regions— the German Bundesrat, American Senate, etc. (see Chapter 11);[5] (*b*) all constitutions, be they written or unwritten, need to contain an element of flexibility, and as a result even in federal systems it is possible for the national government to alter the powers and responsibilities of sub-national governments. The capacity of those executives to alter the status quo is, however, generally heavily constrained through the imposition of stringent procedural requirements for amendment (see Chapter 12);

(c) finally, many federal polities contain a 'Supreme' or 'Constitutional' court with the capacity to preserve the equilibrium of the constitution through the mechanism of judicial review.[6] It is in this context that courts around the world play a major role in articulating and regulating the boundaries within which executives must govern (the focus of Chapter 13).

These three features can be viewed as anti-majoritarian institutions due to the manner in which they seek to impose a degree of constitutional rigidity in order to protect the division of powers within a federal polity: 'They are guarantors of federalism rather than components of federalism'.[7] In order to understand the divisions of power to be found within different countries, and particularly the existence of subtle gradations, Lijphart employed a fivefold classification system. The first criterion that forms the two extremes of this system is whether states have a formal federal constitution or not. This criterion provides a basic distinction between federal and unitary systems that can then further be divided into centralized and decentralized subcategories. An intermediate class of semi-federal systems is needed for a few countries that cannot be unambiguously classified as either federal or unitary (see Table 10.1).

Table 10.1 Degrees of federalism and decentralization in thirty-six democracies, 1945–96

Federal and decentralized [5.0]
Australia, Canada, Germany, Switzerland, United States, Belgium (after 1993)
Federal and centralized [4.0]
Venezuela Austria [4.5] India [4.5]
Semi-federal [3.0]
Israel, Netherlands, Belgium [3.1] (before 1993) Papua New Guinea Spain
Unitary and decentralized [2.0]
Denmark, Finland, Japan, Norway, Sweden
Unitary and centralized [1.0]
Bahamas, Jamaica, Barbados, France [1.2] Botswana, Comobia, Costa Rica, Italy [1.3] Greece, Iceland, Ireland, Trinidad [1.2] Luxembourg, Malta, Mauritius New Zealand, Portugal, United Kingdom

Source: Lijphart (1999) *Patterns of Democracy*, 189.

Table 10.1 assigns a score for each category in order to create a quantitative index of federalism, and it illustrates into which, or between which categories each of the thirty-six countries fall. Relatively straightforward classifications are listed to the left of Table 10.1, and those more complex cases that fall between the categories are listed to the right. Two features of Table 10.1 are particularly significant: (*a*) there are relatively few federal states; and (*b*) the federal–unitary and centralized–decentralized differences are related—federal systems tend to be decentralized and unitary states tend to be centralized. Consequently, the vast majority of countries tend to be bunched around the two extremes but as unitary and centralized countries outnumber federal and decentralized countries by over 2:1 the mean federalism index score is 2.3 and the median is 1.6 (i.e. significantly closer to the 1.0 score for unitary–centralized countries). As Table 10.1 reflects, the United Kingdom has always been characterized as a highly centralized unitary state in which the governmental structures at the local and regional level are subservient to the national level and enjoy no constitutionally entrenched rights or powers. It therefore receives a federalism index score of 1.0 with no variation between the two time periods 1945–96 and 1971–96. Section 10.2 examines how the division of power within the UK was altered during 1997–2007.

10.2 Devolution 1997–2007

New Labour was elected in May 1997 with a commitment to devolve power away from Whitehall and Westminster. Their 1997 General Election manifesto was, however, explicit about the fact that devolution would be delivered *within* the parameters of a unitary state, 'Our proposal is for devolution not federation. A sovereign Westminster Parliament will devolve power to Scotland and Wales'. Any division of powers that might occur was always therefore intended to be operationalized within the contours of the Westminster Model. And yet, it would be a mistake to view any recent division of power solely through the lens of New Labour's period in office. As such, devolution post-1997 needs to be understood as the latest instalment in a long-running chronicle of how to accommodate distinct political and cultural identities within a single-state structure in which England is dominant. This line of argument is closely associated with the scholarship of Mitchell who has consistently portrayed the UK as a 'Union State' in which specific and perennial challenges exist due to the heritage of unions agreed between England and the other constituent nations of the UK over four centuries.[8]

The division of power that occurred in the UK during 1997–2007 came about for a number of reasons and this, in turn, explains the asymmetrical nature of the devolution measures. In Scotland, the popularity of devolution was driven to a great extent by the centralization of power that had occurred during 1979–97, an issue exacerbated by the lack of Conservative Party representation in Scotland during that period. In Wales, devolution was a less salient issue. In Northern Ireland, the need to find a solution to the long-standing sectarian conflict formed the key driver behind the devolutionary process, whereas in England regional devolution was viewed primarily in economic terms as a method for increasing coordination and achieving regional economic and social development.

These variations in the logic and social pressures behind devolution help explain the results of the pre-legislative referendums that were held in advance of devolution. In Northern Ireland, the referendum on the Belfast Agreement, of which devolution was a core element, saw a large majority (71.1%) vote in favour of the agreement on a high turnout (81.1%). Although at 60.4 per cent the turnout was much lower in the pre-legislative referendum on devolution to Scotland, the result still indicated a high degree of public support, with 74.3 per cent voting in favour of establishing a Scottish Parliament (and 63.5% wanting it to also have tax raising powers). Historically, support for devolution had never been as strong in Wales, and this was reflected in the weaker form of executive devolution that was proposed. As a result, the pre-legislative referendum was approved by a tight margin with 50.3 per cent voting on a turnout of just 50.1 per cent. The resulting measures to devolve power have been extensively documented elsewhere, and it is neither necessary nor possible to provide a detailed account of each measure in this chapter. In order to provide a richer account of change, this section sets out the basic framework of devolution in Table 10.2 and then focuses on three core elements or features of the existing division of powers that are either restraining or promoting the transformation of democracy in the UK: (*a*) the meta-constitutional framework; (*b*) the dynamics of change; and (*c*) the centralization of the core.

10.2.1 *The meta-constitutional framework*

Possibly, the most significant element of the devolution process is the manner in which it has been carefully designed to exist within the broader

Table 10.2 Asymmetrical devolution in the UK

Nation	% UK pop.	% UK GDP	Relevant legislation	Form of government
England	83.6	85.7	*Regional Development Agencies Act 1998*	Direct rule from Westminster with growing regional administration of central government policies, but no elected regional government, except in London.
London	12.2	19.1	*Greater London Authority Act 1998*	Greater London Authority with responsibility for strategic policy coordination, economic development, policing, and fire services; elected executive Mayor held to account by separately elected Assembly.
Scotland	8.6	8.1	*Scotland Act 1998*	Scottish Parliament with primary legislative powers in matters not reserved to Westminster (most fields of domestic policy); limited fiscal autonomy; majoritarian government.
Wales	4.9	3.9	*Government of Wales Act 1998*	National Assembly for Wales with secondary legislative powers dependent on Westminster legislation; majoritarian government displacing initial vision of 'corporate body'.
Northern Ireland	2.9	2.2	*Northern Ireland Act 1998*	Northern Ireland Assembly with primary legislative powers in matters not reserved to Westminster (or not temporarily held back by Westminster subject to the security situation); proportional government top secure cross-community balance; embedded in international relationships with Republic of Ireland.

framework of parliamentary sovereignty. In this sense, the UK rejects federal theory. The devolved institutions are explicitly designed to be subservient rather than equal to Parliament at Westminster, and future governments retain the right to repeal or amend the legislation through which devolution has been delivered. In this sense, the constitutional flexibility of the UK's constitution has been retained and New Labour were unwilling to inject the constitutional rigidity that is commonly found in federal systems as a way of embedding and protecting the position of sub-national tiers of government. And yet, the capacity of an executive to alter the division of power within a polity depends upon a blend of formal and informal factors. In this sense, although it is true that there may not be any formal constitutional barriers to prevent a future government repealing, for example, the Scotland Act 1998, their capacity to act and their constitutional flexibility will be restrained through contextual social factors that may militate against change. William Hague, then Leader of the Conservative Party, admitted in 1998 that devolution was an element of change that a future Tory government would have little choice, but to accept. The assessment of the impact of devolutionary measures within a majoritarian state must therefore attempt to weigh the absence of constitutional limits on the executive against the existence of social and institutional dynamics that increase the potential costs of seeking to claw back those powers.

This notion of social and institutional dynamics alerts us to the fact that devolution remains a process rather than a settlement in the UK and it could be argued that the momentum behind devolution and the trajectory of developments within a relatively short time makes it unlikely (though not impossible) that a future government would seek to repeal any of the devolution legislation. The nature of change and particularly the notion of spillover are examined in Sub-section 10.2.2.

10.2.2 *The dynamics of change*

Devolution is a process rather than an event and, as such, devolutionary measures frequently take on a dynamic quality. A well-known pattern can be identified across a number of countries, whereby regional devolution has created a 'snowball' or 'ratchet' effect in which weaker regions seek to acquire the powers of more autonomous regions. In Spain, for example, a division of powers based upon an asymmetrical pattern of devolution was introduced in the late 1980s. Although certain regions—'historic communities'—(Catalonia, Galicia, the Basque Country, and (later) Andalucia) originally acquired more autonomy and devolved powers, this stimulated a process whereby those regions with less autonomy demanded constitutional parity with the historic communities. The Spanish government has attempted to control these centrifugal dynamics by moving towards a standardizing of devolution arrangements, but this has been resisted by the historical communities who see this as undermining their special status and, as a result, have petitioned for even greater powers.[9] In the UK a similar ratchet effect can be identified.

This is arguably clearest in relation to devolution in Wales. An operational review of the NAW 2001 led to the introduction of a government-opposition model, and in 2002 the First Minister launched an Independent Commission to look into the powers and electoral arrangements of the NAW. The (Richard) Commission's report was published in March 2004 and it recommended a staged move towards full primary legislative powers, with interim measures to widen the NAW's autonomy under secondary legislative powers. The government's response, *Better Governance for Wales*, in June 2005 announced that it intended to legislate immediately for the transfer of primary legislative powers to the NAW (although those powers would have to be 'unlocked' through an affirmative public vote in a referendum). In the meantime, an interim procedure would be introduced to increase the legislative capacity of the NAW through Legislative Competence Orders that allowed the transfer of powers from Westminster to Cardiff. Although, a referendum could only be triggered with the approval of two-thirds of AMs and a majority of both Houses of Parliament, in July 2007 the Labour-Party–Plaid-Cymru coalition announced their commitment to holding a referendum on full legislative powers by 2011.

The work of the All Wales Convention, established to promote a 'yes' vote, is likely to benefit from the fact that public opinion in Wales has always favoured full legislative devolution (i.e. the Scottish Model) more than the Assembly model of secondary legislative powers.[10] As such, the devolution dynamic appears strong in Wales:

> ...a more solid, parliamentary edifice is emerging, and emerging much more rapidly than could have been imagined a decade ago...Moreover this edifice is emerging with the broad support of the Welsh population and well as most—though not all—of the nation's political class.[11]

What is noteworthy in terms of constitutional dynamics and the 'ratchet-effect' discussed earlier is the manner in which the arguments of the Richard Commission were frequently couched in terms of 'adopting the Scottish model' and therefore engaged in a strategy Osmond calls 'kilt streaming'.[12] The devolution dynamic is less intense in Northern Ireland. This reflects the long-standing sectarian tensions within the province and also the fact that devolution was, after a stuttering start, suspended during 2002–7. This period of suspension ensured that debates focused not on the dynamics and pace of change (as in Wales), but on whether the consociational principles on which devolution had been engineered through the Belfast Agreement of 1998 could actually produce a stable and workable division of powers. It appeared that devolution was simply not working. Critically, the consociational theory that had shaped devolution in Northern Ireland did not flow into inclusive discussion and negotiations over either the distribution of departments or the chairmanship (and deputy chairmanship) of assembly committees. Instead, via the d'Hondt procedure, these posts were decided by a 'process akin to the pulling of political straws'.[13] At the same time, the third largest political party, the

Democratic Unionist Party (DUP), claimed its legal entitlement to two cabinet positions but then refused to sit with the full twelve-member executive. This 'ministers in opposition' strategy combined with the dual-premiership which was an explicit expression of power-sharing encapsulated the real-world prize of engineering, an inclusionary consociation. Moreover, as Chapter 5 illustrated, post-devolution voting patterns exhibited a very clear polarization amongst the sectarian communities. In this context, Wilson suggested that the competing ethno-national constitutional visions in the province (Northern Ireland as British versus Northern Ireland as Irish) left precious little common ground, in terms of a shared territorial commitment, on which to build a governing consensus.

The contrast between Wales and Northern Ireland during 1997–2007 was therefore marked, and yet both processes raised distinct questions about the future of the UK as a union or unitary state. A comparative perspective provides a valuable reference point from which to engage with these questions about the capacity or resources of majoritarian governments to control devolutionary dynamics, once an initial degree of statutory decentralization has occurred. Political parties, for example, can be viewed as a critical form of organizational social capital through which national governments can seek to retain a degree of control or leverage at the sub-national level through informal networks and patronage powers. And yet, the introduction of devolution based on a proportional form of electoral system greatly reduced the likelihood of any one party dominating at the sub-national level. At the same time, the Labour Party in Wales and Scotland has been forced to try and develop a distinct sense of popular identity separate to that of the national party—the 'clear red water' strategy discussed in Chapter 6.

In Scotland, these intra-party dynamics and a ratchet-like effect are also observable. The election of a SNP minority government in 2007 provided a powerful glimpse of the potentially major cleavages that may, over time, occur. Within weeks of winning office, the SNP executive published a white paper, promoting independence and calling for a referendum on the topic to be held by 2011. Although surveys suggest that the Scottish public do not want independence, and nor do the unionist parties that hold a majority in the Scottish Parliament, there is general support for increased powers.[14] As such, although the unionist parties have refused to engage with the SNP's 'national conversation' about Scotland's future they have established a separate Constitutional Commission to explore possible adjustments to the original devolution settlement.

189

The analysis of developments in Scotland and Wales might be interpreted as an example of significant change in relation to the division of powers within the UK. And yet, the post-1997 pattern of devolution has been highly imbalanced and has led to what Jeffrey refers to as 'the lopsided state'.[15] This imbalance relates to the fact that although significant levels of devolution have been implemented at the geographical periphery, the largest component nation within England, remains highly centralized. This in itself raises significant questions about the statecraft of New Labour, and particularly about whether the division of powers within the UK was ever forged on a coherent or explicit set of values.

10.2.3 *The centralisaization of the core*

English regional government, with the exception of London, proved an apparently insurmountable constitutional conundrum for New Labour during 1997–2007. It was simply never able to build a consensus within or beyond the Labour Party, or articulate a shared vision more generally about how, why, and what powers should be devolved to the English regions.[16] Appointed Regional Chambers were established under the Regional Development Agencies Act 1998 with the role of feeding business-related opinions into the RDAs. As Chapter 9 noted, although the role of regional chambers has been subsequently expanded, they have not formed the basis of a democratic regional framework.

In May 2002, the government published *Your Region, Your Choice*, outlining its plans for elected regional assemblies which involved a modest range of powers and the use of an AMS electoral similar. The Regional Assemblies (Preparations) Act 2003 made provisions for pre-legislative referendums to be held to create such assemblies, but in November 2004 voters in the North-East of England emphatically rejected the proposals by 78 per cent to 22 per cent. As a result, the government abandoned plans for similar referendums in two other English regions. Two factors help explain this emphatic public rejection: (*a*) the referendum was held at the end of the 2001–5 parliament when the government was deeply unpopular, not least about the Iraq War, and it may therefore have formed something of a lightning-rod for broader anti-government sentiment at the time; (*b*) research also suggests that the public were sceptical that the proposed assembly would be anything other than 'just another expensive talking shop' due to its limited powers.[17]

The paradox of this position is that the only existing directly elected regional assembly—the Greater London Assembly (GLA)—had by this point proved itself as a powerful actor. Although the specific model of devolution offered to the English regions was slightly different to that implemented under the Greater London Authority Act 1998, the GLA still governed through a similar model of 'strategic' powers that were dependent upon other agencies for delivery. The establishment of the GLA was approved by 72 per cent of Londoners, and it has played a key role in relation to introducing congestion charges, reducing crime, and securing the 2012 Olympics, and this has been translated into high public confidence and satisfaction levels.[18] And yet, it appears that regional government of a similar form was not considered a credible governance tool beyond London. In July 2007, the government published proposals to alter the structure of English regional governance with the result that Regional Assemblies will be abolished in 2010 with their executive functions transferring to RDAs, the responsibilities for spatial strategies moving to central government, and smaller 'Regional Leaders Forums' will take over responsibility for scrutinizing the RDAs in each region.[19] The division of powers within the UK appears then to be moving in quite different directions: devolution and decentralization in relation to Scotland, Wales, and Northern Ireland, but centralization in relation to England—by far the greater part of the UK in terms of population and economy.

Returning to Lijphart's Index of Federalism (Table 10.1), however, underlines that an important change in the nature of democracy in the UK has occurred. From the index score of 1.0 for 1945–96, the devolutionary reforms since 1997 have led to the creation of an institutional structure somewhere between Lijphart's 'Unitary and Decentralized' category (2.0) and a 'Semi-federal' structure (3.0). The quasi-federal nature of the UK's division of powers would therefore receive an index score of 2.5, which takes it much closer to the mean score of 2.3 for all thirty-six countries within Lijphart's study. So, significant change has undoubtedly occurred, and yet locating these changing patterns of governance back within the broader theories of federalism and the discourse of constitutionalism reveals a number of issues, anomalies, and inconsistencies.

10.3 The shadow of majoritarianism

Tomaney is probably correct to suggest that 'historians assessing the achievements of Tony Blair's 'New' Labour government will doubtless place devolution. . . . near the head of the list'.[20] And yet, it is equally important to acknowledge where the logic of decentralization was not applied. This chapter has attempted to provide a balanced assessment of both decentralization and centralization during 1997–2007, and it has identified the potential for further political mobilization of long-standing territorial cleavages within the UK. This section drills down still further and reflects upon what this chapter's examination of V6 suggests about (a) the governing logic of New Labour, and (b) how this connects with other variables on the federal–unitary dimension.

The culture and values of majoritarianism are embedded deep within the UK's political tradition. Sharing power is therefore an unfamiliar experience that is likely to provoke certain majoritarian impulses. This was particularly evident in 1998, when New Labour sought to use its powers of party patronage to foist their preferred candidates into devolved leadership positions (Frank Dobson in London and Alun Michael in Wales). More broadly, however, the devolution legislation has been carefully designed *within* the contours of parliamentary sovereignty. The devolved institutions are neither treated nor intended to be coequals with Parliament. The dispersal of power is contingent; not constitutionally guaranteed or entrenched. In this regard, the constitutional rigidity that is a feature of many consensual polities has been declined in favour of flexibility and, as such, the devolution legislation possesses no 'higher order' status and can be altered by parliamentary majorities. The fact that the legislation was approved by a popular referendum, and that a clear centrifugal dynamic exists in Scotland and Wales does increase the political costs associated with any future attempt to limit or reduce the division of powers, but that does not change the fact that the shadow of majoritarianism hangs over the devolutionary process.

The implications of 'executive devolution' rather than any form of federalism takes on added emphasis when observed alongside the fact that devolution within the UK has been a peripheral process: England remains highly and increasingly centralized. Although Rokkan and Urwin argue that 'any attempt to solve one peripheral problem cannot be insulated from the rest of the state: a spillover effect is almost inevitable' the situation in the UK seems to suggest both spill-over (notably in relation to Wales and Scotland) and spill-back (in relation to the English regions).[21] The bulk of the UK, therefore, remains governed in a highly centralized manner.

Reflecting on the overall process of devolution throughout 1997–2007 allows us to identify a number of governing traits that can be located within the arguments regarding bi-constitutionality and constitutional anomie that were made in the first part of this book. Alterations to the division of powers within the UK since 1997 have not occurred alongside any detailed constitutional analysis or theorizing, and this argument can be justified at a number of levels. At the mechanical or micro-political level, despite the fact that Mitchell has consistently emphasized how 'asymmetrical devolution creates asymmetrical problems' New Labour consistently failed to assess how devolution in one sphere would have knock-on consequences for other elements of the constitutional configuration.[22] Scotland, Wales, Northern Ireland, and the English regions were all viewed and acted upon in isolation. The relationship between devolution and the composition and processes of both Houses of Parliament, the structural implications of devolution for the territorial ministerial departments, the West Lothian question, or questions surrounding financial redistribution—to mention just a few issues—were never addressed in a coherent or pre-emptive manner. For a government that has been rhetorically committed to 'joined-up' government and theoretically informed policy-relevant research, the failure to examine devolution 'in the round' seems particularly anomalous.

And yet, above these institutional issues lay a number of much broader meta-constitutional questions about which the government has been equally silent. First, there has been little explicit comment about the limits of devolution. How much difference is possible, or manageable within a common state? What limits need to be set, and how might they be policed? What are the principles and values of unionism in the twenty-first century? What is the purpose of 'shared statehood'? What are the rules of the game? During 1997–2007, however, the government refused to engage with these issues. This failure to articulate the limits, values, and principles underpinning the devolution process flows into a second concern regarding the mechanisms for conflict resolution. In the wake of devolution the pre-existing mechanisms of conflict resolution—ad hoc informal bi-lateral negotiations conducted in an atmosphere of collegiality and goodwill—continued. It appeared that as long as the same party was in government throughout the devolved institutions, a degree of policy congruence, informality, and intra-party benevolence would lubricate the system. Observers, however, highlighted that those conditions were unlikely to persist, and at some point a more formalized system of conflict resolution was likely to prove necessary.[23]

The 2007 elections did deliver 'governments of different political persuasions', but the core executive's mechanisms for inter-governmental conflict resolution are yet to be renewed. Further, the government has rejected recommendations targeted at the formalization of inter-governmental relations on the basis of a belief that ministers and officials from the territories involved will continue to work together in a constructive and largely informal manner in the way they do now as 'second nature irrespective of the political persuasion of the administration involved'.[24] The government is therefore relying on the 'good chaps theory of government' instead of engaging in detailed constitutional theorizing and planning. And yet, 'what is clear is that the status quo is not much of an option ... The scale of the dysfunctions of the current arrangements and their as yet unchecked centrifugal logic suggests that muddling through will not be enough'.[25]

Devolution has therefore been significant; especially true when viewed against the innate conservatism of the UK's constitutional tradition. In terms of gauging and understanding the extent of this reform, it may well be that analysts are still close to the actual events to comprehend their true impact which may only become apparent in the medium- or long-term as future governments struggle to stem the flow of consequences arising from the initial devolutionary measures implemented during 1997–2007. However, V6 should not be viewed in isolation. Lijphart's framework emphasizes the existence of relationships between the division of power and the other four variables that form the federal–unitary dimension. This reflects the manner in which constitutionalism is predicated on the notion that there should be certain limits on executive action. These limits protect a certain domain or set of authoritative values that are viewed as central to the effective functioning of a democracy. As a result, certain antimajoritarian institutions or 'auxiliary precautions' may be established to interpret, regulate, and enforce that sphere of action. Federalism on its own is therefore viewed as insufficient to guarantee that future governments could be trusted to abide by the letter and spirit of the constitution, and for this reason federal polities commonly make use of a number of mechanisms in order to embed the division of powers and constrain the constitutional flexibility of the national government.

A degree of constitutional rigidity is therefore achieved through mechanisms including a strong second chamber with a role in promoting the views of the regions, a demanding constitutional amendment processes, and a Supreme Court with the capacity to strike down legislation. Examining how New Labour approached the issues of bicameralism (V7, Chapter 11), constitutional amendment (V8, Chapter 12), and judicial review (V9, Chapter 13) therefore provides critical insights into the changing nature of democracy in the UK, as well as the underlying logic or statecraft behind this process.

V6 Index of federalism conclusion

Lijphart's UK score 1945–96	1.0
Lijphart's UK score 1971–96	1.0
Updated UK score 1997–2007	2.5

Notes

1. Gamble, A (2002) 'Divided, Different, But Not a Disaster', *The Times Higher*, 4 January, p. 22.
2. Norris *op. cit.* (2002), p. 881.
3. Lijphart *op. cit.* (1999), p. 185.
4. Elazar, D (1997) 'Contrasting Unitary and Federal Systems', *International Political Science Review*, 18(3), 237–51.
5. See Watts, R (2001) 'Models of Federal Power Sharing', *International Social Science Journal*, 53(167), 23–32; Russell, M (2001) 'What Are Second Chambers For?' *Parliamentary Affairs*, 54(3), 442–58; Vaubel, R (1996) 'Constitutional Safeguards Against the Centralisation of Power in Federal States', *Constitutional Political Economy*, 7(2), 79–102.
6. Horowitz, D (2006) 'Constitutional Courts', *Journal of Democracy*, 17(4), 125–37; La Porta, R et al. (2004) 'Judicial Checks and Balances', *Journal of Political Economy*, 112(2), 445–70; Hirschl, R (2008) 'The Judicialization of Mega-politics and the Rise of Political Courts', *Annual Review of Political Science*, 11, 93–118.
7. Lijphart *op. cit.* (1999), p. 188.
8. Mitchell, J (2008) *Devolution in the United Kingdom*. Manchester: Manchester University Press.
9. Giordano, B and Roller, E (2004) 'Te Para Todos? A Comparison of the Process of Devolution in Spain and the UK', *Environment and Planning A*, 36, 2163–181.
10. Scully, R, Wyn Jones, R, and Dafydd, T (2004) 'Turnout, Participation and Legitimacy in Post-Devolution Wales', *British Journal of Political Science*, 34(3), 519–38.
11. Wyn Jones, R and Scully, R (2009) 'Welsh Devolution: The End of the Beginning, and the Beginning of . . . ?' in A Trench, ed., *The State of the Nations 2008*. Exter: Imprint, pp. 57–87.
12. Osmond, J (2008) 'Charter 88: A Welsh View from the Periphery'. Paper to the Charter 88 Twentieth Anniversary Conference, University of Oxford, 3–4 July.
13. Wilford, R (2008) 'Consociational Government: Inside the Devolved Northern Ireland Executive', in R. Taylor, ed., *Consociational Theory*. London: Routledge.
14. See Jeffery, C (2009) 'The Dynamics of Devolution', in M Flinders, et al., eds., *The Oxford Handbook of British Politics*. Oxford: Oxford University Press.
15. Jeffery, C (2006) 'Devolution and the Lopsided State' in P Dunleavy, R Heffernan, P Cowley, and C Hay, eds., *Developments in British Politics 8*. London: Palgrave, pp. 138–59.

16. Sandford, M (2005) *The New Governance of the English Regions*. Basingstoke: Palgrave Macmillan.
17. Rallings, C and Thrasher, M (2006) 'Just Another Expensive Talking Shop', *Regional Studies*, 40, 927–36.
18. Margetts, H and Dunleavy, P (2005) *The 2004 GLA London Elections Study*, Devolution Briefings No. 33.
19. HM Treasury (2007) Review of Sub-National Economic Development and Regeneration.
20. Tomaney, J (2002) 'End of the Empire State?' *International Journal of Urban and Regional Research*, 24, 675.
21. Rokkan, S and Urwin, D (1983) *Economy, Territory, Identity*. Sage: London, p. 187.
22. Mitchell, J (2002) 'England and the Centre', *Regional and Federal Studies*, 36, 760.
23. HL 28 (2002–3) *Devolution: Inter-Institutional Relations in the United Kingdom*, Select Committee on the Constitution, Session 2002–3, p. 5.
24. Cm. 5780 (2003) *Government's Response to the Second Report of the Select Committee on the Constitution*, p. 3.
25. Jeffery *op. cit.* (2009).

Chapter 11

V7. Unicameralism–Bicameralism

The whole issue [Houe of Lords reform] seemed to bore the Prime Minister
[Tony Blair], who gave no clear indication of his views.[1]

Chapter 10 examined the division of powers within the UK and how it had changed significantly during 1997–2007. However, it also emphasized how these devolutionary measures had been implemented *within* rather than *instead of* the majoritarian Westminster Model. How the centrifugal forces of devolution could be managed within the centripetal logic of this model was a concern that had not been accompanied by any official constitutional analysis or theorizing concerning the future of the union. New Labour's approach to devolution and the division of powers consequently provides a critical case of Marquand's critique concerning 'a revolution of sleepwalkers who don't quite know where they are going or why'.[2] This notion of 'constitutional sleepwalking' provides the link between V6 and V7.

Although it has embarked on a process of reform in relation to the structure, composition, and processes of bicameralism in the UK the government has never been able to articulate exactly what it is seeking to achieve in relation to the Upper House. More significantly, it is possible to identify a gap between the government's stated *principles* and its actual *practice* in relation to this V7 which (again) can be explained with reference to the influence of the Westminster Model as the prism or framework through which the executive has interpreted the limits of reform. Of particular significance, in the context of this book's emphasis on the challenges of political analysis in relation to constitutional change, is the existence of a scholarly debate concerning an appropriate index score for bicameralism during 1997–2007. The parameters of this debate are, however, fairly narrow.

Flinders' conclusion that the UK has moved from a system of 'between medium strength and weak bicameralism' to one 'which could now be better described as simply weak bicameralism or even a 'one and a half chamber system' has been challenged by Russell, who suggests that the relative strength of the Second Chamber has not been weakened and may even have been strengthened during 1997–2007. This difference of opinion is important for two main reasons: (*a*) it provides insights into the challenges of political analysis where resource-dependencies and exchanges are generally played out through informal channels and where the executive has clear reserve powers, but may be reluctant to deploy them too often; (*b*) it is possible to argue that the Index Score for Bicameralism is of added importance due to the conclusion in Chapter 7 regarding 'executive dominance'. In this sense, the role of the Second Chamber as an anti-majoritarian institution takes on added significance.

This chapter concludes that during 1997–2007, the UK's bicameral system remained somewhere between 'medium strength' and 'weak' and as such, a score of 2.5 remains valid. This conclusion suggests that Flinders' earlier assessment under-estimated the vigour and dynamism that members of the 'interim' House of Lords have displayed since 'Stage One' reform of the Second Chamber in 1998. It also reflects the fact that Flinders overlooked one critical element of Lords reform where power clearly was transferred away from the executive—power in the form of patronage-capacity through the creation of the House of Lords Appointments Commission (HLAC). At the same time, it seeks to locate Russell's more buoyant assessment against the latent capacity and *real politik* of executive politics. In order to justify this conclusion, this chapter is divided into three sections. The first section reviews Lijphart's approach to this variable, and how in particular he derived an index score of bicameralism. The second section briefly describes the process of change in relation to V7 during the decade following 1997, which feeds into an analysis of the degree to which these measures should be interpreted as a transition away from a power-hoarding in the third section. The final section also locates the analysis of V7 within the context of emerging patterns of bi-constitutionalism and the related constitutional anomie thesis.

11.1 Concentration versus division of legislative power

The majoritarian model with its power-hoarding emphasis calls for the concentration of legislative power in one single legislative chamber, thereby removing the number of potential veto points within the constitutional configuration. The consensus model, by contrast, with its power-sharing emphasis, is characterized by a bicameral legislature in which power is formally divided between two differently constituted chambers. The concentration versus division of legislative power is therefore connected with the broader topic of constitutional flexibility and rigidity as the Second Chamber is likely to form some form of constraint upon the executive. Comparative constitutional history therefore reveals countries either shifting from unicameralism to bicameral structures (Morocco 1996) or vice versa (e.g. New Zealand 1950, Denmark 1953, Sweden 1970, Iceland 1991), as perspectives on the utility of centralized governance shift within those polities.[3] Clearly, however, attempts to alter the balance of power within a polity need not involve a wholesale shift from one basic model of legislative design to another but may, more commonly, involve measures that are designed to transfer resources in such a way so as to amend or adjust the existing distribution of power in some way.

It is for this reason that Lijphart's methodological framework employs three variables in order to derive an index score of bicameralism, and thereby assign a score to each of the countries in his study. These are:

Variable 1. Bicameral versus unicameral systems.
Variable 2. Symmetrical versus asymmetrical systems.
Variable 3. Congruent versus incongruent systems.

The two chambers of bicameral legislatures may vary in a number of ways in relation to composition and role. Most generally, the Second Chambers tend to have: (*a*) smaller memberships than the first chambers (the UK proving a notable exception); (*b*) longer legislative terms of office, with the UK again being notable through the use of life membership; and (*c*) frequently employ staggered election processes.[4] More important, however, in relation to the relative balance of power between the two houses (and therefore the V7 scoring), is the formal constitutional powers that the two chambers possess. As the House of Lords' powers are restricted to being able to only delay most bills by around one year, it fits within a general pattern in which the Second Chamber is subordinate to the first chamber and an element of this relationship involves the first chambers' capacity to overturn negative votes. In the UK the formal powers of the House of Lords indicates clearly that Parliament is an asymmetrical or highly unequal model of bicameralism, and this is reflected through the manner in which executive is primary responsible to the lower house.

Although formal constitutional powers are clearly important in determining the strength of bicameralism within any polity, it would be overly simplistic to rely on them as a sole indicator of the nature of resource-dependencies. The method of selecting members in particular can be critical in relation to whether a Second Chamber seeks to use its formal powers of rejection or delay, or indeed whether it seeks to embellish these powers through creative discretion or explicit actions that are constitutionally ultra vires (i.e. beyond its formal powers). As the second section of this chapter examines in some detail, the recent history of the House of Lords provides a critical case of this selection and self-perception dynamic.

Appointed Second Chambers arguably lack the democratic legitimacy of an elected chamber, and as a result may adopt a certain self-restraint or 'voluntary impotence' vis-à-vis the elected chamber.[5] This is likely to be greater in cases where the members have been appointed for life, and as a result may have no relationship with the current government. However, perceived inadequacies in the constitutional balance, particularly concerning an extremely dominant executive within a majoritarian polity, may cultivate a more vigorous and energetic attitude amongst members of the Second Chamber and a new-found willingness to use powers that they may have possessed for some time, but had been reluctant to use due to an awareness of their lack of democratic legitimacy. Conversely, the direct election of a Second Chamber may empower it with not only a degree of democratic legitimacy, but also the expectation that it should play an active role in legislative politics.

This notion of rectifying or balancing out constitutional relationships leads into the fact that in many countries the role of the Second Chamber is to over-represent certain minorities or geographical areas. This is clearly linked to the precepts of consociational or power-sharing constitutional logic, and generally leads to an incongruent relationship in terms of the membership between the two chambers, as federal chambers over-represent the smaller component units of the country.[6] This over-representation can be based on a simple principle of equality (e.g. United States, Switzerland), or a graded model in which the distribution of seats is not equal but smaller units are over-represented (as with the German Bundesrat and Canadian Senate). Countries with federal Second Chambers or where certain societal interests have a formal role in the selection of representatives (like France) are therefore incongruent in selection terms. Congruent systems would, conversely, elect members to both chambers by similar methods. As noted here, Lijphart uses the distinction between bicameralism and unicameralism, symmetrical and asymmetrical divisions of power, and congruent and incongruent selection methods to construct the classification system set out in Table 11.1.

Table 11.1 Cameral structure of legislatures, 1945–96

Legislative type	Index score	Examples
Strong bicameralism (symmetrical and incongruent chambers)	4.0	US Switzerland
Medium-strength bicameralism (symmetrical and congruent)	3.0	The Netherlands
Medium-strength bicameralism (asymmetric and incongruent)	3.0	Canada France
Between medium strength and weak bicameralism	2.5	UK Botswana
Weak bicameralism (asymmetrical and congruent chambers)	2.0	Jamaica Trinidad
One-and-a-half chambers	1.5	Norway Iceland
Unicameralism	1.0	Finland Greece

Source: Adapted from Lijphart, A (1999) *Patterns of Democracy* Yale University Press, p. 212.

As Table 11.1 suggests, using this system, the United Kingdom received a consistent index score of 2.5 (on a scale from 1.0 to 4.0, with the latter being strong bicameralism and the former unicameralism) for the period 1945–96 (no change was identified for the period 1971–96). Lijphart justified this score in the following terms,

> ... although the British bicameral legislature deviates from the majoritarian model [by not being unicameral] it does not deviate much: in everyday discussion in Britain 'Parliament' refers almost exclusively to the House of Commons, and the highly asymmetric bicameral system may also be called near uni-cameralism.[7]

In coming to this conclusion, Lijphart echoed the work of Sartori who had similarly described the UK as 'extremely weak bicameralism' which 'shades into unicameralism'.[8] Table 11.1 aids understanding in relation to the Flinders–Russell debate because although both scholars begin their analysis from an acceptance of Lijphart's variable score of 2.5 for V7, they depart in their interpretations of how the trajectory of the UK has evolved since May 1997. Flinders suggests a weakening of bicameralism to the point somewhere between 'weak bicameralism' and a 'one-and-a-half-chamber system (and for this reason records a variable score of 1.75). Whereas, Russell argues that the trajectory of change has been in the opposite direction towards a stronger model of bicameralism. In terms of locating this debate within the wider literature, what is distinctive about Russell's position is that it challenges the general thrust of opinion. Although exceptions do exist—Brazier suggests, for example, that '[the interim House of Lords] has become the only counterweight in the constitution to elective dictatorship'.[9] Most journalistic comment and academic analysis argued that the House of Lords Act 1999 would lead to a weaker and more pliant Second Chamber due to the removal of the largely Conservative hereditary members (see later).[10] This leads us to examine how the nature of bicameralism has unfolded in the UK during 1997–2007.

11.2 New Labour and the House of Lords

Reform of the House of Lords formed a key strand of the Labour Party's 1997 General Election campaign, and their manifesto stated the party's intention to make 'the House of Lords more democratic and representative'.[11] The 1999 House of Lords Act duly removed all but ninety-two hereditary peers from the Lords, and was designed to be 'Stage One' of a reform process that would eventually lead to exclusion of the remaining hereditary peers when reforms to introduce an elected component (i.e. 'Stage Two') were implemented.[12] A Royal Commission, the Wakeham Commission, was established to examine the topic, and its final report of January 2000 recommended that:

(1) a future Second Chamber should have 550 members of which 67, 87, or 195 should be elected;
(2) an independent Appointments Commission should be established to appoint members; and,
(3) that the Commons should remain the principal house of Parliament with the final say on all major issues of public policy.[13]

The government accepted the 'principles underlying the main elements of the Royal Commission', and in May 2000 the PM announced the membership of a non-statutory Appointments Commission for the House of Lords.[14] Plans to create a joint committee of both Houses to take forward the Royal Commission's recommendations were, however, abandoned due to a lack of cross-party consensus. The lack of consensus was not only *between* the parties, but also *within* the main parties, not least the Labour Party. Under New Labour there has never been a clear vision of the role, responsibilities, or composition of a reformed Second Chamber. This reflects traditional tensions within the Labour Party that whilst committed to abolishing the hereditary principle could not agree what to replace it with.

Having won the 2001 General Election with an increased Commons majority, the government sought to proceed with 'Stage 2' reform with the publication of a further white paper—*The House of Lords: Completing the*

Reform—in November 2001. This proposed that one-fifth (120 of 600) of the members of a future Second Chamber should be elected by proportional representation for a term of fifteen years, or possibly less.[15] The proposals received widespread criticism, and 303 (including 165 Labour backbenchers) signed an Early Day Motion supporting a 'wholly or substantially' elected Second Chamber. Of particular significance was the rejection by the government of the Wakeham Commission's recommendation that the independent Appointment Commission should make *all* appointments, even those representing the political parties, and in this sense the government's proposals sought to maintain a critical source of party political patronage. In February 2002, a parliamentary committee added to the pressure on the government by criticizing the government's plans, and by May the government had withdrawn the white paper and had delegated the issue of Lords reform to a Joint Committee of both Houses.[16] The final report of the Joint Committee was published six months later and included a menu of seven options for the composition of a revised Second Chamber.[17] Both Houses voted on these options in February 2003, plus an additional resolution that the Lords be abolished. As Table 11.2 shows, the House of Commons could not reach an agreement on the future composition of a reformed Lords although the general thrust of the votes was in favour of a significant elected component.

While the Commons rejected all the options for change, the wholly appointed 'interim' House of Lords voted in favour of a fully appointed Second Chamber. Not only did this leave the government's plans in disarray, but the free vote also exposed the extent of divisions within the government, with the PM and Lord Chancellor voting in favour of a fully appointed Second Chamber, while the Leader of the House and several other ministers voted in favour of a significant

Table 11.2 Votes in the House of Commons (including tellers) on Lords reform, 4 February 2003

	Abolish	Elect zero	Elect 20%	Elect 40%	Elect 50%	Elect 60%	Elect 80%	Elect all
Aye	174	247	0	0	0	255	283	274
Did not vote	29	23	0	0	0	22	26	30
No	392	325	595	595	595	318	286	291
Majority	−218	−78	−595	−595	−595	−63	−3	−17

Source: McLean, Spirling, and Russell (2003) 'None of the Above', *Political Quarterly*, 74(3), 299.

elected component. The failure of the vote to identify an area of consensus and the obvious intra-executive friction was further exacerbated by the fact that 174 MPs, far more than expected, voted to abolish the Second Chamber completely.[18]

The Joint Committee was reconvened and given the task of exploring how to proceed, but in light of the February 2003 votes, the committee requested that the government provide it with an indication of the executive's current thinking on the role and composition of a revised Second Chamber.[19] The government's response, published in July 2003, encapsulated the extent of frustration and confusion by bluntly stating 'there is no consensus about introducing any elected element in the House of Lords' which provided little by way of a constitutional compass through which the committee could orientate its approach.[20] The relationship between the government and the Joint Committee became even more strained three months later when the Department for Constitutional Affairs published a further consultation paper on the topic—*Constitutional Reform: Next Steps for the House of Lords*—without any advance consultation with the committee.

This document recommended a fully appointed House of Lords, the removal of the ninety-two remaining hereditary peers, and the creation of a statutory Appointments Commission to replace the existing advisory body, and the Queen's Speech in 2003 duly noted the government's intention to bring forward a Bill during the next session. This was a significant development for three reasons. (*a*) First, it indicated the government's intention to proceed on the basis of a purely appointed Second Chamber, and as such formed part of a gradual but consistent drift towards this position within the Labour Party. Secondly, publication without any prior consultation, not even with the Joint Committee fuelled concerns about the government's lack of probity in relation to constitutional reform. The government was perceived as acting in a rather desperate manner in which there was little evidence of a coherent or systematic vision of what it was trying to achieve, or how reform of the Second Chamber had implications for other constitutional actors. The issue of governmental integrity was a particular issue due to the manner in which the government had initially secured the support of the Conservative Party in the Lords through an informal agreement that the ninety-two hereditary peers would not be removed until 'stage two' to democratize the Second Chamber had been completed. In bringing forward proposals to abolish the remaining hereditary members, but without making the future composition of the Second Chamber any more democratic, the government was widely condemned for attempting to renege on an inter-party agreement that had been widely acknowledged and had cost the Leader of the Conservatives in the Lords, Lord Cranborne, his post.[21]

Following on from this (and thirdly), the publication of yet another white paper contributed to a growing sense that New Labour was not committed to moving away from a power-sharing model of democracy. This suspicion gained credence through the fact that the removal of the hereditary peers had been to the Labour government's statistical advantage in terms of composition as it effectively removed the Lords long-standing Conservative majority (Figure 11.1).

In March 2004, the Secretary of State for Constitutional Affairs announced that a decision had been taken not to proceed with the House of Lords Bill, but that the government would return to the issue in their manifesto for the next general election. Nearly three years later, in February 2007, the government published another white paper—*The House of Lords: Reform*—which contained the recommendations of a cross-party working group that had been chaired by Jack Straw in his capacity as

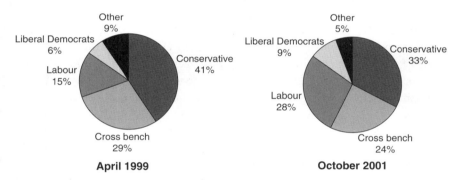

Figure 11.1 Composition of the House of Lords by party, before and after the House of Lords Act 1999

Party	April 1999		October 1999	
	Members	Per cent	Members	Per cent
Conservative	471	41	232	33
Labour	179	15	200	28
Liberal Democrat	72	6	67	9
Cross Bench	353	29	174	24
Other	112	9	38	5
Total	1187	100	711	100

Source: House of Commons Library, Research paper 01/77 (2001), p.12.

Leader of the House.[22] The central recommendation was for a hybrid Second Chamber consisting of an equal number of appointed and elected members. In March 2007, both houses debated and voted on this recommendation, but the Commons voted by a significant majority for an all-elected Second Chamber—while the Lords voted, by an even larger majority, for an all-appointed House. Tony Blair's decade as PM therefore came to an end with the future of the House of Lords appearing as unclear and confused at it had been at the beginning.

Having described the process of reform that has occurred in relation to V7 during 1997–2007, it is straightforward to understand why the vast majority of observers, in general, and Flinders in particular, have come to the conclusion that the balance of power shifted towards the lower house, and therefore a weaker model of bicameralism. The removal of the hereditary peers, while not providing the Labour government with a majority in the Second Chamber, did at least remove 'the permanent Conservative majority' that had previously existed, and which Lijphart had acknowledged.[23] 'Stage One' could therefore be interpreted as achieving a significant weakening or dilution of a potential constitutional veto-point. And yet, the danger of this interpretation is that it risks *assuming* rather than *proving* a correlation between reform and behaviour; it presupposes that a Second Chamber in which no party has overall control would be more amenable to a Labour government than one with an inbuilt Conservative majority. And yet, existing evidence challenges this assumption. The law of unintended consequences can throw up counter-intuitive constitutional dynamics that take us back to the notion of auto-limitation discussed earlier, while also preparing us for questions about constitutional anomie and morality which form the focus of later chapters. Section 11.3 looks beyond descriptions and assumptions by examining the evidence on how the relationship between the House of Commons and House of Lords evolved as a result of the reforms that have been outlined in this section.

11.3 Unintended consequences

It is possible to argue that the issue of reforming the Second Chamber encapsulated New Labour's general approach to constitutional reform during 1997–2007. The government adopted a particularistic approach to democratic renewal rather than a systematic approach, and this left them strategically and intellectually isolated and unable to articulate a clear vision of either their ambitions for the Second Chamber or how a reformed Lords would complement other elements of the reform programme.[24] The diagnosis of constitutional anomie that is developed in this book was therefore palpable in relation to reform of the Lords throughout 1997–2007. Of particular significance, in light of Lijphart's models of democracy is the manner in which New Labour's approach to this issue was always tightly bound within an explicit commitment to maintaining the Westminster Model, and particularly the pre-eminence of the Commons. And yet, committing themselves to establish a more representative and democratic Second Chamber while not threatening the position of the Commons created three interconnected challenges:

1. Making the Second Chamber 'more representative and democratic' would clearly empower the Second Chamber with a heightened sense of legitimacy vis-à-vis the House of Commons.
2. This heightened sense of legitimacy would have to be accompanied with the exercise of an appropriate range of powers which ascribed the Second Chamber with a meaningful practical role.
3. The heightened democratic legitimacy of the Second Chamber, the likelihood that its members would assume they had a duty and right to play an active legislative role, the provision of specified powers alongside a clear statement of roles and duties must all be delivered without threatening the ultimate supremacy of the Commons.

These circuitous challenges refocus our attention on the debate outlined earlier between Flinders and Russell, as to whether Stage One reform of the Lords weakened or strengthened the position of the Second Chamber vis-à-vis the Commons. Two factors weigh on the side of Russell's interpretation. These are, first, the number of legislative defeats suffered by the government in the Lords since 1998 which certainly reflects a more active and less pliant Second Chamber, and, secondly, the transfer of patronage-resources away from the executive to an independent Appointments Commission. Flinders' interpretation, by contrast, is supported by changes to the composition of the Lords, and a refusal by the government to countenance reforms that would increase the formal powers of the Second Chamber.

There is little doubt that removing the vast majority of hereditary peers affected the political composition and political culture of the Lords because it left no party with an overall majority (Table 11.2). Prior to the House of Lords Act 1999, the Conservatives held 471 seats to Labour's 179, while the Liberal Democrats held 72, and the cross benchers 353, but the removal of all but 92 hereditary peers left the Labour, Conservative, and the crossbencher groupings with roughly 200 seats, and the Liberal Democrats with around 70. In addition to flattening out the party distribution within the Lords, removing most of the hereditary members also had a significant cultural affect on the chamber. In this sense, the Lords felt empowered with a certain legitimacy and confidence to play a more active role. This led King to wonder whether 'perhaps the very fact that the reformed House of Lords was dismissed as transitional made its members feel somewhat demob happy'.[25]

Russell therefore bases her argument on an analysis of divisions in the Lords since 1999, which shows that government suffered a total of 390 defeats in the Lords between 'Stage One' reform and 2007.[26] On its own, the data for defeats in divisions is a fairly crude indicator of V7 because it fails to acknowledge that the Lords does not, unlike the Commons, generally vote on whole government bills at second and third reading. Votes are on specific amendments, and therefore one single Bill may be responsible for a great number of defeats. In this sense, the statistical outcome of Russell's analysis risks portraying a more active or influential Second Chamber than actually exists. Moreover, the executive, through tight party control in the Commons, generally enjoys the capacity to overturn any amendment made in the Lords when a Bill returns to the Commons.

Russell's research takes these factors into account by examining the number of occasions on which the Lords insisted on their amendments. This reveals thirty-three such occasions between the House of Lords Act 1999 and 2007 when the Lords resisted the Commons' attempts to remove their amendments. Many of these defeats resulted in significant changes to government policy, and it is therefore possible to construct an argument that V7 has been changed significantly due to the unintended consequences of reforms to the Lords. It is in this vein that Russell explicitly challenges Lijphart's description of the UK as a 'near-unicameral' legislature and Tsebelis' classification of the UK as having only one veto player—the governing party.[27] Although the Lords do not possess an absolute veto, Russell argues that 'Stage One' of the reform process has affectively increased the number of veto players, thereby 'creating a far more plural system at Westminster'.[28] Accepting this thesis would logically lead to a revision of Lijphart's variable score in a manner that suggested a more balanced relationship between the Upper and Lower Houses: a score that sought to reflect a degree of modified majoritarianism. And yet, there exists a powerful antithesis.

The primary element of this counter-thesis is that the House of Commons remains the pre-eminent chamber for four reasons:

1. It provides the executive (and can remove it).
2. It is popularly elected.
3. It has the sole responsibility for raising and spending taxation.
4. The formal powers of the Lords have not been increased.

This pre-eminence is reflected not only in the procedures of Parliament, but also in the convention that the Commons will prevail over the Lords. As a result, the Commons always has the last word over legislation and may seek to overturn Lords' defeats when a Bill returns there for approval. Although Russell's research suggests that during 1999–2007, the government only overturned around 40 per cent of defeats, this does not change the basic fact that the executive generally has the capacity to reverse any defeats it suffers in the Lords should it wish to do so. This forces any analysis to take into account the existence of *latent* or *potential* powers within a constitutional arrangement; which Russell clearly does, but in a rather unidimensional manner: 'the chamber [Lords] has not changed its formal powers, but seems more willing to use them'. And yet, this veils the counterfactual that the Commons remains the pre-eminent chamber and a future government may well be more willing to use its control of the House of Commons to reverse amendments or even reform the Second Chamber in a weakening manner.

The second element of this counter-argument steps back from the legislative process and reviews how recent reforms have affected the Lords' capacity to play a role in the full range of Parliament's responsibilities. Parliament has two central functions: a legislative function and a scrutiny function. Although 'Stage One' reform may have enhanced the Lords willingness to play a greater role in the legislative process, as reflected in the number of government defeats, there is little evidence to suggest that the balance of power has shifted between the Lords and the executive in relation to its scrutiny capacity. The argument promoted by Russell therefore risks overstating the extent of change in relation to just one facet of the Lords' work.

Finally, there is a basic issue of causation to be addressed. Russell assumes a direct relationship between defeats in the Lords and the government revising or abandoning (often major) Bills. The actual correlation between these two political phenomena is actually extremely complex. The government may decide to revise or amend a piece of legislation in response to a range of pressures, of which defeat in the Lords may well be one factor, but this is quite different from inferring a direct relationship. The examples that Russell deploys in support of her thesis, 'the *Lords blocking* a new offence of religious hatred, preventing the merger of the criminal justice inspectorates, and adding judicial safeguards to anti-terrorist legislation' (emphasis added) display this tendency to assume causation. Although, the Lords may well have been one actor operating within the policy networks surrounding each policy, it was certainly not unique in voicing opposition or alternative measures. Put slightly differently, the position of the Lords in relation to the Commons was strengthened by a highly political context, but the executive may have been less willing to concede ground had the Lords not been one element of a broader critical orchestra.

In essence, the debate between Flinders and Russell is quite simple and rests on a different approach to how Lijphart's themes of congruence (composition) and symmetry (power) are assessed. The negative assessment of Flinders is based on (*a*) a change in the composition of the Lords which removed the inbuilt Conservative majority and (*b*) a refusal by the government to countenance reforms that would increase the formal powers of the Second Chamber. The positive assessment of Russell, by contrast, rests on the contention that removing the (largely Conservative) hereditary peers advantaged specific sections within the Lords (specifically the Liberal Democrats), while also engendering a cultural change by which its members felt more legitimate and as a result were more willing to assert themselves against the Lower House. 'Using Lijphart's terms, this moves Britain in the direction of consensus democracy'.[29] Russell's research is persuasive and although it might be over-stating the case to argue that the Lords has been strengthened during 1997–2007, the available research does suggest that Flinders' previous assessment is problematic. It is therefore possible to conclude by accepting Russell's account and inserting a variable score of 2.5—'Between Medium Strength and Weak Bicameralism' (Table 11.1)—that does not suggest that the Lords has been weakened.

Indeed, it is possible to draw upon an alternative source of evidence to bolster Russell's argument that 'Stage One' reform of the Lords has not weakened bicameralism in the UK. The HLAC recommends individuals to the Queen for appointment as non-party-political life peers and scrutinizes all those individuals nominated by political parties. The creation of the HLAC in May 2000 therefore reduced the executive's patronage capacity. The manner in which the government had effectively created a new constitutional veto player was made very clear in March 2006, when several of the Labour Party's nominations for life peerages were rejected by the HLAC. It was later revealed that they had loaned large amounts of money to the Labour Party with the implication that the offer of a peerage had formed the incentive for the loan.

Irrespective of the Crown Prosecution Service's final decision not to pursue criminal charges against individuals associated with New Labour, the 'Cash for Peerages' scandal forms an important part of this chapter's analysis of bicameralism during 1997–2007 due to the manner in which it provides an insight into the mentality and statecraft of New Labour. The government had created the HLAC with a remit to impose an explicit regulatory framework for appointments to the Second Chamber in order to respond to public concern regarding political patronage and corruption. It had also introduced tight rules on party funding through the Political Parties, Elections, and Referendums Act 2000 in order to address public concerns regarding private donations and party funding. To then seek to circumvent this legislation by exploiting a statutory ambiguity through which loans are not classed as donations was clearly unprincipled. Reform of the House of Lords was intended to demonstrate the government's propriety, and yet evidence of the link between party political loans and the Labour Party's list of nominations may well have undermined, rather than enhanced, public trust.

Set in the context of Lijphart's original research, an Index of Bicameralism score of 2.5 represents 'No Change'. This conclusion for V7 corresponds with the findings of alternative methods for measuring this variable drawn from the fields of comparative politics and policy performance.[30] Looking at the issue of V7 more widely, in terms of statecraft and executive marginalization and veto-capacity, it is reasonably clear that although New Labour may have been *rhetorically* committed to strengthening and democratizing the House of Lords during the run-up to the 1997 General Election, this rhetoric veiled a far more ambiguous position. Lord Richard's (Leader of the House of Lords between May 1997 and July 1998) reflections reveal that he simply could not persuade the cabinet to support any measures that may have significantly altered the balance of power.[31] And yet, it is possible to identify the 'Blair paradox' in relation to V7 because New Labour were willing to devolve power, in this case to the HLAC, while at the same time seeking to retain powers through ministerial opt-outs, vetoes, or, in this case, evading the principles and processes that it had recently implemented.

Having now examined V6 and V7, it is possible to look for the first indications of inter-connectedness or internal consistency along the federal–unitary dimension. As Lijphart found, there is usually a strong

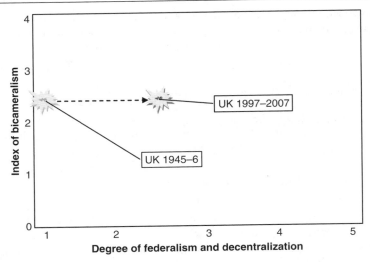

Figure 11.2 Relationship between V6 (division of power) and V7 (unicameralism–bicameralism) for the UK

empirical correlation between V6 and V7. Figure 11.1 shows the position of the UK for 1997–2007 (and 1945–96), when the two indexes of federalism and bicameralism are correlated.

Figure 11.1 reflects the existence of significant change along the federal–unitary axis, but stability along the unicameralism–bicameralism axis. The inconsistency arising from the position of the UK for 1997–2007 arises from the expectation that an increase in V6 would be accompanied by an increase in the index score for V7. The relationship between federalism and bicameralism is therefore generally positive. This internal discrepancy is not significant on its own, but may become so if the scores for V8, V9, and V10 reveal similar anomalies which would, in turn, aid in understanding and help us dissect with greater precision this book's arguments concerning bi-constitutionality and constitutional anomie.

V7 Index of bicameralism conclusion

Lijphart's UK score 1945–96	2.5
Lijphart's UK score 1971–96	2.5
Updated UK score 1997–2007	2.5

Notes

1. King *op. cit.* (2007), p. 303.
2. Marquand, D (1999) 'Populism or Pluralism? New Labour and the Constitution'. Mishcon Lecture, UCL.
3. See Tsebelis, G and Money, G (1997) *Bicameralism*. Cambridge: Cambridge University Press; Kettere, J (2001) 'From One Chamber to Two: The Case of Morocco', *Journal of Legislative Studies*, 7(1), 135–50.
4. See Borthwick, R (2001) 'Methods of Composition of Second Chambers', *Journal of Legislative Studies*, 7(1), 19–26.
5. Shell, D (1999) 'To Revise and Deliberate', in S Patterson and A Mughan, eds., *Senates: Bicameralism in the Contemporary World*. Ohio: Ohio State University.
6. Russell, M (2001) 'The Territorial Role of Second Chambers', *Journal of Legislative Studies*, 7(1), 105–18.
7. Lijphart *op. cit.* (1999), p. 18.
8. Sartori, G (1994) *Comparative Constitutional Engineering*. Basingstoke: Macmillan, p. 188.
9. Brazier, R (2008) *Constitutional Reform*. Oxford: Oxford University Press, p. 70.
10. See, for example, *The Guardian*, 9 February 1999.
11. Labour Party (1997) *New Labour: Because Britain Deserves Better*. London: Labour Party, p. 32–3.
12. Cm. 4183 (1999) *Modernising Parliament: Reforming the House of Lords*; for a detailed discussion, see Cockerill, M (2001) 'The Politics of Second Chamber Reform', *Journal of Legislative Studies*, 7(1), 119–34.
13. Cm. 4534 (2000) *A House for the Future*.
14. HL (2000) *Hansard*, 610, col. 912, 7 March.
15. Cm. 5291 (2001) *The House of Lords: Completing the Reform*.
16. HC 494 (2001–2) *The Second Chamber—Continuing the Reform*. Fifth Report from the Public Administration Select Committee, Session 2001–2.
17. HL 17/HC 171 (2002–3) *House of Lords Reform*. First report of the Joint Committee on House of Lords Reform, Session 2002–3.
18. For a detailed analysis of this vote, see McLean, I, Spirling, A, and Russell, M (2003) 'None of the Above', *Political Quarterly*, 74(3), 298–310.
19. HL 97/HC 668 (2002–3) *House of Lords Reform*. Second report of the Joint Committee on House of Lords Reform, Session 2002–3.
20. HL 155/HC 1027 (2002–3) *House of Lords Reform: Government Reply to the Committee's Second Report*. Second special report of the Joint Committee on House of Lords Reform, Session 2002–3.
21. See http://news.bbc.co.uk/1/hi/uk_politics/3237430.stm
22. Cm. 7027 (2007) *The House of Lords—Reform*.
23. Lijphart *op. cit.* (1999), p. 203.
24. Walters, R (2003) 'The House of Lords', in V Bogdanor, ed., *The British Constitution in the Twentieth Century*. Oxford: British Academy.

25. King *op. cit.* (2007), p. 307.
26. Russell, M and Sciara, M (2007) 'Why Does the Government Get Defeated in the House of Lords?' *British Politics*, 2(3), 300.
27. Tsebelis, G (2002) *Veto Players: How Political Institutions Work*. Princeton: Princeton University Press.
28. Russell and Sciara *op. cit.* (2007), p. 319.
29. Russell, M (2009) 'A Stronger Second Chamber? Assessing the Impact of House of Lords Reform in 1999, and the Lessons for Bi-cameralism', *Political Studies*, 58, 1–24.
30. Vatter, A (2005) 'Bicameralism and Policy Performance', *Journal of Legislative Studies*, 11(2), 194–205.
31. Richard, I and Welfare, D (1999) *Unfinished Business*. London: Vintage.

Chapter 12

V8. Constitutional Amendment

The risk, however, is that a Government with a secure majority in the House of Commons, even if based on the votes of a minority of the electorate, could in principle bring about controversial and ill-considered changes to the constitution without the need to secure consensus support for them.[1]

This chapter examines the constitutional amendment process in the UK. It does this by employing the notions of constitutional *flexibility* and constitutional *rigidity*. In the former, a constitution can be changed by simple-majority votes in the legislature, while in the latter, the same amendment would involve a number of more stringent requirements to be achieved. Democracies around the world employ a range of mechanisms or constitutional safeguards to both impose a degree of constitutional rigidity, and also demonstrate the 'higher order' status of constitutional provisions. The baseline question of this chapter is—to what degree did the degree of constitutional flexibility in relation to constitutional amendments (V8) alter during 1997–2007?

In order to answer this question, the first section of the chapter reviews Lijphart's original research in relation to this variable and specifically his method for devising an Index Score of Constitutional Rigidity. The second section seeks to reapply this methodology to the UK by examining three distinct aspects of constitutional amendment processes: (*a*) the role of the House of Commons; (*b*) the role of the House of Lords; and (*c*) the role of referendums—and this book examines the degree to which each element evolved during the decade. The evidence suggests that the degree of constitutional flexibility in relation to V8 did not change during 1997–2007; the implications of this conclusion are the focus of the final section.

12.1 Amendment mechanisms

Although, democracies around the world use a wide range of processes and mechanisms to give their constitutions differing degrees of flexibility or rigidity, Lijphart reduces the variety of provisions to four basic types. This is based on the distinction between approval by ordinary majorities— indicating complete flexibility—and by larger majorities. Next, three categories of rigidity can be distinguished:

1. Approval by *less* than two-thirds majority (but more than an ordinary majority) for instance, a three-fifths parliamentary majority or an ordinary majority plus a referendum.
2. Approval by two-thirds majorities—a common rule for constitutional amendment based on the idea that the supporters should outnumber the opponents of a measure by at least two-to-one.
3. Approval by *more* than two-thirds majority, such as a three-fourths majority or a two-thirds majority, plus approval by state legislatures.

In the imposition of special majorities (sometimes referred to as 'extraordinary majorities' or 'super majorities'), the nature of the national electoral system is clearly important. Parliamentary systems employing simple-plurality electoral systems are disproportional (see Chapter 8) and as a result may return large legislative single-party majorities on the basis of a minority of the electorate. Therefore, supermajorities are clearly less constraining in countries using simple-plurality electoral systems compared to those using proportional systems. To take this feature into account, plurality systems are classified in Table 12.1 in the category below the one to which they technically belong. However, Lijphart acknowledges that the need for adjustment does seem to have been recognized by many plurality countries themselves through the imposition of a very high threshold. Therefore, the only countries that require three-quarter plus parliamentary majorities for constitutional amendment are all plurality systems (Bahamas, Jamaica, Mauritius, Papua New Guinea, and Trinidad).

As Table 12.1 shows, most countries fit somewhere within the two middle categories because they require more than simple-ordinary majorities for constitutional amendment but no more than two-thirds majorities or their equivalent.[2] On an index of 1.0–4.0 (with the former characterizing systems in which a simple majority was required to sanction a constitutional amendment compared with super-majority greater

Table 12.1 Majorities and supermajorities required for constitutional amendment in thirty-six democracies

Super-majorities greater than two-thirds [4.0]	
Australia, Canada, Japan, Switzerland, United States	Germany [3.5]
Two-thirds majorities or equivalent [3.0]	
Austria, Bahamas, Belgium, Costa Rica, Finland, India, Jamaica, Luxembourg, Malta, Mauritius, Netherlands, norway, papua New Guinea, portugal, spain, Trinidad	
Between two-thirds and ordinary majorities [2.0]	
Barbados, Botswana, Denmark, Greece, Ireland, Italy, Venezuela,	France [1.6], (Columbia after 1991), (France after 1974), (Sweden after 1980)
Ordinary majorities [1.0]	
Iceland, Israel, New Zealand, United Kingdom	Columbia [1.1], Sweden [1.3], (Colombia before 1991), (France before 1974), (Sweden before 1980)

Note: The indexes of constitutional rigidity are in square brackets.
Source: Lijphart, *Patterns of Democracy* (1999), 220.

than two-thirds in the latter), Lijphart predictably ascribed the UK a score of 1.0 for the period 1945–96. (The mean index score for constitutional rigidity is 2.6, and the median is 3.0.)

In order to demonstrate the distinctiveness of a particular constitutional feature, it is useful to provide some reference points or markers against which judgements concerning idiosyncratic qualities can be made. In the context of V8, the United States, Australia, Canada, Switzerland, and Japan provide counterparts due to their constitutional rigidity that raise specific questions about the constitutional flexibility that Lijphart associated with the UK. The constitution of the United States is the least flexible because amendments require two-thirds majorities in both houses of the legislature, as well as approval by three-quarters of the states. In Australia and Switzerland, amendments require approval in referendums with double-thresholds (a majority of the popular electorate plus support in a majority of the states or cantons). This allows a majority of states of cantons, which may in fact have a combined population of less that 20 per cent of the total, to veto proposals. The Japanese constitution requires two-thirds majorities in both houses of the legislature, as well as a popular referendum. Section 12.2 focuses on the values and principles underpinning the flexibility of the UK's constitution and particularly whether a greater degree of rigidity was imposed under New Labour.

12.2 Constitutional amendment in the UK

In relation to the UK any discussion of the procedures and mechanisms through which the constitution can be amended immediately flounders against the fact that the specific contours of the constitution are both opaque and highly contested.[3] 'With no written constitution there is no way of distinguishing between 'constitutional' enactments and others'.[4] As a result, amending the constitution is not conducted by reference to any accepted set of 'higher order' statutes or principles, but is simply a question of bringing forward new legislative proposals. As noted earlier, although other countries generally require special majorities, popular referendums, or other safeguards to ensure that the constitution remains protected from day-to-day partisan manipulation, the constitution of the UK is notable due to the absence of these auxiliary precautions. An ordinary legislative majority can approve any constitutional amendment brought forward in the form of legislation by the executive.

It would be wrong, however, to suggest that amendments to the constitution are treated just like 'ordinary' acts. Convention dictates that 'bills of first-class constitutional importance' take their committee stage on the floor of the House of Commons, and the period 1997–2007 involved a large number of popular referendums on specific constitutional reforms. This period also witnessed the creation of a new parliamentary actor with an explicit role in terms of examining and reviewing the constitutional significance of legislative proposals. And yet, as observed in the following paragraphs, these mechanisms are features of a parliamentary state in which the executive remains dominant. As a result, whether a bill is referred to a committee of the whole house, whether a referendum is held, or whether the recommendations of the Lords Committee on the Constitution are actually accepted, are decisions for the executive to make on its own. There are precious few constitutional safeguards which are imposed, formalized, and obligatory, that combine to limit the flexibility of a dominant executive when it comes to amending the constitution. In order to substantiate this statement, it is necessary to examine what, through a comparative perspective, could be interpreted as the three key mechanisms through which a degree of constitutional rigidity in relation to V8 is generally imposed—special procedures in the lower house, special procedures in the upper house, and the use of referendums as a societal validation device.

12.2.1 *The role of the House of Commons and first-class constitutional bills*

Unlike most ordinary bills which are automatically committed to a Standing Committee after second reading, a convention exists whereby bills of 'first-class constitutional importance' are committed to a committee of the whole house. Before 1945, all bills usually had their first committee stage on the floor of the House but after this date and following a recommendation of the Procedure Committee, ordinary bills were referred to Standing Committees for detailed consideration, leaving just 'exceptional' bills raising first-class constitutional issues to be considered by a committee of the whole House.[5] The aim of the Procedure Committee was to achieve a sense of balance between allowing the House to manage the heavy legislative programme that was likely to be brought forward in the period of post-war reconstruction, while at the same time retaining a special procedure for 'great measures' like the Parliament Act 1911, and Statute of Westminster 1931.[6] From 1945 onwards, Erskine May stated that 'it is the regular practice for Government bills of first class constitutional importance to be committed to a committee of the whole house'. Hazell notes, however, that after 1997 this convention was diluted with the word 'common' replacing 'regular' in the text cited above, and adding, 'although there is no invariable rule to that effect, nor any settled definition of what "first class" constitutional importance should be taken to mean'.[7] From the inception of this convention, the precise definition and understanding of 'first class constitutional significance' has been highly contested. However, after surveying the history of this convention, Seaton and Winetrobe suggest that,

> Any proposed legislation relating to the basic existence of the UK as a political and geographical entity (such as Northern Ireland or devolution legislation); the structure, operation, and powers of Parliament and the Crown (in its political, official, and monarchical contexts, elections and the franchise, emergency powers, innovations such as referendums or bill of rights), and major issues of foreign policy (for example EU treaties), would generally be regarded as prima facie constitutional matters.[8]

Using this definition, they suggest that thirty-five constitutional bills took their committee stage on the floor of the Commons during 1945–97. Hazell deploys a slightly more expansive definition to construct a list of fifty-five bills passed during 1997 and 2005 that could reasonably be regarded as being 'constitutional', of which thirty-two took their committee on the floor of the Commons (of which three were split).[9] Of these thirty-two bills, six bills were taken on the floor because they were so short that they did not require detailed scrutiny and ten were 'urgent'. Because some of the 'urgent' bills, such as the emergency measures to control terrorism, were also of constitutional importance, Hazell suggests that it is reasonable to conclude that twenty bills took their committee stage on the floor of the House because they were considered to be of 'first-class' constitutional significance.

Of those twenty that were interpreted as being of 'first-class' significance (Table 12.2), it is reasonable to suggest, as Hazell does, that only six of these bills fulfil the level of importance that was intended by both the Procedure Committee and the Leader of the House of Commons in 1945. These would be the three main devolution acts, namely, Human Rights Act, House of Lords Act, and the Constitutional Reform Act (discussed in Chapter 13).

This identification of what might be termed 'first-class' from 'second-class' or even 'third-class' constitutional bills raises critical questions concerning the process and actors involved in the process of assessing constitutional significance. Why were the bills, for example, that would become the Freedom of Information Act 1998, Regional Development

Table 12.2 Legislation subject to the procedure for measures of 'first-class constitutional significance'

Topic	Legislation
Devolution	*Scotland Act 1998* *Government of Wales Act 1998* *Northern Ireland (Elections) Act 1998* *Northern Ireland Act 1998* *Greater London Authority Act 1998* *Northern Ireland Act 2000*
Referendums	*Northern Ireland (Elections) Act 1998* *European Parliamentary Elections Act 1997* *Greater London Authority (Referendum) Act 1998* *Regional Assemblies (Preparations) Act 2003*
Elections	*Northern Ireland (Elections) Act 1998* *European Parliamentary Elections Act 1999* *Political Parties, Elections and Referendums Act 2000* *Representation of the People Act 2000*
Europe	*European Communities (Amendment) Act 1998* *European Communities (Amendment) Act 2002* *European Union (Accessions) Act 2003*
Human rights	*Human Rights Act 1998*
House of Lords reform	*House of Lords Act 1999*
Supreme Court/Lord Chancellor	*Constitutional Reform Act 2005*
Emergency legislation	*Anti-Terrorism, Crime and Security Act 2001* *Prevention of Terrorism Act 2005*

Source: Derived from Hazell, R. (2006) 'Time for a New Convention: Parliamentary Scrutiny of Parliamentary Bills, 1997–2005', *Public Law*, 247–66.

Agencies Act 1998, or the Bank of England Act not classified as being of 'first-class' constitutional significance? The answer exposes the unprincipled nature of the UK's constitution and notably the lack of any accepted or reliable rules. In effect, decisions are made by one-part principled criteria and two-parts political calculation by the dominant executive.

As Chapter 7 demonstrated at length, the balance of power between the executive and legislature (V3) was not significantly amended during 1997–2007. In theory, it is for the House of Commons to decide upon its own procedures, powers, and actions, but it has been recognized for some time that *in practice* it is the government, through the posts of Leader of the House and Chief Whip and supported by a generally compliant majority, that take decisions regarding the business of the House. Whether a bill is recognized as being of 'first-class' constitutional importance, and therefore as representing an amendment to the constitution, is a matter for the executive to decide rather than the legislature. If a debate ensues and the House takes a vote on the issue, the executive's support on the backbenches will in all, but the rarest circumstances ensure that the government's interpretation is upheld. This is a critical point in terms of constitutional rigidity and flexibility. The position of the UK in relation to V8 was already very flexible due to the absence of any formal requirement for a super-majority, popular referendum, or affirmation by subnational political actors. The only mechanism for recognizing a constitutional amendment is procedural, non-statutory, and internalized. Internalized in the sense that the constitutional balance of power effectively allows the government of the day whether or not to channel a proposal into the procedure for examining a constitutional amendment (i.e. by having it recognized as being of 'first-class' significance).[10]

The framework of incentives and sanctions within the legislature actually encourages the government to adopt a narrow definition regarding 'first class' constitutional measures because referring bills to the floor of the House for their committee stage can consume significant amounts of precious parliamentary time. With their first devolution measure, the Government of Wales Bill, New Labour sought to reduce the amount of time consumed on the floor by seeking to refer the majority of clauses 'upstairs' to a Standing Committee, while only examining those clauses that raised issues of principle on the floor of the House.[11] Although all the parties represented in Wales favoured splitting the Bill in this way, and the government won the division on the motion to adopt this process, the government relented and entered an informal agreement with the Conservative Party through which the whole Bill was examined on the floor of the House but within an agreed period of no more than seven days.

Between 1997–2005, 'first-class' constitutional bills were therefore managed by the executive in two ways: (*a*) by agreeing a programme motion with the opposition whereby a timetable was agreed which limited the amount of time a bill would be debated on the floor of the House; or (*b*) by splitting the committee stage between a Standing Committee and the Committee of the Whole House. The use of Programme (timetabling) Motions by the executive to impose time-limits on the debate surrounding proposals of 'first-class' constitutional importance provides an insight into the executive–legislative relationship that supports the conclusion of Chapter 7. New Labour's large parliamentary majority allowed it to maintain tight control over the timetable for individual bills, and by the end of the 1997–2001, opposition parties had become frustrated with the government's use of programme motions to strictly limit the committee stage on the floor of the House. Hazell notes, 'It is difficult to resist the conclusion that the Committee of the Whole House procedure has become a dignified part of the constitution'.[12] The evidence would therefore suggest that although a convention exists in relation to bills of 'first-class' constitutional significance, the subsequent procedure for amendments to the constitution contributes very little in terms of limiting the constitutional flexibility of the executive vis-à-vis V8. This, in turn, places greater weight on the role and capacity of the Second Chamber as a potential veto-point.

12.2.2 *The Role of the House of Lords as a 'constitutional long-stop'*

In many countries, one of the main roles of the second chamber is to act as a 'constitutional long-stop', ensuring that changes are not made to the constitution without full and open debate and an awareness of the consequences.[13] Table 12.3 illustrates that the form and nature of the powers held by second chambers varies around the world.

Second chambers also frequently play a formalized role not just in examining proposals for constitutional amendments, but also in reviewing the operation of the constitution more generally. The Australian Senate has a Legal and Constitutional Legislation Committee, the Israeli Knesset has a Constitution, Law, and Justice Committee. The Polish Sejm and the Japanese House of Councillors have more focused committees on constitutional affairs in the form of the Standing Committee on Constitutional Accountability and the Research Commission on the Constitution, respectively. Comparative studies therefore reveals that second chambers

Table 12.3 Role of the Upper House in passing constitutional amendments

Country	Legislative process in the Upper House	Chamber's power to call referendum	Other safeguards
Australia	Must pass by absolute majority (1) but Senate may be overruled after a delay.	None.	All constitutional changes are subject to referendum.
Canada	Senate can delay for six months.	None.	All constitutional changes are subject to agreement by provincial legislatures.
France	Pass by simple majority only, but Senate has absolute veto (1).	None.	All constitutional changes subject to referendum or approval by joint parliamentary sitting.
Germany	Must pass by a two-thirds majority (1).	None.	None.
Ireland	Same as ordinary legislation.	None (2).	All constitutional changes are subject to referendum.
Italy	Must pass twice, second time by an absolute majority (1).	If not passed by two-thirds majority in both houses, one fifth of Senators may request referendum (1).	In some circumstances, referendum may also be called by 500,000 electors or five regional assemblies (3).
Spain	Must pass by a three-fifths majority (1)—or else by two-thirds majority in lower house and absolute majority in Senado (4).	One-tenth of Senators may request referendum within fifteen days (1).	None.
United Kingdom	Same as ordinary legislation, except House of Lords has veto of bill to extend the life of a parliament.	None.	None.

Notes: (1) Same applies in the lower house. (2) Seanad has power to petition for a referendum on any bill of 'national importance', but a referendum is automatic on constitutional change. (3) A similar provision also allows for referendums to propose the repeal of any existing law. (4) Major constitutional changes including changes to the status of the monarchy, or citizen's rights, this process must be followed by dissolution of both houses of parliament, and repeated after fresh elections. They are then subject to a referendum.

Source: Russell M. (2001) 'Responsibilities of Second Chambers: Constitutional and Human Safeguards', *Journal of Legislative Studies*, 7(1), 65.

frequently have responsibility of monitoring constitutional change, although their specific powers vary. In Germany, France, Italy, and Spain, the second chambers can act as a real veto-point over constitutional change. In Canada, Australia, and Ireland the limited powers of the second chamber are off-set to some extent by the requirement to achieve popular support at the sub-national level. In Australia, this is achieved through a referendum that must be supported by at least half of those voting in at least four of the six states. It must also be supported by a majority of voters overall. In Canada, all constitutional amendments must be approved in provincial referendums, and in Ireland a national referendum is required to change the constitution. Recourse to popular referendums is therefore a form of precautionary mechanism to prevent ill-considered or highly partisan constitutional amendments, where the second chamber has limited powers.

As both Tables 12.1 and 12.3 indicate, there are few constitutional safeguards in the UK in the sphere of constitutional amendment.[14] Apart from where a government is seeking to extend its own life, the House of Lords has no special powers, and constitutional measures are not subject to either a higher voting threshold or any compulsory form of referendum. There are no requirements to demonstrate that proposals have cross-party or public support. There are no procedures in place through which actors in either House (or within sub-national political institutions) or members of the public can utilize trigger mechanisms to compel the government to hold a referendum. Unlike many other countries (e.g. Spain, Germany, France), the House of Lords has no capacity to challenge the constitutionality of proposals by referring them to a Constitutional Court.[15]

The Lords has historically attempted to act as a form of constitutional guardian, notably through its absolute veto power over the dismissal of key office holders, like judges, and through its delaying powers.[16] In this context, it is relevant that on each of the five occasions since 1911, when Acts have been passed under Parliament Act procedures they have each dealt with what were broadly 'constitutional' matters. The Wakeham Commission on the future of the House of Lords did not, however, recommend that a reformed second chamber should have increased powers in relation to constitutional legislation. It also cited the existence of an unwritten constitution and the principle of parliamentary sovereignty as militating against the creation of a specified Constitutional Court in the UK to arbitrate on disputes over whether a particular piece of legislation was or was not of 'first-class' constitutional significance. The Commission's terms of reference, specifically the requirement 'to maintain the position of the House of Commons as the pre-eminent chamber of Parliament', effectively prevented it from supporting any measures that were designed to impose a greater degree of constitutional rigidity. The Commission did, however, recommend the establishment of an 'authoritative' Constitutional Committee to act as a focus for the Lords' interest in (and concern for) constitutional matters. This recommendation was accepted, and a Constitution Committee was established in February 2001 with a remit to examine the constitutional implications of all public bills coming before the House, and to keep under review the operation of the constitution.[17]

If Lords' reform stimulated measures that were designed to increase the capacity of the House of Lords in relation to its role as a 'constitutional long-stop', then incorporation of the ECHR created a similar dynamic. In December 1998, the government announced its intention to ask both Houses of Parliament to establish a Joint Committee on Human Rights (JCHR) *inter alia*, to 'conduct inquiries into general human rights issues, the scrutiny of remedial orders [and] the examination of draft legislation where there is doubt about compatibility with the ECHR'.[18] The creation of these two specialist committees has bolstered the role of the Lords in relation to identifying and scrutinizing any proposals that are, in reality, constitutional amendments. In this sense, the Lords has been confirmed as the defender or monitor of the constitution, but, once again, this change has occurred very much within the confines of a Westminster Model in which the executive is dominant. In addition, the negative executive mentality makes it unlikely that the government will volunteer information about the full constitutional implications of a proposal or its compatibility with the Human Right Act. 'The onus remains mainly on members to confront the minister with the right question to trigger an answer'.[19]

The Constitution Committee and the JCHR also lack formal powers. Put slightly differently, the committees do possess certain resources in terms of specialist advisers and the capacity to draw attention to an issue through the publication of a critical report, but they have no constitutional 'power to force their views on an unwilling executive'.[20] For example, although the Constitution Committee was adamant that the Legislative and Regulatory Reform Bill 2006 was of 'first-class constitutional significance', the proposals were not subject to pre-legislative scrutiny and the committee stage was not taken on the floor of the House of Commons.[21]

The creation of the Lords Constitution Committee and the JCHR may have slightly improved the capacity of the Lords to scrutinize the government's proposals, but the process for constitutional amendment remains conspicuous by the absence of formal veto points which raises the question of whether any other restraints exist beyond the legislature that may impose a degree of constitutional rigidity in relation to V8. As Table 12.3 illustrates, in Canada, Australia, and Ireland, the limited powers of the legislature are offset to some extent by the requirement to achieve popular support through the use of referendums.

12.2.3 *The use of referendums*

The process for amending the constitution in a number of polities frequently involves not only achieving a super-majority within the legislature, but may also involve some broader display of societal or public approval. And yet, the use of referendums should not be viewed in isolation: constitutional amendment processes frequently involve a blend of precautionary measures (super-majorities within the legislature *and* popular approval through a referendum). As Lijphart notes, 'If majority approval in a referendum is the only procedure required for constitutional amendment, the referendum serves as a majoritarian device'.[22] The more common blend of auxiliary precautions in countries with a written constitution involves a prescribed referendum in addition to legislative approval by ordinary or extraordinary majorities; thereby making amendments more difficult to adopt and constitutions more rigid (the blend of mechanisms together serving as an anti-majoritarian device). In Italy, for example, Article 75 of the constitution provides that certain laws must be put to a referendum if there is sufficient public demand and the turnout at any referendum must be equal to at least 50 per cent plus one of the total electorate for the result to be binding. In Denmark, the constitution requires at least 40 per cent of the electorate to vote in favour of an amendment; the Australian constitution requires a double threshold based on popular and geographical criteria, as did the 2005 referendum on electoral reform in British Columbia.[23] Butler and Ranney's *Referendums Around the World* (see Table 12.4) demonstrates the manner in which referendums are a prescribed and binding element of constitutional change in many countries, and that the constitution in the UK is conspicuous due to the relative absence of constitutional constraints.

This absence of constraints fits within the political tradition of the UK in terms of its emphasis on stability, control, and a limited role for the public in between elections. The constitution was, as earlier chapters emphasized, based on a strict demarcation between the governors and the governed, and a normative preference in favour of unfettered governing capacity. It is in this context that Birch noted in his *Representative and Responsible Government* (1964) that 'It has occasionally been proposed that a referendum might be held on a particular issue, but the proposals do not appear to have been taken seriously'. This in itself reflected certain elite assumptions regarding the capacity of the masses to understand 'complex'

Table 12.4 Referendums in Western European Constitutions

	Referendums mentioned in the constitution?	Referendums required for constitutional amendments?	Con. provision for refs. in reply to: non-con. leg.?	Who triggers?	Provision for qualified majority?	Adv. or binding
Austria	Yes	Yes	Yes	Govt. or ML	No	Binding
Belgium	No	No	No	Govt.	No	Advisory
UK	No	No	No	Govt.	Yes	Advisory
Denmark	Yes	Yes	Yes	ML	Yes	Binding
Finland	Yes	No	Yes	Govt.	No	Advisory
France	Yes	Yes	Yes	Govt.	No	Binding
Germany	Yes	No	No	NA	No	Binding
Greece	Yes	No	Yes	H	No	Binding
Iceland	Yes	No	Yes	H	No	Binding
Ireland	Yes	Yes	Yes	H and ML	Yes	Binding
Italy	Yes	No	Yes	E	Yes	Binding
Netherlands	No	No	No	NA	No	NA
Norway	No	No	No	Govt.	No	Binding
Portugal	Yes	No	Yes	H	No	Binding
Spain	Yes	Yes	Yes	Govt.	No	Binding
Sweden	Yes	No	Yes	Govt. or ML	Yes	Binding & Advisory
Switzerland	Yes	Yes	Yes	E	Yes	Binding

Notes: NA—Not available; E—Electorate; H = Constitutional head of state; ML—Minority of the legislature.

socio-political issues or comprehend what was in their own best interests. In this context, the recent increase in the use of referendums in the UK highlights a certain dimension of the 'Blair paradox'. There is no requirement for a government to hold a referendum over any matter. There are no formal constitutional mechanisms, 'triggers', through which societal minorities can force the government to hold a referendum, like the referendum-plus-initiative in Switzerland. At the same time, informal political pressure to hold a referendum in all but the most extreme cases, can be channelled and diverted through the executive's tight control of its legislative majority. In this sense, the executive remains highly insulated from public pressure—a hallmark of the stability and distance promised (and cherished) by majoritarian democratic theory—and the constitution continues to offer an extreme degree of constitutional flexibility. Even when a referendum has been held, there is no formal requirement for a government to accept the outcome of a referendum—they possess a purely advisory role.[24] And yet, the role and societal influence of popular referendums should not be understated. This is because the use of a referendum polarizes public opinion and raises public expectations that a certain issue will be addressed in one way or another.

Even where referendums involve no formal constitutional powers, in terms of plenipotentiary powers, they do create and exert a degree of political leverage which, depending on the specific result, may make it very hard, if not impossible, for an executive to marginalize the end result. As such, one of the most critical elements of the politics of referendums focuses not on their practical implementation (e.g. the use of popular or geographic thresholds), but on the power of 'non-decision making' (i.e. which political actors have the capacity to ensure that certain issues do not become the topic of referendums). In this context, the increased use of referendums in the UK during 1997–2007 raises a number of questions about the executive mentality and the evolving constitution. As Table 12.5 indicates, since the 1970s, referendums have become a relatively frequent constitutional device, but few have been votes on a nationwide scale. The use of referendums has been a particularly distinctive element of constitutional decision-making processes under New Labour.

The increased use of referendums in the UK since 1997 has stimulated a discussion regarding whether there is a need for some form of threshold in order to ensure the legitimacy and broad societal acceptance of a measure. The idea of a threshold reflects the view that major constitutional change is more important than ordinary elections and should therefore be

Table 12.5 Referendums in the UK, 1973–2007

Referendum	Date	Scale	Threshold	Result %
Northern Ireland Border Poll	8 Mar. 1973	Sub-national	No	98.9 Yes 58.6 turnout
Terms of Continuing UK Membership of the EEC	5 Jun. 1975	Nationwide	No	67.2 Yes 64.5 turnout
Devolution for Scotland	1 Mar. 1979	Sub-national	Yes	51.6 Yes 63.8 turnout
Devolution for Wales	1 Mar. 1979	Sub-national	Yes	79.7 No 58.8 turnout
Establishment of the Scottish Parliament	11 Sept. 1997	Sub-national	No	74.3 Yes 60.4 turnout
Establishment of the National Assembly for Wales	18 Sept. 1997	Sub-national	No	50.3 Yes 50.1 turnout
Belfast (Good Friday) Agreement	22 May 1998	Sub-national	No	71.1 Yes 80.9 turnout
Establishment of a Greater London Authority	7 May 1998	Sub-national	No	72.0 Yes 34.1 turnout
Establishment of an Elected Regional Assembly in the North East	4 Nov. 2004	Sub-national	?	77.9 No 47.1 turnout

approved by more than a simple plurality of votes.[25] As the 1996 Commission on the Conduct of Referendums concluded,

> The main difficulty in specifying a threshold lies in determining what figure is sufficient to confer legitimacy e.g. 60%, 65% or 75% and whether the threshold should relate to the total registered electorate or those who choose to vote. Requiring a proportion of the total registered population to vote 'Yes' creates further problems because the register can be so inaccurate. Some of the electorate may believe that abstention is equal to a 'No' vote. Thus the establishment of a threshold may be confusing for voters and produce results which do not reflect their intentions. A turnout threshold may make extraneous factors, such as the weather on polling day, more important.[26]

The issue of thresholds was debated in the run-up to the referendum on membership of the EEC in 1975. The government considered specifying a minimum of the total registered electorate, but decided that 'it will be best to follow the normal electoral practice and accept that the referendum result should rest on a simple majority—without qualifications or conditions of any kind'.[27] 'Normal electoral practice' was, however, to change in 1979 with the inclusion of thresholds for the referendums on Scottish and Welsh devolution. The '40% rule' is still a highly contentious issue and was blamed by the pro-devolution camp as the main reason for the failure of the 1970s campaign.[28] With this in mind, it is significant that during the mid-1990s, the Labour Party consistently rejected the logic of thresholds—'no tricks. No fancy franchise. The test will be a straightforward majority of the votes cast'.[29]

The situation regarding referendums and thresholds became confused, however, in 2003 in relation to the planned regional referendums on elected regional government. The Regional Assemblies (Preparations) Act 2003 did not stipulate a threshold, but the responsible minister insisted that the government would not approve the creation of assemblies in regions where the turnout was 'derisory'.[30] The level at which turnout would become 'derisory' was never formally clarified, but the overwhelming 'No' vote relieved the government of any need to clarify the situation in that specific case. In March 2004, however, the government was forced to clarify its position as a result of a Private Members Bill, the Referendums (Thresholds) Bill which proposed that in future all referendums be subject to a 50 per cent threshold of the electorate in order to demonstrate extensive public support, and thereby empower that measure with a higher degree of legitimacy than ordinary legislation. The government refused to support the bill with the responsible minister arguing,

> It would be too rigid and inflexible and approach to apply the fifty per cent threshold for all referendums in all circumstances. It is important that every referendum is considered on its merits. On principle, it would be wrong to have a fifty per cent threshold, thereby allowing non-voters effectively to veto a 'Yes' vote or even a 'No' vote, depending on how one viewed a threshold. That is a fundamentally undemocratic approach. People who wanted a 'No' vote could campaign for abstentions.[31]

The government has been consistent in maintaining this position, and as a result the draft Single European Currency (Referendum) Bill commits the government to hold a referendum on a single currency once five economic tests have been fulfilled, but does not stipulate any threshold.

As Table 12.4 suggests, the 'trigger' or decision-making capacity for holding a referendum rests solely with the government of the day. There exist no mechanisms through which the public can compel the government to hold a referendum at the national level. Popular control mechanisms have, however, been created at the local level. Under Local Government Act 2000, local authorities are obliged to adopt new executive arrangements which institute a clearer separation of powers. Referendums form a central element of this process and must be held in a *binding* form where: (*a*) the council proposes an elected mayor; (*b*) where 5 per cent of the local electorate petition the council for a referendum on an elected mayor; or (*c*) where a council fails to either bring forward proposals or to consult adequately, and as a result the Secretary of State may formally require a referendum. The turnout data on the thirty-five local referendums held between June 2001 – September 2007 (Table 12.6) provides an insight into the use of thresholds at the local level. The Local Government Act 2000 imposed no minimum threshold, but in the majority of cases, turnout has hovered around 25 per cent (the lowest 'Yes' vote was based upon just 10% of the electorate).

The introduction and use of referendums at the local level should not be conflated with any dilution of the constitutional flexibility that continues to exist at the national level. The capacity of the government to dismiss demands for a referendum was clear in relation to the debate concerning a constitution for the European Union in 2004 and 2005. The specific arguments concerning the difference between the original draft constitution for the EU and the subsequent Lisbon Treaty are less important than the fact that the government was able to reject all demands for a national referendum on the topic. A vote demanding a referendum on the Lisbon Treaty was vetoed by the government through tight party management (311 votes to 247).

The debate concerning the European-Constitution–Lisbon-Treaty suggests that even where a government has been elected on a commitment to hold a referendum, it may well participate in strategic game-playing to avoid a public vote. And yet, the notion of 'strategic game-playing' connects with the broader theme of public trust and political engagement because one of the consequences of political promises concerning constitutional reform and democratic renewal is that they heighten public expectations about the performance and form of politics that can be expected, and particularly about the level of popular engagement and political dialogue. Put slightly differently, the failure to deliver on commitments to facilitate public involvement is arguably more detrimental to public confidence in politics than would otherwise have been the case because:

Table 12.6 Turnout for local referendums held under the Local Government Act 2000

Council	Date	Result	For	Aginst	Turnout (%)
Berwick-upon-Tweed	7 Jun. 2001	No	3,617	10,212	63.8*
Chelteham	28 Jun. 2001	No	8,083	16,602	31.0
Gloucester	28 Jun. 2001	No	7,731	16,317	30.8
Watford	12 Jul. 2001	Yes	7,636	7,140	24.5
Doncaster	20 Sept. 2001	Yes	35,453	19,398	25.0
Kirklees	4 Oct. 2001	No	10,169	27,977	13.0
Sunderland	11 Oct. 2001	No	9,593	12,209	10.0
Hartlepool	18 Oct. 2001	Yes	10,667	10,294	31.0
Lewisham	18 Oct. 2001	Yes	16,822	15,914	18.0
North Tyneside	18 Oct. 2001	Yes	30,262	22,296	36.0
Sedgefield	18 Oct. 2001	No	10,628	11,869	33.3
Middlesbrough	18 Oct. 2001	Yes	29,067	5,422	34.0
Brighton and Hove	18 Oct. 2001	No	22,724	37,214	31.6
Redditch	8 Nov. 2001	No	7,250	9,198	28.3
Durham City	20 Nov. 2001	No	8,327	11,974	28.5
Harrow	7 Dec. 2001	No	17,502	23,554	26.0
Harlow	24 Jan. 2001	No	5,296	15,490	36.4
Plymouth	24 Jan. 2001	No	29,559	42,811	39.8
Southwark	31 Jan. 2002	No	6,054	13,217	11.2
Newham	31 Jan. 2002	Yes	27,263	12,687	25.9
West Devon	31 Jan. 2002	No	3,555	12,190	41.8
Shepway	31 Jan. 2002	No	11,357	14,435	36.6
Bedford	21 Feb. 2002	Yes	11,316	5,537	15.5
Newcastle under Lyme	2 May 2002	No	12,912	16,468	31.5
Oxford	2 May 2002	No	14,692	18,686	33.8
Hackney	3 May 2002	Yes	24,697	10,547	31.9
Stoke on Trent	3 May 2002	Yes	28,601	20,578	27.8
Mansfield	3 May 2002	Yes	8,973	7,350	21.0
Corby	26 Sept. 2002	No	5,351	6,239	30.9
Ealing	11 Dec. 2002	No	9,454	11,655	9.8
Ceredigion	20 May 2004	No	5,308	14,013	36.3
Isle of Wight	5 May 2005	No	28,786	37,097	62.4*
Torbay	14 Jul. 2004	Yes	18,074	14,682	32.1
Crewe & Nantwich	4 May 2006	No	11,808	18,768	35.3
Darlington	27 Sept. 2007	No	7,981	11,226	24.7

Note: * Same day as General Election.

Source: British electroal facts 1832–2006 (updated).

1. Public expectations had been inflated to a level that now makes the 'performance gap' even greater.
2. The measures themselves were designed to counter evidence of a lack of public trust in politics, and therefore the failure to deliver manifesto commitments will underline and accentuate pre-existing socio-political concerns.

New Labour's position on the Lisbon Treaty was perhaps as important for its symbolic value, than for its practical importance. It provided a brutal illustration of the realities of executive government within a majoritarian polity. Viewed through a historical frame, it formed the latest occurrence of a relatively clear pattern of executive politics, whereby the holding of a referendum is dictated by intra-party political dynamics and rational calculations, rather than overarching constitutional precedents, requirements, or principles. In 1975 and 1996, the Labour Party and Conservative Parties (respectively) were divided over the issue of Europe and the decision to hold (or in the latter case commit itself to) a referendum was a leadership strategy designed to maintain party unity and vent certain pressures. During 1997–2007, referendums were held not due to a critical sense of constitutional morality, but due to a process of political cost–benefit analysis that led some referendums to occur (specifically in relation to devolution), but other referendum commitments (e.g. electoral reform, economic and monetary union) to be marginalized; while other 'first-class' elements of the constitutional reform agenda—Human Rights Act, House of Lords reform, etc.—have not been subject to referendums. The contours of the constitution are therefore blurred when it comes to holding referendums on constitutional amendments in the UK and the executive can exploit this situation to either open up or close off political debate about when, how, or whether a referendum should be held. As King notes, 'The arguments you deploy may be good or bad in themselves, but their merits or demerits have nothing whatsoever to do with your reasons for deploying them...The debate on whether or not to hold a referendum in any given case is mostly a charade'.[32]

This section's analysis of constitutional rigidity leads to the conclusion that Lijphart's score for the UK for the period 1945–96 has not altered significantly during 1997–2007. The capacity of the Commons to constrain the executive is commonly eviscerated due to the existence of large parliamentary majorities, the potential of the Lords to act as a veto player is limited by a straightforward lack of powers, and referendums remain very much a tool of the executive rather than an independent component of the broader constitutional configuration. Having come to this conclusion, it is necessary to explore some its broader implications in terms of the evolving constitution.

12.3 Implications and assessment

This chapter has examined the extent to which the degree of constitutional rigidity altered during 1997–2007. The evidence suggests it has changed very little, if at all. The UK's arrangements for amendments to the constitution remain highly flexible, and procedures for amending the constitution tend to be subject to much sterner thresholds in other countries. This finding matters because it may aid understanding in relation to the constitutional anomie thesis that has been developed throughout this book. The absence of explicit and stringent constitutional amendment procedures may partially account for the way in which New Labour's constitutional reforms have so often been criticized for being rushed, ill-considered, and deficient in terms of consultation. The evolution of the constitution since 1997 has therefore become associated with the 'Tommy Cooper' or 'just like that' school of reform, 'each successive reform apparently pulled out of a hat, leaving the rest of us to gape in astonishment and wonder how it all happened'.[33] In this context, a greater degree of constitutional rigidity, the existence of more numerous potential veto points may have slowed down the process, and forced the government to engage in a more principled and rounded manner.

The use of referendums during 1997–2007 is particularly significant in the context of broader debates concerning the 'Blair paradox'. Referendums may well have been held relatively frequently during 1997–2007, but only in relation to issues where the government could confidently predict an acceptable result. In this sense, referendums were strategically deployed to facilitate or prevent reform. In some circumstances, referendums were used to circumnavigate the veto capacity of other actors; whilst in other instances referendums were avoided in order to bypass potential veto capacity of the public. The use of referendums was therefore a strategic tool of the executive rather than a principled and consistent element of constitutional thought and practice. Exposing this fact sensitizes observers to the inter-play and dialectical relationship between *strategic action* by agents, on the one hand, and the *strategically selective context*, on the other.

All political games and strategies incur certain costs. These costs can assume a variety of forms (financial, reputation, legislative support, etc.), and political calculations about the relative costs versus benefits of each strategy will effect their subsequent deployment. In this context, referendums involve certain costs. They also bring with them an element of risk due to the fact that the behaviour of the public can never be predicted with absolute certainty. A key element in terms of assessing the political costs of holding a referendum relates to the degree to which a decision that has been ratified in a popular referendum should be perceived as being superior to decisions arising through the ordinary legislative process. Phrased slightly differently, is the political cost of putting a decision to a referendum a reduction in the political flexibility of that or future governments in terms of amending that feature of the constitution? Can referendums entrench certain decisions in a way that effectively undermines, or at the very least limits, traditional notions of parliamentary sovereignty? These questions are particularly appropriate in the context of the UK in light of the various referendums outlined in Table 12.5. Does the fact that several elements of New Labour's reform programme have been ratified directly by the public designate them as 'higher order' laws that effectively curtail or significantly delimit the contours of the UK's traditional flexibility?

Ackerman's distinction between 'monistic' and 'dualistic' accounts of democracy may help us unravel these questions.[34] 'Monistic' accounts are based on the belief that democracy requires the grant of plenary law-making powers to the winner of the last general election, and is therefore rooted in a power-hoarding conception of democracy. 'Dualistic' account, by contrast, embrace the notion of 'higher order' laws that exist above general legislation due to the direct mandate they have received from the public in the form of a referendum. Decisions by the people to create a 'higher law' provides a form of enhanced legitimacy which acts as a constitutional buffer and is therefore insulated from erosion, amendment, or repeal through 'normal' politics. Bogdanor is therefore adopting an implicitly dualistic account when he states that referendums have become 'an instrument of entrenchment... a graphic illustration of how a barrier to fundamental change can be constructed in a country without a codified constitution'.[35]

For Ackerman, the challenges faced by a dualistic democracy include: how to specify the process for making 'higher law' in order to delineate the occasions on which a piece of legislation has earned a special status, how to structure the process for making 'normal law' to create incentives for public engagement and consultation, and how to establish 'preservation mechanisms' to protect the considered judgements of the mobilized people from illegitimate erosion by normal constitutional government. Ackerman's work can be used as a conceptual bridge between this chapter's focus on constitutional amendment (V8) and the analysis of Chapter 13 on the changing role of judicial review within the evolving constitution due to the fact that several scholars have suggested that the UK now has a dualistic democracy in which certain laws are de facto 'higher order' laws. And yet, both the Labour Party and Conservative Party maintain that parliamentary sovereignty—a neo-Diceyan monistic form of democracy in which no government can constrain its successor—remains. This clash between dualistic claims and monistic perseverance (even doggedness) regarding the evolving constitution forms the focus of Chapter 13.

V8 Index of constitutional rigidity

Lijphart's UK score 1945–96	1.0
Lijphart's UK score 1971–96	1.0
Updated UK score 1997–2007	1.0

Notes

1. Cm. 4534. (2000) *A House for the Future*, p. 48.
2. Lijphart *op. cit.* (1999), p. 222.
3. This section draws upon the research of the Constitution Unit, notably that published by Hazell, R (2006) 'Time for a New Convention', *Public Law*, 247–66.
4. Cm. 4534 *op. cit.* (2000), p. 50.
5. HC 9 (1945–6) *First Report of the Select Committee on Procedure*. Session 1945–6. See Donnelly, K. (1997) 'Parliamentary Reform', *Parliamentary Affairs*, 50(2), 246–62.
6. See Seaton, J and Winetrobe, B. (1998) 'The Passage of Constitutional Bills in Parliament', *Legislative Studies*, 4(2), 33.
7. Hazell *op. cit.* (2006).
8. Seaton and Winetrobe *op. cit.* (1998), p. 3.
9. Hazell *op. cit.* (2006).
10. HC (1981) *Hansard*, 996, col. 750, 12 January.
11. See Smith, N and Hazell, R (1996) *Delivering Constitutional Reform*. London: Constitution Unit.
12. Hazell *op. cit.* (2006), p. 21.
13. See Tsebelis, G and Money, J (1997). *Bicameralism*. Cambridge University Press.
14. See Cm. 4534. (2000) *A House for the Future*, pp. 48–57.
15. See Russell, M (2000) *Reforming the House of Lords: Lessons from Overseas*. Oxford: Oxford University Press.
16. Donnelly *op. cit.* (1997), p. 260.
17. HL 11 (2001–2) *Reviewing the Constitution*. First Report of the Constitution Committee, Session 2001–2.
18. HC (2008) *Hansard*, 14 December.
19. Feldman, D (2002) 'Parliamentary Scrutiny of Legislation and Human Rights', *Public Law*, 323–48.

20. Ibid.
21. HL 194 (2005–6) *Legislative and Regulatory Reform Bill*. Eleventh report from the House of Lords Select Committee on the Constitution, Session 2005–6.
22. Lijphart *op. cit.* (1999), p. 230.
23. Flinders, M and Curry, D (2009) 'Deliberative Democracy, Elite Politics and Electoral Reform', *Policy Studies*, 29(4), 371–92.
24. In 1975, at the time of the referendum on whether Britain should remain in the EC, Edward Short, the Leader of the House of Commons, declared that 'the Government will be bound by its result, but Parliament, of course, cannot be bound by it ... Although one would not expect honourable members to go against the wishes of the people, they will remain free to do so'. HC Debs. (1975), 888, col. 293, 11 March. Noted in Bogdanor, V (2004) 'Our New Constitution', *Law Quarterly Review*, 120, 3.
25. See Gay, O (2004) *Thresholds in Referendums*. House of Commons Library, Standard Note SN/PC/2809.
26. Electoral Reform Society (1996) *Report of the Commission on the Conduct of Referendums*, p. 42.
27. Cmnd. 5925 (1979) *Referendum on UK Membership of the European Community*, para. 6.
28. Bogdanor, V. (1980) 'The 40 Per Cent Rule', *Parliamentary Affairs*, 33(1), 252–5.
29. Scottish Labour Press Notice (1996) 12 June.
30. See *The Independent* (2002) 4 November, 8.
31. HC Deb. (2004) 27 February, col. 587.
32. King *op. cit.* (2007), p. 279.
33. Hennessy, P (2001) *The Prime Minister*. London: Penguin, p. 510.
34. Ackerman, B (2004) 'Constitutional Economics—Constitutional Politics', *Constitutional Political Economy*, 10(4), 415–24.
35. Bogdanor *op. cit.* (2004), p. 3.

Chapter 13

V9. Judicial Review

The principle of parliamentary sovereignty means neither more nor less than this, namely, that Parliament . . . has, under the English constitution, the right to make or unmake any law whatsoever.[1]

One of the main reasons for creating a written constitution is to set down a number of core principles or tenets that should frame the socio-political governance of a country. Written constitutions can therefore be associated with explicating a sense of constitutional morality, whereby certain values or rules are viewed as being of such importance that they should exist, in all but the most exceptional circumstances, beyond the reach of politicians. That is not to say that countries without a written constitution do not exhibit their own constitutional morality, but simply that in those cases it can be far harder to identify the precise borders of the constitution. The absence of a written constitution is generally a reflection of a conscious choice by a political elite to avoid the increased rigidity that is associated with judicial review; and although judicial review can occur in countries without a written constitution, the courts generally have less to 'bite on' in terms of legitimating their decisions through recourse to constitutional principles.

If a written constitution exists, it reflects a certain logic that those stipulations included in the document are of a higher status than other elements of the political system. This, in turn, brings with it a presumption that (unless clearly stated otherwise) constitutional prerequisites should be protected. Conversely, one of the socio-political effects of having an unwritten constitution, notably in relation to the political history of the UK, is that the idea of external constitutional adjudication is unfamiliar (even alien) to dominant cultural understandings of good governance.[2] This stems from the UK's evolution as a *political* constitution. Towards the end of the twentieth century, the logic and value of this model was questioned by a range of actors who drew upon continental case law and jurisprudence to argue in favour of limiting the capacity of politicians through judicial mechanisms. The logic of these arguments was based in the belief that *judicial* constitutions increase the degree of constitutional rigidity by seeking to locate some basic rights, values, or principles beyond the reach of elected politicians.

It is at this point that the bridge between V8 and V9 provided by Ackerman on 'monistic' and 'dualistic' accounts of democracy become obvious: reformers were seeking to promote a 'dualistic' account, while the executive sought to defend a 'monistic' approach in which all laws have equal status, and no actor has the capacity to deny the legitimacy of executive action. Dualistic accounts are in line with a legal model of constitutionalism that is common in both North America and continental Europe. In this model, the existence of 'higher order' or 'fundamental' laws act as a constitutional buffer and are insulated from erosion, amendment, or repeal through 'normal' politics. This chapter's focus on judicial review (V9) is therefore couched within broader debates concerning:

1. 'Monistic' and 'dualistic' visions of democracy.
2. Power-hoarding and power-sharing polities.
3. Judicial and political constitutions.

For much of the twentieth century, the UK's position in relation to each of these three (inter-related) dimensions would have been straightforward: it was a monistic power-hoarding polity based firmly upon a political constitution. The central ambition of this chapter is to assess the degree to which this has changed. Its main conclusion is that change has been significant, but not fundamental. Furthermore, the manner in which change has occurred has created a hybrid model of democracy which resonates with this book's broader arguments concerning bi-constitutionality and constitutional anomie. In order to justify and tease apart the implications of this conclusion, Section 13.1 reviews Lijphart's methodology for generating an Index Score for Judicial Review. Section 13.2 examines developments in the UK during 1997–2007 through the lens of this methodology, and the final section locates the specific findings of this chapter within a number of broader themes.

13.1 Judicial review

As Lord Hailsham wrote in *The Dilemma of Democracy* (1978), the critical element of the theory of limited government was that it 'prescribed limits beyond which governments and parliaments must not go, and it suggests means by which they can be compelled to observe those limits'.[3] Earlier chapters have analysed the existence and capacity of certain limits or what have been termed 'anti-majoritarian institutions'. This chapter develops this line of analysis by examining the degree to which the boundaries of the constitution in the UK are policed by judicial mechanisms. The nature and extent of judicial review varies around the world, and it is in this context that Lijphart noted that the Greek constitution states that 'the courts shall be bound not to apply laws, the contents of which are contrary to the constitution'.[4] Some countries, like the Netherlands do have written constitutions, but explicitly remove the jurisdiction of the courts from constitutional oversight. As a result, the legislature is the primary protector of the constitution in those countries without a written constitution and those where a written constitution exists, but where judicial review is not utilized. Although consideration in the ordinary courts is the most common form of judicial review, some countries (including Austria, Germany, Italy, Spain, Portugal, and Belgium) have created specialized constitutional courts to which the ordinary courts can refer cases for a decision regarding constitutionality. France also has a constitutional court (known as a 'council') to which cases can be referred, but this is an offshoot of the political rather than judicial system. Referrals to the French Constitutional Council can be made by the President, Prime Minister, the presidents of the two chambers, and (since 1974) small minorities in the legislature. As a result, the legislature is no longer the sole interpreter of the constitution and France possesses a form of centralized constitutional review.

In order to locate all these different constitutional designs within one framework, Lijphart designed an Index of Judicial Review based upon a fourfold classification based upon (a) the distinction between the presence and absence of judicial review, and on (b) three degrees of activism in the assertion of this power by the courts.

The general pattern for V9 shown by Table 13.1 is one of generally weak judicial review. The mean score is 2.2 and the median is 2.0. Table 13.1 does, however, contain elements that suggest a trend towards a stronger judicial review. The evolution of judicial review in Canada, Belgium, Colombia, Italy, and France (second column Table 13.1) reflects a consistent transition from lower to higher degrees of strength. This trend resonates with Hirschl's comparative analysis of the 'judicialization of politics' and theories suggesting a contemporary transition from 'democracy' to 'juristocracy'.[5] This body of work emphasizes the manner in which constitutional courts and strong systems of judicial review now exist in over one hundred countries. This includes post-authoritarian regimes in the former Eastern Bloc, Latin America, Asia, and Africa (like Russia, Poland, Hungary, Ukraine, Venezuela, Mexico, South Africa); alongside more established democracies (Italy, Germany, Canada).[6] 'Even such countries as Britain, Canada, Israel, and New Zealand—not long ago described as the last bastions of Westminster-style parliamentary sovereignty—have rapidly joined the trend towards constitutionalization'.[7] Leaving aside the *degree* to which the UK has followed this trend (the focus of this chapter), one of the more general outcomes of this transformation has been an increasing reliance on courts and judicial processes for assessing core socio-political questions, public-policy dilemmas, and moral predicaments. A diverse range of what can, using the framework set out in Chapter 2 (Table 2.1), be interpreted as 'meta-' or 'mega-constitutional' issues have been increasingly framed as matters for the courts, not politicians or the public.[8]

The 'judicialization of politics' is a socio-political phenomenon with direct implications for debates regarding democratic renewal and majoritarian-modification, both in the UK and more broadly, because it seeks to attempt and explain the re(distribution) of power within constitutional configurations. Lijphart identifies a clear correlation between judicial

Table 13.1 The strength of Judicial Review in thirty-six democracies (1945–96)

Strong Judicial Review [4.0]	
Germany, India, United States	Canada (after 1982)
Medium Strength Judicial Review [3.]	
Australia, Austria*, Mauritius, Papua New Guinea, Spain*	Canada [3.3] Italy [2.8] (Belgium after 1984*) (Canada before 1982) (Colombia after 1981) (France after 1974*) (Italy after 1956*)
Weak Judicial Review [2.0]	
Bahamas, Barbados, Botswana, Costa Rica, Denmark, Greece, Ireland, Iceland, Jamaica, Japan, Malta, Norway, Portugal,* Sweden, Trinidad, Venezuela	Belgium [1.5] Colombia [2.4] France [2.2] (Colombia before 1981) (Italy before 1956)
No Judicial Review [1.0]	
Finland, Israel, Luxembourg, Netherlands, New Zealand, Switzerland, United Kingdom	(Belgium before 1984) (France before 1974)

Note: The indexes of judicial review are in square brackets.
* Centralized judicial review by constitutional courts.
Source: Lijphart (1999), Patterns of Democracy, 226.

review and constitutional rigidity because both rigidity, in terms of subjecting constitutional amendments to special processes and judicial review are anti-majoritarian devices. Flexible constitutions and the absence of judicial review, by contrast, permit unconstrained majoritarian rule. Constitutional rigidity and judicial review are also mutually reinforcing in terms of one without the other would be largely ineffective. As such, a great deal of the literature on the changing relationship between law and politics is framed in terms of non-majoritarian or counter-majoritarian mechanisms.[9]

The relationship between V9 and constitutional evolution is complex due to the fact that it often rests on the *latent* influence of the potential for judicial review. As Table 13.1 suggests, a distinction needs to be made between the existence of formal mechanisms of judicial review and the actual use of those mechanisms. A distinction also needs to be made between the absence of formal mechanisms of judicial review and the *de facto* development of judicial safeguards, and attempts by the judiciary to encroach upon new constitutional terrain. This latter point feeds into a potential criticism of Lijphart's assessment of the UK in relation to V9 for the period 1945–96: the role and assertiveness of the senior judiciary altered towards the end of the twentieth century. Although this did not reflect the outcome of any formal amendment to the constitution, it did reflect, often explicitly, concerns within sections of the senior judiciary regarding the lack of rigidity and the behaviour of the executive, and manifested itself in an increase in judicial review decisions going against the government. In light of this, Lijphart's scoring of 1.0 indicating 'No Judicial Review' for both 1945–96 and 1971–96 could be criticized for overlooking a subtle, yet critical shift in the executive–judicial relationship during the latter period. How this relationship evolved during 1997–2007 is examined in Section 13.2.

13.2 Legal constitutionalism

The constitution of the UK has historically rejected the public law frameworks that are common in other countries. It was, and some could argue it still is, a political constitution. The executive is responsible to the legislature, parliamentary sovereignty remains (theoretically at least) absolute, and the courts have no formal capacity to reject legislation with reference to 'higher order' laws. It was for politicians, not judges, to make decisions about the acceptable limits of political action and decisions concerning the 'public interest'.[10] The political constitution is therefore simple: the executive may remain in office so long as it enjoys the support of the majority of the legislature. The political constitution was reflected in the institutional configuration of the constitution and particularly the casualness with which it approached the separation of powers. The political constitution was therefore a key element of the majoritarian power-hoarding democracy, because it not only empowered the executive with a degree of control over the legislature, but it also rejected the notion of placing judicially regulated constitutional limits on executive action.

The executive–judicial relationship was forged on an implicit constitutional understanding that the judiciary would not seek to expand their sphere of competence as long as politicians did not seek to encroach upon the independence of the judiciary, and as long as a coherent argument could be made that the legislature was able to fulfil its constitutional responsibility of holding the executive to account.[11] The political constitution was therefore founded on an implicit political relationship in which judges were reluctant to rule on politically salient issues, and where a decision was unavoidable, the notion of ultra vires (i.e. acting beyond one's powers) allowed them to claim that they were simply upholding the will of parliament.

The basis of this traditional relationship eroded during the 1990s because sections of the judiciary came to believe that judicial independence had been eroded and effective parliamentary accountability no longer existed.[12] As a result, a debate developed concerning the merits of legal constitutionalism. Legal constitutionalism encapsulates a normative preference for judicial regulation of political and administrative behaviour as a way of constraining the executive, which explains its relationship with Lijphart's interest in anti-majoritarian mechanisms and constitutional rigidity. In essence, legal constitutionalism argues in favour of demarcating the boundaries, expectations, and values of the constitution and then empowering the judiciary with the capacity to compel the executive to operate within those contours, thereby recognizing that there must be limits on the notion of parliamentary sovereignty.[13] Modern legal constitutionalist views therefore argued that politics should be enclosed within what Loughlin has described as the 'straitjacket of law'—a phrase with a direct resonance to notions of constitutional rigidity and anti-majoritarianism.[14]

The logic and promotion of legal constitutionalism was an explicit response to the perceived failure of the political constitution. Although the Liberal Democrats had for some time favoured a more robust system of judicial review in the UK, as one element of a much broader commitment to moving from a power-hoarding to a power-sharing polity, the Labour Party had throughout its history been committed to the political constitution. The position of the Labour Party, however, altered in the mid-1990s. In *The Blair Revolution—Can Labour Deliver* (1996), for example, Mandelson and Liddle praised the strength of 'their [the judiciary] strictures against the excesses of the Conservative government in recent years' which were such as 'to have convinced even the most prejudiced class warrior not to question the judges' independence and integrity'.[15] This shift in attitude was also reflected in the output of the Joint Consultative Committee on Constitutional Reform between the Labour Party and Liberal Democrats (1996–7) which recommended a incorporation of the European Convention on Human Rights (ECHR) into UK law, noting, 'Incorporation of the ECHR would represent a very significant strengthening in practice of what amounts to the UK's *fundamental law*[emphasis added]'.[16]

This recommendation was subsequently included within the Labour Party's 1997 General Election manifesto and was implemented via the Human Rights Act 1998. Incorporation was important as it imported a set of legal safeguards in the form of human rights which the judiciary were therefore obliged to protect. Put slightly differently, it gave the judiciary a firmer foundation on which to make judgements in defence of certain 'higher order' values. The Human Rights Act was, however, carefully designed and implemented within the contours of the Westminster Model and, as a result, did not give the courts the power to 'strike down' legislation that was found to be incompatible with the ECHR. The form of judicial review was therefore far weaker than that found in many other European countries or in North America.

The role of the judiciary is limited to issuing 'declarations of incompatibility'. where legislation cannot be interpreted as being in accordance with the ECHR. The executive then has the opportunity to review the declaration and either amend the legislation, or account to Parliament for its decision not to alter the legislation. Two critical points arise from this procedure: (*a*) the legislation remains in force until it has been reviewed by the government; and (*b*) the executive is under no obligation to alter the legislation. This framework has been instituted to protect and maintain the political constitution. Final decisions over the appropriateness of legislation must be made by members of the executive who must then account to the legislature for their decision.

Although the position of the judiciary may have been strengthened as a result of the Human Rights Act the 2005 case against the government regarding indefinite detention without trial of foreign terrorist suspects, it displayed the continuing realities of executive government. The House of Lords found that the legislation authorizing the detention was a breach of Article 5 of the ECHR. It also found that the government's derogation from the ECHR in order to pass the Anti-Terrorism, Crime and Security Act 2001 was also unlawful. In explaining this judgement, Lord Bingham rejected the argument of government counsel that 'matters of this kind here fall within the discretionary area of judgement properly belonging to the democratic organs of the state' and went on to note that 'it is wrong to stigmatise judicial decision-making as in some way undemocratic'.[17] The court found in favour of the appellant and issued a 'declaration of incompatibility'. This decision did not lead to the release of any suspects. The detained individuals were held in custody until new legislation (the Terrorism Act 2005) was passed, which gave the responsible minister new powers to detain them at home through the use of control orders.[18]

If the Human Rights Act has increased the capacity of the judiciary to challenge the position of the executive, it is also noteworthy that the judiciary has shown a great deal of restraint in making use of this capacity (see Table 13.2). Numerous judgements have argued that it would be wrong for unaccountable judges to supplant the position of elected politicians.[19] This sentiment was developed in Lord Bingham's 2007 judgement against the second challenge by the Countryside Alliance to the Hunting Act 2004, 'The democratic process is liable to be subverted if, on

Table 13.2 Declarations of incompatibility under the Human Rights Act 1998

Since the Human Rights Act 1998 came into force on the 2 October 2000, 25 declarations of incompatibility have been made. Of these:

- 16 have become final (in whole or in part), and are not subject to further appeal.
- 8 have been overturned on appeal, of which 2 remain subject to further appeal; 1 remains subject to appeal.

Of the 16 declarations of incompatibility that have become final

- 10 have been remedied by later primary legislation (which in relation to 2 cases is not yet in force).
- 1 has been remedied by a Remedial Order under Section 10 of the Human Rights Act.
- 3 relate to provisions that had already been remedied by primary legislation at the time of the declaration.
- 1 is subject of public consultation (in conjunction with the implementation of a judgement of the European Court of Human Rights).
- 1 is under consideration as to how to remedy the incompatibility.

Source: Ministry of Justice (11 November 2008).

a question of moral and political judgement, opponents of [legislation] achieve through the courts what they could not achieve in Parliament.'[20]

In order to understand this apparent caution on the part of the judiciary, it is useful to reflect on whether the Human Rights Act 1998 should itself be interpreted as representing a body of 'higher order' or 'constitutional' law existing above and beyond normal day-to-day legislation. In this context Maer has argued that,

> [C]onstitutional law is growing into a more distinct body of fundamental law. Although technically these constitutional laws have no higher status, politically they are entrenched in a way that ordinary statute law is not ... however much David Blunkett [the then Home Secretary] may dislike the Human Rights Act, that too is politically entrenched ... human rights once recognised in statute, cannot easily be taken away.

Against this position, Weir and Byrne have highlighted the manner in which New Labour used their parliamentary majority to push through parliament the Anti-Terrorism, Crime and Security Act 2001, which involved derogating from Article 5 of the European Convention on Human Rights less than two years after in enactment in the Human Rights Act.[21] Since the Human Rights Act was passed, and particularly since the 9/11 attack in the United States and the London bombings of July 2005, the context in which decisions regarding rights-based questions has shifted significantly. This is reflected in a series of statutes that have sought to increase the capacity of the state to limit individual freedoms in the name of protecting the public from terrorist attacks. New Labour therefore focused on the introduced human rights legislation during its first term, but they brought forward a draft of statutory restrictions on personal and political freedoms during its second term. Consequently, Tomkins concludes that a 'close examination of the case law reveals that little has been achieved by way of increasing judicial protection of civil liberties'.[22] In many ways the extent of judicial deference should not come as a surprise.[23] During the passage of the Human Rights Bill the Lord Chief Justice observed that,

> Those who hope for a surge in judicial activism may be disappointed ... I think that judges will continue to accord a very considerable margin of appreciation to political and office decision makers. ... To do so would certainly help to allay the fears of those who see incorporation as an objectionable judicial usurpation of democratic authority.[24]

The evolving constitution is therefore complex as it relates to V9 and is riddled with paradoxes and contradictions: there has been no straightforward shift from a political to a judicial constitution in the UK. It is more accurate to interpret developments as involving an attempt to move towards a modified majoritarianism in which the position of the judiciary was enhanced, but very much within the precepts of a political constitution. Such hybrid constitutionalism creates theoretical and practical challenges, many of which have become clearer as the implications of the initial reforms have taken root. In this sense, the period 1997–2007 displays a degree of policy momentum or spillover which raises questions about executive capacity to control change once initial concessions have been made. The position of the Lord Chancellor, for example as a member of the executive, legislature, and judiciary became more problematic with incorporation of the ECHR. Article 6 of the convention stipulates that a fair trial must involve an impartial and independent judge (and not therefore a member of the same government bringing the case). The Human Rights Act therefore had broader implications for both the composition of the executive and the future of the reformed Second Chamber.

In June 2003, the government unexpectedly announced its intention to address three longstanding concerns regarding the constitution: (*a*) the lack of a distinct separation of powers; (*b*) anxieties regarding the independence of the judiciary; and (*c*) concern about the social diversity of the judiciary. This would be achieved by removing the Law Lords from the reformed Second Chamber, transferring judicial patronage powers from the executive to an independent Judicial Appointments Commission, and abolishing the post of Lord Chancellor.[25] The announcement of these measures failed to reflect the inclusive style of politics that New Labour had suggested which would underpin its approach to politics. The announcement that took the form of a press release was not preceded by any form of consultation, no detailed plans were available, and several members of the Cabinet were unaware of the proposals.[26] The subsequent Constitutional Reform Bill was not published in a draft form which fuelled accusations that the government was acting in a high-handed manner in relation to democratic renewal and, furthermore, doing so in a manner devoid of any obvious appreciation of the implications that reform in one area may have for other aspects of the constitutional infrastructure.[27] This lack of detailed planning, sharpened through the constructive criticism generally garnered through pre-legislative scrutiny and consultation, created a number of obstacles both within and beyond the Palace of Westminster.

Within the House of Lords in Parliament, the Bill was referred to a select committee, against the government's wishes, and when the committee's final report was debated in July 2004, an amendment was passed to retain the post of Lord Chancellor.[28] Beyond Parliament, the government became embroiled in a dispute with the Law Lords concerning not just the powers of the planned Supreme Court, but also where it would be physically located. The government's plans included no measures to increase the formal powers of the judiciary vis-à-vis the executive. The Court would not, therefore, be 'supreme' in the sense of being able to strike down legislation, and for this reason was pejoratively labelled 'second-class' by the Lord Chief Justice.[29]

Nevertheless, the Constitutional Reform Bill received Royal Assent as one of the final legislative acts of New Labour's second term of office. But only after the government had been forced to accept that the office of Lord Chancellor should be retained, and a new concordat had been signed between the Lord Chancellor and the Lord Chief Justice setting out the division of functions and responsibilities. The Act provided for the creation of a Supreme Court, disqualified judges from membership of the reformed Second Chamber, created new machinery for judicial appointments, and confirmed that the Lord Chancellor would no longer sit as a judge.[30] The drift towards legal constitutionalism under New Labour was tightly bound within a commitment to parliamentary sovereignty. This raises the question of the degree to which the creation of a Supreme Court without the existence of a rigid constitution and the judicial capacity to veto legislation amounts to a meaningful alteration of a political system. At the same time, the symbolic value of establishing a Supreme Court and removing judges from the legislature should not be dismissed lightly. Section 13.3 evaluates these reforms through the prism of Lijphart's methodology. It also seeks to locate this chapter's focus on V9 within a number of broader themes and issues in relation to majoritarian modification and constitutional change.

13.3 Hybrid constitutionalism

Griffith's 'The Political Constitution' (1979) provides a critical reference point for debates concerning judicial review and the evolution of democracy in the UK because it represented an impassioned plea to preserve the existing constitutional framework, while also rejecting the logic of legal constitutionalism.[31] In many ways Griffiths' thesis (and its anti-thesis) became increasingly relevant over the subsequent decades due to a combination of internal and external factors. Internally, the behaviour of the

Conservative governments during 1979–97 cultivated a belief that the logic of auto-limitation and a hidden constitution was failing and as a result a move towards legal constitutionalism, in which the capacity of the executive was restrained, was necessary. So, whereas in 1917 Lord Dunedin could reflect on the power-hoarding nature of the constitution and conclude that although, 'the danger of abuse is theoretically present; practically, as things exist, it is in my opinion absent', by the end of the century many had come to a quite different conclusion.[32] This shift in attitudes occurred with an ideational context in the decades that spanned the millennium that viewed the judicialization of politics as a normatively positive development.

And yet, this chapter has provided an account of a *partial* shift; a shift that has been conceived in strictly Diceyan terms; a shift that exhibits elements of paradox and contradiction. This includes a judicial branch that has claimed and sought more power over representative institutions, but has then resorted to a largely deferential relationship with politics; and an executive that is willing to establish a 'Supreme Court' while at the same time emphasizing the sovereignty of Parliament. This hybrid constitutionalism and the partial shift between models of constitutionalism was encapsulated by the Lord Justice Laws,

> In its present state of evolution, the system may be said to stand at an intermediate stage between parliamentary supremacy and constitutional supremacy. Parliament remains the sovereign legislature; there is no superior text to which it must defer; there is no statute which by law it cannot make. But at the same time, the common law has come to recognise and endorse the notion of constitutional or fundamental rights.[33]

To this statement, and particularly the reference to an 'intermediate stage', the Lord Chancellor replied, 'I do not join in that prediction. The present arrangements were crafted as a settlement. They represent our reconciliation of effective rights protection with parliamentary sovereignty...a limited form of constitutional review'.[34] It is the notion of 'a settlement' that is likely to prove problematic. As with devolution, reforms that have altered the executive–judicial relationship are likely to evolve and take on a degree of constitutional momentum. Moreover, the idea of 'limited' constitutional review is arguably indicative of an executive mentality that fails to comprehend the aims and logic of legal constitutionalism. Bogdanor has foretold a possible 'constitutional crisis' in the future due to an attempt to combine arguably incompatible constitutional doctrines (i.e. parliamentary sovereignty and legal constitutionalism).[35]

We return to the issue of momentum, spillover, and dynamics in Part III, but it is now necessary to return to Lijphart's Index of Judicial Review (Table 13.1). The UK received a score of 1.0 (No Judicial Review) with no variance identified between the periods 1945–96 and 1979–96. At first glance, the creation of a Supreme Court moves towards a more distinct separation of powers, and the incorporation of the ECHR suggests a significant shift towards a power-sharing model of democracy. A more detailed analysis of the manner in which these measures have been implemented, however, suggests that New Labour's approach to strengthening judicial review as an anti-majoritarian mechanism are much weaker than the situation found in many consensual political systems due to the dominance of the concept of parliamentary sovereignty. Although the theoretical capacity of the judiciary to play a greater role as a constitutional 'long-stop' may have been increased, this has been offset to a large extent by a judicial culture of continuing deference and a reluctance to engage in explicit and detailed constitutional discourse. The constitution of the UK has definitely evolved away from the political constitution, but the degree of this shift is far more limited than the rhetoric of Labour ministers, as some 'Revolutionary Theorists' suggest. Reapplying Lijphart's methodology for V9 results in an updated index score of 1.5, suggesting a move from 'No Judicial Review' to 'Weak Judicial Review'.

This conclusion does, however, fit with Lijphart's argument about a global trend towards more and stronger forms of judicial review. Countries including Canada, Belgium, Colombia, France, Italy, and the UK reflect a constant transition from lower to higher degrees of strength for this variable. And yet, this chapter has revealed how a government may embark upon an apparently wide-ranging programme of constitutional reform with little actual commitment to changing the nature of democracy—what could be termed 'cosmetic reform'. More accurately, this chapter has illustrated how a government may wish to shift the balance of power within the constitutional configuration of a country to some degree, while still retaining control *over* core components and power centres, such as the voting system, legislature, and judiciary—'moderate reform'. Pushing the analysis further—what else can this chapter tell us about the statecraft and executive mentality of New Labour and particularly about the role of Tony Blair as a constitutional entrepreneur? Is the revised score for V9 internally consistent with the other score along this dimension?

In terms of statecraft, the findings of this chapter can be located within the contours of both the bi-constitutionality thesis and the argument concerning constitutional anomie. The creation of a Supreme Court and incorporation of the ECHR have created a new constitutional paradigm based upon the 'bi-polar sovereignty of the Crown in Parliament and the Crown in the Courts'.[36] This is bi-constitutionality along a second dimension. As the analysis of the first five variables revealed, New Labour has attempted to forge devolution on a power-sharing model, while retaining a form of modified majoritarianism at the national level. This *modified* majoritarianism at the core involves bi-constitutionalism based upon an attempt to operationalize incongruent models of democracy (i.e. a Political Constitution and a Legal Constitution).

However, identifying the existence of bi-constitutionality along any dimension raises the question of whether this occurred through chance or by design, and it is at this point that the constitutional anomie thesis becomes relevant. The nature of democracy in the UK *drifted* throughout 1997–2007: it was not reconfigured on the basis of any clear or coherent plan. What is especially significant about V9 is the manner in which it underlines the lack of a 'constitutional entrepreneur' with the capacity to adopt a clear position and lead change. The sudden announcement in June 2003 of the decision to create a Supreme Court and abolish the position of Lord Chancellor represented Tony Blair's attempt to take control of the constitutional reform agenda after years of criticism.[37] It therefore occurred at the same time as a Cabinet reshuffle in which Lord Irvine was replaced by Lord Falconer. Instead of rebuilding confidence in the government's capacity to engage in considered and rational planning, the raft of measures only served to exacerbate long-standing concerns, 'it is difficult to resist the conclusion that the reforms [were] the product of policy making on the hoof. They [did] not square with statements from government ministers; nor, for that matter, were the reforms mentioned in the 2001 Labour Party election manifesto'.[38]

The theme of consistency brings us back to a consideration of Lijphart's framework and particularly the interrelationship between specific variables. There are many reasons to expect V8 (constitutional rigidity) and V9 (judicial review) to display a correlation; (*a*) rigidity and judicial review are both anti-majoritarian devices and, conversely, completely flexible constitutions are unlikely to feature robust judicial review; (*b*) both variables are also logically related—judicial review can only be effective if supported by constitutional rigidity (and vice versa). Figure 13.1 shows the empirical relationship between V8 and V9. The correlation remains significant, and although the UK has

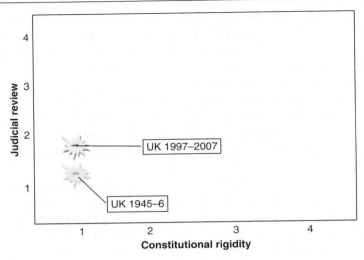

Figure 13.1 Relationship between V8 (constitutional rigidity) and V9 (judicial review) for the UK

V9 Index of judicial review conclusion	
Lijphart's UK score 1945–96	1.0
Lijphart's UK score 1971–96	1.0
Updated UK score 1997–2007	1.5

shifted slightly along the vertical axis it remains clearly within the majoritarian quadrant of the diagram. Before it is possible to explore this finding in more detail it is necessary to examine the last variable (V10)—central bank independence.

Notes

1. Dicey, A (1885) *The Law of the Constitution*. London, p. 39.
2. See Harlow, C (2000) 'Disposing of Dicey', *Political Studies*, 48(2), 356–69.
3. Lord Hailsham (1978) *The Dilemma of Democracy*. London: Collies, p. 13.
4. Lijphart *op. cit.* (1999), pp. 223–4.
5. Hirschl, R (2004) *Towards Juristocracy*. Cambridge: Harvard University Press; see also Shapiro, M and Stone Sweet, A (2002) *On Law, Politics and Judicialization*. New York: Oxford University Press; Stone Sweet, A (2000) *Governing with Judges*. Oxford: Oxford University Press.
6. Ginsburg, T (2003) *Judicial Review in New Democracies*. Cambridge: Cambridge University Press.

7. Hirschl, R (2008) 'The Judicialization of Mega-Politics and the Rise of Political Courts', *Annual Review of Political Science*, 11, 94.

8. See Miller, R (2004) 'Lords of Democracy', *Washington Lee Law Review*, 61, 587–662.

9. See, for example, Graber, M (1993) 'The Non-Majoritarian Difficulty', *Studies in American Political Development*, 7, 3–73; Graber, M (2006). 'From the Counter-Majoritarian Difficulty to Juristocracy and the Political Construction of Judicial Power', *Massachusetts Law Review*, 65, 1–14.

10. Bellamy, R (2007) *Political Constitutionalism*. Cambridge: Cambridge University Press.

11. Drewry, G (1992) 'Judicial Politics in Britain', *West European Politics*, 15(3), 17.

12. For a review of this literature, see Flinders, M. (1999) *The Politics of Accountability in the Modern State*. London: Ashgate.

13. Tomkins, A (2005) *Our Republican Constitution*, London: Hart, p. 11.

14. Loughlin, M (2000) *Sword and Scales*. Oxford: Hart, p. 5.

15. Mandelson, P and Liddle, R (1996) *The Blair Revolution*. London: Faber & Faber, pp. 195–6.

16. *Report of the Joint Consultative Committee* (1997), para. 23.

17. See Rosenberg, J (2004) 'The Right to Liberty Cannot be Overstated', *The Telegraph*, 17 December.

18. See Ewing, K (2007) 'The Political Constitution of Emergency Powers', *International Journal of Law in Context*, 3, 313–318.

19. *R v DPP ex p Kebeline* (2000) 2 AC 326, p. 381. See Ewing, K (2009) 'The Judiciary', in M Flinders et al., eds., *Oxford Handbook of British Politics*. Oxford: Oxford University Press.

20. *R (Countryside Alliance) v Attorney General* 2007 UKHL 52.

21. Weir, S and Byrne, I (2004) 'Democratic Audit', *Parliamentary Affairs*, 57(2), 453–68.

22. Tomkins, A (2008) 'The Rule of Law in Blair's Britain', *University of Queensland Law Journal*.

23. See Edwards, R (2002) 'Judicial Deference under the Human Rights Act', *Modern Law Review*, 65 (6), 859–82.

24. Lord Bingham (1998) 'Incorporation of the ECHR', 2 *Jersey Law Review*, 257.

25. Le Sueur, A (2003) 'New Labour's Next (Surprisingly Quick) Steps in Constitutional Reform', *Public Law*, (Autumn), 368–77.

26. Ahmed, K (2003) 'Cabinet Ignored Over Historical Legal Reforms', *The Observer*, 15 June.

27. See HC 48 (2003–4) *Judicial Appointments and a Supreme Court*. Select Committee on Constitutional Affairs, Session 2003–4, para. 188. Also HL Deb, col.1211–344.

28. HL 125 *Constitutional Reform Bill (HL)*. Select Committee on the Constitutional Reform Bill.

29. Woolf, Lord (2004) 'The Rule of Law and a Change in Constitution'. Squire Centenary Lecture, Cambridge University.

30. See Woodhouse, D (2007) 'The Constitutional Reform Act 2005', *International Journal of Constitutional Law*, 153; Windlesham, Lord (2005) 'The Constitutional Reform Act 2005', *Public Law*, 806.

31. Griffiths, J A G (1979) 'The Political Constitution', *Modern Law Review*, 42(1), 16.

32. Quoted in Ewing, K (2000) 'The Politics of the British Constitution', *Public Law*, 142.

33. *International Transport Roth GmbH and Other v Secretary of State for the Home Department* (2002) 3 WLR 344, para. 71.

34. Irvine, Lord (2002) 'The Human Rights Act Two Years On', Durham University, 1 November.

35. Bogdanor, V (2006) 'The Sovereignty of Parliament or the Rule of Law?' Magna Carta Lecture, 15 June.

36. See Sedley, S (1996) 'Human Rights: A Twenty First Century Agenda', *Public Law*, 386.

37. See Norton, P (2007) 'The Constitution', in A Seldon ed., *Blair's Britain*. Cambridge: Cambridge University Press.

38. Le Sueur *op. cit.* (2003), p. 368.

Chapter 14

V10. Central Bank Independence

What governs our approach is a clear desire to place power where it should be: increasingly not with politicians, but with those best fitted in different ways to deploy it. Interest rates are not set by politicians in the Treasury but by the Bank of England. This depoliticising of key decision-making is a vital element in bringing power closer to the people.[1]

The previous four chapters (covering Variables 6–9) appear to demonstrate that more change has occurred along the federal–unitary dimension than along the executive–parties dimension. This updated analysis is also beginning to reveal how changes and reforms have occurred very much within the contours of a majoritarian framework. The fifth and final variable of the federal–unitary dimension concerns central banks and their degree of independence from governments. The governance of central banks provides an important indicator of the kind of democracy in which these institutions operate. This is because, giving central banks a high degree of independence and autonomy forms another mechanism for sharing power and fits the cluster of 'divided power characteristics' (the second dimension) of the consensus model of democracy.[2]

Once again, the empirical research presented in this chapter reveals change. Whereas Lijphart's original studies identified comparatively low levels of central bank independence in the UK, this chapter concludes that the score for V10 has increased significantly. In order to explain and justify this conclusion, this chapter is divided into three sections. Lijphart's methodology for arriving at an Index Score for Central Bank Independence and his original assessment of the UK provides the focus of Section 14.1. This flows into an account of change and the generation of an updated index score in Section 14.2. The final section examines the degree to which the specific findings of this chapter exhibit relationships with other variables that form the federal–unitary dimension.

14.1 Financial gatekeepers

The analysis of central banks as an element of constitutional political analysis or public-law scholarship is somewhat alien in the UK. Research and writing on the politics and governance of independent central banks is primarily found within the sub-disciplines of public administration and political economy, and it remains true that within recent mainstream studies of the UK's constitution, V10 is rarely treated with anything more than a fleeting reference. King's *The British Constitution* (2007), Bogdanor's *The British Constitution in the Twentieth Century* (2003), Oliver's *Constitutional Reform in the UK* (2003), Jowell and Oliver's *The Changing Constitution* (2007), Hazell's *Constitutional Future Revisted* (2008), and McDonald's *Reinventing Britain* (2007) underline the point that the analysis of monetary policy and central bank independence still tends to occur beyond the contours of 'traditional' constitutional studies. In the United States, by contrast, the discipline of constitutional political economy has evolved to offer a broader and epistemologically distinct approach to the nature of incentives and sanctions in institutional design. A central strand of this approach locates independent central banks at the constitutional interface of politics and economics. This highlights many of the distinctive qualities of political studies and public-law scholarship in the UK that were highlighted in Chapter 4 and to which this book is intended to be a departure.

Quasi-autonomous institutions of economic management at both the national and international levels represent key actors in the emerging architecture of global governance. Moreover, the governance arrangements and discretion levels of central banks provides a critical indicator in relation to judging the nature and form of a democracy, and is particularly relevant to a polity's evolution. In contextual terms, this is reinforced by dominant ideational conceptions of 'good governance', promoted by institutions like the World Bank and International Monetary Fund, which tend to interpret the existence of an independent central bank as a core foundation of a modern and effective democracy. Put slightly differently, in the twenty-first century the logic of distancing macro-economic management from elected politicians is viewed as a defining element of any country's claim to be a *credible* democracy. This is particularly evident in relation to European Union governance where candidate countries must be able to demonstrate a domestic institutional architecture that includes an independent central bank. During the 1990s, it was possible to identify a global trend in which more than thirty countries passed legislation increasing the legal independence of their central banks.[3]

The transfer of decision-making responsibility for macro-economic issues offers a direct correlation with the distinction between power-hoarding and power-sharing democracies. Strong and independent central banks form a critical element of the diffusion of powers generally associated with consensual or power-sharing democracies. When central banks are dependent branches of the executive and therefore relatively weak, there is likely to be a correlation with other variables, such as a weak legislature and high levels of constitutional flexibility, that tend to be features of a power-hoarding majoritarian polity. Delegating powers to central banks is simply another way of dividing power.

Central banks are generally responsible for monetary policy; that is the regulation of interest rates and the supply of money. These two levers have a direct (if imperfect) effect on price stability and the control of inflation which, in turn, are critical variables in relation to unemployment levels, economic growth, and financial stability. The powers of central banks are commonly set out in statutes and not through constitutional provisions. Nevertheless, such is the contextual pressure on politicians not to be seen to interfere with central bank independence that these statutes tend to be treated with a higher status than 'ordinary' legislation: they tend to have a 'quasi-constitutional force'.[4] In terms of measuring the degree of central bank independence in a given country, Lijphart draws upon three strands of research:

1. Cukierman, Webb, and Neyapti.
2. Grillo, Masciandaro, and Tabellini.
3. The analysis of governor turnover rates.

The Cukierman, Webb, and Neyapti (CWN) index of central bank independence analyses sixteen variables (relating to the appointment and tenure of the Bank's governor, policy formulation, central bank objectives, and limitations on spending) concerning legal independence.[5] The highest (most independent) score, for example, would be given to a governor who is appointed for eight years or longer and cannot be removed, and who may not simultaneously hold other offices in government. The lowest (most dependent) score would be given to governors who are appointed for less than four years, who can be dismissed at the discretion of the executive, and who is not disqualified from holding another government appointment. In relation to limitations on spending the CWN index would ascribe a high independence score to those banks with the capacity to lend only to central government and when they control the terms of the lending; conversely, they are least independent when they can lend to all levels of government, to public enterprises, and to the private sector and when the terms of lending are decided by the executive and not the bank.

The CWN research examined central bank independence in each of the decades from the 1950s to the 1980s, and the set of scores contained in the second column of Table 14.1 represent either the average of these four ratings or the averages of the ratings for the relevant later decades for countries that were not independent or democratic in the middle of the twentieth century. Lijphart then utilized two further indexes in order to fill in missing data and draw upon a wider expertise base. These being the Grilli–Masciandaro–Tabellini (GMT) index of political and economic independence and the rate of turnover in the governorship of the central bank.[6] These two additional indexes were adjusted by Lijphart to the zero-to-one scale used by the CWN index, and are shown in the third and fourth columns of Table 14.1. The final column of Table 14.1 shows the mean of the two separate indexes of independence for the twenty-eight of the thirty-six central banks and the one index that is available for the remaining eight central banks. The values in the final column therefore constitute the comprehensive index score for V10 that was used by Lijphart, and is updated in this chapter.

Comparative analysis of this data for V10 reveals that although the theoretical range runs from 0 to 1.0, the actual empirical range is only around half as wide. Only five countries achieve the threshold of <0.5 that the CWN indexing scheme categorizes as 'semi-independence'. The midpoint of the empirical range is 0.43, but the mean and median are lower (0.38 and 0.36, respectively) indicating that more countries are located in the lower half of the empirical range.[7] The data also suggests that even those central banks that are widely viewed as the strongest in the world—those in Germany, Switzerland, and the United States—are partners in an arm's-length relationship with politicians and are by no means completely independent. Of particular importance for the focus of this chapter is the UK's score of 0.31 and 0.28 (for the periods 1945–96 and 1971–96, respectively) leading to an overall index score of 0.30.

This score reflects the outcome of the historical relationship between the Westminster Model and central bank independence.[8] Even when a number of mainland European countries (e.g. France, Belgium, Spain) were moving towards granting independence to their central banks in the 1990s, as part of the move towards Economic and Monetary Union and the establishment of a European Central Bank, the UK adopted a distinct position. As late as 1993, the Conservative PM, John Major, used

Table 14.1 Central bank independence in thirty-six democracies

Country	CWN index	GMT index	Governors' turnover rate index	Mean
Germany	0.69	0.69	—	0.69
Switzerland	0.56	0.64	—	0.60
United States	0.48	0.64	—	0.56
Austria	0.63	0.48	—	0.55
Canada	0.45	0.58	—	0.52
Netherlands	0.42	0.53	—	0.48
Denmark	0.50	0.42	—	0.46
Mauritius	—	—	0.43	0.43
Australia	0.36	0.48	—	0.42
Papua New Guinea	0.36	—	0.47	0.42
Ireland	0.44	0.37	—	0.41
Malta	0.44	—	0.39	0.41
Bahamas	0.41	—	0.39	0.40
Barbados	0.38	—	0.43	0.40
Costa Rica	0.47	—	0.31	0.39
Israel	0.39	—	0.39	0.39
Trinidad	—	—	0.39	0.39
Greece	0.55	0.21	—	0.38
India	0.34	—	0.35	0.35
Jamaica	—	—	0.35	0.35
Iceland	0.34	—	—	0.34
Colombia	0.27	—	0.39	0.33
Luxembourg	0.33	—	—	0.33
Botswana	0.33	—	0.31	0.32
France	0.27	0.37	—	0.32
Venezuela	0.38	—	0.27	0.32
United Kingdom	0.30	0.32	—	0.31
Sweden	0.29	—	—	0.29
Finland	0.28	—	—	0.28
Portugal	0.41	0.16	—	0.28
Belgium	0.16	0.37	—	0.27
Italy	0.25	0.27	—	0.26
Japan	0.18	0.32	—	0.25
Spain	0.23	0.27	—	0.25
New Zealand	0.22	0.16	—	0.19
Norway	0.17	—	—	0.17

Source: Lijphart (1999) *Patterns of Democracy*, pp. 236–7.

the announcement of a new Governor of the Bank of England to reaffirm that the government remained opposed to the idea of an independent central bank.[9] This view reflected the UK's traditional approach to monetary policy which held that the Chancellor of the Exchequer and not the Bank of England as ultimately responsible.[10] For this reason, as Table 14.1 shows, in comparative terms, the Bank of England was ranked as being highly dependent on the government. This score would appear to complement the statement made by a former Chancellor of the Exchequer, Sir Stafford Cripps, that, 'The Bank is my creature'.[11] Section 14.2 considers whether the Bank of England remains a creature of the executive after ten years of New Labour government.

14.2 Monetary policy, 1997–2007

The idea of a new role for the Bank of England had been an element of New Labour's strategic planning since the mid-1990s, and was subsequently included in the 1997 election manifesto: 'we will reform the Bank of England to ensure that decision-making on monetary policy is more effective, open, accountable and free from short-term political manipulation'.[12] And yet, the pace at which the government brought forward this reform surprised many commentators. Just five days after their election victory (and before the first Labour cabinet meeting), the Chancellor of the Exchequer, Gordon Brown, wrote to the Governor of the Bank of England setting out new arrangements for monetary policy making which transferred operational independence to the Bank.[13] These plans were confirmed later in a statement to the House of Commons and subsequently legislated for through the Bank of England Act 1998.[14]

The logic and rationale for this alteration in policy making lay in a number of strands of thinking which, taken together, formed a confluence of analysis and prescription. Central amongst these were Downsian arguments concerning the political marketplace and the rationalities of political behaviour.[15] The incentives and opportunities for politicians to interfere in the economy for short-term political benefits created a credibility gap which discouraged investment and increased inflation.[16] The delegation of tasks to quasi-autonomous institutions that are indirectly controlled by politicians has been promoted as an effective response to these rational choice theoretic assumptions concerning political behaviour.[17] The incentive for politicians to delegate a degree of control in relation to monetary policy is that it: (*a*) may provide an effective tool of inflation control; while also (*b*) affording opportunities for 'blame-shifting' should problems occur.[18] It was in this ideational context that the Bank of England Act 1998 sought to amend the 'nationalization' legislation of 1946 in order to achieve what HM Treasury described as 'a new departure in economic policy making'—the 'depoliticization' of policy making.[19]

Institutionally, the main reform came in the form of a new organization, the Monetary Policy Committee (MPC), which would be responsible for setting monetary policy. Section 11 of the Bank of England Act 1998 sets out the formal role and constitution of the MPC. In relation to monetary policy, the objectives of the Bank of England are: (*a*) to maintain price stability; and (*b*) to support the economic policy of the government, including its objectives for growth and employment. The government reviews and announces the inflation target for the Bank at the time of the budget and the MPC has operational independence about how it meets the inflation targets. The Bank of England Act 1998 therefore gave the MPC 'instrument independence' in the sense that it is free to pursue its policy goals without (formal) interference from outside political pressures, but the government and HM Treasury retain 'goal independence' in the sense of setting the targets that the MPC is expected to achieve.[20] The membership of the MPC includes the Governor and two Deputy Governors of the Bank of England, two members appointed by the Governor after consultation with the Chancellor, and four outside 'expert' members appointed by the Chancellor. The MPC has a two-day meeting on a monthly basis and all decisions on interest rates are announced immediately after the last day. The proceedings of the meetings, including votes, are published within two weeks.[21] The centrifugal thrust of delegating powers to the MPC is reconciled with the centripetal force of the convention of ministerial responsibility to Parliament through the existence of executive 'reserve powers'. This allows the Chancellor to intervene in previously delegated operational issues where those directions are 'required in the public interest and by extreme economic circumstances'.[22] However, the capacity and flexibility of the executive to intervene is restrained by the requirement that any intervention must be approved by both Houses of Parliament within twenty-eight days.

How to achieve an appropriate and proportionate balance between legislative scrutiny and operational independence had been a contested issue since the Treasury and Civil Service Committee first recommended increasing the independence of the Bank of England in 1994.[23] Although New Labour were willing to concede a need for legislative approval for the use of emergency reserve powers, it was not willing to formally strengthen the capacity of the House of Commons vis-à-vis the MPC or Bank of England in any other way. The Chancellor's statement to the House regarding granting operational independence to the Bank of England stimulated an inquiry by the Treasury Select Committee on how an acceptable degree of accountability could be secured. The committee recommended that the Bank of England Bill should make provisions for nominations to the MPC to be subject to confirmatory hearings by the committee in order to ensure that all appointees fulfilled the specified criteria.[24] Although the government rejected this recommendation on the basis that such a process risked politicizing candidates and undermining the responsibility of ministers, the Treasury Committee decided to implement a series of non-statutory confirmation hearings for all appointments to the MPC.[25]

The Treasury's decision to implement a formal system for non-statutory confirmation hearings for appointments to the MPC raises questions about the executive's capacity to control the legislature, even in highly majoritarian polities. Concerns regarding the politicization of appointments have not proved founded as the committee has restricted itself to issues of demonstrable professional competence, rather than broader political affiliations. Although the government has persisted with the appointment of a small number of individuals about whom the committee has raised concerns, the existence of a formal legislative arena in which an appointee will be examined is likely to exert a significant anticipatory effect on the executive to ensure that all candidates are 'above the bar' in professional terms.[26] The Treasury Committee's confirmation hearings also exhibit elements of constitutional 'spillover' in two ways: (*a*) a number of other select committees have established similar procedures for scrutinizing ministerial appointments to the various agencies, boards, and commissions that they are charged with overseeing;[27] (*b*) the government's July 2007 *Governance of Britain* green paper stated that the House of Commons should play an expanded and strengthened role in relation to a number of ministerial public appointments (discussed further in Chapter 16).

The independence of the Bank of England is therefore protected not only by formal mechanisms (statute law, parliamentary ratification of 'reserve power', etc.), but also by informal mechanisms, like the non-statutory confirmation hearings, that also serve to bolster the position of the MPC and limit the flexibility of the executive. As a result reassessing the governance of the Bank of England through the lens of Lijphart's methodology for 1997–2007 reflects this increased level of central bank independence with a statistical score of 0.45 (using the mean of the CWN and GMT indexes) as opposed to the score of 0.31 for 1945–96. This conclusion is in alignment with the comparative research of de Sousa who employed a different methodology to measure central bank independence, but came to a similar conclusion regarding the extent of change in the UK.[28] The extent of this shift is underlined when viewed against the data shown in Table 14.1. A score of 0.45 in 1996 for V10 would have positioned the UK almost exactly mid-point (0.43) on the empirical range. Having identified a significant change in relation to V10, it is necessary to explore the existence of correlations with other variables, as well as examine the link between this variable and the core arguments concerning bi-constitutionality and constitutional anomie made in this book.

14.3 Squaring the Circle?

Throughout the twentieth century, the view was taken by consecutive governments that the UK's constitution was incompatible with the concept of central bank independence. New Labour departed from this position and instead sought to square the circle by granting independence, but within the contours of the Westminster Model. This demonstrates how the specific incorporation of global trends are framed and implemented differently by various national systems. The notion that the Bank of England was ever simply a 'creature' of the executive throughout the twentieth century veils the existence of a far more complex relationship. However, the evidence presented in this chapter suggests a significant shift in the governance of the UK as it relates to V10 which has implications at a number of levels. The first implication being that New Labour utilized the malleability of the constitutional framework in order to legitimate a transfer of power beyond the core. This is a significant point. Throughout the 1980s and 1990s, the Conservative governments maintained that the conventions of collective and individual ministerial responsibility to the legislature demanded that functions be exercised within the parameters of a ministerial department of state.[29] This led to a rejection of the logic of an independent central bank. New Labour adopted a different interpretation: an interpretation that did not see the delegation of monetary policy as incompatible with the convention of ministerial responsibility. Finance ministers remained accountable to the legislature for fiscal matters, but not necessarily responsible in the sense of being to blame. The

chain of delegation between the legislature, the executive, and state officials had therefore become more tenuous, but was not necessarily broken.

The timing of New Labour's decisions and the drivers behind this process are also critical explanatory variables in understanding the process of
change, especially as the granting of operational independence to the
Bank of England came a decade after the start of the trend in central
bank independence.[30] Accepting the logic of monetary delegation was
the result of a number of domestic and international factors. During the
early and mid-1990s, when many countries around the world were granting independence to their central banks, the UK's voluntary exclusion
from the Exchange Rate Mechanism (except for 1990–2) and the opt-
out from Economic and Monetary Union slowed down the process of
ideational diffusion and alleviated the pressure for 'institutional isomor-
phism'.[31] The Labour Party's history of governing was, however, marred by
an association with financial crisis (the sterling crisis of 1947, the devalua-
tion of 1967, and the International Monetary Fund loan in 1976), which
created a need to reassure the business community and financial markets
that 'New' Labour could implement a stable and credible monetary policy.
This instrumental political need on the part of the Labour Party dovetailed
with the activity of a powerful epistemic community and pattern of ideational diffusion, promoted the benefits of central bank independence.[32]

At a slightly broader level, it is possible to argue that the logic of central
bank independence corresponded with New Labour's approach to reform
and modernization. Lijphart's analysis displays a strong correlation
between central bank independence and federalism.[33] The five central
banks with the greatest independence (shown in Table 14.1), all operate
in federal systems. The representation in Figure 14.1 of changes to V6 and
V10 in the UK during 1997–2007 also suggests a degree of internal consistency due to the manner in which both measures combine to generate
diagonal evolution from the bottom/left quadrant (power-hoarding) towards the top/right quadrant (power-sharing).

Figure 14.2 reveals a similar, but less-pronounced direction of travel in
relation to the relationship between central bank independence (V10) and
judicial review (V9). In simple terms, Figures 14.1 and 14.2 reveal that
moderate reform has occurred in relation to the division of powers within
the UK (V6), the position of the judiciary vis-à-vis the executive (V9), and
in relation to the Bank of England (V10). The variable scores for bicameralism (V7) and constitutional rigidity (V8) reflect no change, and therefore
suggest that the nature of majoritarian modification in the UK during
1997–2007 has been unbalanced.

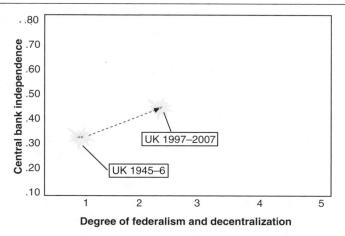

Figure 14.1 Relationship between V6 (federalism) and V10 (central bank independence) for the UK

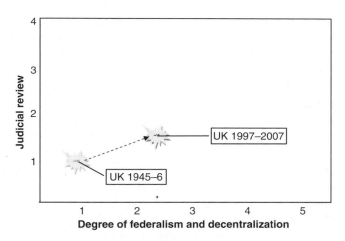

Figure 14.2 Relationship between V9 (judicial review) and V10 (central bank independence) for the UK

The notion of majoritarian modification feeds into a number of related issues that could be interpreted as elements of 'mega-politics' (see Chapter 2) which each in their own ways open up questions concerning political disengagement and the issue of trust in politics. The first of these issues concerns the rationalization of power transfers to non-elected actors. Dominant ideational perspectives promote the transfer of decision-making capacities to judges (V9) and financial experts (V10) on the basis that politicians cannot be trusted. Put slightly differently, judicial review and independent central banks are anti-majoritarian institutions, or what Goodhart describes as 'commitment devices', that utilize *appointed* rather than *elected* actors in the governance of modern democracies.[34] The delegation of functions away from elected politicians is frequently tied to the perceived benefits of 'depoliticization' as a valuable tool of modern governance. However, the use of anti-majoritarian institutions as a way of sharing power and regulating the behaviour of politicians—core elements of consensual politics—creates dilemmas at a number of levels. At a fairly basic level, the transfer of powers beyond elected politicians not only creates issues in terms of ensuring accountability and controlling patronage, but it also generates deeper questions concerning the boundaries of 'the political' and what constitute 'core' political tasks that should always lie in the hands of elected politicians.[35]

Scholars have arguably focused on the former set of more obvious questions to the detriment of the analysis of those deeper questions that are actually likely to become key debates in the twenty-first century. What are the choices faced by politicians in relation to democratic and administrative reform? Locating the issue of choice back within the sphere of public contestation is arguably critical as certain implicit assumptions, many tied to the variables studied in this book, have become almost uncontested. Marcussen suggests that the logic of central banking, for example, has transcended even depoliticized modes of governance, and has reached the point where it has been *apoliticized*, in that there is no longer a debate about even the principle of depoliticization, and it is difficult to foresee a situation in which politicians would seek to move back to a direct mode of governance.[36] A process of 'scientization' has allowed some policy areas to almost transcend politics through their redefinition as technical issues to be directed by experts. Apoliticization therefore signifies a shift in authoritative status, and a process in which the scientific knowledge of 'experts' is preferred to the electoral legitimacy of politicians.

In this sense, the interpretation of the law (V9) and the optimal choice of interest rates (V10) are viewed as technical matters, and responsibilities are subsequently delegated away from politicians to prevent political interference. Although this shift in powers may be understandable against the context of declining trust, and in politicians it poses distinctive questions about the fundamental aims and ambitions of political processes (i.e. issues of mega-politics concerning the basic values, identity, and fabric of a polity). This creates questions about the nature of democratic legitimacy and the capacity of political actors to borrow the legitimacy of other social groupings that have not been affected by the apparent tainting of conventional politics. While also feeding back into more basic questions regarding how those anti-majoritarian actors to which power has been delegated can be effectively held to account.

Engaging with these broader questions is facilitated by the fact that this chapter has produced an updated data score for Lijphart's tenth and final variable. This allows us to fulfil two of the aims of this book that were discussed in the opening chapters. Namely (a) to trace and plot the nature of democratic drift in the UK for the period 1997–2007 on the conceptual map of democracy; (b) from this to gain a deeper understanding of the cumulative impact of New Labour's reforms. These goals form the focus of Chapter 15.

V10 Index of central bank independence conclusion

Lijphart's UK Score 1945–96	0.31
Lijphart's UK Score 1971–96	0.28
Updated UK Score 1997–2007	0.45

Notes

1. Falconer, Lord (2003) Speech to the Institute for Public Policy Research, London.
2. Lijphart *op. cit.* (1999), p. 233.
3. See Maxfield, S (1997) *Gatekeepers of Growth*. Princeton, NJ: Princeton University Press.
4. Elster, J (1994) 'Constitutional Courts and Central Banks: Suicide Prevention or Suicide Pact?' *East European Constitutional Review*, 3(4), 68.
5. Cukierman, A, Webb, S, and Neyapti, B (1994) *Measuring Central Bank Independence and its Effect on Policy Outcomes*. San Fransciso: ICS.
6. Grilli, V, Masciandaro, D, and Tabllini, G (1991) 'Political and Monetary Institutions and Public Finanacial Policies in the Industrial Countries', *Economic Policy*, 6(2), 342–92.
7. Lijphart *op. cit.* (1999), p. 239.
8. Busch, A (1994) 'Central Bank Independence and the Westminster Model', *West European Politics*, 17(1), 53–72.
9. *The Times* (1993) 23 January.
10. See Busch *op. cit.* (1994).
11. See Hirsch, F (1965) *The Pound Sterling: A Polemic*. London, p. 142.
12. See Labour Party (1995) *A New Economic Future for Britain*. London: Labour Party. For a historical account, see King, M (2005) 'Epistemic Communities

and the Diffusion of Ideas: Central Bank reform in the United Kingdom', *West European Politics*, 28(1), 94–123.

13. HM Treasury Press Release (1997) 6 May.

14. HC Deb (1997), 20 May 294, cols. 507–11.

15. See Downs *op. cit.* (1957); Brittan, S (1975) 'The Economic Contradictions of Democracy', *British Journal of Political Science*, 5(2), 129–59; Alesina, A (1989) 'Politics and Business Cycles in Industrial Democracies', *Economic Policy*, 8, 55–98.

16. Cobham, D, Papadopoulos, A, and Zis, G (2004) 'The Cost of Political Interference in Monetary Policy', *International Finance*, 7(3), 471–93; Forder, J (2000) 'Central Bank Independence and Credibility', *International Finance*, 3(1), 167–85.

17. Bergman, T, Muller, W and Strom, K (2003) *Delegation and Accountability in Parliamentary Democracies*. Oxford: Oxford University Press; Braun, D and Gilardi, F (2006) *Delegation in Contemporary Democracies*, London: Routledge; Epstein, D and O'Halloran, S (1999) *Delegating Powers*. New York: Cambridge University Press; Thatcher, M and Stone Sweet A (2003) *The Politics of Delegation*. London: Frank Cass.

18. Hood, C (2002) 'The Risk Game and the Blame Game', *Government and Opposition*, 37(1), 15–37.

19. HM Treasury (2002) *Reforming Britain's Economic and Financial Policy*. London: Palgrave, pp. 82 and 355. For a historical account and contestation of this position, see Burnham, P (2007) 'The Politicisation of Monetary Policy Making in Post-War Britain', *British Politics*, 2(3), 395–420; Buller, J and Flinders, M (2005) 'The Domestic Origins of Depoliticisation in the Area of British Economic Policy', *British Journal of Politics and International Relations*, 7(4), 526–44.

20. Spiegel, M (1998) 'Central Bank Independence and Inflation Expectations', *FRBSF Economic Review*, 1, 3–14.

21. Available at www.bankofengland.co.uk/monetarypolicy/overview.htm

22. *Bank of England Act 1998*, Section 19(1).

23. HC 98 (1993–4) *The Role of the Bank of England*. First Report from the Treasury and Civil Service Committee, Session 1993–4, para. 79.

24. HC 282 (1997–8) *Accountability of the Bank of England*. First report by the Treasury Select Committee, Session 1997–8, paras. 46–8.

25. HC 502 (1997–8) *Accountability of the Bank of England: The Response of the Government and the Bank of England*. Third special report from the Treasury Committee, 1997–8; HC 571 (1997–8) *Confirmation Hearings*. Third report from the Treasury Committee, Session 1997–8; HC 822 (1997–8) *The Monetary Policy Committee of the Bank of England*, Sixth Report of the Treasury Select Committee, Session 1997–8.

26. Flinders, M (forthcoming 2010) 'The Politics of Patronage and Public Appointments', *Governance*.

27. For a detailed review, see Flinders, M (2008) *Delegated Governance and the British State*. Oxford: Oxford University Press.

28. De Sousa, P (2001) 'Independent and Accountable Central Banks and the European Central Bank', *European Integration Papers Online*, 5(9).
29. This logic appeared specific to fiscal matters as the Conservative governments did not apply the same constitutional logic in relation to other policy spheres. See Barker, A (1982) ed. *Quangos in Britain*. London: Macmillan; Greve, C, Flinders, M, and Van Thiel, S (1999) 'Quangos—What's In a Name?' *Governance*, 12, pp. 129–47; Hogwood, B. (1995). 'The Growth of Quangos', in F Ridley and D Wilson (eds.) *The Quango Debate*, Oxford: Oxford University Press.
30. Widely seen as starting with the 1989 reform of the Reserve Bank of New Zealand.
31. Quaglia, L (2005) 'An Integrative Approach to the Politics of Central Bank Independence', *West European Politics*, 28(3), 549–68.
32. King *op. cit.* (2005).
33. Lijphart *op. cit.* (1999), pp. 240–2.
34. Goodhart, C (2002) 'The Constitutional Position of an Independent Central Bank', *Government & Opposition*, 37(2), 200.
35. See Flinders *op. cit.* (2008).
36. Marcussen, M (2006) 'Transcending Politics', in P Lægreid and T Christensen, eds., *Autonomy and Regulation: Coping with Agencies in the Modern State*. London: Edward Elgar.

Part III:

Bi-constitutionalism and the Governance of Britain

Chapter 15

Bi-constitutionalism

The British tend to ignore big constitutional change. They behave like a patient who submits to surgery under anaesthetic, but only considers whether he wants the operation some time later when he begins to feel the consequences.[1]

This book has attempted to look beneath the institutional reforms of New Labour in order to reveal their deeper statecraft or guiding public philosophy in relation to democratic change. The two chapters that together constitute Part III of this book use the data generated in Part II to assess the cumulative impact of New Labour's constitutional and democratic reforms (Chapter 15), and then examine the broader comparative, executive, and socio-political implications of these findings (Chapter 16). In essence, the next two chapters ask: what have we found? Does the evidence support the arguments regarding bi-constitutionality and constitutional anomie? What are the implications of these findings for future governments? How does the UK compare to the evolution of other democracies over the same period? Why does any of this matter?

This chapter is focused on updating the position of the UK on Lijphart's conceptual map of democracy, and then using these findings to develop the arguments relating to bi-constitutionalism and anomie. It argues that the UK's revised position on the map provides an empirical reflection of not only the bi-constitutional nature of UK governance at the beginning of the twenty-first century, but it also provides new insights into the 'Blair paradox'. This argument points to a potential weakness in Lijphart's framework because the debate in the UK has become polarized around a binary distinction *between* consensual or majoritarian meta-constitutional orientations, when in fact the contemporary reality is far more complex. The 'Blair paradox' actually reflects not a simple shift in orientations (i.e. from majoritarian power-hoarding to consensus power-sharing), but a multifaceted attempt to overlay a new meta-constitutional orientation, in terms of a set of core values, principles, and assumptions about the distribution of power and the relationship between political actors, on top of the existing version. This is the creation of a multilevel polity based upon a more consensual model of democracy *within* an increasingly frail conception of the Westminster Model (i.e. modified majoritarianism). And it is this constitutional engineering, or more precisely the attempt to blend arguably incompatible meta-constitutional orientations that explains: (*a*) the specific manner in which certain reforms have been implemented; (*b*) why the government has sought to block or marginalize certain issues; and (*c*) the academic polarization of opinion.

In order to examine these issues this chapter is divided into three sections. The first section focuses on updating Lijphart's work on the UK for the decade 1997–2007. This flows into an evaluation of the relationship between the revised position of the UK and this book's arguments concerning bi-constitutionalism and constitutional anomie in the second section. The final section then seeks to expose the origins of these phenomena by analysing the theoretical and ideological foundations of New Labour.

15.1 Analysis

Lijphart's framework for understanding political systems offers a valuable tool for understanding how democracy in the UK has been altered by the constitutional reforms enacted by New Labour between 1997 and 2007. In addition to allowing scholars to gauge the actual extent of change, it also provides an overview of the changing constitutional terrain, as well as differences in emphasis between certain dimensions of change. Table 15.1 brings together the updated scores for each of the variables examined in Part II of this book.

The revised index scores for both dimensions are the used to reposition the UK on the Conceptual Map of Democracy (Figure 15.1). This reveals that democracy in the UK did change under New Labour, but that this change has been one-sided. There has been a clear shift along the federal–unity dimension—reflecting primarily devolution, incorporation of the ECHR, and reform of the Bank of England—but no equivalent shift on the executive–parties dimension. On the contrary, the change on this dimension suggests a slight increase or greater concentration in executive power since 1997. This finding complements Riddell's view that under

Table 15.1 Auditing reform in the UK under New Labour: Lijphart's ten variables and two dimensions

Variable	Majoritarian	Consensus	1945–96	1971–96	1997–2007	Extent of change (nationally)	Post-devolution (sub-nationally)
V1. Party system	Two party system.	Multiparty system.	2.11	2.20	2.28	No change	3.84
V2. Cabinets	Single party majority cabinets.	Power-sharing multiparty coalitions.	96.7	93.3	100.0	No change	25.0
V3. Executive–legislative relationship	Dominant executive.	Executive–legislature balance of power.	5.52	5.52	6.78	No change / more majoritarian	3.5
V4. Electoral system	Disproportional first-past-the post system.	Proportional representation.	10.33	14.66	17.00	No change / more majoritarian	6.87
V5. Interest groups	Informal pluralist interest group interaction.	Coordinated and 'corporatist' interest group interaction.	3.38	3.50	3.50	No change	2.6
V6. Federal–unitary dimension	Unitary and centralized government.	Federal and decentralized government.	1.0	1.0	2.5	Significant change	—
V7. Unicameralism–bicameralism dimension	Concentration of power in a unicameral legislature.	Division of power between two equally strong, but differently constituted houses.	2.5	2.5	2.5	No change	—
V8. Constitutional amendment	Flexible constitution that can be amended by simple majorities.	Rigid constitutions that can be changed only by extraordinary majorities.	1.0	1.0	1.0	No change	—
V9. Legislative supremacy	Legislature has the final word on the constitutionality of legislation.	Legislation subject to a judicial review of their constitutionality by a supreme or constitutional court.	1.0	1.0	1.5	Moderate change	—
V10. Central bank	Dependent on the executive.	Independent central bank.	0.31	0.28	0.45	Significant change	—
D1. Executive–parties			1.21	1.39	1.62	No change / more majoritarian	0.28
D.1 Federal–unitary			1.12	1.19	0.42	Significant change	N/A

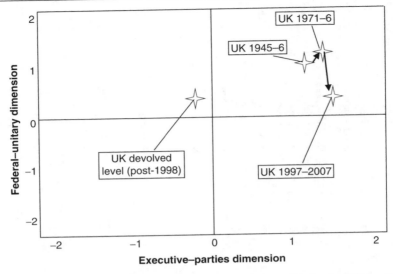

Figure 15.1 Two-dimensional conceptual map of democracy in the UK (national and devolved)

New Labour, 'There was, and remains, a sense that it was all very well to adopt a more pluralist framework away from London, but not within the Palace of Westminster' and Beetham's conclusion that 'ministers are determined to hold onto all their traditional powers at the centre'.[2]

Figure 15.1 confirms Norris' 2002 prediction that if Lijphart's seminal work was updated for the UK that it would reveal that, 'the federal–unitary dimension of British government has been transformed far more than the executive–party dimension ... Like Harold Lloyd dangling in midair on a skyscraper ledge, one hand has slipped but the other retains its grip.'[3] This result stimulates a number of questions:

1. Can this be accepted as a valid result in terms of reflecting the changed nature of democracy in the UK?
2. How does this result fit within the academic polarization between the 'Fundamental Camp' and the 'Sceptical Camp' (discussed in Chapter 4)?
3. How can this result be used to develop the bi-constitutionality thesis?
4. What is the relationship between this result and the 'Blair paradox'?
5. How can we drill down still further in order to understand the roots of New Labour's statecraft?

6. Does a deeper understanding of New Labour's statecraft provide new insights into the argument regarding constitutional anomie?

This section examines the first two questions, Section 15.2 focuses on the third and fourth questions, and Section 15.3 of this chapter explores the last two questions.

Are the results set out in Table 15.1 and illustrated in Figure 15.1 valid? As Chapter 4 acknowledged, the generation of quantitative scores to capture interpersonal and inter- and intra-institutional relationships is not unproblematic. For this book, this specific epistemological and methodological challenge has been managed through a process of triangulation, using cognate research projects that have analysed the same variables using different techniques, and through a system of peer review. The results can therefore be accepted as both credible and precise. That is not to say that debates do not exist about the specific scorings, but the extent of these debates are marginal and would not drastically effect the overall position of the UK. In terms of the selection of variables, it could be argued that the ten variables in Lijphart's framework are problematic because they underestimate the commitment to change, and downplay the existence of a strong institutional bias towards inertia over time. Several variables might be interpreted as not actually being open to purposeful constitutional engineering (e.g. V1 'Party System' and V5 'Interest Groups'). The argument being that, the impression of the degree of change generated by Lijphart's framework may be more due to the differing susceptibility to constitutional modification of the variables rather than the constitutional lethargy of the government. Although this argument raises a valid point, it risks downplaying the capacity of governments to legislate or simply govern in a manner that would stimulate change. For example, although the government cannot legislate to create more political parties, it can legislate to change to a more proportional electoral system that would be likely to return a greater number of parties. Reflecting on the theoretical and conceptual utility of Lijphart's framework still further, the latter point concerning the interrelationship between variables does appear to expose a critical weakness in the methodology—the absence of any weighting. Several variables (notably V1, V2, and V3) are heavily dependent upon the electoral system (V4), and yet the methodology is based upon an equal weighting-score that does not seek to differentiate between what could be called 'primary' or 'root' characteristics as opposed to 'secondary' elements.

A common technique for validating the reliability of variable sets from different forms of internal and external bias, however, is to compare their findings against a number of alternative indicators to either confirm or raise questions about the observed pattern of results. The existence of freedom of information legislation (FOI), for example, could be used as an indicator of either power sharing (reflected in the existence of a robust externally regulated statutory regime) or power hoarding (the absence of statutory FOI measures). In the case of the UK during 1997–2007, FOI provides a variable that fits very much within the contours of the argument regarding executive dilution made in this book, and particularly regarding the distinction between New Labour's *rhetoric* and *reality*. A radical and potentially far-reaching regime was initially promised by New Labour, but the subsequent Freedom of Information Act 2000 implemented a far weaker statutory right to access and maintained executive reserve powers (discussed further in Chapter 16).[4] A similar pattern of dilution and evisceration can be observed in relation to the *Governance of Britain* agenda under Gordon Brown (discussed in Chapter 16), but raising the issue of reserve powers introduces another dimension of constitutional analysis that deserves comment.

Calculating changes or shifts in the nature of political power in the UK during 1997–2007 is difficult due to New Labour's commitment to retaining the reserve powers that the Westminster Model offers any government. In many areas—FOI, central bank independence, incorporation of the ECHR, etc.—the radical potential of measures has to some degree been reduced by the executive's insistence that reserve powers and an executive veto capacity must be retained in order to protect the twin conventions of ministerial responsibility and parliamentary sovereignty. New Labour sought to play down the relevance of these reserve powers by emphasizing that it could be trusted not to abuse these powers, and would only deploy them in 'exceptional circumstances'. In a sense, therefore, New Labour were asking the public to trust them and establishing their own version of the 'good chaps theory of government'. This approach was problematic for at least three interlinked reasons: (*a*) it reflected either a rejection or a misunderstanding of the theory of limited government and the utility of legal constitutionalism in terms of imposing explicit and externally regulated boundaries on political behaviour; (*b*) it overlooked the fact that large sections of the public no longer trusted politicians; (*c*) it was a short-sighted approach because even if New Labour could be trusted to self-regulate its behaviour, there was no guarantee that future governments would be as virtuous. In terms of constitutional political analysis, the challenge arises from how to score variables where the executive still has reserve powers, but insists they will rarely, if ever, be deployed.

A final analytical challenge that could be levelled against the research framework used in this book is that it fails to acknowledge the long-term consequences of reforms that in the short-term may appear limited. Put slightly differently, is it too early to fully understand the consequences of those measures introduced during 1997–2007? Understood in these terms, the importance of the Human Rights Act 1998 and the Constitutional Reform Act 2005, for example, may lie not in the number of 'declarations of incompatibility' that have been issued, or other such indicators, but in the symbolic importance of incorporating human rights within UK law, while also shifting to a sharper separation of powers. It could therefore be argued that the potential capacity of the judiciary has been significantly increased irrespective of whether they have as yet decided to utilize this capacity. It is in this vein that Jowell notes that 'it may take some time, provocative legislation and considerable judicial courage for the courts to assert the primacy of the Rule of Law over parliamentary sovereignty'.[5] A great deal also depends on the dynamics of the territorial constitution and the way in which the prevailing conception of the appropriate relationship between Westminster and the regions evolves over time (an issue discussed in Chapter 16).

Having accepted, however, that within a minimal margin of error, the results outlined in Table 15.1 and illustrated in Figure 15.2 provide an accurate account of change, it is possible to consider this finding within the contours of the debate between those who believe New Labour have fundamentally changed the nature of democracy in the UK (the Revolutionary Camp) and those who admit a degree of change but who also emphasize the retention of core aspects of the Westminster Model, and are therefore more doubtful about 'revolutionary' interpretations (these were described as the Sceptical Camp in Chapter 4). Figure 15.1 suggest that both groupings have sought to emphasize two sides of the same process. This is a statecraft strategy based upon constitutional coexistence and the parallel operation of markedly different models of democracy within one polity. Neither academic grouping is correct or incorrect because, as mentioned earlier, such a crude binary distinction is of little value in this context. What this book has revealed is a statecraft based upon blending, or the parallel deployment of different forms (or models) of democracy.

15.2 Bi-constitutionalism and the 'Blair paradox'

The central argument developed in this chapter is that democracy in the UK has *not* shifted from one distinct model to another (i.e. majoritarian *to* consensual), which is the dominant conceptual lens that has shaped debates to date, but that New Labour (either by accident or design) sought to develop and institute a new meta-constitutional orientation at the sub-national and local levels based upon a more consensual and participatory model of democracy, while maintaining (and defending) a quite different meta-constitutional orientation at the national level. This argument is shown in Figure 15.1 in the distance *between* the existing types of democracy at the national level compared against that at the sub-national devolved level. In simple terms, Figure 15.1 clarifies the point emphasized throughout Part II of this book that devolution has engineered a quite different form of democracy in relation to executive politics. This is statistically shown in a variable score of 1.62 at the national level for the executive–parties dimension compared to −0.28 at the devolved level.

Labour's hybrid approach or 'bi-constitutionalism' dovetails with this book's thesis concerning constitutional anomie because the government appears unable or unwilling to explain why it feels a more pluralistic form of governance is appropriate at the devolved level, but not at the national level. This line of argument could be extended to pose distinct questions about New Labour's governance reforms at other constitutional levels. Dunleavy notes,

> In some areas the pull of the Westminster model has been extended, notably in local government with the introduction of local cabinets . . . By leaving plurality-rule elections for councils intact, these supposed 'democratisation' changes in fact created mini-Westminster systems, where previously a somewhat less-elitist model had managed to survive.[6]

King also picks up this theme by stating 'There can be few countries in the world—perhaps there are none—which have within themselves a variety of governing institutions that are based on such fundamentally divergent constitutional conceptions'.[7] In fact, Figure 15.1 suggests that the bi-constitutionalism has developed along two quite distinct dimensions: (*a*) along a territorial dimension with different models at the national and devolved levels; and (*b*) at the national level itself where power-sharing measures have been implemented in some areas, but the logic and principles have not been transferred elsewhere. Indeed, what both Table 15.1 and Figure 15.1 convey is that the reform process has been internally inconsistent—more pluralist in some areas, more centralized in others.

At the level of principles, one of the most enduring criticisms of New Labour has been that its programme of constitutional reform has lacked any ideological foundation or principled coherence. And yet, the analysis set out earlier could be interpreted as suggesting that there was a clear rationale sustaining the reform programme as a whole—a commitment to modified majoritarianism. This is reflected in change along one dimension, but not along the other. It may not have been that New Labour was unprincipled in their approach, as Marquand, for example has argued, but that their *implicit* guiding principles were so incongruent with their *explicit* rhetoric that they could not be admitted or articulated. After attacking the Westminster Model for so long in opposition, New Labour could not admit that its 'constitutional revolution' was actually 'conceived in strictly Diceyan terms'.[8] This, in turn, may explain: (*a*) why the government refused to be drawn into debates about the principled basis of its reforms; and (*b*) why ingenious attempts were made to create a more consensual system *within* a majoritarian framework. And yet, identifying the existence of bi-constitutionalism is not the same as establishing that this hybrid statecraft actually matters, or that it can be taken as evidence of constitutional anomie.

The deployment of different models or forms of democracy at different levels within one polity is not innately problematic as long as the constitutional configuration can accommodate and legitimate the existence of difference. In this regard, Norris is correct to suggest that 'the UK is becoming more like the political systems in Australia and Canada'. The problem with this comparison is that it overlooks the fact that the UK formally remains a unitary (not a federal) state, and the assimilation of different meta-constitutional orientations is therefore more problematic. Put differently, federal states could be interpreted as facilitating bi-constitutionality through their accommodation of ideational shifts that have not become prevalent at the national level. It is in this vein that Lusztig isolates a distinctive 'Western' mega-constitutional orientation at the Canadian provincial level which remains, and has been for some time, distinct from the dominant majoritarian orientation at the federal level.[9] Federalism might therefore be interpreted as allowing the adoption of different models of democracy without creating any constitutional friction or contradiction in a way that is not possible in a formally unitary state like the UK. Different constitutional configurations may therefore facilitate, difference, or militate against difference by 'locking-in' certain beliefs or assumptions about the nature of democracy.

Indeed, the existence of chains of democratic arenas within multilevel governance frameworks may extend far beyond *bi*-constitutionalism and display elements of *multi*-constitutionalism. An awareness of meta-constitutional orientations and the existence of bi-constitutionality may therefore enhance our understanding of evolving models of multilevel governance. Debates and tensions between actors that are involved in territorially over-arching policy networks may well originate in quite different positions concerning the legitimate boundaries of the state, the extent of citizen engagement, or the appropriate boundaries between, for example, the principles of efficiency and accountability. The EU provides a critical case of a polity formed around a highly distinctive meta-constitutional orientation (arguably indirect, highly elitist, depoliticized, insulated, and non-participatory), and yet many scholars argue that as the very nature of the EU differs from that of nation states a different idea of 'democracy'—and arguably a different meta-constitutional orientation—is appropriate.[10]

Counter-arguments which seek to 'upload' elements of national meta-constitutional orientations (essentially a 'thicker' model of democracy) not only help underline the value of the concept by sensitizing us to issues of constitutional momentum and spillover, but also how different orientations may have markedly different understandings of core terms such as 'participation' and 'representation'.[11] Scharpf's dissection of the concept of legitimacy illustrates that different orientations may adopt quite different positions. Consensual democracy, with its emphasis on citizen and group representation, may deliver high levels of *input*-based legitimacy, but a trade-off occurs in relation to *output*-based legitimacy as the compromise and participatory requirements of consensus may impede flexibility, optimum solutions, and dynamism. By contrast, the centralized and relatively unimpeded framework of majoritarian democracy facilitates *output*-based legitimacy but at the expense of *input*-based legitimacy, which suggests that different approaches inculcate certain normative beliefs regarding different forms of legitimacy. From this perspective, New Labour arguably switched from an emphasis on *input*-based legitimacy during its first term but shifted to an *output*-based understanding during its second term.

Although the existence of different meta-constitutional orientations *between* distinct political parameters (i.e. between different countries or between different provinces in federal systems) might be rationalized (or at least explained) according to national traditions or the precepts set out in a written constitution, the situation is more complex where bi-constitutionalism has been established *within* a unitary state. This raises questions concerning constitutional stability and the capacity of the executive to either prevent or facilitate further reform. The argument being made is that seeking to accommodate bi-constitutionality within the bounds of a unitary state is likely to prove unstable. This is due to the existence of constitutional momentum and spillover, which can, in itself, take many forms.

Institutionally, the operation of proportional electoral systems in Scotland, Northern Ireland, Wales, and England is likely to emerge (or spillover) as a significant issue in the short-term, especially as the Labour government seems unwilling (or unable) to explain why a more consensual model of democracy and a different electoral system is appropriate for the sub-national level (and indeed supra-national), but not for the national level. Culturally, the existence of a more consensual system at the devolved level is, as Judge has argued, likely to produce 'normative sub-systems' and 'deviant cultures' that will increasingly challenge, or at least stand in stark contrast to the established meta-constitutional orientation at Westminster.[12] Bi-constitutionalism is also likely to prove volatile for the simple reason that it has created anomalies and dynamic forces that are likely to destabilize and eviscerate core tenets of the Westminster Model over time (e.g. devolution, Supreme Court, etc.). A period of constitutional reflection and restabilization is therefore likely to form a key component of the Blair legacy to any future government (a topic examined in Chapter 16). And yet, although this chapter has sought to tease apart the bi-constitutional nature of New Labour's statecraft and some of its implications, it is necessary to seek to identify the origins of this condition. In order to do this, Section 15.3 seeks to identify whether an inconsistency existed within the ideological and theoretical foundations of New Labour.

15.3 The Third Way and constitutional anomie

So far this chapter has updated the UK's position on Lijphart's conceptual map of democracy, and then discussed this repositioning in the context of debates and arguments concerning bi-constitutionality and the 'Blair paradox'. This section looks within the theoretical and ideological foundations of New Labour in an attempt to trace the origins of New Labour's approach to constitutional and democratic reform. It argues that the roots of New Labour's hybrid or bi-constitutional statecraft can be located within 'Third-Way' theory.

New Labour's governing strategy was always focused on results rather than principles; it was a pragmatic political philosophy. This point and its relationship with the tension identified earlier is clear in the writing of Giddens, who although arguing for a 'widening and deepening of democracy', also emphasized the need for 'philosophic conservatism'.[13] This led Sheldrick to conclude that, 'there is little in the Third Way for those who

Table 15.2 Meta-constitutional orientations: core tenets

	Consensus	Third way	Majoritarian
Power	Distributed	Bounded rationalism	Concentrated
Executive type	Multiparty	Mixed	One party
Electoral system	Proportional	Mixed	Disproportional
State	Decentralized	Hybrid	Unitary
Constitution	Codified	Quasi-codified	Unwritten
Executive–legislative relationship	Balance	Loyalty	Dominance
Public participation	Inclusion	Moderate	Exclusion
Political culture	Participatory	'Philosophic conservatism' (elite)	Elite
Normative priority	Fairness	Delivery	Governability

hope for a more radical impetus towards democratisation'.[14] And yet, Figure 15.1 does indicate that significant changes have occurred. Not only have they occurred, but they have been shaped by the clashing imperatives of 'Third-Way' theory. This theoretical framework represented an amalgam or fusion of two distinct orientations that drew upon the centrifugal emphasis of a consensual model, while retaining aspects of a majoritarianism (see Table 15.2). For this reason, the development of a new form of politics or the 'democratization of democracy' was at the same time wedded to an 'Old Labour' commitment to retaining elements of the Westminster Model.

This framework could be used to suggest that New Labour were *outcome-contingent* during the early to mid-1990s, when the party felt its chances of winning a workable majority were slim but became *act-contingent* as public opinion surveys indicated they could win a full majority. Put simply, when New Labour believed their chances of governing under the Westminster Model were slight, they developed and embraced an alternative meta-constitutional orientation, the outcome of which would have been a more balanced distribution of power. As the party became aware that it could win under the existing system, their commitment to a more consensual system waned, but they maintained a rhetorical commitment to fundamental constitutional reform in order to benefit from the perceived electoral benefits of such a position.

The 'Third Way' was always therefore hybrid, and provided the ideological seeds that would later germinate to produce the perplexing institutional reforms the second part of this book analyses in detail. As such, although New Labour ministers claimed to have overseen 'the most radical programme of constitutional change since the Great Reform Bill of 1832', their meta-constitutional orientation was never genuinely 'radical' as it did not involve a break with key elements of the pre-existing fundamental principles.[15] It is for this reason that Weir claims 'New Labour is just a smokescreen. Broadly, what we have is pretty Old Labour party in terms of its pragmatism and its acceptance of the status quo politically'[16] and Evans concludes that 'third-way democracy is elite democracy in disguise'.[17] In *Where Now for New Labour?* (2002) Giddens expresses a degree of frustration (even disappointment) with Labour's failure to embrace a distinctly new meta-constitutional orientation. After criticizing the 'top–down' nature of the reform process, and lamenting the manner in which a disparate range of constitutional reforms had been implemented without any attempt to embed them in an explicit set of revised constitutional principles, Giddens writes, 'Difficult though these questions and others may be to answer, they will not go away . . . far better to confront them openly than to muddle along in a constitutional limbo.'[18]

Although, confronting the current 'constitutional limbo' identified by Giddens is the focus of Chapter 16, identifying and teasing apart both the centripetal and centrifugal aspects of New Labour's statecraft at this stage aids understanding in relation to the marked shift in governing styles that can be identified particularly between 1997–2001 and 2001–5. During its first term, a number of factors (e.g. the energy of a new government, public expectations, policy momentum, legislative space, etc.) conspired to encourage the government to emphasize consensual or pluralist measures. By New Labour's second term, however, ministers began to feel frustrated with the pace of public sector performance and reform, particularly in light of the increased resources that had been made available, and felt that constitutional issues had consumed too much ministerial energy and parliamentary time for little public reward. This shift of emphasis towards the benefits of 'strong government' in terms of delivery capacity was further augmented by the terrorist attacks of 2001 and 2002 which in a different way also underlined the benefits of executive capacity.

Although Tony Blair identified a need to 'construct a new and radical politics to serve the people in the new century ahead . . . where power is pushed down to the people instead of being hoarded centrally', the cumulative analysis offered in this chapter suggest that reform has been significant (rather than radical) and one-sided.[19] Most importantly, there has been no discernible conception of an alternative constitution and it has been argued that the existing constitutional configuration is likely to prove unstable. The next and final chapter explores the broader comparative, executive, and socio-political implications of these findings.

Notes

1. Wilson, R (2005) 'Constitutional Change: A Note by the Bedside', *Political Quarterly*, 76(2), 281.
2. Riddell *op. cit.* (2007), p. 42.
3. Norris, *op. cit.* (2001), p. 881.
4. See Flinders, M (2000) 'The Politics of Accountability', *Political Quarterly*, 71(4), 422–36.
5. Jowell, J (2007) 'The Rule of Law Today', in J Jowell and D Oliver, eds. *The Changing Constitution*. Oxford: Oxford University Press.
6. Dunleavy, P (2006) 'The Westminster Model', in P Dunleavy, C Hay, Heffernan, R. and, Cowley R. eds., *Developments in British Politics 8*. London: Palgrave, p. 327.
7. King *op. cit.* (2007), p. 352.
8. Harlow, C (2000) 'Disposing of Dicey?' *Political Studies*, 48(2), 356–9.
9. Lusztig, M (1995) 'Federalism and Institutional Design', *Publius*, 25, 35–50.
10. See Majone, M (1994) 'The Rise of the Regulatory State in Europe', *West European Politics*, 17, 78–102; Moravcsik, A (2002) 'In Defence of the Democratic Deficit', *Journal of Common Market Studies*, 40, 603–34.
11. Scharpf, F (1998) 'Interdependence and Democratic Legitimation'. MPIfG Working Paper, 98/2.
12. Judge, D (2006) 'This is What Democracy Looks Like', *British Politics*, 1(3), 391.
13. Giddens, A (1998) *The Third Way*. Cambridge: Polity, p. 69.
14. Sheldrick, B (2002) 'New Labour and the Third Way', *Studies in Political Economy*, 67, 133–43.
15. Irvine, Lord (1998) *Lecture to the Centre for Public Law*. Cambridge University.
16. Quoted in Morrison *op. cit.* (2003), p. 527.
17. Evans *op. cit.* (2003), pp. 312–27.
18. Giddens, A (2002) *Where Now for New Labour?* London: Fabian Society, p. 45.
19. Blair, T (1996) 'My Vision for Britain', in G Radice, ed., *What Needs to Change*. London: Harper Collins, p. 3.

Chapter 16

Democratic Drift

It has been said of Christopher Columbus that when he set sail, he did not know where he was going; that when he got there, he did not know where he was; and when he got back, he did not know where he had been. Blair appeared to adopt Columbus' approach, though without the benefit of finding a new world. He set off with an agenda in which he had little interest, he generated a set of constitutional changes that do not hang together, and he bequeaths to his successor an absence of any coherent view of what type of constitution is appropriate for the UK.[1]

The statement by Lord Norton (above) encapsulates the argument that has been made in this book. Democracy in the UK is drifting. At the end of the first decade of the twenty-first century the UK is 'constitutionally speaking, in a half-way house' or as King more starkly concludes 'a mess'.[2] It is neither one thing nor another. This critique has formed the backbone of this book, and has been developed using the concept of constitution anomie. Lijphart's methodology for assessing the position and evolution of democratic models has been used to develop and interrogate this critique which, has in turn, allowed us to develop the analytical precision of the bi-constitutionality thesis.

The simple conclusion of this book is that New Labour altered the nature of democracy from a purely majoritarian model to a form, most accurately described, as 'modified majoritarianism'. Modified in the sense that power-sharing reforms were introduced, but that these were designed and implemented within the contours of what remains a power-hoarding democracy. More precisely, an approach to statecraft was deployed based upon constitutional co-existence and the parallel operation of markedly different models of democracy within one polity. To label this approach as a 'strategy' risks suggesting a degree of executive capacity, thought, and planning that did not in fact exist. In reality, a series of reforms were implemented with little appreciation of what (in the long run) the government was seeking to achieve; or how reform in one sphere of the constitution would have obvious and far-reaching consequences for other elements of the constitutional equilibrium. The result has been a situation of constitutional anomie in which long-standing principles or rules have been jettisoned or corrupted, but not replaced. In this sense, the UK has drifted to its current position on Lijphart's conceptual map of democracy (Figure 15.1).

The aim of this chapter is to situate the specific findings of this book about the changing nature of democracy in the UK during 1997–2007 within a much broader context; to look outwards and forward instead of backwards. More specifically, this chapter is structured around four interconnected questions:

1. How can we develop the analytical traction and leverage of 'constitutional anomie'?
2. What evidence is there that Gordon Brown's *Governance of Britain* initiative has been able to offer the 'new narrative' demanded by many observers to underpin and explain the changing nature of the constitution?
3. Does the Conservative Party's current policy platform offer a coherent view of what type of constitution is appropriate for the UK?
4. Does a comparative perspective suggest that there is anything particularly distinctive about the recent evolution of democracy in the UK?
5. Is there a link between constitutional anomie and declining levels of public trust and public engagement in politics?

16.1 Constitutional anomie and morality

This book has developed an argument relating to constitutional anomie and has sought to demonstrate this line of reasoning through the utilization of a distinctive methodology drawn from comparative political science. Put simply, this argument suggests that under New Labour it was not possible to identify or understand the public philosophy, political ideology or basic principles on which democracy in the UK was recast. Some scholars could reject this argument on the basis that the constitution in the UK is (in)famous for being 'unwritten' or 'unprincipled', but they would be wrong. The constitution of the UK throughout the twentieth century may have been unwritten in the sense of not being set out in one definitive source, but it was far from unprincipled. Parties of both the left and the right accepted the logic and principles, and therefore the institutional framework, of the Westminster Model. The UK's constitutional morality was therefore relatively clear—Lijphart described it as a 'blueprint'—and embraced the principles of power-hoarding, unionism, stability, control, distance, etc.[3] The Westminster Model provided the dominant, almost totemic, meta-constitutional orientation in terms of the core values and assumptions about the distribution of power and the relationship between political actors.

Constitutional morality is therefore the opposite or anti-thesis to constitutional anomie. Where the latter suggests a sense of frustration, confusion, or anxiety regarding the nature of a democracy, particularly regarding the absence of a constitutional compass, the former indicates a reasonably clear and coherent set of socio-political principles which in turn direct and underpin a polity's institutional arrangements. Constitutional morality is by no means a new concept. In *Representative Government* (1861), John Stuart Mill referred to constitutional morality as 'the ethics of representative government'. For Mill, 'constitutional morality' forms the basic foundation of any polity through its encapsulation and protection of those basic values, principles, and assumptions that are viewed as paramount. The importance of this constitutional morality is twofold. First, it performs a self-regulating function, whereby governments understand that their behaviour must confirm to certain expectations regarding appropriate conduct. As Mill explained,

> The very existence of some governments, and all that renders others endurable, rests on the practical observance of doctrines of constitutional morality; traditional notions in the minds of the several constituted authorities, which modify the use that might otherwise be made of their powers...we may truly say that only by the regard paid to maxims of constitutional morality is the constitution kept in existence.

Constitutional morality also plays a critical role in maintain and regulating the relationship between the governors and the governed. In this sense, it provides a basis for socio-political understandings. The Westminster Model therefore provided an organizing perspective, not just regarding how the UK's political system operated, but also how it *should* work. It is possible to continue along a rich seam of writing throughout the nineteenth and twentieth centuries—a path that would pass through Dicey's *An Introduction to Study of the Law of the Constitution* (1885), which

examined how accepted conventions 'make up the constitutional morality of the day, to Maitland's *Constitutional History of England* (1965), Dunham's work on the 'Spirit of the Constitution' (1971), and then on to
Marshall's (1984) *Constitutional Conventions* and many other respected
texts—that each in their own way discussed constitutional morality as
the glue, conscience, or the accepted meta-constitutional orientation of
a polity.

The concept of constitutional morality is therefore quite nebulous, but
this chimes with Hirschl's comment (Chapter 2) that working with the
under-pinning values of a polity is to some degree likely to be 'intuitive
and context-specific rather than analytical'. And yet, applying the concept
to the empirical experience of reform under New Labour provides a degree
of grounding. New Labour deconstructed the UK's long-established constitutional morality, its 'traditional' constitution, but did not offer an
alternative set of governing values or principles. More than this, their
approach to reform was confused and inconsistent. The old rules do not
appear to suit the new game, and yet the government continues to insist
that the old rules still apply.

It is in this context that Hazell called for Tony Blair's successor to offer a
'new narrative' that can offer a 'better justification for the first wave of
reforms than the bland word of modernisation'.[4] This plea resonates
with the notion of constitutional anomie because it explicitly recognizes
not only the need to join-up the various institutional reforms, but also the
need to locate that process within a broader public discourse that can
inform and legitimate current socio-political relationships. It was against
this background that Gordon Brown made the issue of public trust and
democratic renewal the topic of not only his May 2007 leadership campaign, but also his first public statement as PM and his government's first
policy document—*Governance of Britain*.

16.2 Brown and the *Governance of Britain*

The *Governance of Britain* initiative represents an explicit acknowledgement by Gordon Brown of not only the existence but also the need to
address the condition of constitutional anomie. The aim of this section
is to review this initiative and assess the degree to which it represents a
coherent reform with the capacity to offer a 'new narrative'. It concludes
that the *Governance of Britain* agenda represents more continuity than
change and little in terms of a coherent view of what type of constitution

is appropriate for the UK in the twenty-first century. The *Governance of Britain* green paper was published in July 2007 with the intention of forging 'a new relationship between government and the citizen, and begin the journey towards a new constitutional settlement'.[5] Its proposals fall into four main areas:

1. Limiting the powers of the executive (e.g. reforming the Royal Prerogative, increasing parliamentary scrutiny of appointments, reviewing the role of the Attorney General).
2. Making the executive more accountable (e.g. revising the Ministerial Code).
3. Reinvigorating democracy (e.g. increasing public participation in local government, moving election days to weekends, reviewing the right to protest in the vicinity of Parliament).
4. Examining the UK's future (e.g. by stimulating a debate about national values and possibly a British Bill of Rights).

In essence, the *Governance of Britain* initiative attempts to construct a form of constitutional morality with the capacity to: (*a*) underpin those reforms that have already been implemented and those which may be delivered in the future; while also (*b*) delivering a form of social glue in the sense of forging a shared identity and cultivating a sense of shared rights, duties, and obligations. A series of consultation papers were published on various aspects of the proposals, and in March 2008 the Government published a white paper—*Governance of Britain: Constitutional Renewal*—and draft Bill.[6] A joint committee was established to conduct pre-legislative scrutiny on the draft Bill and its findings relate directly to this book's argument regarding constitutional anomie,

> We recognise that the draft Bill is a first step in a wider programme of reforms to the constitution. However, we have found it difficult to discern the principles underpinning the draft Bill and we ask the government to reflect further on whether 'Constitutional Renewal' is an appropriate title.[7]

It is not necessary for the purposes of this section to examine any of the proposals in great deal, as it is more important to reflect upon the extent of the changes being proposed; the evolution of the reform process under Brown; and the challenges confronted by any attempt to forge a new constitutional morality.[8]

In terms of the extent of the changes being proposed, it is difficult to avoid the conclusion that they represent modest, even superficial, adjustments to the current constitutional order. Returning to Lijphart's ten variables provides a frame of reference to support this evaluation. Although the government published a review of the voting systems in the UK in January 2008, it remains opposed to electoral reform for Westminster (V4 and strongly influencing V1, V2, and V3). Many of the proposals seek to increase the role and capacity of the House of Commons vis-à-vis the executive (V3) but taken together are unlikely to *significantly* shift the current balance of power. Apart from stressing the notion of 'Britishness', the government has not articulated its view on the appropriate relationship between Westminster and the regions (V6) but has instead appointed Sir Kenneth Calman to chair a commission to review the Scotland Act 1998. In relation to V7, the government published a white paper in July 2008—*An Elected Second Chamber: Further Reform of the House of Lords*—proposing an elected component of between 80 and 100 per cent with non-renewable terms of twelve to fifteen years.[9] The government intends to include this as a manifesto commitment at the next General Election, but in terms of models of democracy the current proposals reiterate that the primacy of the commons is 'acknowledged beyond debate' (V9).[10] The government is also clear that the powers of the Lords should not be strengthened and as a result the path to 'Stage Two' reform appears long and convoluted.

Furthermore, the *Governance of Britain*'s contribution to the development of a sense of constitutional morality is arguably circumscribed by its failure to engage with deeper questions about: what the government is seeking to achieve; how future reforms might dovetail with recent measures; or the underpinning principles that will inform future developments. In fact, the initiative is arguably more significant for the issues it either omits completely or seeks to marginalize. The challenge of constitutional anomie is rather greater than the *Governance of Britain* agenda appears to recognize: 'If we are to restore trust to the political process we need a far more wide-ranging debate'.[11]

What is equally significant about the *Governance of Britain* initiative is not, however, its limitations in terms of breadth and depth, but also the manner in which it continues to exhibit tendencies that were prominent under New Labour. Specifically: (*a*) the dilution and eviscerated of proposals by the government as they pass through the policy-making process; (*b*) a gap between ministerial rhetoric and political reality; and (*c*) the programme appears internally confused. Two examples demonstrate the theme of dilution. First, the original proposal to introduce legislation to transfer war-making powers from the PM to Parliament was replaced with a convention that the executive should in future seek a parliamentary resolution on the deployment of the armed forces. Secondly, while claiming to support a sharper constitutional separation of powers, the government retreated from its initial plans to radically reform the position of the Attorney General and instead decided to maintain the office holder as a member of the executive, a member of the legislature, and the government's chief legal advisor. This pattern of weakening initial plans did not go unnoticed. Freedland remarked that there were 'tell-tale water stains all over the white paper and the draft bill—clear signs of dilution' while *The Guardian* highlighted the manner in which 'the reforms are bound up with exceptions and the gap between ministerial rhetoric and what is being offered is unfortunate'.[12] The official response of the Political Studies Association of the UK was equally critical, suggesting that the majority of the reforms were 'cosmetic' and together constituted 'a rag-bag of potentially clashing proposals, aspirations and objectives'.[13]

The *Governance of Britain* initiative did, however, contain one component that is designed to respond to the constitutional anomie thesis, at least in a somewhat oblique way. This took the form of a willingness to start a 'national conversation' about a Bill of Rights, the notion of 'Britishness', and the concept of citizenship.[14] The relationship between this agenda and the argument regarding constitutional anomie outlined above was set out in Gordon Brown's 2006 speech on the future of Britishness in which he emphasized how rediscovering 'the shared values that bind us together and give us a common purpose' would allow us to be 'far more ambitious in forging a new and contemporary settlement of the relationship between state, community and the individual . . . a common purpose without which no society can flourish'.[15] He went on to highlight the exceptionalism of the UK in having no constitutional statement or declaration enshrining 'our objectives as a country; no mission statement defining purpose; and no explicitly stated vision of our future'.[16] In the context of Tony Blair's widely perceived failure to offer any sense of direction in terms of constitutional reform, this point arguably forms not only an implicit criticism of Blair's leadership during 1997–2007, but also an explicit acknowledgement of the need to address a sense of constitutional anomie. The government's belief that 'Britishness' may offer some form of modernized constitutional morality was explicit when Brown went on to state,

> I believe that out of a debate [about Britishness], hopefully leading to a broad consensus about what Britishness means, flows a rich agenda for

change: a new constitutional settlement . . . giving more emphasis to the common glue.

The existence of bi-constitutionalism, however, makes providing a coherent 'new narrative' more difficult in a number of ways. A Bill of Rights may play a role in providing a rhetorical form of constitutional morality, but it would be problematic in practice due to specific internal arguments about what precisely the Bill of Rights should contain, and external questions of compatibility vis-à-vis the ECHR. These challenges are reflected in the government's failure to publish a consultation paper on a British Bill of Rights due to difficulties with devolved governments and Whitehall departments.[17]

A less formal and legalistic focus on Britishness, possibly augmented through the introduction of specific mechanisms that were designed to foster a more explicit sense of citizenship—like those suggested in Lord Goldsmith's report of March 2008 *Citizenship: Our Common Bond*—may provide an alternative strategy for promoting a form of constitutional morality. But again, even these measures do not sit comfortably with recent devolutionary reforms that have increased the nationalistic identities of the Scottish, Welsh, and Northern Irish, and have further weakened (or at the very least relegated) any sense of 'British' national identity outside the English.[18] The capacity of 'Britishness' as a binding narrative therefore appears limited at a historical point when the cultural and political strength of the concept is at its weakest. The dilemma of this situation was crudely exposed by the tone of many responses to Lord Goldsmith's review, and particularly by the manner in which some of its suggestions were received by nationalist groupings. The Leader of the SNP, Alex Salmond, immediately announced that his party would use their devolved powers to block any moves to introduce an Oath of Allegiance to Queen and country, while a nationalist politician in Northern Ireland declared the idea 'divisive and dangerous'.[19]

These comments exposed the difficulty of consolidating a national 'British' identity as a form of social glue or constitutional morality in a time of major constitutional and demographic change. In this regard devolution (alongside other elements of the 'first wave' of constitutional reforms) and the concept of 'Britishness' appear to take quite different directions and the government may have to take a quite different strategic direction if it is to counter the challenges of constitutional anomie. 'Critics might thus assert that devolution gnaws at British national identity from within'.[20] Stimulating debates about 'Britishness', citizenship or a 'common statement of values' might, therefore, be regarded as somewhat weak and oblique responses to the challenges of constitutional anomie set out in this book. The *Governance of Britain* initiative appears to confirm rather than challenge arguments regarding constitutional anomie. It also suggests that the government is content to engage with meso- or micro-constitutional level reform, but not mega-political change that would lead to a more fundamental shift in power.

> The constitutional reforms do nothing to alter the hermetic insulation of Parliament from the people because they are dealing with the distribution of power between what one might call 'the officer class'. The reforms redistribute power between elites, not between elites and the people... Frankly much in the Constitutional Reform Bill is merely a shifting of the institutional furniture. It will not have much effect on popular grievances.[21]

If the *Governance of Britain* initiative appears to offer little guidance in terms of articulating the contours of the constitution as it currently exists, or explaining what the government is actually trying to achieve, then this will clearly have implications for future governments. Phrased differently, the winning party at the 2010 General Election will inherit low levels of trust and confidence in political processes, institutions, and politicians and a constitution in 'limbo', to use Giddens' description. As opinion polls suggest that the Conservative Party *may* win the next General Election, it is necessary to examine the degree to which they appear capable of offering a coherent view of what type of constitution is appropriate for the UK.

16.3 Cameron's Conservatives

Conservative political thought has traditionally been bound to majoritarian notions of democracy. This stems, in part, from the commitment to preserve and defend established institutions that have evolved through adaptation, and largely served the country well. The Conservative Party therefore has a long history of scepticism about programmes of constitutional reform, and opposed most major changes.[22] As such, the approach of New Labour during 1997–2007 represented nothing less than a threat to the stability and unity of the country and were interpreted as acts of 'constitutional vandalism', even 'the rape of the constitution'. The possibility of a transition from opposition to government poses an acute dilemma for the party because it must now clarify exactly how it intends to

Table 16.1 Conservative options for change

Option	Direction	Content
1.	Pure Majoritarianism	Reverse New Labour's reforms in order to move the UK back towards a 'pure' model of majoritarian democracy.
2.	Modified Majoritarianism	Seek stability in terms of attempting to stem dynamic pressures while reinforcing core elements of the Westminster Model
3.	Consensualism	Conclude that the Westminster Model has been damaged beyond repair and accept the trajectory of change towards consensualism as a pragmatic response.

respond. This section concludes that the Conservative Party has remained remarkably stable in its commitment to the values and institutions of the Westminster Model. They neither present a vision of a 'new' constitution nor any detailed plans for how they would manage or address the constitutional anomalies and tensions they may inherit. In terms of understanding the position of the Conservative Party vis-à-vis constitutional reform and democratic renewal, it is possible to identify three main options and then chart them on Lijphart's conceptual map of democracy (see Table 16.1 and Figure 16.1). These options correspond (respectively) with Norton's 'Reactionary', 'Conservative', and 'Radical' paths.[23]

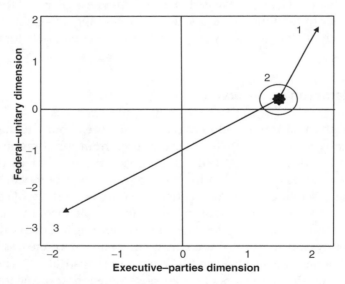

Figure 16.1 Conservative Party—options for change

If Option 1 were selected a Conservative government would attempt to re-construct the majoritarian constitution and repair the 'damage' wrought by New Labour. This strategy would offer three main benefits: (*a*) it would allow the government to articulate a clear and coherent vision of the constitution—impose a form of constitutional morality and thereby avert the accusations of constitutional anomie that blighted New Labour; (*b*) following the rationale of majoritarianism would impose a degree of internal coherence within the constitutional configuration. The anomalies and inconsistencies that have been created by attempting to forge a more consensual polity *within* the contours of a majoritarian polity would be addressed, thereby clarifying currently confused boundaries and relationships; (*c*) this option would find support within 'reactionary' elements of the Conservative Party.

The theory of path dependency alerts us to the manner in which certain options incur more costs than others. The benefits of adopting Option 1 must therefore be off-set against the costs involved, and for a future Conservative government these take two forms: (*a*) several reforms implemented after 1997 would be very difficult to reverse (e.g. devolution) and there are other elements that a future Conservative administration is unlikely to want to reverse (e.g. operational independence to the Bank of England); (*b*) possibly the most powerful pressure against Option 1 is the need for the party leadership to present a 'modern' image of an outward-looking party that can deliver change in light of new public expectations. Internationally, the general direction of democratic change is away from 'pure' power-hoarding majoritarianism and it would therefore be highly problematic for any party to counter this trend and advocate a shift *back* to an essentially elitist model of democracy. If Option 1 delivers a clear narrative, it is certainly not a 'new' one.

Option 2 focuses on stability, preservation, and adaptation and would, therefore, be in alignment with classic Conservative thought. It offers the benefit of relieving the party of the need to articulate a clear strategy. However, for a number of reasons, 'doing nothing' is possibly not an option because having spent the last decade *inter alia* attacking New Labour for lacking a 'joined-up' approach to the constitution, bemoaning the dominance of the executive over the legislature, emphasizing the 'English question', and creating a Democracy Taskforce, the party has created the expectation that some reforms will be advanced. Option 2 would also be problematic due to two institutional factors: there are long-marginalized elements of 'unfinished business' that any future government will have to resolve; and the dynamic nature of many of the measures instigated since 1997 will need to be carefully managed and channelled (e.g. further devolutionary pressures, the impact of establishing a Supreme Court). Conserving the constitution in the sense of preserving the institutionalized distribution of powers is therefore problematic due to a range of endogenous and exogenous variables that are likely to make change unavoidable. This, in turn, emphasizes the need for the party to have a clear and coherent strategic position on assuming office.

Option 3 involves a far-reaching shift in the nature of democracy in the UK from a power-hoarding to a power-sharing model. This option would certainly: add a distinct dimension to any party 'rebranding' strategy; indicate a stark departure from the past; and, add credibility to Conservative pronouncements concerning 'new politics'. It would represent a fresh approach to governing; but not necessarily one that resonates with traditional Conservative values. There may however be a rationale for adopting this option without offending traditional Conservative thought. A future administration may, possibly after a period pursuing Option 2, conclude that in terms of effective government the attempt to establish anti-majoritarian institutions (Supreme Court, independent central bank, etc.) within an essentially majoritarian framework was not sustainable. It could therefore embrace 'common sense' and accept that the Westminster Model has been fatally altered and for this reason engineer quite a different form of democracy.

There are, however, a number of costs or barriers against reforms of this nature. Even if a future Conservative government wanted to embark on Option 3, it is likely to face an intra-party structure that would oppose it. This is because although Conservative thought cherishes the notion of pragmatism, this is tied to a belief in organic change. For Conservatives, constitutions are not made, and definitely not 'engineered', but evolve out of socio-political interactions over time. It is therefore possible to suggest that only an extreme situation could create the drive necessary to persuade a Conservative government to select this option. As Chapter 2 stressed, such 'mega-political' change is generally driven by a dramatic event—such as a civil war or invasion—which leads to a seismic shift in attitudes, variables that are unlikely to play a role in determining the strategy of a Conservative government in the near future. Indeed, all the evidence is that constitutional reform is not a salient public issue.

Framed in terms of the options set out in Table 16.1, the Conservative Party appears content to adopt Option 2. This involves a pragmatic approach to reform based upon the desire to maintain core tenets of the Westminster Model wherever possible. From 1997 onwards, the

Conservative Party has maintained a consistent position on the constitution based upon rebuilding the role of Parliament and protecting the concept of parliamentary sovereignty. Even though David Cameron attempted to stimulate fresh thinking on the topic—'the time is right for a serious and thoughtful programme of Conservative institutional and constitutional reform'—the output of the Democracy Task Force (2006–8) examined a relatively narrow range of issues and arrived at recommendations that: (*a*) overlapped with Labour's *Governance of Britain* agenda; (*b*) had already been proposed by other actors (such as the Hansard Society); (*c*) were insufficiently developed and created as many problems as they solved (like the 'solution' to the West Lothian Question); and (*d*) were clearly designed to clarify and rebalance relationships in order to rebuild the Westminster Model.[24]

The Democracy Taskforce was in fact placed in an invidious position, being charged with orchestrating a general debate about a range of options, while at the same time expected to operate within the margins of established Conservative policy. The leadership's demand for 'new ideas' therefore obscured the existence of a Conservative Party whose position on many issues was relatively fixed. The Party opposed: electoral reform for Westminster, federalism, empowering the Lords, constitutional amendment procedures, a greater role for the judiciary; and it had no interest in altering the governance of the Bank of England. At the same time, the constraining influence of the Westminster Model removed the Taskforce's capacity to engage in those more innovative and dynamic (power-sharing) political processes that are being developed in other countries under the rubric of 'deliberative democracy' or 'participatory governance'.

The paradox of this situation is that while the Taskforce adopted a restricted approach to constitutional reform and democratic renewal, the Leader of the Party and the Shadow Justice Secretary, Nick Herbert, were promoting a more radical agenda focused on a new approach to human rights based upon a British Bill of Rights. The case for this measure rests on a belief that judgements made under the Human Rights Act 1998 have over-emphasized the rights of individuals, and under-emphasized an individual's responsibilities vis-à-vis their country of residence. A British Bill of Rights would, the Conservative Party suggests, rebalance this relationship by providing a domestic constitutional doctrine, similar to the German Basic Law, which would give, through the 'margin of appreciation', the judiciary, at all levels, a more explicit nationally defined reference point against which to make judgements.

The Conservative contradiction between this policy and Conservative thinking, however, stems from the plan to entrench the Bill of Rights. Cameron has suggested that 'one of the options is the removal of powers under the Parliament Act for the Commons alone to amend or repeal the Bill of Rights'.[25] But by seeking to entrench a British Bill of Rights, the Conservatives would at the same time weaken the notion of parliamentary sovereignty, by seeking to limit the capacity of future governments. It would continue a pattern, whereby reforms are implemented which actually eviscerate core components of the Westminster Model. But this puzzle possibly forms the results of a much deeper tension surrounding both the core tenets and the public image of the Conservative Party.

The interest from 2008 onwards in 'progressive conservatism' signals an attempt to not only develop fresh thinking about social justice and mobility, but also to re-engage those sections of society that have lost faith in conventional politics.[26] Elements of this project, such as allowing the public to trigger parliamentary debates through the submission of petitions, mark a stark departure from the logic of majoritarianism, and towards a more participatory and consensual style of governing.[27] This nascent emphasis within Conservative Policy has been orientated within a rhetorical position that promises a 'new politics', as emphasized by Cameron in March 2008 when he stated: 'The change we need is not just from Labour's old policies to our new policies...It's about a change from old politics to new politics'.[28] And yet, the deployment of this 'new politics' narrative by the Conservative Party is problematic for a number of reasons: (a) it was deployed by Tony Blair in the mid-1990s, and formed a central element of Gordon Brown's leadership campaign in 2007, and the public may therefore have become somewhat sceptical about whether the espoused *principles* will be translated in political *practice*; (b) this last point may be particularly poignant for those members of the public who remember the style of governing adopted by the Conservative governments in the 1980s and 1990s; (c) public suspicion may also be fuelled by the fact that the Conservative Party has no detailed information regarding how their participatory mechanisms would be implemented in practice. Moreover, the wider policy platform of the party is clearly aligned with maintaining, and restoring where possible, the Westminster Model which is essentially a power-hoarding system that would grate against the notions of direct democracy.

In conclusion, the Conservatives' position has evolved to encompass three main strands—parliamentary reform, a British Bill of Rights, and an increased degree of direct democracy. Returning to the three options set out in the second section, it is possible to suggest that the Conservative Party's position is therefore midway between Option 1 and 2—a form of modified majoritarianism. What is crucial in terms of broader debates concerning political disengagement is the degree to which the party's position overlaps with that of the current Labour government. The *Governance of Britain* agenda is also structured around shifting the balance of power between parliament and the executive, experimenting with direct democracy, and orchestrating a debate about Britishness and a Bill of Rights. It is not surprising, therefore, that the Conservatives have been accused of copying Labour's approach to constitutional reform.[29]

Having examined the positions of both the Labour Party and Conservative Party on constitutional reform and democratic renewal, it would appear that that the current condition of constitutional anomie within UK politics is unlikely to be resolved in the near future: 'muddling through' remains the dominant approach to constitutional design. However, before examining the link between this condition and evidence of increasing public disenchantment with conventional politics, it is necessary to locate the analysis offered in this book within a broader comparative perspective.

16.4 Deviant democracies

This book has explored the tension between two competing models of democracy. Within this frame of reference, it has analysed how the nature of democracy in the UK altered during 1997–2007. This revealed a one-sided pattern of change involving significant change along the federal–unitary dimension, but no change along the executive–parties dimension (Figure 15.1). This section locates this finding within comparative research in order to identify global trends and whether there is anything particularly distinctive about the recent evolution of the UK. In order to tease apart those elements of a comparative perspective that are particularly relevant to the UK this section focuses on what might be termed 'extreme politics'. 'Extreme' in the sense of focusing on countries that have traditionally been viewed as archetypal examples of either consensual or majoritarian politics (specifically Switzerland and New Zealand in this case) or 'extreme' in the sense of exhibiting a fundamental shift in the nature of democracy (Ireland). Figure 16.2 locates this book's analysis of the UK against the trajectory of these countries.

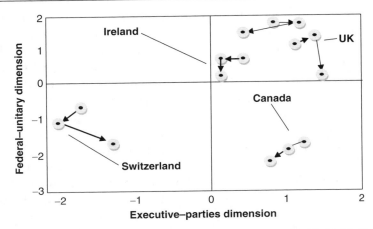

Figure 16.2 Democratic change from a comparative perspective (1945–96, 1971–96, 1997–2007)

Not only does Figure 16.2 underline the continuing theoretical and empirical value of Lijphart's framework, but it also poses certain questions about the extent, pace, and drivers of change in different countries. New Zealand's Westminster constitution, for example, before the mid-1990s had been characterized as an 'executive paradise'.[30] The 1986 Royal Commission on the Electoral System Report, *Towards a Better Democracy* led to the introduction of a mixed-member proportional (MMP) electoral system in 1993, the outcome of which was to make it much less likely that any one political party would achieve a majority in Parliament. The overall effect has been to dilute executive power and make the executive less dominant. The rejection of a plurality electoral system in favour of MMP reflected public concern with the predominance of the executive, evidence of the vagaries of a highly disproportional electoral system, and a desire for a more responsive and accountable system of government.[31]

The impact of MMP should not be overstated. The Westminster traditions of majoritarianism and adversarialism persist, and secure majorities (single- or multi-party) can still control the house to a greater or lesser extent through strict party discipline.[32] However, majorities of this type are less frequent, and as a result the overall dominance of the executive has been tempered and Parliament's role has been enhanced (backbench government MPs are more willing to criticize ministers, select committees no longer include ministers and rarely have an inbuilt government majority, MPs who chair select committees now receive an additional salary). Palmer and Palmer conclude,

What MMP has done has been, in political terms, to break up the monopoly on power enjoyed under the FPP [first-past-the-post] system in Westminster by the party in government. In other words it has put an end to what Lord Hailsham called, when he was in opposition, 'the elective dictatorship'.[33]

Consequently, Palmer's *Unbridled Power?* (1979) was re-titled *Bridled Power* for its fourth edition (2004) to reflect the changed dynamics of executive–legislative relationships. Canada shares with New Zealand a constitutional and political heritage arising from its colonial links with the UK and as a result was classified by Lijphart as a majoritarian–federal country. However, institutional attempts to deal with political expressions of ethnic–cultural divisions in Canada have led some observers to describe it as 'semi-consociational'.[34] Critical factors in this assessment include: the development of Canadian federalism; the rejection of the Meech Lake Accord (1990) and the Charlottetown Accord (1992); increased attention to the claims of Aboriginal peoples; increased demands for the relaxation of party discipline within the legislature; increased controversy over the use and impact of judicial review; and, critically, the perennial problem of national unity. Studlar and Christensen's re-application of Lijphart's methodology for the period 1997–2006 lead them to conclude that although it remains a federal–majoritarian polity 'over the past decade Canada has become somewhat less majoritarian on both dimensions'.[35]

Moving to the other extreme, Figure 16.2 indicates that Switzerland has also shifted away from its traditional position and characterization as 'the clearest prototype' of a consensus democracy.[36] The reasons for this alteration include: amendments to the federal constitution in 1999; a new division of powers between the federal authorities and the cantons in 2004; and changes to the party-composition of the government (Federal Council) during 2003–7. As a result of these changes, Vatter concludes that instead of representing a 'pure' form of consensus democracy 'that at the beginning of the twenty-first century Switzerland is on the way to becoming an average consensus democracy'.[37]

What is interesting about the evolution of democracy in New Zealand, Canada, and Switzerland is that, like the UK, the extent of reform has been significant, but at the same time restricted within the parameters of a distinct meta-constitutional orientation. Reform has therefore taken place within the contours of a bounded rationality. The experience of Ireland also supports this theme, but in a manner that is particularly relevant in relation to this book's focus on modified majoritarianism and executive control capacity.

Ireland was integrated into the UK in 1801, and until 1921 its constituencies were represented at Westminster. The Constitution of the Irish Free State (1922), apart from adopting a proportional electoral system, conformed to the Westminster Model. The power-sharing effect of proportional representation was undermined by the existence of nationalist cleavages which acted to promote two dominant nationalist parties and resulted in there being 'absolutely no curb on the untrammelled power of the executive'.[38] This situation altered in December 1937 when a new Constitution of Ireland came into force after being passed by a national plebiscite the previous July. This created a Supreme Court and a President with the power to refer legislation to it, and required that the constitution could only be amended by referendum. As a result, Ireland became an 'intermediary' case of majoritarianism in Lijphart's framework. More specifically, reforms were introduced to moderate the perceived defects of a purely majoritarian system, but not to replace the system.

During the middle of the twentieth century, cultural and institutional dynamics impelled Ireland towards a more consensual polity. What is significant about the Irish case is the manner in which this adaptation evolved over time. There was a significant shift on the executive–parties dimension between the first and second periods, but a greater shift on the federal–unitary dimension between the second and third periods. The initial shift arose from formal institutional measures introduced under the 1937 constitution; whereas the second shift stemmed more from the cultural factors (e.g. a changing in the attitude of the judiciary, changing norms regarding the use of referendums, the use of 'social partnership agreements' with interest groups, etc.). And yet, although Bulsara and Kissane find that the 'Westminster Model is clearly in decline, and there is now more consensus politics on both sides of the Irish border', they also emphasize the manner by which power remains centralized at the core.[39] Ireland remains a two-party system (V1), the electoral system remains simple plurality FPTP (V4), a unitary and heavily centralized system (V6), and the second chamber (the Seanad) remains weak (V7). As a result, Bulsara and Kissane conclude their Lijphartian analysis by stating, 'Since 1937 power [in Ireland] has become more diffuse, but not enough to call the state a consensual democracy'.[40] This finding underlines Lijphart's conclusion regarding the entrenched nature of majoritarian impulses and cultures. It also relates to this book's analysis of the 'Blair paradox' due to the manner in which twentieth century Irish political history provides an example of a constitutional reform programme, De Valera's 1937 constitution, in which powers were decentralized along one dimension, but at the same time centralized in other areas.[41]

This brief discussion of New Zealand, Canada, Switzerland, and Ireland is valuable because it provides some comparative reference points from which to reflect back upon the changing nature of democracy in the UK. The first and most basic insight gleaned from this brief review is that the nature of democracy within a country evolves over time as institutions, conventions, and cultures change. However, what is also clear from Figure 16.2 is that, as Lijphart found, 'fundamental constitutional changes are difficult to effect and therefore rare'.[42] In this sense, reform trajectories tend to be bounded by certain accepted precepts that act as a form of bounded rationality (reflected in reform processes tending to occur within distinct quadrants). What Figure 16.2 does suggest, however, is that a degree of convergence is occurring around the mid-point whereby the number of 'intermediate' polities is increasing as the number of 'extreme' or 'classic' cases of consensual or majoritarian democracies orientate towards the central axis. This is by no means a perfect pattern and exceptions exist, but certainly in terms of Lijphart's original 'exemplars' there has been a shift away from 'extreme' politics.[43] Indeed, what is interesting about the nature of this re-orientation is that it generally occurs in a uni-dimensional or 'one-sided' manner; resulting in directional movements that are either vertical (i.e. operationalized along the federal–unitary Dimension) or horizontal (i.e. vice versa) but rarely diagonal, in the sense of moving directly towards or away from a pure consensual or majoritarian form.

What then can we take from this short comparative discussion in terms of deepening our understanding about the likely evolution of form, its drivers, and particularly what is distinctive about the UK's current position? Two issues stand out: the first pertaining to process and the second to distinctiveness. In terms of process, a comparative perspective underlines the manner in which a dialectical and iterative relationship exists between cultural change and institutional change. Institutional change can stimulate cultural changes, which may, in turn, promote further institutional changes. This was particularly significant in relation to the Irish case (stated earlier) where, although initial democratic alterations occurred through formal institutional change, later changes occurred through attitudinal and cultural modifications. The possible implication for the UK being that over time, the significant changes that have occurred in relation to the federal–unitary dimension may well create cultural and attitudinal pressures that spillover to make change along the executive–parties dimension inevitable.

This notion of spillover or momentum relates to what is arguably the distinctive element of governance in the UK when viewed through a comparative perspective—bi-constitutionality. In this sense the UK is distinctive due to the existence of so many anomalies, and particularly due to the attempt to adopt an approach to statecraft based upon the co-existence and parallel operation of markedly different models of democracy within one polity. Some constitutional configurations may posses institutional or procedural techniques (like federalism) that may offer the capacity to manage and legitimate the existence of difference. In the UK, however, the constitution has become fractured and its malleability exhausted. There is no 'new' constitution but an inter-mediate transitional phase of development which, due to the existence of widening fault lines, may, at some point, lead to a more coherent and far-reaching re-appraisal of the nature of democracy in the UK. Some observers may reject this point on the basis that the UK has always been distinctive *exactly* due to its capacity to sustain political cohesion despite difference, anomalies, and asymmetry and in this sense the UK has 'always suffered from deep intellectual incoherence'.[44]

What this book has revealed, however, is that the extent of 'difference' has now grown to the point that the governing efficiency and effectiveness of the polity is likely to become increasingly fragile. There are simply too many 'rough edges'—the proliferation of voting systems is a little too odd, the models for devolution are so different in concept and design, the future of the Lords remains unknown, the policies on human rights and counter-terrorism are conflicting, increasing juridification grates against the logic of parliamentary sovereignty, etc.[45] However, a constitutional reappraisal, a mega-political debate, is unlikely to occur in the near future. This view is supported by the future forecasting analysis led by Hazell that concluded that major constitutional changes are unlikely to occur in the short to medium term, 'This will come as a bitter disappointment for constitutional reformers who have fought so long for the complete transformation of the Westminster Model'.[46] The economic gloom arising from the global economic crisis has in the UK at least pushed constitutional reform and democratic renewal down the government's agenda. As noted earlier, the draft Constitutional Renewal Bill was widely acknowledged as lacking in terms of dynamism and ambition, which may explain why it was not included in the Queen's Speech at the beginning of the 2008–9 session of Parliament. A similar pattern of slippage surrounds the government's plans in relation to a British Bill of Rights. The government initially promised to publish a consultation paper by the spring of 2008, this was put back to the summer, and then to the autumn. In August 2008, the parliamentary Joint Committee on Human Rights published their own proposals and a draft bill with the intention of pressuring the government to act—but to no avail.[47] As of May 2009, the government's proposals were still to appear and with financial cutbacks looming over all government departments and a general election approaching, Gordon Brown's opportunity for re-energizing the constitutional reform programme, with a Bill of Rights at the core, may well have passed. What then is the likely impact of this conclusion in terms of democratic drift, constitutional anomie, and public trust in politics?

16.5 Drift, anomie, and trust

This is a wide-ranging book and, like painting on a large canvas, this has required the use of a fairly broad brush, in analytical, comparative, and conceptual terms. It has, however, explored two related arguments—the first pertaining to bi-constitutionality, and the second relating the constitutional anomie. This final section locates these arguments within the broader literature and data evidence on 'disaffected democracies' that was highlighted in the opening chapter. In this sense, the book has come full circle and in many ways it is possible to identify a self-perpetuating cycle of political disenchantment. It is exactly these links between political disengagement and constitutional anomie, and between constitutional anomie and the 'swing thesis' that this section seeks to emphasize.

Political parties that promise to institute far-reaching changes to the nature of a democracy if elected into office but then renege upon, marginalize, or dilute those promises once in office create what can be termed an 'expectations gap'. Having inflated public expectations, the subsequent performance of those politicians undermines public confidence, thereby fuelling disenchantment and apathy. The issue of Freedom of Information provides a case in point. In February 2009, the Secretary of State for Justice announced his decision to invoke the ministerial veto in order to block the release of information concerning the invasion of Iraq in 2003, despite the decisions by both the statutory Information Commissioner and the Information Tribunal that recommended disclosure. When the Shadow Secretary of State for Justice told the House of Commons that '[T]he public have had their expectations about openness raised by Labour's spin and propaganda, only to be brought down to earth by the intrusion of the realities of government' he was not attempting to make a simple partisan argument (the Conservative Party supported the use of the veto) but was actually referring to the distance and implications of the rhetoric–reality gap that has tended to dilute New Labour's measures in the sphere of constitutional reform and democratic renewal.[48] Therefore, the swing from a rhetorical commitment to consensual politics in opposition to a practical steadfastness to executive government in office contributes to a general cynicism about the trustworthiness of politicians—an argument that resonates with Hay's work on 'why we hate politics' and Stoker's analysis of why politics in mass democracies seems 'destined to disappoint'.[49]

The *supply-side* of politics (i.e. the behaviour of politicians) therefore affects the *demand-side* (i.e. the behaviour of the public) in a negative manner and this is reflected in survey evidence that suggests that 83 per cent of the public do not trust politicians and 72 per cent feel disconnected from Parliament.[50] This data veils more dramatic signs of political inequalities; the turnout gap between the highest and lowest income quintile in 1964 was 7 per cent, by 2005 it had nearly doubled to 13 per cent; in 1970 there was an eighteen-point difference between the 18–24 age group and those over sixty-five, in 2005 the gap was forty points. Moreover, a lack of public faith in politicians, political institutions, and political structures can produce a situation in which the public become so jaded in their view of politics that they are unwilling or unable (or both) to appreciate and believe that in some policy areas promises are being delivered—a 'perception gap'—and in this context it is noteworthy that two-thirds of those surveyed by MORI in 2007 believed that, in general, New Labour had not kept its promises.

The reasons for the evidence of contemporary public trust in conventional politics and disengagement from traditional forms of political activity (e.g. voting, membership of a political party, etc.) are complex, and it would be facile to lay the emphasis on any one factor but it is at the same time reasonable to suggest a link between the 'expectations gap' and a downturn in public trust in politics, in general, and interest in constitutional reform, in particular. The Hansard Society's 2008 audit of political engagement provides empirical evidence to support this point: public interest in politics is falling; more than half the public claim to know very little or nothing at all about politics; the number of people who think that governance in the UK works well is declining; around half of the public have never heard of, or know very little about the constitutional arrangements governing the UK; and out of eleven key constitutional issues there were none where more than half the public thought they understood them. The report concludes, 'Taking all the figures into account, this year's are the most negative to date, although the decline has come from a relatively low base of satisfaction'.[51]

This negative public context is critical in relation to this book's focus on. (*a*) constitutional anomie; (*b*) the apparent weaknesses of the government's *Governance of Britain* agenda; and (*c*) the unlikelihood of major reforms in the short to medium term (i.e. the next decade). The Brown government's current package of reforms and those promised by the Conservative Party are too insubstantial to resonate with the public. They also lack a strong central theme with the capacity to unite those reforms (and their consequences) that have gone before it. And yet, rectifying this situation through the design and dissemination of a broadly accepted narrative of change (a 'constitutional morality'), demands skills that the political elite in the UK arguably lack. These include, as King emphasizes, a mindset of constitutional-thinking and design, the capacity to look across departmental boundaries and understand the inter-relationships between various elements of the constitutional configuration, and a cultural predisposition which is not disparaging (if not totally opposed) to the role of constitutional theory or jurisprudence as a blueprint or route map for reform.[52] It is not until these skills have been developed and honed that the challenges outlined in this book—challenges concerning democratic drift, constitutional anomie, and declining public trust—can start to be addressed.

Notes

1. Norton, P (2007) 'Tony Blair and the Constitution', *British Politics*, 2, 269.
2. Bogdanor, V (2002) 'Conclusion', in V Bogdanor, ed., *The British Constitution in the Twentieth Century*. London: British Academy, p. 719; King *op. cit.* (2007), p. 345.
3. Lijphart *op. cit.* (1984), p. 210.
4. Hazell, R (2007) 'The Continuing Dynamism of Constitutional Reform', *Parliamentary Affairs*, 60(1), 3–25.
5. Cm. 7170 (2007) *Governance of Britain*, p. 5.
6. Cm. 7342 (2008) *Governance of Britain: Constitutional Renewal*.
7. HL166/HC551 (2008) *Draft Constitutional Renewal Bill*. Joint Committee on the Draft Constitutional Renewal Bill, 1.
8. For a detailed analysis, see Maer, L (2008) *Governance of Britain: An Update*. London: House of Commons Library; Ministry of Justice (2008) *Governance of Britain: One Year On*.
9. Cm. 7438 (2008) *An Elected Second Chamber: Further Reform of the House of Lords*.
10. Ibid., 4.
11. Hay, C and Stoker, G (2007) 'Who's Failing Whom?' in Political Studies Association (PSA), eds., *Failing Politics? A Response to the Governance of Britain Green Paper*. Newcastle: PSA, p. 8.

12. Freedland, J (2008) *The Guardian,* 26 March.

13. Political Studies Association (PSA) (2007) *Failing Politics? A Response to the* Governance of Britain *Green Paper*, Newcastle: PSA, p. 6.

14. See Brown, G (2004) 'British Council Annual Lecture', 7 July; Brown, G (2006) 'The Future of Britishness'. Speech to the Fabian Society, Imperial College, London, 14 January; Brown, G (2004) 'The Golden Thread that Runs Through Our History' *The Guardian,* 8 July.

15. Brown, G (2006) 'Who Do We Want to Be? The Future of Britishness'. Fabian New Year Conference, Imperial College, London, 14 January.

16. In making this point the Prime Minister referred to Jonathan Freedland's (1999) book, *Bringing Home the Revolution.* London: Fourth Estate.

17. See HL 165/HC 150 *A Bill of Rights for the UK?* Joint Committee on Human Rights.

18. See Park, A et al. (2008) *British Social Attitudes: The 24th Report.* London: Sage.

19. Ford, R (2008) 'Scots Lead Rebellion Against Oath of Allegiance', *The Times,* 12 March, 1.

20. Citrin, J (2007) 'Constitutional Reform and British National Identity', in A. McDonald, ed., *Reinventing Britain.* London: Politicos, p. 212.

21. Bogdanor, V (2008) 'The Significance of the Constitutional Reform Bill'. Speech to the British Academy, 16 June.

22. Hague, W (2000) 'A Conservative View of Constitutional Change'. Lecture given at Magdalen College, Oxford, 13 November.

23. Norton, P (2005) 'The Constitution', in K. Hickson, ed., *The Political Thought of the Conservative Party since 1945.* London: Palgrave, pp. 93–112.

24. For a detailed review, see Flinders, M (2009) 'Conserving the Constitution', *Political Quarterly.*

25. Cameron, D (2006) 'Balancing Freedom and Security: A Modern British Bill of Rights'. Speech 26 June.

26. Cameron, D (2009) 'Making Progressive Conservatism a Reality'. Speech at Demos, London, 22 January.

27. Cameron, D (2008) 'Fixing Britain's Broken Politics'. Speech to the Welsh Conservative Party, Llandudno, 1 March.

28. Ibid.

29. Tempest, M (2006) 'Cameron Denies Copying Brown on Constitutional Reform', *The Guardian,* 6 February.

30. Zines, L (1991) *Constitutional Change in the Commonwealth.* Cambridge: Cambridge University Press, p. 47.

31. See Mulgan, R (1994) *Politics in New Zealand.* Auckland: Auckland University Press.

32. Barker, F and McLeay, E (2000) 'How Much Change?' *Party Politics,* 6(2):131–54.

33. Palmer, G and Palmer, M (2004) *Bridled Power.* Auckland: Oxford University Press, p. 370.

34. McRae, K (1997) 'Contrasting Styles of Democratic Decision-making', *International Political Science Review*, 18, 279–95.

35. Studlar, D and Christensen, K (2006) 'Is Canada a Westminster or Consensus Democracy?' *PS: Political Science and Politics*, 39(4), 837–41.

36. Lijphart *op. cit.* (1999), p. 33.

37. Vatter, A (2008) 'Swiss Consensus Democracy in Transition', *World Political Science Review*, 4(2), 31.

38. Former Irish minister, quoted in Kissane, B (2007) 'Eamon de Valera and the Survival of Democracy in Inter-war Ireland', *Journal of Contemporary History*, 42 (2), 212.

39. Bulsara, H and Kissane, B (2009) 'Arend Lijphart and the Transformation of Irish Democracy', *West European Politics*, 32(1), 186.

40. Ibid., p. 192

41. See Mair, P (2004) 'De Valera and Democracy', in T Garvin, M Manning, and R Sinnott, eds., *Dissecting Irish Politics*. Dublin: UCD Press, p. 31–45.

42. Lijphart, A (2008) *Thinking About Democracy*. London: Routledge, p. 178.

43. See Flinders, M and Vatter, A (2009) 'Democratic Extremism Revisited'. Mimeo, University of Sheffield.

44. McLean, I and McMillan, A (2005) *State of the Union*. Oxford: Oxford University Press, p. 256.

45. Falconer, Lord (2006) Speech to the ESRC Devolution and Constitutional Change Programme, London, 10 March.

46. Hazell, R (2008) *Constitutional Futures Revisited*. Houndmills: Basingstoke, p. 297.

47. HL 15/HC 145 (2008–9) *A Bill of Rights for the UK?* Third report of Session 2008–9.

48. HC (2009) *Hansard*, 24 February, col. 156.

49. Hay, C (2007) *Why We Hate Politics*. London: Polity Press; Stoker, G. (2007) 'Politics in Mass Democracies: Destined to Disappoint?' *Representation*, 42(3), 181–94.

50. Data taken from, Lodge, G (2008) 'Options for Britain II—Challenges for a New Constitutional Settlement'. Paper delivered at Nuffield College, Oxford.

51. Hansard Society (1998) *Audit of Political Engagement 5*. London: Hansard Society, p. 6.

52. King *op. cit.* (2007), pp. 88–9.

Index

Index